Certainty in Action

Also available from Bloomsbury

Ethics after Wittgenstein, edited by Richard Amesbury and Hartmut von Sass
Portraits of Wittgenstein, edited by F.A. Flowers III and Ian Ground
Wittgenstein on Internal and External Relations, by Jakub Mácha
Wittgenstein, Religion and Ethics, edited by Mikel Burley

Certainty in Action

Wittgenstein on Language, Mind and Epistemology

Danièle Moyal-Sharrock

BLOOMSBURY ACADEMIC
LONDON • NEW YORK • OXFORD • NEW DELHI • SYDNEY

BLOOMSBURY ACADEMIC
Bloomsbury Publishing Plc
50 Bedford Square, London, WC1B 3DP, UK
1385 Broadway, New York, NY 10018, USA
29 Earlsfort Terrace, Dublin 2, Ireland

BLOOMSBURY, BLOOMSBURY ACADEMIC and the Diana logo
are trademarks of Bloomsbury Publishing Plc

First published in Great Britain 2021
This paperback edition published in 2022

Copyright © Danièle Moyal-Sharrock, 2021

Danièle Moyal-Sharrock has asserted her right under the Copyright,
Designs and Patents Act, 1988, to be identified as Author of this work.

For legal purposes the Acknowledgements on p. ix constitute an
extension of this copyright page.

Cover design by Charlotte Daniels Cover image: *Winter Landscape with
Ice Skaters*, Hendrick Avercamp, c. 1608, Photo by: Sepia Times/
Universal Images Group via Getty Images

All rights reserved. No part of this publication may be reproduced or transmitted in any
form or by any means, electronic or mechanical, including photocopying, recording,
or any information storage or retrieval system, without prior permission
in writing from the publishers.

Bloomsbury Publishing Plc does not have any control over, or responsibility for, any
third-party websites referred to or in this book. All internet addresses given in
this book were correct at the time of going to press. The author and publisher
regret any inconvenience caused if addresses have changed or sites have
ceased to exist, but can accept no responsibility for any such changes.

A catalogue record for this book is available from the British Library.

Library of Congress Cataloging-in-Publication Data

Names: Moyal-Sharrock, Danièle, 1954-author.
Title: Certainty in action: Wittgenstein on language, mind and
epistemology / Danièle Moyal-Sharrock.
Description: London; New York: Bloomsbury Academic, 2021. |
Includes bibliographical references and index. |
Identifiers: LCCN 2020051506 (print) | LCCN 2020051507 (ebook) |
ISBN 9781350071292 (hb) | ISBN 9781350071308 (epdf) |
ISBN 9781350071315 (ebook)
Subjects: LCSH: Wittgenstein, Ludwig, 1889-1951. | Act (Philosophy)
Classification: LCC B3376.W564 M69 2021 (print) |
LCC B3376.W564 (ebook) | DDC 192–dc23
LC record available at https://lccn.loc.gov/2020051506
LC ebook record available at https://lccn.loc.gov/2020051507

ISBN: HB: 978-1-3500-7129-2
PB: 978-1-3502-2889-4
ePDF: 978-1-3500-7130-8
eBook: 978-1-3500-7131-5

Typeset by RefineCatch Ltd, Bungay, Suffolk

To find out more about our authors and books, visit
www.bloomsbury.com and sign up for our newsletters.

For my mother, Esther Moyal,
who gave me and taught me life, and the love of it.

Contents

Preface	viii
Acknowledgments	ix
Abbreviations of Works by Wittgenstein	xi
Introduction: Discovering Wittgenstein	1

Part 1 Language

1	Wittgenstein's Grammar: Through Thick and Thin	19
2	Universal Grammar: Wittgenstein versus Chomsky	33
3	'Words as Deeds': Wittgenstein's 'Spontaneous Utterances' and the Dissolution of the Explanatory Gap	49
4	Literature as the Measure of our Lives	65

Part 2 Mind

5	From Deed to Word: Gapless and Kink-Free Enactivism	81
6	Wittgenstein and the Memory Debate	99
7	Wittgenstein on Psychological Certainty	117

Part 3 Epistemology

8	Wittgenstein on Knowledge and Certainty	137
9	Too Cavellian a Wittgenstein: Wittgenstein's Certainty, Cavell's Scepticism	155
10	Fighting Relativism: Wittgenstein and Kuhn	169
11	Beyond Hacker's Wittgenstein	181

Notes	201
References	237
Index	251

Preface

This selection of essays represents a distillation of twenty years of work in which my understanding and appreciation of Wittgenstein's genius was guided by three exceptional philosophers: Avrum Stroll paved my way to *On Certainty*; John V. Canfield illuminated Wittgenstein's philosophical psychology, and Peter Hacker shed an indispensable light on the *Philosophical Investigations*. While Peter Hacker is prominent in this volume as a guide and an ally, he is also present as an admired and energizing opponent.

I am also deeply indebted and grateful, both for their friendship and their intellectual input over the years, to Anat Biletzki, Louise Barrett, Christiane Chauviré, Frank Cioffi, David Cockburn, Annalisa Coliva, Raimond Gaita, Ken Gemes, Hans-Johann Glock, Laurence Goldstein, Ian Ground, Bernard Harrison, Lars Hertzberg, Daniel D. Hutto, Olli Lagerspetz, Sandra Laugier, Anat Matar, Brian McGuinness, Volker Munz, Erik Myin, Alois Pichler, Nigel Pleasants, Duncan Pritchard, Constantine Sandis, Genia Schönbaumsfeld, Paul Standish, David Stern, Michel ter Hark, Meredith Williams and Michael Williams. It is to my husband, Peter Sharrock, who had F. R. Leavis as a teacher at Cambridge, that I owe my discovery of Wittgenstein. This, along with his unswerving confidence and support, and his intellectual stimulation, have enabled me to become the philosopher that I am.

A special note of thanks to Colleen Coalter, my publisher at Bloomsbury, for her encouragement and advice in the publication of this volume, and for her long-time support of the British Wittgenstein Society.

Acknowledgements

This volume draws on previously published material, some of which has been updated. Where pertinent, I am grateful to the publishers and editors for permission to reprint either extracts or the entirety of my original articles:

'**Wittgenstein's Razor: The Cutting Edge of Enactivism**', *American Philosophical Quarterly,* 50 (3) 3 July 2013: 263–79.

'**The Myth of the Quietist Wittgenstein**' in *Wittgenstein and Scientism*, eds Jonathan Beale and Ian Kidd. (London: Routledge, 2017), 152–74. Reproduced with permission of Informa UK Limited through PLSclear.

'**Realism, but not empiricism: Wittgenstein versus Searle**' in *A Wittgensteinian Perspective on the Use of Conceptual Analysis in Psychology*, eds Timothy P. Racine and Kathleen L. Slaney (Basingstoke: Palgrave Macmillan, 2013), 153–71. Reproduced with permission of Springer Nature.

'**Wittgenstein's Grammar: Through Thick and Thin**' in *wittgensteinian (adj.): Looking at things from the viewpoint of Wittgenstein's Philosophy*, eds S, Wuppuluri and N. da Costa (Cham: Springer, 2020), 39–54. Reproduced with permission of Springer Nature through RightsLink.

'**Universal Grammar: Wittgenstein versus Chomsky**' in *A Companion to Wittgenstein on Education: Pedagogical Investigations*, eds M. A. Peters and J. Stickney (Cham: Springer, 2017), 573–600. Reproduced with permission of Springer Nature through RightsLink.

'**"Words as Deeds"': Wittgenstein's "Spontaneous Utterances" and the Dissolution of the Explanatory Gap**', *Philosophical Psychology,* 13 (3) (September 2000): 355–72. Reproduced with permission of Taylor & Francis through RightsLink.

'**Literature as the Measure of our Lives** in *Wittgenstein and the Limits of Language*, ed. Hanne Appelqvist (Abingdon: Routledge), 270–87. Reproduced with permission of Taylor and Francis Group LLC (Books) US through PLSclear.

'**From Deed to Word: Gapless and Kink-free Enactivism**' in *Radical Views of Cognition* in *Synthese* (2019). https://link.springer.com/article/10.1007/s11229-019-02218-5#citeas Reproduced with permission of Springer Nature through RightsLink.

'Wittgenstein and the Memory Debate' in *New Ideas in Psychology* Special Issue, eds. Ulrich Mueller & Tim Racine, Mind, Meaning and Language: Wittgenstein's Relevance for Psychology 27 (2009), 213–27. Reproduced with permission of Elsevier through PLSclear.

'Wittgenstein on Psychological Certainty' in *Perspicuous Presentations: Essays on Wittgenstein's Philosophy of Psychology*, ed. Danièle Moyal-Sharrock (Basingstoke: Palgrave Macmillan, 2007), 211–35. Reproduced with permission of Springer Nature BV through PLSclear.

'Wittgenstein on Knowledge and Certainty' in *Blackwell Companion to Wittgenstein*, eds Hand-Johann Glock and John Hyman (Oxford: Wiley-Blackwell, 2017), 547–62. Reproduced with permission of John Wiley & Sons through RightsLink.

'Too Cavellian a Wittgenstein: Wittgenstein's Certainty, Cavell's Scepticism' in *Wittgenstein and Modernism*, ed. Anat Matar (London: Bloomsbury, 2017), 92–112. Reproduced with permission of Bloomsbury Academic US, an imprint of Bloomsbury Publishing Inc.

'Fighting Relativism: Wittgenstein and Kuhn in *Realism – Relativism – Constructivism*, eds. C. Kanzian et al (Berlin: Walter de Gruyter, 2017), 215–32. Reproduced with permission of Walter de Gruyter.

'Beyond Hacker's Wittgenstein'. Discussion Paper for Peter Hacker's 'Wittgenstein on Grammar, Theses and Dogmatism' *Philosophical Investigations* 35 (1), January 2012: 1–17. In *Philosophical Investigations,* October 2013, 36 (4): 355–80. Reproduced with permission of John Wiley & Sons through RightsLink.

Abbreviations of Works by Wittgenstein

AWL *Wittgenstein's Lectures: Cambridge, 1932–1935,* from the notes of A. Ambrose and M. MacDonald. A. Ambrose (ed.). Oxford: Blackwell, 1979.

BB *The Brown Book* in *The Blue and Brown Books*, 2nd ed. Oxford: Blackwell, 1969.

BT *The Big Typescript: TS 213*, ed. and tr. C. G. Luckhardt & M.A.E. Aue. Oxford: Blackwell Publishing, 2005.

CE 'Cause and Effect: Intuitive Awareness' in *Philosophical Occasions: 1912–1951*, ed. J. C. Klagge and A. Nordman. Indianapolis: Hackett Publishing, 1993, 371-426.

CV *Culture and Value*, ed. G. H. von Wright in collaboration with H. Nyman, tr. P. Winch, amended 2nd ed. Oxford: Blackwell, 1980.

EL *Letters from Ludwig Wittgenstein, With a Memoir* by Paul Engelmann. Oxford: Basil Blackwell, 1967.

GB 'Remarks on Frazer's *Golden Bough*', in *Philosophical Occasions: 1912–1951*, ed. J. C. Klagge and A. Nordman. Indianapolis: Hackett Publishing, 1993, 119–55.

LE 'A Lecture on Ethics' in *Philosophical Occasions: 1912–1951*, ed. J.C. Klagge and A. Nordman. Indianapolis: Hackett Publishing, 1993, 37–44.

LFM *Wittgenstein's Lectures on the Foundations of Mathematics, Cambridge 1939,* from the notes of R. G. Bosanquet, N. Malcolm, R. Rhees and Y. Smythies, ed. C. Diamond. Hassocks: Harvester Press, 1976.

LPE Notes for Lectures on "Private Experience' and 'Sense Data' in *Philosophical Occasions: 1912–1951*. J. C. Klagge and A. Nordman (eds). Indianapolis: Hackett Publishing, 1993, 202–367.

LPP *Wittgenstein's Lectures on Philosophical Psychology 1946–47*, notes by P. T. Geach, K. J. Shah and A. C. Jackson, ed. P.T. Geach. Hassocks: Harvester Press, 1988.

LW I *Last Writings on the Philosophy of Psychology*, vol I, ed. G. H. von Wright and H. Nyman, tr. C. G. Luckhardt and M. A. E. Aue. Oxford, Blackwell: 1982.

LW II *Last Writings on the Philosophy of Psychology*, vol. II, eds G. H. von Wright and H. Nyman, tr. C. G. Luckhardt and M. A. E. Aue. Oxford: Blackwell, 1992.

LWL	*Wittgenstein's Lectures, Cambridge 1930–1932*, from the notes of J. King and D. Lee, ed. Desmond Lee. Oxford: Blackwell, 1980.
MWL	Moore's *Wittgenstein Lectures in 1930–1933*, in J. C. Klagge & A. Nordman (eds), *Philosophical Occasions: 1912–1951*, 46–114. Indianapolis: Hackett Publishing, 1993.
NB	*Notebooks 1914–16*, ed. G. E. M. Anscombe and G. H. von Wright, tr. G. E. M. Anscombe, 2nd ed. Oxford: Blackwell, 1979.
NL	Notes on Logic. Appendix 1, in eds G. E. M. Anscombe and G. H. von Wright, tr. G. E. M. Anscombe, *Notebooks 1914–16*, 2nd ed., 93–107. Oxford: Blackwell, 1979.
OC	*On Certainty*, ed. G. E. M. Anscombe and G. H. von Wright, tr. D. Paul and G. E. M. Anscombe. Amended 1st ed. (reprinted with corrections), Oxford: Blackwell, 1997.
P	'Philosophy' (sections 86–93 of the Big Typescript) in *Philosophical Occasions: 1912–1951*, ed. J. C. Klagge and A. Nordman. Indianapolis: Hackett Publishing, 1993, 160–99.
PG	*Philosophical Grammar*, ed. R. Rhees, tr. A. Kenny. Oxford: Blackwell, 1974.
PI	*Philosophical Investigations*, tr. G. E. M. Anscombe. 2nd ed. Oxford: Blackwell, 1997.
PLP	*The Principles of Linguistic Philosophy* by F. Waismann, ed. R. Harré, 2nd ed. London: Macmillan, 1997.
PO	*Philosophical Occasions: 1912–1951*, ed. J. C. Klagge and A. Nordman. Indianapolis: Hackett Publishing, 1993.
PR	*Philosophical Remarks*, ed. R. Rhees, tr. R. Hargreaves and R. White. Oxford, Blackwell, 1975.
RC	*Remarks on Colour*, ed. G. E. M. Anscombe, tr. L. L. McAlister and Margarete Schättle. Oxford, Blackwell, 1980; 1st Ed. 1977.
RFM	*Remarks on the Foundations of Mathematics*, eds G. H. von Wright, R. Rhees and G. E. M. Anscombe, tr. G. E. M. Anscombe. 3rd rev. ed. Oxford: Blackwell, 1978.
RPP I	*Remarks on The Philosophy of Psychology*, vol. I, ed. G. E. M. Anscombe and G. H. von Wright, tr. G. E. M. Anscombe. Oxford: Blackwell, 1980.
RPP II	*Remarks on the Philosophy of Psychology*, vol. II., eds G. H. von Wright & H. Nyman, tr. C. G. Luckhardt and M. A. E. Aue. Oxford: Blackwell, 1980.
TLP	*Tractatus Logico-Philosophicus*, tr. D. F. Pears and B. F. McGuinness. London: Routledge & Kegan Paul, 1961.

VOW	L. Wittgenstein & F. Waismann, *The Voices of Wittgenstein: The Vienna Circle,* ed. G. Baker, foreword by B. F. McGuinness. London: Routledge, 2003.
WVC	*Ludwig Wittgenstein and the Vienna Circle*, shorthand notes recorded by F. Waismann, ed. B. F. McGuinness. Oxford: Blackwell, 1979.
Z	*Zettel,* eds G. E. M. Anscombe and G. H. von Wright, tr. G.E.M. Anscombe. Berkeley, CA: University of California Press, 1970.

Giving grounds, however, justifying the evidence, comes to an end; – but the end is not certain propositions striking us immediately as true, i.e. it is not a kind of seeing on our part; it is our acting, which lies at the bottom of the language-game.

Ludwig Wittgenstein (*On Certainty* 204)

Introduction

Discovering Wittgenstein

I came to Wittgenstein from literature. Being an admirer of F. R. Leavis,[1] I was intrigued by his affirmation of Wittgenstein's genius. Leavis knew Wittgenstein personally, invited him to his home, went on boat trips with him, and wrote a chapter recording their relationship in which he says that they never discussed philosophy and that he found Wittgenstein's interest in literature to be 'rudimentary'.[2] This, however, did not stop him from affirming his 'very positive sense of the nature of [Wittgenstein's] genius' (Leavis 1982; 143). Leavis (uncharacteristically) gave no substantive reasons for this impression, but his judgement was enough to prod my curiosity. Yet, when I decided to study philosophy, at the University of Geneva, no course was offered on Wittgenstein. Armed with Leavis's comment, I approached one of my professors, and got him to agree to teach an extra-curricular course on Wittgenstein. He taught the *Tractatus*; I failed to see the genius and decided to undertake a PhD in the philosophy of literature.

The question I wanted philosophy to answer was: what is the great thing about literature? Why are we drawn to it? My immediate answer was similar to Aristotle's and Kant's: *cognitive pleasure*. But the problem with cognition is its kinship with knowledge; and justified true belief was *not* what I was looking for. The kind of cognition that literature affords us is not susceptible of strict justification but of a more fundamental and indubitable grasp. I then got my hands on a book of Wittgenstein's that had received very little attention: *On Certainty*. And this is where I found the genius that Leavis was talking about.

On Certainty is Wittgenstein's last 'work'.[3] And so, as I also like to say, I came to Wittgenstein through the backdoor. This gave me a perspective on his philosophy that I would not have had, had I started with the *Investigations*. From the vantage point of the *culmination* of Wittgenstein's thought, I was better able to track the objectives on the way and penetrate the cohesiveness and coherence of the journey. It is this cohesiveness and this coherence that inform the title of this volume: 'Certainty in Action.' A title that flags Wittgenstein's constant and consistent introduction of *action* and ways of acting in his later philosophy to supplant the misleading dominance of mental representations in our understanding of human thought, language and behaviour. And a title that reflects the various ways in which nonreflective, animal *certainty* – 'hinge certainty', as I call it[4] – is at the basis of all human thought and action.

But before delving into that, I'd like to linger a little on discovering Wittgenstein – for that, too, takes one beyond, or rather deeper than, the intellect.

Discovering Wittgenstein was a turning point for me, both in philosophy and in life. It prompted a 'conversion' in my basic understanding of what it is to think, to remember, to use language, to mean something. The shift was gradual and difficult, so engrained were my assumptions that the mind is in the brain; that thought is something that happens before it is put in words; that it, along with the will, feelings, consciousness, knowledge, self-knowledge, memory etc. are stored and processed *in the brain, by the brain*. Discovering Wittgenstein enabled me to veer away from this *brain-centred* view of thought, intelligence, behaviour, language, knowledge and memory to a *person-centred* view, focused on ways of acting that are universally embedded in a human form of life and diversely embedded in innumerable forms of human life.[5]

I came to understand that we are more than the sum of our parts, and that this irreducible 'extra' is neither physical nor metaphysical; that our thoughts, intelligence, will, memory, self-knowledge etc. are not ghostly processes that materialize, through some kind of decoding, into action or words but, rather ways of acting that have their source in our interactions with the world. I understood that no amount of thought, intelligence, will, memory or self-knowledge *could* come from the brain; that although the brain is a necessary *mechanical* enabler, making thought etc. possible in the same way it makes walking or digestion possible, it is unable to create, store or grasp meaning. Only a person can do that; and she does it through living in the world and interacting with others. All of this took some time to assimilate intellectually, and even longer to apply unreflectively. It required the initially conscious correction of automatisms, and the application in every aspect of my life of what is easily described as a paradigm shift.

Of course, discovering Wittgenstein affected my philosophical along with my personal stance. I learned from him that our urge to reify the nonphysical – such as our thoughts, desires, or memories – is a *metaphysical* urge; and that this urge is but a sublimated version of what we might call a *physicalist or scientistic presumption*: the presumption that everything must have a physical cause and can be reduced to it. I came to see that the notion of a person's mind – which Wittgenstein realized amounts to that of a person having and exercising certain dispositions, capacities or abilities, such as thinking, remembering, recognizing, hoping, loving, grieving, being afraid, feeling pain) which are enabled by, but not reducible to, the brain[6] – has been subjected to this physicalist presumption. A presumption Wittgenstein questioned at its core:

> I saw this man years ago: now I have seen him again, I recognize him, I remember his name. And why does there have to be a cause of this remembering in my nervous system? Why must something or other, whatever it may be, be stored-up there *in any form*? Why *must* a trace have been left behind? Why should there not be a psychological regularity to which *no* physiological regularity corresponds? If this upsets our concepts of causality then it is high time they were upset.
>
> RPP I, 905

Of course, as we shall see,[7] Wittgenstein does not deny that we need brain activity for thinking or remembering, just as we do for walking; and so, in that limited sense, our thoughts etc. *are* causally dependent on the brain – on brain structures in different brain areas and on synaptic modifications in these areas. What he denies is that these structures are *representations* of particular thoughts, memories, feelings or emotions, generated by the brain and stored and encoded in the brain. Where then – it might be asked – are our thoughts, memories, feelings and emotions, and what is their source? The answer that I have learned from Wittgenstein is that our thoughts, memories, feelings and emotions exist only in their occurrences – that is, in our thinking, speaking, remembering, desiring, loving, giving, caressing, suffering, hurting, writing, painting, playing the piano etc. – and they have their source in the stream of our lives. This is their physical manifestation; and it is not – nor can it be – a *physicalist* manifestation. Let's try to flesh this out.

1. The disease of philosophy

Wittgenstein is the first philosopher to have precisely diagnosed the disease of philosophy: 'the tendency to explain instead of merely describing' (RPP I , 256). The disease of philosophy is caused by its propensity to *explain* rather than *describe* – to *think* (that is, *over*think) without *looking* (that is, without *over*looking). In its efforts to look *deeply*, philosophy overlooks the surface, what is in plain sight; and in its will to explain, it emulates explanation as practised by science:[8]

> Philosophers constantly see the method of science before their eyes, and are irresistibly tempted to ask and answer questions in the way science does. This tendency is the real source of metaphysics, and leads the philosopher into complete darkness. I want to say here that it can never be our job to reduce anything to anything, or to explain anything. Philosophy really *is* 'purely descriptive'. (Think of such questions as 'Are there sense data?' and ask: What method is there of determining this? Introspection?)
>
> BB 18

Explanation, when philosophy practises it, often results in metaphysics – that is, sublimated physics: the postulating of the basic entities and processes – such as sense data (or, more currently, internal representations) – that compose reality. When philosophy emulates science, the 'crystal does not appear as an abstraction; but as something concrete, indeed, as the most concrete, as it were the *hardest* thing there is' (PI 97). Plato's *Forms*, Descartes' *Consciousness*, Hegel's *Being* and the early Wittgenstein's *Logical Form*[9] are not offered as abstractions, but as hard crystals, allegedly ontologically robust entities, faculties, etc., that have crucially informed, or rather misinformed, philosophy throughout its history, perpetuating the explanatory, mythopoeic stance of the pre-Socratics. Plato reified predication, giving predicates *existence*, and indeed privileged existence. Aristotle corrected him but got entangled in his own *form*. And so it goes. Wittgenstein properly diagnosed this metaphysical malady, and its source in scientism; and against these he prescribed conversion to a method focused on description – one that engages *looking* and *describing* rather than speculative thinking or *explaining*: '... don't think, but look!' (PI 66). It is the task of the scientist to explain; the philosopher must only describe: 'Philosophy simply puts everything before us, and neither explains nor deduces anything. – Since everything lies open to view there is nothing to explain. For what is hidden ... is of no interest to us' (PI 126). It is the temptation, heightened by the traps of language, to treat philosophical problems as if they were empirical problems that misleads philosophers into trying to get beneath phenomena to uncover the 'hidden'.

Wittgenstein viewed philosophy as conceptual or grammatical[10] elucidation: 'The philosophical problem is an awareness of disorder in our concepts, and can be solved by ordering them' (BT 309). What we, in our scientistic attitudes, have traditionally taken to be metaphysical problems are linguistic confusions: 'The characteristic of a metaphysical question being that we express an unclarity about the grammar of words in the *form* of a scientific question' (BB 35). This is why, in keeping with Wittgenstein's 'modern' way of philosophizing (MWL 113), the philosopher should rid herself of the urge to approach problems scientifically, and engage in the task of conceptual elucidation and rearrangement which alone can 'bring words back from their metaphysical to their everyday use' (PI 116):

> The problems are solved, not by giving new information, but by arranging what we have always known. Philosophy is a battle against the bewitchment of our intelligence by means of language.
>
> PI 109

Wittgenstein's *descriptive* philosophy enables us to see simply and directly – thanks to the philosopher's conceptual elucidations or 'perspicuous presentations' (PI 122) – what is always before our eyes but made invisible by familiarity or blurred by misconception or preconception (PI 89; 122). This descriptive approach acts as a counter to traditional philosophy's *explanatory* fairy tales, often involving metaphysical entities, that lead to centuries of confusion and false problems. Rather than *presume* the existence of entities such as consciousness (which will then give rise to the so-called 'hard problem of consciousness'), the descriptive philosopher will start by 'reminding'[11] us that these 'entities' do not exist, and that presuming their 'existence' only obstructs rather than clarifies our understanding of ourselves. (We will come back to this in section 4, 'The importance of conceptual elucidation'.)

2. Wittgenstein's *realism without empiricism*

Wittgenstein's emphasis on conceptual elucidation does not, as is often believed, make him a linguistic idealist,[12] for he understood that 'words have meaning only in the stream of life' (LW I, 913). There is, for Wittgenstein, no Platonic or metaphysical Third Realm of meaning; meaning can be embedded only in use, in context, in life. He expressed this in one of his most brilliant and best-known aphorisms: 'the meaning of a word is its use in the language' (PI 43), usually abbreviated as 'meaning is use'. Indeed, his insistence that mind, thought, meaning, emotion can be manifest only in the stream of life, and attributed to persons (and, to a lesser extent, animals), makes Wittgenstein a realist, not an idealist, but his realism is of a soft kind; it is a realism without empiricism: 'Not empiricism and yet realism in philosophy, that is the hardest thing'[13] (RFM VI, 23, p. 325). Where realism *is* an empiricism – such as in John Searle's *biological naturalism*, all that we are – as physical, mental, social beings – 'bottoms out' in (is reducible to) electrons and neurons. Searle points out that this suggests an apparent paradox:

> How can we give an account of ourselves, with our peculiar human traits – as mindful, rational, speech-act performing, free-will having, social, political human beings – in a world that we know independently consists of mindless, meaningless, physical particles? How can we account for our social and mental existence in a realm of brute physical facts?
>
> 2010, ix

For Searle, this is a real question – one that genuinely seeks the means of producing a physicalist account of ourselves, and assumes that our achieving it is a matter of time – not one that disparages the very attempt. Searle's urge to produce a physicalist account of our social and mental existence exemplifies the disease of philosophy that Wittgenstein warned us against. What I would say in response to Searle is that there is no paradox in accounting for our social and mental existence in a realm of brute physical facts because our world is not *merely* a realm of brute physical facts; it does not consist only of mindless, meaningless, physical particles – for I am not a mindless, meaningless, physical particle and I am part of what the world consists of. Nor can my thoughts be reduced to mindless, meaningless, physical particles. And if they can't be thus reduced, there is no paradox about an account of our social and mental existence in a world of brute physical facts. As Peter Hacker writes: 'No amount of physics, chemistry or biology can explain why Hannibal did not attack Rome itself after the battle of Cannae, why increasing wealth is accompanied by falling birthrates, let alone why Raphael painted the figure of Democritus in *The School of Athens* with boots on. But we do know the answers to these questions' (2015a, 99).

For Searle, even collective intentionality – because it is a type of intentionality – must be mental (that is, caused by and realized in neurobiology): 'If you understand electrons and elections right you will see why some electrons have to participate in elections. No electrons, no elections' (2011, 2). So that although institutional facts – the products of collective intentionality such as marriage, academia, the economy, politics – have themselves no physical realization, they still need, on Searle's view, to bottom out in the entities of physics and chemistry. And what better, or who better, to serve that purpose than human beings? The brute facts, in the case of institutions, are 'actual human beings and the sounds and marks that constitute the linguistic representations' (2010, 109) that generate and maintain normative constraints. For Wittgenstein too, rule-following is a matter of the 'quiet agreement' of a community of people, but the importance of the individual in Wittgenstein's communal picture does not reside, as it does for Searle, in her having a brain and thus being a biological generator of '*standing Directives*' or speech-acts (2010, 158). Rather, her quiet agreement needs no bottoming out – which is not to say that brute physical facts are disregarded, but only that they are not regarded as generative or explanatory of social institutions.

In a sense, there is no question that society or social institutions are *caused* by human beings: human beings do bring social institutions about; they cause them to exist. And, of course, human beings have neurobiological structures and processes, and indeed could not create or cause anything at all, or even think, without these. But it does not follow from the necessity of such structures and processes for thinking that our thoughts are isomorphic or reducible to them. Thinking about quantum physics, talking about my savings or voting in an election are not dependent on anything molecular other than in the instrumental sense that I am dependent on molecules, but those molecules – just as any other neurobiological conditions for life – are *enabling*, not *determinant*; where an enabling condition is, as Anthonie Meijers puts it: 'one that makes possible a phenomenon, without determining its actual characteristics' (2000, 158)[14]. The conflation of these – expressed by William Ramsey as 'the characterization of any functional architecture that is causally responsible for the system's performance … as *encoding* the system's knowledge-base, as *implicitly representing* the system's know-how' (2007, 3–4; my emphasis) – is what Wittgenstein warned us against.[15] So, yes, Wittgenstein too would say: 'no electrons, no elections', and would agree with Searle that 'mental states, such as my present state of consciousness, are caused by a series of neurophysiological events in my brain' (1991, 144), but there is a huge, unwarranted, leap from saying *that* to saying that 'brains cause minds' (1990, 29)[16].

A passage from Bennett and Hacker's reply to Searle clearly illustrates the confusion in Searle's analogy:

> Professor Searle suggests that the question 'Where do mental events occur?' is no more philosophically puzzling than the question: 'Where do digestive processes occur?' So, he argues, digestive processes occur in the stomach, and consciousness occurs in the brain. This is mistaken. Being conscious, as opposed to unconscious, being conscious of something, as opposed to not noticing it or not attending to it, do not occur *in* the brain at all. Of course, they occur *because of certain events in the brain*, without which a human being would not have regained consciousness or had his attention caught. 'Where did you become conscious of the sound of the clock?' is to be answered by specifying where I was when it caught my attention, just as 'Where did you regain consciousness?' is to be answered by specifying where I was when I came round.
>
> Both digesting and thinking are predicated of animals. But it does not follow that there are no logical differences between them. The stomach can be said to be digesting food, but the brain cannot be said to be thinking. The stomach is the digestive organ, the brain is no more an organ of thought than it is an organ of locomotion. If one opens the stomach, one can see the food being digested there. But if one wants to see thinking going on, one should look at the *Penseur* (or the surgeon operating, or the chess player playing or the debater debating) not at his brain. All his brain can show is what goes on there *while he is thinking*.
>
> 2007, 143

'Consciousness' cannot be found in the brain for the simple reason that it is not a thing or substance but a state of a person or animal. Here again, as Wittgenstein and Ryle (1949) realized, we are mistaking states and dispositions of a person (e.g., being conscious, unconscious, half-conscious etc.) for substances ('consciousness'), and then wondering where these reside in the brain so as to work out their causal efficacy. The 'hard problem of consciousness' is only one of the many self-created, illusory problems that philosophers and scientists are still intent on solving. (We will come back to this in section 4, 'The importance of conceptual elucidation'.)

In any case, why should we go micro? Why – when there are other perfectly viable options – should we go micro in any account of ourselves as mindful, social beings? Especially as Searle himself concedes that there is no micro account (yet) available:

> ... a deep understanding of consciousness would require an understanding of how consciousness is caused by, and realized in, brain structures. Right now nobody knows the answers to these questions: how is consciousness caused by brain processes and how is it realized in the brain?
>
> 2010, 26

Why insist that any account of our mindful, speech-act performing, social selves *must* go all the way down when even science is unable to demonstrate that that's the way to go. If attention is to be paid by philosophy to science, shouldn't it be to scientific *results* rather than to scientific hypotheses that are nourished by a preconception of how things must be? Yet this doesn't stop Searle from stating what is a hypothesis as unquestionable: '... it is just a plain fact that neuronal processes do cause feelings, and we need to try to understand how' (2005 online).

Even if, *per impossibile*, a micro account were available (I say '*per impossibile*' because it seems to me logically impossible that my mental life can be caused by a configuration of molecules rather than result from my interactions with fully fledged people, events and things out there in the world: there is no physical or logical room in those molecules for the world), how would it be more adequate or relevant than a Wittgenstein-type account? How would it be a more *perspicuous presentation* of our human form of life? Water is not relevantly reducible to H_2O other than in very limited contexts, such as chemistry classes and labs: we do not think of, or refer to, as H_2O the stuff we splash in at the beach, or the stuff we add to our whisky or admire in Monet paintings or pray to the rain god for. Indeed those of us who pray to the rain god have probably never even heard of H_2O. Moreover, not all H_2O is water: some H_2O we call ice; other H_2O we call steam or vapour.[17] And so if even water is not – except in very limited contexts – *relevantly* reducible to its molecular configuration, why should our meanings, feelings and behaviours be? Why should my awareness that I am enjoying the sun, or a Château Pétrus '82, or that I am slowly losing consciousness, be things that I would want to attribute to my molecules or thank them for? Or indeed find relevance or adequacy in *any* account of myself as a minded and social being that would do so? Anyone must agree that we can have no elections without electrons, but what is the explanatory relevance of neuronal processes for our understanding of ourselves as minded beings, or for our understanding of the nature of institutions and our participation in institutions such as elections? As Dan Hutto puts it; 'Something may have to be the case for certain things to happen; but it can be irrelevant to the explanation we need' (in conversation).

So to Searle's question about how human beings can create such marvellous features as elections, and how they can maintain these in existence once created, I would answer – as he also partly does – through language and practices; but then *I* would go no further. For to go further is to take part in the shadow play of reductionism; and, as Raimond Gaita reminds us, the most fundamental aspect of Wittgenstein's legacy is that we cannot purify our concepts of their embeddedness in human life without being left with only a shadow play of the grammar of serious judgement (1990, xii). That shadow play is reflected, it seems to me, in the dance of neurons and electrons that make up Searle's dehumanized world.

3. Wittgenstein's *enactivism*: the primacy of action

In contrast to Searle's (and physicalists' generally) bottoming out of facts in neurons and electrons, Wittgenstein sees the basis of our human form of life in action or behaviour: 'In the beginning was the deed' (CE 395; CV 31; OC 402). Action, in Wittgenstein, is everywhere – not only at the origin of thought and language for the human species and for all individual human beings, but at the origin of any human thought or utterance.[18] That is, it has regained its rightful place in the description of our human mindedness; a place usurped by an inflated intellect and brain, in the form of content, propositions, representations or intelligent neurons. Action – rather than any of these – is, for Wittgenstein, at the logical foundation of thought. This is not merely to say that we need to be alive to think (or that thinking is an act), but that much – not all, but much – of what we have always regarded as thinking is only acting or behaving in a certain way.

This is what brings me to say that Wittgenstein is – and should be recognized to be – at the root of the important contemporary philosophical movement called *enactivism*,[19] along with its relatives *embodiment, embeddedness* and *extensiveness*: movements (all encapsulated in what I like to call 'the e-turn'[20]) that his work has explicitly or implicitly inspired. Enactivism, broadly understood,[21] is the view that mentality is 'rooted in engaged, embodied activity as opposed to detached forms of thought'; a view that favours 'the primacy of ways of acting over ways of thinking when it comes to understanding our basic psychological and epistemic situation' (Hutto 2014, 281). On this Wittgenstein-inspired view, to say that living beings have minds is not to say that they have brains that process representational states and their contents but rather that these beings have and exercise certain dispositions, capacities and abilities such as thinking, understanding, remembering, recognising, hoping, fearing, hurting etc.; and that these are not abilities and activities of the *brain*, but embodied and situated abilities and activities, causally, but not contentfully, enabled by the brain. One of the most recent versions of enactivism is Dan Hutto and Erik Myin's 'radical enactivism', which:

> ... holds that it is possible to explain a creature's capacity to perceive, keep track of, and act appropriately with respect to some object or property without positing

internal structures that function to represent, refer to, or stand for the object or property in question. Our basic ways of responding to worldly offerings are not semantically contentful. ... the great bulk of world-directed, action-guiding cognition exhibits intentional directedness that is not contentful.

2013, 82

There is nothing here that cannot be traced back to Wittgenstein.[22]

I want to stress that Wittgenstein's enactivism is not anything added but rather what is left when our superfluous, unsubstantiated, explanation-hungry enhancements have been erased from the straightforward picture of human action and cognition. The chapters in this volume will show how Wittgenstein's Razor[23] has pared off the excess in our approaches to language and thought, mind, memory, knowledge – thereby impacting not only philosophy but also psychology, neuropsychology, primatology, language acquisition and literature. Wittgenstein's Razor can be seen at work on the subjects of perception, belief, knowledge, language, consciousness, memory, feelings, sensations, emotions and of course action, wherever we have traditionally inserted an intellectual process or state – be it a thought, a description, an interpretation, an inference, a judgement or a justified true belief – that turns out to be, upon scrutiny, superfluous. Here are some passages from Wittgenstein that succinctly exemplify this:

The squirrel does not infer by induction that it is going to need stores next winter as well. And no more do we need a law of induction to justify our actions or our predictions.

OC 287

You don't need any *knowledge* to find a smell repulsive.

LW I 758

It is not as if he had only indirect, while I have internal direct evidence for my mental state. Rather, he has evidence for it, (but) I do not.

LW II, p. 67

... to say one knows one has a pain means nothing.

OC 504

If I let my gaze wander round a room and suddenly it lights on an object of a striking red colour, and I say 'Red!' – that is not a description.

PI p. 187

My attitude towards him is an attitude towards a soul. I am not of the *opinion* that he has a soul.

PI 287

... we can see *from their actions* that [people] believe certain things ...

OC 284; my emphasis

In all these passages – and note, in passing, the simple, incontrovertible way in which they encapsulate and deal with major philosophical problems – Wittgenstein pares away the superfluous thought or process supposed to lie behind all our doxastic and psychological states, behind a spontaneous utterance, or our attitude to someone, or our reaction to something. Meaning, believing, thinking, understanding, reasoning, calculating, learning, following rules, remembering, intending, expecting, longing – there is hardly anything, traditionally thought to be emergent from, underwritten by, or reducible to, a mental process or state, that Wittgenstein has not subjected to the razor of enactivism; that is, shown to be primitively embodied or enacted rather than originating in propositions, theories of mind, or ghostly processes. This may sound like behaviourism, but it isn't. Wittgenstein does not do away with the inner; he merely revises its importance and its nature[24].

In fact, more than a razor, Wittgenstein has taken an axe to much of philosophy. Much of the motivation for this volume was to show how this axing of ghostly mental processes and the problems they generate are crucial to realist or realistic philosophy, as opposed to physicalist and metaphysical philosophy.

4. The importance of conceptual elucidation

Wittgenstein was not alone in alerting us to the damage caused by the physicalist/explanatory/metaphysical stance in philosophy and its origin in 'the misinterpretations of our forms of language'[25] (PI 111), but he is unequalled both in fleshing out the ways and consequences of the damage, and in making conceptual elucidation the sole task of philosophy: 'Philosophy. The clarification of the use of language. Traps of language' (P 183/ BT 311). To say that conceptual philosophy is the sole task of philosophy is not to say that philosophy is not concerned with the world, for language is necessarily embedded in the stream of life. It *is* to say that 'philosophical problems arise when language *goes on holiday*' (PI 38; original emphasis), and this includes the temptation, as philosophers, to misinterpret and misuse our forms of language:

> Philosophical troubles are caused by not using language practically but by extending it on looking at it. We form sentences and then wonder what they can mean. Once conscious of 'time' as a substantive, we ask then about the creation of time.
>
> AWL 15

It is crucial that we not underestimate, as is often done by Wittgenstein's many detractors, the damage produced by conceptual confusion and the related importance of conceptual elucidation.[26] Tim Crane, for example, thinks some of these 'supposed [intellectual] confusions' to be 'so banal that it is quite incredible that any serious thinker should be taken in by them' and he dismisses the linguistic nature of philosophical confusion:

> ...to ask whether time flows (for example) ... is not to have your intelligence bewitched by language; it is not to misunderstand what Wittgenstein called the

'grammar' of the word *time*. Rather, it is to grapple with questions that are at once simple to grasp – what is it for some things to be in the past, and some in the future? – and also of great complexity: how our actual temporal experience of the world is related to the picture of time and space that we have acquired from physics.

2016

Note that Wittgenstein would not be averse to grappling with precisely the questions Crane lists here; what he is really concerned about in the AWL passage above – and Crane fails to address – is that because of language (i.e. 'time' being a substantive), we are confused into thinking that time is a thing (and therefore ask about its creation). As Wittgenstein makes clear: 'it is the use of the substantive 'time' which mystifies us. If we look into the grammar of that word, we shall feel that it is no less astounding that man should have conceived of a deity of time than it would be to conceive of a deity of negation or disjunction' (BB 6). Such mystification – often, as here, in the form of reification – is neither rare nor of *superficially* linguistic importance. Because they are substantives, we are mystified into taking 'time', but also 'mind', 'memory' or 'consciousness', to be entities or faculties having discrete existence and location. Because 'consciousness' is a noun, we think it must stand for a nominatum – a thing it names. Also, it is all too tempting a step to infer, from the fact that we are sometimes conscious, the *existence of an entity* called consciousness. This out-dated residue of the Platonic reification of states and qualities has been blown out of all proportion: the 'problem of consciousness' being 'arguably the most central issue in current philosophy of mind' – consciousness being viewed by many philosophers as a physical entity that can only be understood by investigating the brain.[27] William Seager's worry, that 'despite recent strides in neuroscience and psychology that have deepened understanding of the brain, consciousness remains one of the greatest philosophical and scientific puzzles' (2016, i), is telling.

The attempt to capture the human person in microphysics has plagued philosophy since, perhaps, the pre-Socratics (the atomists), but it seems more pervasive today than ever. Raymond Tallis invokes the current 'neuromania', as he calls it, 'based on the incorrect notion that human consciousness is identical with activity in the brain, that people are their brains, and that societies are best understood as collections of brains', rightly adding that 'while the brain is a necessary condition of every aspect of human consciousness, it is not a sufficient condition – which is why neuroscience, and the materialist philosophy upon which it is based, fail to capture the human person' (2012).[28]

When philosophers like Tim Crane object that reification – being nothing but an innocuous, figurative way of speaking – does not mystify us, they are profoundly wrong: reification often impacts and reflects our understanding of some mental concepts as *physical* entities or places in the brain. Of course, this is not dismissive of reification; it only flags our vulnerability to it. Crane's suggestion that we should accept transfers and extensions of meaning as part of the essence of our language (2015, 258) is platitudinous. Wittgenstein is only combating the extensions that are taken *literally*. As Peter Hacker aptly quips, there is 'nothing wrong with talking about the *foot* of a mountain – as long as one does not wonder whether it has a shoe' (Bennett et al, 2007, 154). However, Ian Ground is right to stress (in conversation) that we must not dismiss such linguistic confusions (e.g., thinking of *the inner* as being *inside* our head) as merely silly or superficial, but recognize them for the deep, far-reaching, inevitable confusions they are and be on our guard against them given that we cannot eliminate them.[29]

Wittgenstein was well aware that such confusions would 'seem trivial' (AWL 98) to philosophers. But they are far from trivial. Like all our unquestioned assumptions and many of our powerful pictures, conceptual confusions by default inform empirical research. Taking the mind and the brain as synonyms or as co-extensive has repercussions on how we conduct research and treat mental illness; for example, by privileging – through acknowledgement, reward and funding – the physiological approach that de-contextualizes psychiatric disorders and treats them as discrete, drug-treatable, brain conditions rather than as products of nurture which deserve increased attention and funding. John Searle's suggestion that human beings are 'embodied brains' (Bennett et al, 2007, 120ff) does not smack of the innocuously figurative. Such figurative expressions can mislead us into thinking that a problem is a scientific one when in fact it is not. Scientism can mystify us in different ways, mostly through the uncritical adoption of scientific ways of thinking and images, and their systematic transfer and application to realms outside science.[30]

By calling attention to grammatical mystification, Wittgenstein called attention to the absence of clarity which has, for centuries, often led the empirical and human sciences astray. The scientist crafts new theories about the natural world by using accumulated data, as well as the resources of her laboratory often supplemented by those of her imagination. But in crafting her theories she is not always conceptually circumspect, as Wittgenstein notes:

> In a scientific investigation we say all sorts of things, we make many statements whose function in the investigation we don't understand. For not everything is said with a conscious purpose; our mouth simply runs. We move through conventional thought patterns, automatically perform transitions from one thought to another according to the forms we have learned.
>
> RPP II, 155

There is no scientific investigation that is not informed by language, and so rather than unquestioningly adopt 'the picture of time and space ... acquired from physics' (Crane 2016) or the picture of memory acquired from neuropsychology, it is the philosopher's task to conceptually investigate those pictures and call attention to conceptual confusions and their repercussions so as to ensure that the scientist enter the lab or the consultation room with clear concepts.[31] Is this a two-way street? 'Is scientific progress useful to philosophy?' – asks Wittgenstein, and he replies: 'Certainly. The realities that are discovered lighten the philosopher's task, imagining possibilities' (LW I, 807). Certainly, my own philosophical work has found in empirical research some examples or evidence to bolster my conceptual task, as amply evidenced in this volume,[32] but the philosopher's task remains a conceptual one – albeit, one firmly planted in the stream of life.

The extent of confusion about the nature of philosophy is evidenced by the current trend on the *uselessness* of philosophy,[33] which often shows up the widespread confusion about its dividing line with science. Stephen Hawking and Leonard Mlodinow's claim that because 'philosophers have not kept up with modern developments in science' 'philosophy is dead' and scientists have become the sole 'bearers of the torch of discovery in our quest for knowledge' (2010, 13), evinces the currency of the false view that philosophy is meant to add to our knowledge. But as Wittgenstein makes clear, it is a crucial misconception to see philosophers as involved in the quest for knowledge at all. Knowledge, as commonly defined in philosophy, is 'justified true belief' – that is, evidence based – and therefore not the aim of philosophy; for philosophy is an endeavour that clears the conceptual path for the search of evidence. Philosophy's role is *not* to bring us new knowledge but rather to set us on the clear path to knowledge: 'One might also give the name "philosophy" to what is possible *before* all new discoveries and inventions' (PI 126).

To Crane's dismissal of the value of Wittgenstein's 'new method' of doing philosophy, and his urge that we stick to traditional philosophy as a 'straightforwardly intellectual endeavour in pursuit of the truth', we can retort that if traditional philosophers have achieved some great insights, they have also largely succumbed and contributed to conceptual confusion. Wittgenstein has given us the tools to address this, and those are conceptual elucidation and perspicuous presentation. However, the Wittgensteinian philosopher does not only wield these tools – as Locke would have it – as an 'under-labourer . . . removing some of the rubbish that lies in the way to knowledge' (1689), but as giving 'new direction to scientific investigation' by giving 'a new order', 'a new arrangement' to its descriptions (RPP I, 950). And so, on Wittgenstein's view, the philosopher's perspicuous presentation *can* bring new understanding – only let's not confuse that with knowledge.

5. Certainty in action

In fact, it is another important aim of this book to show that Wittgenstein not only put knowledge in its right conceptual place, but that it is one of his major achievements to have diminished its pervasiveness in our accounts of human thought and action. To the so-called 'problem of other minds' – the problem of knowing (i.e. of *being in the position of justifying* the common belief) that others have minds, and are capable of thinking or feeling, just as we do – Wittgenstein's response is that we don't *know*, just as we don't *know* that the world exists or that other people exist, and just as I don't *know* that I am sitting here typing these words or that I speak French or that I am in pain or that I have two hands. On Wittgenstein's view, we don't *know* these things, not because we can always doubt them, but because doubt about them is, in default circumstances, *logically* impossible. Outside of pathological circumstances, there is no epistemic gap, and therefore no room for doubt, between these things and our assurance of them. Wittgenstein introduces the concept of nonepistemic 'certainty' – 'hinge certainty', as I call it – to describe the kind of indubitable, unreasoned or 'animal' assurance that is at work here[34]. It is an *enactive* certainty, a *certainty in action*, which lies at the basis of all our thinking and acting: 'I want to say: it's not that on some points men know the truth with perfect certainty. No: perfect certainty is only a matter of their *attitude*' (OC 404; my emphasis).

In fact, if I had to name Wittgenstein's single most important contribution to philosophy, it would be that he revived the animal in us; the animal that is there in every fibre of our human being, and therefore also in our thinking and reasoning. By this I mean that he pushes us to realize that we are animals not only genealogically, but as evolved human beings – whether neonate, or language-possessing, civilized, law-abiding, fully-fledged adults. Constitutionally, and in everything we do, we are still *fundamentally* animals. Wittgenstein's evocation of the 'animal' in us is strewn, more or less implicitly, throughout his philosophy, but it is clearly articulated in *On Certainty*, where he says he wants to conceive of our basic certainty 'as something that lies beyond being justified or unjustified; as it were, as something animal' (OC 359). By this he means: as something instinctive, thought-free, reflex-like. So that, in grasping the world's 'furniture',

> [c]hildren do not learn that books exist, that armchairs, exist, etc., etc., – they learn to *fetch* books, *sit* in armchairs, etc., etc.
>
> Later, questions about the existence of things do of course arise. 'Is there such a thing as a unicorn?' and so on. But such a question is possible only because as a rule no corresponding question presents itself. For how does one know how to set about satisfying oneself of the existence of unicorns? How did one learn the method for determining whether something exists or not?
>
> OC 476

A child's first 'grasp' of a chair is not intellectual, but enactive – she deals with the chair's existence *in action*, not in thought – thinking about its existence comes later, if at all. One does not learn a method of figuring out whether something exists or not until a question presents itself; and a question does not *normally* present itself as to whether I (or the chair I am sitting in) exist. It *does* normally present itself about unicorns, or about whether there are chairs in the *next* room. What Wittgenstein is doing here is deproblematizing or de-intellectualizing what we have problematized and intellectualized: 'Does a child believe that milk exists? Or does it know that milk exists? Does a cat know that a mouse exists?' (OC 478). If a cat doesn't need to know that a mouse exists before chasing it, a child doesn't need to know that milk exists before drinking it. And nor does an adult need to know that a house exists before entering it. For Wittgenstein, grasping and navigating the world is *by default* done primitively – not epistemically, or indeed propositionally. Here, perception – be it of the milk, the mouse or the house – is, as Dan Hutto puts it, 'not contentful but enabling' (2014, 81). And contrary to 'the widely endorsed thesis that cognition always and everywhere involves content' (Hutto and Myin 2013), Wittgenstein regards cognition as starting always and everywhere not with knowing but with a certainty that is unreflective, animal: 'For why should the language-game rest on some kind of knowledge? (OC 477). Hinge certainty makes an appearance in every chapter of this volume because the notion of a basic, nonintellectual, or *animal*, certainty – rather than knowledge – as underpinning all that we say and do has enlightened my understanding of language, mind and epistemology, and helped me dissolve some of the important problems in these areas of thought.

6. Conclusion

I have conceived this volume as a *vade mecum* in the literal sense – that is: Latin for *go with me* – wishing to take the reader through my journey of understanding, inspired by the extraordinary intelligence and insight that permeate almost all that Wittgenstein wrote.[35] You will find ample testimony of this in the abundance of passages from his work that inform and bolster my arguments in this volume, which I have endeavoured to make accessible to the general reader. This is in keeping with my aim, since discovering Wittgenstein and realizing that he had been sidelined by most philosophers (particularly in the UK and the US), to (re-)awaken, both within and outside philosophy, awareness of his genius. My passionate determination over the years to counter attempts to diminish the importance and validity of Wittgenstein's work materialized not only in my philosophical work but also in the foundation, in 2007, of the British Wittgenstein Society. The goal of the BWS was to revive Wittgenstein's intellectual presence both for philosophers and nonphilosophers, and to ensure that it continues to play a fertile and creative role in twenty-first-century thought. This is done through regular lectures and annual conferences bringing philosophers, as well as practitioners of various other disciplines, to testify to, and debate, the pertinence and application of Wittgenstein's philosophy in their respective areas of thought. A rekindling of interest in Wittgenstein was also effected, I believe, by my drawing attention to what I identified as a 'third Wittgenstein' – a post-*Investigations* Wittgenstein[36] – and calling especially for his last work, *On Certainty*, to be given the attention it deserved. This has culminated in my inception, with Annalisa Coliva and Duncan Pritchard, of a now flourishing branch of epistemology called 'Hinge Epistemology' which has more widely opened mainstream epistemology to Wittgenstein's work.[37]

It is crucial that we keep Wittgenstein's philosophy alive and influential, for who better can save us from the still prevalent view that human life, thought and spirit are reducible to electrons and neurons? Such a view has rendered remarks such as these, by Richard Dawkins, all too common: 'the deep and universal questions of existence and the meaning of life are scientific matters which should properly be dealt with in science classes' (1993); and by Francis Crick: '"You", your joys and your sorrows, your memories and your ambitions, your sense of personal identity and free will are, in fact, no more than the behaviour of a vast assembly of nerve cells and their associated molecules' (1994, 3). It is the task of the Wittgensteinian philosopher to make perspicuous the nonsense that these remarks perpetuate.[38]

Part One

Language

Like Aristotle, Wittgenstein's leitmotif was action. Wittgenstein saw action (or behaviour) as the root, manifestation and transmitter of language and meaning. He makes clear the regress in viewing the proposition, or any kind of mental representation, as a necessary precursor to thought and action, and points out the superfluity of such shadowy inner precursors when instinct and practices can easily be seen to be at the foundation of all our thoughts and actions: 'In philosophy one is in constant danger of producing a myth of symbolism, or a myth of mental processes. Instead of simply saying what anyone knows and must admit' (Z 211). Wittgenstein urges us to see the differences in meaning that are often hidden by the uniform appearance of language, famously insisting that meaning is dependent on use or context. Just as Aristotle in the Categories *gave Plato's Forms a linguistic status, so Wittgenstein took a linguistic turn from his predecessors, giving metaphysics a grammatical reading: both showed that concepts are not entities existing in isolated splendour in some metaphysical realm but simply abstractions from our use of language; and as Wittgenstein also makes clear, nor do concepts and grammar exist in the brain. Indeed, we shall see in this section that Wittgenstein gives our grammar and concepts an anthropo-logical and enactive twist: they are conditioned by our form(s) of life and manifest in what we do and in what we say. There is, for Wittgenstein, no 'language of thought' or mentalese that then gets verbalized: language is rooted in instinct and behaviour, generated by our practices, and transmitted by enculturation. It can deploy itself in 'inner thinking', in 'thinking out loud' or in speech; but it is not a mere 'vehicle' for some ghostly nonlinguistic thought that craves linguistic expression. However, language is the unparalleled vehicle and evolving repository of human culture, finding its finest and most enactive expression in literature – where, through language, is shown what cannot be said.*

1

Wittgenstein's Grammar:

Through Thick and Thin

This chapter clarifies Wittgenstein's idiosyncratic view of 'grammar' and traces its evolution from the *Tractatus* to *On Certainty*. I distinguish between a 'thin grammar' and an increasingly more fact-linked, 'reality-soaked', 'thick grammar'. The 'hinge certainties' of *On Certainty* and the 'patterns of life' of his *Last Writings in the Philosophy of Psychology* attest to the fact that one of the leitmotifs in the work of the third Wittgenstein is *the grammaticalization of experience*. In moves that exceed anything in *Philosophical Investigations*, the third Wittgenstein makes grammar *enactive*. We shall also see that his conception of the logical as internally linked to the human form of life clashes with traditional conceptions of logical necessity and constrains its limits, thus making possibility *anthropo*-logical.

---

1. Defining grammar

The limits of what makes sense and what does not; what can be said and what cannot, is a leitmotif of Wittgenstein's philosophy. But what determines those limits? Wittgenstein's astonishing answer, already inscribed in the *Tractatus*, is: *grammar*. For him, language – any language – is rule-governed (RC 303); that is, governed by rules of grammar. What Wittgenstein means by 'grammar' is both similar to and different from what we usually mean by grammar. Ray Monk recounts the following (due to Rush Rhees):

> Moore, who attended Wittgenstein's lectures, insisted that 'Wittgenstein was using the word "grammar" in a rather odd sense.... Thus, he argued, the sentence: "Three men was working" is incontrovertibly a misuse of grammar, but it is not clear that: "Different colours cannot be in the same place in a visual field at the same time" commits a similar transgression. If this latter is also called a misuse of grammar, then "grammar" must mean something different in each case.' No, replied Wittgenstein. "The right expression is 'It does not have sense to say...'." Both kinds of rules were rules in the same sense. 'It is just that some have been the subject of philosophical discussion and some have not.'
>
> 1991, 322–3

And what Monk importantly adds here is that grammatical mistakes made by philosophers are more 'pernicious' than ordinary grammatical mistakes. Wittgenstein, then, merely expands our ordinary understanding of grammar rather than altering it: he does not see grammar as comprised merely of syntactic rules, but of any rule that governs 'the way we are going to talk' (MWL 72): 'By *grammatical* rule I understand every rule that relates to the use of a language' (VOW 303). For him, grammar is 'a preparation for description, just as fixing a unit of length is a preparation for measuring'; so that 'A rod has a length' is as much a preparation for description (e.g., 'This rod is three feet long') as the grammatical rule to use 'were' and not 'was' in some cases is a preparation for our intelligible use of language. Wittgenstein is simply more liberal than grammarians as to what he will count as grammar:

> Everything that's required for comparing the proposition with the facts belongs to grammar. That is, all the requirements for understanding. (All the requirements for sense.)
>
> BT 38

Another way of putting this is that grammar consists of the conditions of intelligibility of a language. It is the conventionally established basis on which we can *make sense*: 'Grammar consists of conventions' (PG 138), keeping in mind that conventions here are not due to a concerted consensus, but to an unconcerted agreement in practice.

Now if grammar includes '[a]ll the requirements for sense', it must then also include rules such as 'There exist people other than myself'. For isn't that a requisite underpinning of sense – a preparation for such descriptions as 'There are twenty of us in this room' or 'Vietnam's population is 96.5 million'? Moreover, following Wittgenstein's criterion for the misuse of grammar in his reply to Moore above ('It does not have sense to say . . .'), it has at least as little sense to say 'I can't be sure that anyone exists but me' as to say 'Three men was working'. In fact, people are more likely *not* to understand what you are saying in the first case than in the second. In both cases, they'll understand all the words, but as Monk noted, violations of grammar can be more or less pernicious – so that whereas 'Three men was working' is laughable at worst, 'I can't be sure that anyone exists but me' smacks of the pathological. We'll come back to this.

Grammar, then, is a normatively sanctioned system or method of representation / description; it allows us to use words in order to *intelligibly* represent, describe, express, misrepresent, misdescribe, imagine, pretend, lie about, etc. how things are. I would say that one of the continuous tracks of Wittgenstein's philosophy is the discernment and elucidation of grammar – its nature and its limits. This chapter traces Wittgenstein's evolving notion of grammar from the *Tractatus* to *On Certainty*. We can distinguish in Wittgenstein what I will call a 'thin grammar' – a grammar that governs our use of words independently of facts about the world – from a 'thick grammar' – a grammar that is 'reality-soaked'[1] or fact dependent. It seems to me that Wittgenstein's thick grammar grows increasingly thick; so much so that there occurs in 'the third Wittgenstein'[2] what I call *a grammaticalization of experience*. This is particularly notable in his notion of 'patterns of life' in *Last Writings in the Philosophy of Psychology* and of hinge certainty in *On Certainty*[3]; and it reflects his growing realization that grammar can be anthropo-*logical*, as it were, and that it can manifest itself as *a way of acting*. In moves that exceed anything in *Philosophical Investigations*, the third Wittgenstein makes grammar *enactive*. However, we shall see that his unrelenting, albeit at times hesitant, connection of grammar to the stream of life in no way infringes on the 'autonomy of grammar'. I will now briefly retrace Wittgenstein's drawing of the limits of language in the *Tractatus* as it relates to nonsense and ineffability; for it remains, in this, essentially unchanged and informs what the later Wittgenstein will call grammar.

2. Drawing the limits of language

In 'On Heidegger on Being and Dread', written in 1929, Wittgenstein writes:

> Man feels the urge to run up against the limits of language. Think for example of the astonishment that anything at all exists. This astonishment cannot be expressed in the form of a question, and there is also no answer whatsoever. Anything we might say is *a priori* bound to be nonsense. Nevertheless we do run up against the limits of language.... This running-up against the limits of language is *ethics*.
> WVC 68

Why is anything we might say in explanation of the astonishment that anything at all exists, nonsense? Why would such an attempt constitute a 'running-up against the limits of language? And how is *that* ethics? In his 'Lecture on Ethics' (written in the same year), Wittgenstein writes:

> I see now that these nonsensical expressions were not nonsensical because I had not yet found the correct expressions, but that their nonsensicality was their very essence. For all I wanted to do with them was just to go beyond the world and that is to say beyond significant language. My whole tendency and, I believe, the tendency of all men who ever tried to write or talk Ethics or Religion was to run against the boundaries of language. This running against the walls of our cage is perfectly, absolutely hopeless. Ethics so far as it springs from the desire to say something about the ultimate meaning of life, the absolute good, the absolute valuable, can be no science. What it says does not add to our knowledge in any sense.
> LE 44

At this early period of his thought, Wittgenstein viewed as nonsensical any expression that did not 'add to our knowledge'[4] – that was not a proposition of natural science (6.53). The nonsensical included ethics and aesthetics (6.421), the mystical (6.522) and his own Tractarian sentences (6.54). None of these have sense – none are bipolar propositions susceptible to truth and falsity – and cannot therefore add to our knowledge. Indeed, even his Tractarian sentences do not *inform*; they *elucidate* (6.54), which is the rightful task of philosophy (4.112). It is *their not adding to knowledge* that makes Tractarian *Sätze* technically nonsensical, devoid of sense.

It is clear then that the *Tractatus* advances a *non-derogatory*, indeed *positive*, understanding of the nonsensical,[5] which it was a mistake on the part of New Wittgensteinians to reject.[6] For, preferring a monochrome, 'austere', reading of nonsense as exclusively gibberish meant having to view Tractarian sentences as gibberish – a consequence they embraced, with no enduring success. Already the first sentence in the 'Lecture on Ethics' passage shows Wittgenstein alluding to different uses of nonsense ('I see now that these nonsensical expressions were not nonsensical because I had not yet found the correct expressions, but that their nonsensicality was their very essence'); but he was also later to make this clearer: '... the word 'nonsense' is used to exclude certain things [...] for different reasons' (AWL 64). By the time of the *Investigations*, Wittgenstein uses the terms 'nonsense', 'senseless', 'has no sense' indiscriminately to refer to combinations of words that are excluded from the language, 'withdrawn from circulation' (PI 500), and insists that this exclusion may be for different reasons:

> To say 'This combination of words makes no sense (*hat keinen Sinn*)' excludes it from the sphere of language and thereby bounds the domain of language. But when one draws a boundary it may be for various kinds of reason.
>
> PI 499

But the *Tractatus*, I'd have thought, was clear enough in its distinctions of different kinds of nonsense. Unlike nonsense which (1) results from a *violation* of sense, say, when categorial boundaries are misread and allowed to overlap, as in the question: 'Is the good more or less identical than the beautiful?' (4.003) or in '2+2 at 3 o'clock equals 4' (4.1272)), there is nonsense (call it 'important nonsense') that does not make sense either because (2) it is *impossible to put into words* (e.g., the mystical, ethics and aesthetics[7]) or because (3) it *enables* or *regulates* sense (e.g., 'There is only one 1' (4.1272)) or because (4) it *elucidates* sense – and this includes Tractarian remarks. Nonsense that regulates sense is one of the early manifestations of what Wittgenstein will later call 'grammar'.

Moreover, inasmuch as the Tractarian Wittgenstein takes only truth-conditional utterances to be sayable (6.53)[8], any string of words that does not express a truth-conditional proposition is not, technically speaking, *sayable*. On that count, all nonsense is *ineffable*. However, as regards important nonsense, whereas (2) the mystical, ethics and aesthetics cannot even be put into words, (3) regulative and (4) elucidatory nonsense, though not *sayable* strictly speaking, can be meaningfully formulated for heuristic purposes. That is, they can be formulated to serve as steps towards a clearer understanding of the conditions of sense or 'limit to thought' (TLP Preface). Tractarian remarks must be passed over in silence in that they are not hypothetical propositions, but the 'steps' or 'ladder' to intelligibility or perspicuity (6.54). Once used, the ladder must be thrown away (6.54), for these heuristic aids do not belong to the sphere of language but rather to its delimitation. That is, they belong to what Wittgenstein will later call the *scaffolding of thought* (OC 211). As to elucidatory nonsense, he later makes clear that 'nonsense is produced by trying to express by the use of language what ought to be embodied in the grammar' (MWL 103).

If important nonsense is by definition ineffable, ineffability, too, appears validated. This sheds light on the value for Wittgenstein of 'what we must pass over in silence' (TLP 7); as does this, from Paul Engelmann: 'Wittgenstein passionately believes that all that really matters in human life is precisely what, in his view, we must be silent about'[9] (EL 97). But silence here is not deadening: what really matters cannot be said but it isn't imperceptible; it can *show* itself, make itself manifest, to us. And it often does this *through* language: 'the unutterable will be – unutterably – *contained* in what has been uttered' (EL 7), and we can apprehend it. Our apprehension of significance, as non-propositionally conveyed in a work of literature, is of that kind – it resembles our grasp of wit. But grammar, too, *shows* itself in our use of language.

The later Wittgenstein will extend the list of the *sayable* to include non-truth-conditional uses of language (e.g., spontaneous utterances, questions, imperatives),[10] but he will never give up the idea that some things cannot be *said* in the sphere of language – that is, 'in the flow of the language-game'; or the idea that some things cannot be put into words *at all* but can only show themselves *through* words (and, he will add, through deeds)[11]. In fact, he will add *certainties* to the list of the ineffable – the grammatical ineffable. Like regulative nonsense, certainties cannot be *said* because they constitute the scaffolding of sense, not its object[12]. Basic certainties (e.g., 'There exist people other than myself', 'I have a body', 'Human beings need nourishment') are 'removed from the traffic' (OC 210); they cannot meaningfully be said in the flow of the language-game as if they were open for discussion because they are bounds of sense (rules of grammar), not objects of sense.

In fact, the *Tractatus* sets the stage for what Wittgenstein will later call 'grammar': grammar is that which enables or regulates sense (and so is itself nonsensical) and cannot meaningfully be said in the flow of the language-game but only heuristically articulated. What is also incipient in the *Tractatus* is the idea of philosophy as conceptual or grammatical elucidation:

> Philosophy aims at the logical clarification of thoughts. . . . A philosophical work consists essentially of elucidations. [Indeed, this is what he says his Tractarian propositions are: elucidations (6.54)] Philosophy does not result in 'philosophical propositions', but in the clarification of propositions. Without philosophy thoughts are, as it were, cloudy and indistinct: its task is to make them clear and to give them sharp boundaries.
>
> TLP 4.112

Here again, Wittgenstein will never retract his Tractarian view that conceptual elucidation is the task of philosophy; that '[t]he philosophical problem is an awareness of disorder in our concepts, and can be solved by ordering them' (BT 309). This emphasis on grammatical elucidation has given Wittgenstein a bad name in mainstream philosophy: it seems as if he reduces everything to language, which would make him a linguistic idealist. Does Wittgenstein think philosophers only play games with words? Language-*games*? What philosophers should be primarily interested with is life, not language. Language is for linguists, no? No. Grammatical elucidation is important for life because grammar is inextricable from life. Let's see in what way it is inextricable.

3. Grammar delimits the world

The connection between language and reality has long perplexed philosophers. Is human language the result of our attempts to translate 'nature's own language'? But how can nature have a language? More plausibly, is human language the result of our attempts to facilitate and enhance our relationship with nature, and each other? 'The connection between "language and reality" is made by definitions of words, and these belong to grammar', writes Wittgenstein[13] (PG 97).

There is no such thing in the world, or nature – or however we want to name what Paul Boghossian calls the 'basic worldly dough' (2006, 35) – as an outline, a system or a concept. The system does not reside in the nature of things (Z 357). Nature is conceptually unmarked; it is we who, with our use of language, cut paths or inroads of salience and understanding in order to harness the contingent in ways that produce and govern sense for us. For Wittgenstein, this tracing is not metaphysical, but grammatical: 'One thinks that one is tracing the outline of a thing's nature over and over again, and one is merely tracing round the frame through which we look at it' (PI 114). Boghossian is right: 'we have no choice but to recognize that there must be some objective, mind-independent facts' (2006, 35). However, as linguistic beings, we come to experience and grapple with the world *always already* with language, and there is no getting out of language to compare or measure our outline against bare particulars. At the *conceptual* basis of our confrontation with experience are not bare particulars, but grammar: it is *grammar* that tells us what *kind* of object anything is (PI 373). Wittgenstein's realization that the demarcation is not empirical but grammatical – that the connection between language and world is a grammatical or logical connection (these are synonymous for the later Wittgenstein[14]) – is, as far as I know, unprecedented in the history of philosophy.

Wittgenstein, however, is no linguistic idealist;[15] he does not reduce reality, 'the world' or even 'our world', to language. Though we are responsible for its conceptual outline, the world is not our invention. Is not even the Tractarian Wittgenstein a linguistic idealist? I think not. 'The limits of my language mean the limits of my world' may be read as expressing the view that 'my world' – i.e. my perception of the world – is concept laden. The later Wittgenstein fleshed this out in his many remarks on how enculturation conditions us to perceive the world through a conceptual frame[16]. But what I want to stress here is that our perception being (from a very early age) concept-laden does not make it *judgement* laden: though I must possess the concept of 'grief' to see grief on someone's face, judgement need not come into it.[17] In most cases, I see emotion in someone's face immediately: no judgement, interpretation or inference is needed; and therefore no so-called 'Theory of mind'.[18] Of course, in describing the face as 'sad', I am using a concept, but I am not thereby necessarily making a judgement. That much perception is concept-laden does not make it theory laden. This is important in that it shows the nonempirical and nonepistemic nature of our *basic* conceptual interactions with the world.

When Peter Hacker writes that the post-Tractarian Wittgenstein sees the harmony between language and reality as no longer orchestrated between language and reality but *within* language – that is, by grammar – and that far from reflecting the logical structure of the world, grammar is 'arbitrary', it owes no homage to reality' (2000, 9–19), he should be wary of throwing out the baby with the bathwater. For Wittgenstein, grammar's demarcations, though not accountable to reality,[19] do owe some homage to it. Language (or rather grammar[20]) constitutes *our* world in that it conceptually demarcates *the* world; but that demarcation is itself conditioned by the world.

4. The world's impact on grammar: a 'reality-soaked' grammar

Certainly, Wittgenstein is clear that grammar is not – in fact, *cannot be* – accountable to reality: 'Grammatical conventions cannot be justified by describing what is represented. Any such description already presupposes the grammatical rules' (PR 67). But he is also clear that reality has to impact our grammar or concepts:[21] 'The rule we lay down is the one most strongly suggested by the facts of experience' (AWL 84). Though we don't read off our concepts from nature, our concepts are impacted by natural *facts* which are fundamental or salient for us: 'What we have to mention in order to explain the significance, I mean the importance, of a concept, are often extremely general facts of nature: such facts as are hardly ever mentioned because of their great generality' (PI, p. 56). But what is the nature of this correspondence? 'Would it be correct to say our concepts reflect our life?' he asks; to which he replies: 'They stand in the middle of it' (LW II, 72). This means that our concepts are immersed in our life, intertwined with it in a dynamic interaction: the fabric of life provides the milieu in which our concepts are formed; in turn, our concepts order the fabric of life. Does this mean that the grammar of our language is *justified* by facts? Wittgenstein asks himself this question again and again, from at least 1930.[22] Here is one late formulation of it:

> If we can find a ground [by which Wittgenstein means a 'justification': he uses the German *begründen*] for the structures of concepts among the facts of nature (psychological and physical), then isn't the description of the structure of our concepts really disguised natural science; ought we not in that case to concern ourselves not with grammar, but with what lies at the bottom of grammar in nature?
>
> Indeed the correspondence between our grammar and general (seldom mentioned) facts of nature does concern us. But our interest does not fall back on these *possible* causes. We are not pursuing a natural science … Nor natural history … .
>
> RPP I, 46; cf. PI, p. 230

This[23] makes it clear that when Wittgenstein speaks of the correspondence between concepts and nature, he is talking about the correspondence between the *structures* of concepts – that is, our grammatical rules – our grammar – and facts of nature. Take the concept of pain, some of the 'structures' of that concept can be expressed in grammatical rules such as: 'Human beings are normally susceptible to pain'; 'Tables and chairs don't feel pain'; 'There is psychological as well as physical pain', etc. In these passages, then,

Wittgenstein is saying that of course we are interested in the correspondence between our grammar and very general facts of nature, but not in the way natural scientists or historians are interested in this correspondence. That is, we are not interested in any empirical justification or historical account for our having the grammatical rules we do. Let me give an example.

There are cases where a rule of grammar may have its historical root in an empirical discovery; for example, the realization that men have something to do with the reproductive process (it was long thought that women procreated singly[24]) may well be at the root of the grammatical rule: 'Every human being has two biological parents.' However, such correspondence or justification is of no interest to philosophers; what philosophers are interested in is what *logically* demarcates sense from nonsense, and that cannot be due to justification: 'The essence of logical possibility is what is laid down in language. What is laid down depends on facts, but is not made true or false by them' (AWL 162). Our grammatical rules are not the result of reasoning or justification. So how are facts connected to grammar?

In contrast to what I will call a '*thin* grammar', whose rules are *not* conditioned by facts (e.g., '2 + 2 = 4'; 'A rod has a length'; 'This is (what we call) a table') and are normatively engendered and sanctioned, the rules of '*thick* grammar' (e.g., 'Human beings have bodies, need nourishment, sleep'; 'Human beings can go to the moon') *are* rooted in facts and may be either experientially or normatively engendered and sanctioned. Wittgenstein opposes the terms: 'cause' and 'ground' to distinguish a nonratiocinated rootedness in facts and experience from a justified rootedness. Would it be right to say that my having a body is a bound of sense for me *because* previous experience has taught me so? No, our lifelong experience of having a body may be the 'cause' of it being a bound of sense, but it is not its 'ground' (cf. OC 429; 474). I have not come to the conclusion that I have a body 'by following a particular line of thought' (OC 103). Our *experience* of having a body or of mountains not sprouting up in an hour is not empirical or epistemic; it is either instinctive (as is the case of having a body) or acquired via repeated exposure or conditioning, and so second nature (as is the case with mountains being there immemorially). It may help here to distinguish between 'experiential' (*embedded in* experience) and 'empirical' (*inferred from* experience). Our lifelong experience of ourselves as embodied; our experience of the world as populated by people other than ourselves; our experience of mountains as geological structures that do not sprout up in an hour[25] make such experience part of the scaffolding or background of sense for us. These facts are 'fused into the foundations of our language-game' (OC 558) – that is, they are part of our grammar. And where some thick rules of grammar are originally grounded in fact and articulated as news-breaking propositions (e.g., 'Human beings can go to the moon'), it is only with time and repetition, once they have hardened into a rule, that they belong to the scaffolding of thought.[26]

5. 'The common behaviour of mankind'

While acknowledging the buzzing indeterminacy, spontaneity and irreducibility of human life, Wittgenstein also keeps reminding us of certainties and regularities.

Amongst these are our *shared* natural reactions; what he calls 'the common behaviour of mankind' (PI 206): reactions such as crying when in pain or sad; smiling when glad; jumping when startled; gasping or screaming when afraid; reacting to someone's suffering. He calls these instinctive common reactions or action patterns 'prototype[s] of thought' (RPP I, 916). These prototypes or action patterns are the necessary starting points of language: 'it is characteristic of our language that the foundation on which it grows consists in *steady ways of living, regular ways of acting*' (CE 397; my emphasis). Without certain constantly recurring patterns, our concepts would have no grip; so that our acquiring concepts, such as pain, requires that we have normal prototypical human reactions: 'If a child looked radiant when it was hurt, and shrieked for no apparent reason, one couldn't teach him to use the word "pain"' (LPP 37).

In his last writings on the philosophy of psychology, Wittgenstein delves deeper into these action patterns as they typically, and often internally, relate to feelings and emotions. He introduces the expressions 'patterns of life' and 'patterns of experience'[27] to denote the 'constant repetition' (RPP II, 626), the regular and tell-tale characteristics of our various psychological expressions and behaviours (e.g., those of pain, joy, grief, hope, but also of *simulated* pain, joy grief, hope etc.) – going as far as to suggest that typical physiognomies and constitutive rhythm and tempo attach to them:

> 'Grief' describes a pattern which recurs, with different variations, in the weave of our life. If a man's bodily expression of sorrow and of joy alternated, say with the ticking of a clock, here we should not have the characteristic formation of the pattern of sorrow or of the pattern of joy.
>
> PI, p. 174; cf. LW I, 406

> For pretence is a (certain) pattern within the weave of life. It is repeated in an infinite number of variations.
>
> LW I, 862

> Someone smiles and his further reactions fit neither a genuine nor a simulated joy. We might say 'I don't know my way around with him. It is neither the picture (pattern) of genuine nor of pretended joy'.
>
> LW II, 61

'Patterns of life' refer to recurring – mostly behavioural and facial – expressions characteristic of psychological concepts. There is not only one, or even a handful of 'occasions' that we might call 'grief', but innumerable ones that are interwoven with a thousand other patterns (cf. LW I, 966). And this is so for *all* our psychological concepts, because the 'natural foundation' for the way they are formed 'is the complex nature and the variety of human contingencies' (RPP II, 614). As a result the concepts themselves lack determinacy and have a kind of elasticity; but where most philosophers attempt to tame or reduce the indeterminacy, Wittgenstein wants to capture it: 'I do not want to reduce unsharpness to sharpness; but to capture unsharpness conceptually' (MS 1367, 64). Yet this unsharpness does not mean that our concepts are so elastic as to lack a hard core. Indeed Wittgenstein's depiction of psychological indeterminacy is everywhere bounded not by rules, but by certain *regularities*: an order or pattern emerges from obstinate, though constantly varied, repetition; the evidence has tell-tale *characteristics*, our feelings and behaviours are informed by *typical physiognomies* (see Rosat 2007). Of course, 'there are simple and more complicated cases; and that is important for the concept' (LW I, 967), for it is the simple cases that give the concept its solid centre, its unambiguous core' (RPP II, 614): 'There is an *unmistakable* expression of joy and its opposite' (LW II, 32; original emphasis). The point here is not to eradicate indeterminacy, but to recognize that there are *basic* regularities in the 'hurly burly of human action' (Z 567), and that these are what shape our psychological bedrock or psychological grammar. This, without losing sight of the fact that 'simple language-games [...] are poles of a description, not the ground-floor of a theory' (RPP I, 633). The point is that, though there is an *indefiniteness* or *indeterminacy* essential to the kind of *repetition* in question – for it is a repetition that is embedded in life – there *is* a repetition, a pattern; and our psychological grammar is conditioned by such patterns:

> Seeing life as a weave, this pattern (pretence, say) is not always complete and is varied in a multiplicity of ways. But we, in our conceptual world, keep on seeing the same, recurring with variations. That is how our concepts take it. For concepts are not for use on a single occasion.
>
> Z 568

6. The grammaticalization of experience

The 'hinge' certainties of *On Certainty* and the 'patterns of life / experience' of *Last Writings* attest to the fact that one of the leitmotifs in the work of the third Wittgenstein is what I call the *grammaticalization of experience*. Thick grammar – inasmuch as it is conditioned by our human form of life[28] – is a grammaticalization of experience[29]; one might say it is anthropo-*logical*: 'The basic concepts are interwoven so closely with what is most fundamental in our way of living that they are therefore unassailable' (LW II, 43–4). Unassailable means impregnable and infallible. So that grammar, though impacted by facts, remains autonomous.

The grammaticalization of experience did not come easily to Wittgenstein. As early as 1930, he writes: 'I will count any fact whose obtaining is a presupposition of a proposition's making sense as belonging *to language*' (PR 45)' (by which he means grammar[30]). And indeed in PI, he had gone as far as to count objects such as samples as belonging to grammar.[31] However, in his last notes: *Remarks on Colour* and *On Certainty*, we find him hesitant to apply this to contingent facts: 'Here it could now be asked what I really want, to what extent I want to deal with grammar' (RC 309); and what he'd asserted as a 'correspondence between concepts and very general facts of nature' in PI, is now put in the form of a question, albeit a rhetorical one, in *On Certainty*: 'Indeed, doesn't it seem obvious that the possibility of a language-game is conditioned by certain facts?' (OC 617).

Though comfortable with the idea that some contingent facts condition our grammar, Wittgenstein was uneasy with assigning the expression of these contingent facts a grammatical status – indeed, with recognizing seemingly empirical propositions to be grammatical rules. So much so that, as late as OC, he even contemplates a compromise: 'Is it that rule and empirical proposition merge into one another?' (OC 309). However, his '[inclination] to believe that not everything that has the form of an empirical proposition *is* one' (OC 308) wins the day; in *On Certainty*, he comes to see that the contingent or empirical nature of these propositions is invalidated by their very unassailability or indubitability. In fact, he could have reminded himself of this passage from the *Remarks on the Foundations of Mathematics*: 'To accept a proposition as unshakably certain . . . means to use it as a grammatical rule' (RFM 170). Be that as it may, we can safely say that in *On Certainty*, he is finally reconciled with the fact that some apparent empirical propositions 'form the foundation of all operating with thoughts (with language)' (OC 401). Wittgenstein has understood that grammar can be 'reality-soaked' without being empirical, but the journey was laborious, confirming that 'Not empiricism and yet realism in philosophy' is indeed 'the hardest thing' (RFM 325).

Our concepts delimit the world; but the world has its impact. Realizing the full extent to which – as Cora Diamond puts it, '. . . grammar is to be seen in how we live' (1989, 20), Wittgenstein expands our conception of the logical. He gives grammar/logic an anthropological twist, and thereby redefines its limits. Logic is seen to be 'reality-soaked', but without falling into the traps abhorred by Frege: it is flawed neither by subjectivity (psychologism) nor fallibility (empiricism). This is crucially important for philosophy; it redefines the limits of sense or possibility.

7. Redefining the limits of possibility

Wittgenstein's conception of the logical is internally linked to our human form of life and this does not sit well with traditional conceptions of logical necessity. Stanley Cavell points out this apparent shortcoming:

> Wittgenstein's view of necessity is . . . internal to his view of what philosophy is. His philosophy provides, one might say, an anthropological, or even anthropomorphic, view of necessity: and that can be disappointing; as if it is not really *necessity* which he has given an anthropological view of. As though if the a priori has a history it cannot really be the a priori in question.
>
> 1979, 118–19

On the standard philosophical view, the logical must encompass *all possible worlds*. Most philosophers think, like Bertrand Russell, that 'No logical absurdity results from the hypothesis that the world consists of myself and my thoughts and feelings and sensations, and that everything else is mere fancy' (1912, 10). This, the Tractarian Wittgenstein would have endorsed: 'A thought contains the possibility of the situation of which it is the thought. What is thinkable is possible too' (TLP 3.02). But, on Wittgenstein's anthropo-*logical* view of logic (which would include the grammatical rule: 'There exist people other than myself'), logical absurdity *would* result from such hypotheses or thoughts as 'The world consists of myself alone' – unless meant figuratively or embedded in a fictional context. Conceivability can be equal to possibility in fictional worlds, but in our world, possibility is dependent on the conditions of sense anchored in our human form of life. A thought that has lost its human mooring and runs wild on the uncharted tracks of the imagination is not a possibility, it's a thought. It takes anthropo-*logical* bounds of sense to enable us to discern the *humanly* possible from the merely imaginable. Of course, these reality-soaked bounds of sense are, by definition, *basic* – but it only takes something as basic as the grammatical rule: 'There exist people other than myself' to render senseless the alleged possibility that 'The world consists of myself alone'.

Philosophical speculation should not be deemed sufficiently confined by conceivability; it must be constrained by logical parameters specific to our world. Raimond Gaita echoes Cavell's denunciation of traditional epistemology and logic as a 'denial of the human' because the concepts informing them are 'essentially unconditioned by the fact that they are concepts deployed by human beings' – and, he adds, echoing Winch this time, that 'we cannot purify our concepts of their embeddedness in human life ... without being left with only a shadow play of the grammar of serious judgement' (1990, xi; xii). Wittgenstein decried this purification of our concepts, or as he put it, the 'crystalline purity of logic' (PI 107). For logic to stop being 'empty', it must '[g]et back to the rough ground'! (ibid.).

When the only constraints on logical necessity are a few logical laws pared of any *human* specification, nothing impedes the so-called 'possibilities' that: 'There may exist no one in the world but myself'; 'The world may be five minutes old' and 'Human beings can switch bodies'.[32] To any ordinary person, these are inanities unless uttered in sci-fi contexts; and philosophers shouldn't be in the business of propagating them as possibilities. Hume is right that '[n]othing is more dangerous to reason than the flights of the imagination, and nothing has been the occasion of more mistakes among philosophers[33]' (*Treatise* 1.4.7).

Wittgenstein had a second look at logical necessity and saw that, as Diamond puts it, it has a *human* face (1991, 6, 13). The logical limit of possibility in our form of life has to be an anthropo-*logical* limit. Wittgenstein's extension of logic to incorporate specifically human bounds of sense prevents – or ought to prevent – philosophers from envisaging life-size absurdities as legitimate possibilities.

8. Grammar as enactive

We have seen that grammar can manifest itself in action. All grammar – thin or thick – deploys itself as a technique, a know-how, not as a set of principles that we learn and apply rationally: 'To understand a language means to be master of a technique' (PI 199). In mastering different language-games, a child masters the *grammar* of words; their use in the language: 'How is the word used?' and 'What is the grammar of the word?' I shall take as being the same question (AWL 3).

Wittgenstein's notion of grammar is not more complicated than this. Rules of grammar are simply expressions of the norms of sense that grow out of, and in tandem with, our natural ways of acting and our socio-cultural practices. Grammar does not generate language; nor does it exist independently of language or action; it is embedded and enacted in what we say and do. The proper use of the word 'pain', for example, is manifested in our ways of speaking and acting, and so the child assimilates grammatical rules or norms as it assimilates the language – through exposure to, and guidance in, correct usage. That is, children are habituated into standards of correctness of the practice in question, and thereby formed to act and react in particular ways; they are trained to master a technique through the inculcation of a normative attitude. The assimilation of rules – be they linguistic or mathematical – does not have the features of a *learning that*, but of a *learning how* – of a training or a conditioning, a way of acting.

Wittgenstein's account of the emergence, transmission and practice of language is an enactive account. In teaching a child to replace the natural expression of pain with the word 'pain', adults teach the child 'new pain-behaviour' (PI 244). Language is, in such cases, an extension of an underlying action pattern, a more sophisticated way of acting. So that, in investigating our grammar – thick or thin – the philosopher examines and reflects on the practices, forms of life and patterns of life in which it is inextricably embedded. *Pace* its detractors, grammatical or conceptual investigation is not a philosophical method that ignores reality, but a way of elucidating *our* bounds of sense.

2

Universal Grammar

Wittgenstein versus Chomsky

In memoriam Laurence Goldstein (1947–2014)[1]

The motivations for the claim that language is innate are, for many, quite straightforward. The innateness of language is seen as the only way to solve what has been termed the 'logical problem of language acquisition': the mismatch between linguistic input and linguistic output. In this chapter, I begin by unravelling several strands of the nativist argument, offering replies as I go along. I then give an outline of Wittgenstein's view of language acquisition, showing how it renders otiose problems posed by nativists like Chomsky – not least by means of Wittgenstein's own brand of grammar which, unlike Chomsky's, does not reside in the brain, but in our practices.

---

1. Introduction

A few years ago, I sent Laurence Goldstein a draft entitled 'Coming to Language: Wittgenstein's Theory of Language Acquisition'. Laurence being a Wittgenstein-inspired philosopher, I was astonished when his comments revealed a leaning toward Chomsky's Universal Grammar:

> There is one problem that you mention but don't much discuss, about which I still feel some unease, and that's the 'poverty of stimulus' argument. You deny that there is any such poverty – you talk about the child's 'multifarious practice and repeated exposure', but child developmentalists say that infants are typically exposed to very little language and close to zero correction of grammar by parents. I am also disinclined to ignore Derek Bickerton's evidence for the 'language bioprogram hypothesis'. Bickerton gathered a large amount of data on pidgins and creoles. A pidgin has rudimentary grammar; a creole is grammatically complex, but the transition from one to the other is made within the space of one generation, suggesting that grammar is biologically hard-wired.

However, a week later, Laurence wrote me the following:

> For the last week, I've been hanging around with my first grandchild, now six months old, and so have had the opportunity to assess the poverty of stimulus hypotheses. Of course, that environment, replete with articulate adults bent on amusing the child was unrepresentative. But what struck me, and this would be true too of the linguistically less rich environments, was the variety of 'language-games' to which the child is exposed. Almost all the words it hears are interwoven with action – objects are pointed to, animal sounds are made in the context of stories about country life, the child is lifted and lowered to the accompaniment of 'up we go……down we go' etc.

In saying this, Laurence had replaced the poverty of *grammatically complex* instruction and correction with the richness of exposure to a huge variety of *language-games* where words, behaviour, context and repetition interact with each other to inculcate in a child her native language. In Peter Hacker's words: 'We must not think of understanding a language as mastery of a calculus, but rather as mastery of complex interlocking language-games' (2015b, 11).

In this chapter, I begin by unravelling some strands of the nativist argument, offering replies as I go along. I then give an outline of Wittgenstein's view of language acquisition to see if it doesn't render otiose problems posed by nativists like Chomsky, not least by means of Wittgenstein's own brand of grammar which, unlike Chomsky's, does not reside in the brain, but in our practices.[2]

2. Chomsky's Universal Grammar: The nativist argument

The motivations for the claim that language is innate are, for many, quite straightforward. The innateness of language is seen as the only way to solve the 'logical problem of language acquisition' (LPLA): the mismatch between linguistic input and linguistic output. How is it that children come to know and use – at an incredible speed – linguistic principles they have never been taught (and indeed, that exceed the knowledge of a PhD in linguistics), and how is it they can produce an unlimited number of sentences from the limited data to which they are exposed? This is also known as 'poverty of the stimulus' or the underdetermination of the output. The nativist solution to this problem is that linguistic principles do not have to be input or learned at all; we are born with them – they come in the form of an innate Universal Grammar. For Chomsky, then, knowledge of language is based on a core set of principles embodied in all languages[3] and innately stored somewhere in the mind/brain of every human being. Let's flesh out the nativist argument.

The syntax or structure of any language is so abstruse that it seems impossible that children should learn it – particularly as quickly as they do. As Green and Vervaecke write:

> Constituent hierarchical structure, an almost definitional feature of language, is just not something, by and large, that we come up against in the everyday world; and even when we do, it is darn hard, even for the best and brightest among us, to figure it out. Witness, for instance, the struggles of linguists themselves to

adequately characterize language.... linguists have been unable to discover exactly what the rules are, even after dozens (one might argue hundreds or even thousands) of years of research. By contrast, virtually every child does it within a few years (with far less in the way of specialized cognitive machinery, and control over the quality of the incoming data, it is worth pointing out, than a Ph.D. in linguistics).

1997

The difficulty is compounded by the fact that the child's environment is, allegedly, of hardly any help. As Anderson and Lightfoot note: 'The child masters a rich system of knowledge without significant instruction and despite an impoverished stimulus; the process involves only a narrow range of 'errors' and takes place rapidly, even explosively between two and three years of age. The main question is how children acquire so much more than they experience' (2000, 13-14).

The *poverty of the stimulus* argument strikes at empirical or social theories of language acquisition by claiming that the utterances encountered by the child in experience are too limited[4] for it to be possible to learn the language by generalizing from them, and so we are forced to suppose that the brain contains innate means of creating an unlimited number of grammatical sentences from a limited vocabulary. Hence, Chomsky's stipulation that the child is born with a 'language acquisition device' (LAD) which, when the child starts being exposed to language, recognizes which language it is and sets the correct parameters for that particular language. Thanks to the LAD, the child knows *intuitively* that there are some words that behave like verbs, and others like nouns, and that there is a limited set of possibilities as to their ordering in a sentence. The LAD can enable this because it is equipped with a Universal Grammar (UG) which consists of invariant principles,[5] as well as parameters[6] whose settings vary between languages, and recursive rules to enable productivity or creativity. Thus equipped, the child is able to apply her built-in unconscious knowledge of how language works to the limited number of sentences she hears, and at an otherwise (allegedly) unexplainable speed[7]: 'Learning a particular language thus becomes the comparatively simple matter of elaborating upon this antecedently possessed knowledge, and hence appears a much more tractable task for young children to attempt' (Cowie 2008).

Minimal exposure to 'language evidence' is necessary to trigger the various parameters of Universal Grammar[8] (Cook and Newson 2007, 186). As for vocabulary, writes Chomsky:

You just have to learn your language's vocabulary. The universal grammar doesn't tell you that "tree" means "tree" in English. But once you've learned the vocabulary items and fixed the grammatical parameters for English, the whole system is in place. And the general principles genetically programmed into the language organ just churn away to yield all the particular facts about English grammar[9].

1983

It is, then, through the *interaction* between our genetically-inherited principles and the linguistic environment to which we happen to be exposed that a specific language emerges:

> ... English-speaking children learn from their environment that the verb *is* may be pronounced [iz] or [z], and native principles prevent the reduced form from occurring in the wrong places.
>
> Anderson and Lightfoot 2000, 6

Let's see how this prevention works in practice. According to Anderson and Lightfoot:

> The verb *is* may be used in its full form or its reduced form: English speakers can say either *Kim is happy* or *Kim's happy*. However, certain instances of *is* never reduce: for example, the [is] underlined items in *Kim is happier than Tim is* or *I wonder where the concert is on Wednesday*. Most speakers are not aware of this, but we all know subconsciously not to use the reduced form in such cases. How did we come to know this? As children, we were not instructed to avoid the reduced form in certain places. Yet, all children typically attain the ability to use the forms in the adult fashion, and this ability is quite independent of intelligence level or educational background. Children attain it early in their linguistic development. More significantly, children do not try out the non-occurring forms as if testing a hypothesis, in the way that they "experiment" by using forms like *goed* and *taked*. The ability emerges perfectly and as if by magic.
>
> 2000, 3

On the nativist view, then, the child is faced with a chaotic linguistic environment and scans it – in this case, she is looking for *clitics*: unstressed words that cannot stand on their own (e.g., The contraction of *is*, in 'What's going on?' or the possessive marker *'s* in 'The man's book'). Since clitics and their behaviour are predefined at the genetic level, the child is able to arrive at a 'plausible analysis' following exposure to a few simple expressions: she concludes that no reduction obtains for the second '*is*' in *Kim is happier than Tim is* or in *I wonder where the concert is on Wednesday*, and countless other cases. The child needs no correction in *arriving* at this system: the very fact that *'s* is a clitic, a notion defined in advance of any experience, dictates that it may not occur in certain contexts. She now has a *reason* for the generalization that *is* may be pronounced as *'s* does not hold across the board.[10]

How this in fact goes on in the brain is, of course, far from clear. It is merely *assumed* that the brain is able to produce, store and evoke symbolic representations that inform or instruct the child when, in fact, symbolic representations can be determined only by conventions, not by neurons.[11] It seems also assumed that the child is able to understand a notion like *clitic*, for she is said to come to a conclusion about it. To reply that all the analysis, scanning, inferring and concluding she is said to do occurs unconsciously or intuitively should not exempt the child from understanding, for what would be the sense of saying that the child arrives at a '*plausible analysis*' of something she does not, and *cannot*, understand? Moreover, this is all supposed to add to her antecedent *knowledge* of the language. But what 'knowledge' of 'clitics' can an average child 'already' have at three? Again, adding 'unconscious' to 'knowledge' or replacing 'knowledge' with 'cognizance', as Chomsky was – precisely for such reasons – compelled to do, hardly allows him to retain all the epistemic activity – scanning, analysis, comparing, inferring and concluding – that allegedly goes on in the child's brain.

I suggest, then, that we replace this fantastical child-grammarian scenario with an explanation along the lines of: reducing the 's' in cases such as *Kim is happier than Tim is* makes the sentence incomprehensible; it gives: **Kim is happier than Tim's* – where the contraction misleadingly suggests possession, unlike such correct constructions as 'Sue's liking this'. Failure to communicate meaning may well be what discourages the child from reducing in such cases, besides the fact that she never hears it done in such contexts.

3. Principles not required

It is sometimes difficult to pick out what Chomsky is faulting, not simply because his views have changed considerably over the years, but also because of his lack of clarity. In speaking of language acquisition, Chomsky sometimes speaks of *language* not being acquired but at other times of *principles* not being acquired. So that when he claims children are seldom corrected by parents, one can easily disagree, but it is more difficult to disagree with the view that parents do not teach children linguistic *principles*, which leads Chomsky to conclude that these must be innate. For, on Chomsky's view – shared by nativists generally – to acquire a language, one must know the *principles* of language. Call this Chomsky's 'Principle Requirement'. The poverty of the stimulus argument crucially rests on this misleading requirement; that is, on the false assumption that the only way to *acquire and use* language in all its grammatical diversity is to know it in all its grammatical *complexity*. And as no child, or indeed adult, is ever taught all the grammatical complexity of language, we are forced to stipulate an innate universal grammar which endows the child with this complex knowledge – these principles – for how could she otherwise understand and speak her language?

But surely the fact that children know *language* by age three need not imply that children know *linguistic principles* by age three; what it does – more plausibly – imply is that knowledge of linguistic principles is not needed at all to know or use a language. The idea that children learn languages by discerning grammatical principles – or indeed, that this is the only possible way of acquiring a language – is an unnecessary and unsubstantiated stipulation which goes against all we experience and witness about how native languages are learned; namely, by directed and undirected repeated exposure to use, in a multiplicity of contexts. This basic observation is fleshed out in diverse ways by empirical studies.

Research shows that children systematize the language they hear based on the probability and frequency of forms, not on the basis of principles; they learn probabilistic patterns of word distributions, not syntactic rules; they generalize from cues, not from rules.[12] A series of experiments conducted by Hudson-Kam and Newport (2009) show that children ignore minor variations in linguistic input and reproduce only the most frequent forms – thereby regularizing and systematizing the inconsistent input and standardizing the language they hear around them. As Melodie Dye has also found:

Young children ... act like finely-tuned antennas, picking up the dominant frequency in their surroundings and ignoring the static. Because of this – because toddlers tend to pick up on what is common and consistent, while ignoring what is variable and unreliable – they end up homing in on and reproducing only the most frequent patterns in what they hear. In doing so they fail to learn many of the subtleties and idiosyncrasies present in adult speech (they will come to learn or invent those later).

2010

It is this picking up of the dominant frequency that explains characteristic errors such as children adding the suffix '-ed' to irregular verbs to mark the past, such as 'He hitted me'.[13] Such findings fit within a relatively new approach to language acquisition known as 'statistical learning'; as also 'similarity-based generalization' to explain how children are able to figure out how to use new words by generalizing about their use from similar words they already know how to use (Yarlett and Ramscar 2008). And of course, children also learn from repeated failure.[14] So that word-learning is a probabilistic, success- and error-driven process, rather than a process of implicit rule-application.

Also, the nativist emphasis on the poverty of grammatical instruction and correction seems to rely on a restricted view of these. That children do not learn language with much in the way of *overt instruction*, as Fiona Cowie (2008) contends, is right if by this she means they are not taught linguistic principles or rules of syntax; but that they are often taught *language* is readily observable, as well as argued for by interactionist theorists of language acquisition, such as Lev Vygotsky's (with his notion of *collaborative learning*) and Jerome Bruner (with his *Language Acquisition Support System*).[15] In fact, as Ted Schoneberger (2010) has shown, the crucial nativist claim that children find little linguistic reinforcement or corrective feedback is a myth. There is plenty of empirical evidence that children do encounter corrective data.[16] However, when presented with such evidence, Chomskians reject it on the grounds that whereas only *some* children are exposed to correct data, *all* children learn the correct rule. Indeed, a key justification for a Universal Grammar is that it explains why *all* children pick up the language correctly. As Green and Vervaecke write:

... the single most important datum to capture when modelling language learning is that children *virtually never* fail to learn language correctly, regardless of what kind of linguistic data they are exposed to early in life.

1997

I don't really know what to make of this; it sounds preposterous in that it is obvious that many children *do* fail to learn language correctly and that, in fact, many of them don't improve with age: a ride on the bus, a stroll in a shopping mall or even a university corridor or an hour of TV viewing will easily attest to the fact that many, if not most, people – children and grown children – do not speak grammatically correct English. For instance, we seem to be wiping out adverbs and are now doing 'amazing'. There is hardly a day when I don't hear some of the errors made in the following sentence: 'I'm feeling *more better* than I *done* yesterday though I'm not my *bestest*; but still, I should *of went* to the gym.' And other such common errors could be heard on the lips of many campaigning MPs, including Harriet Harman boasting about something 'we have *showed* [the country]' (2015 TV campaign appearance). Such errors are much too frequent and consistent to be dismissed as slips of the tongue. The point is not whether or not we ought to deplore this state of things – linguistic norms change,[17] like it or not – but that what we call 'grammatical' is not hard wired. Grammar is a mapping of language norms in use, not a map established in the brain in advance of all use, which linguists try to fathom.

Neither we, nor our brain, rely on or need to know any *principles* to form a correct sentence. If Universal Grammar (innate principles) were there to guarantee that the correct parameter is set, why do children (and adults) not eventually systematically produce the correct version of what they hear? Why, when she lives in an adult community which regularly produces expressions such as 'Me and her went to the gym' or 'They hurt theirself', does the child use these mistaken expressions into adulthood? Or, alternatively correct herself if and when guided or exposed to correct usage? The number of adults who speak ungrammatically, and the fact that, as Dabrowska (2010) shows, agreement on well-formedness of complex sentences is far from universal in adults, easily belie the claim that, unless our language organs are severely impaired, we are universally either actual or potential perfect grammatical users of our native languages. What we speak is what we learn.

The poverty of stimulus argument took added impetus from findings by Derek Bickerton's examination of pidgins and creoles (1984). A pidgin has rudimentary grammar;[18] a creole is grammatically complex, but Bickerton found that the transition from one to the other is made within the space of one generation, and without the creole deriving its grammatical principles from the target language (that of the 'masters'), or from any of the substratum languages (one spoken by some subgroup of the labourers), suggesting that grammar is biologically hard wired. Jean-Michel Fortis (2008) has shown Bickerton's evidence to be faulty. The complexification of Hawaiian pidgin seems to have been accomplished by speakers who were more or less passively bilingual, and therefore previously exposed to complex linguistic data; and new evidence shows that the complexification of pidgin to creole is not made within the space of one generation, but two.[19]

Another argument in support of nativism is the alleged 'domain specificity' of the language faculty: its independence from other aspects of cognition. This dissociation of language from the rest of our cognitive abilities is said to be evidenced by children who are linguistically prolific and yet present impaired intelligence; and, inversely, by cases where language ability is impaired in the presence of otherwise normal cognitive ability. The latter is known as 'Specific Language Impairment'. It is conceded, by Anderson and Lightfoot, that the homogeneity of cases that have been grouped under the SLI diagnosis is quite controversial, but this does not prevent them from using the argument. The controversy, I believe, is mostly to do with cases of feral children as the main evidence in support of SLI. The claim being that feral children fail to develop language despite normal cognitive abilities and exposure to language. But the objection that flares up here must be: that *normal cognitive abilities* are attributed to feral children in the first place. If not retarded from infancy and abandoned because of this, the psychological and physical abuse feral children suffered is alone sufficient to preclude normal language development[20]. The child can hardly be seen as growing up in a nurturing environment; the lack of language acquisition in later life may be due to the results of a generally abusive environment before – but also after – the child was found. For, the teaching methods used after the child is taken into care are often limited, if not repressive: the child is kept in (often harsh) experimental conditions, taught a native language by mere ostensive teaching of words rather than normal exposure and habituation in a form of life. It seems to me, then, that what such cases demonstrate is that language acquisition is *not* separable from cognitive development generally.

There is no space here to go into other kinds of case used to justify 'domain specificity', but as a general response, I would say two things: (1) there may be neural structures in the brain that are crucial to linguistic development, and the impairment of these may result in linguistic disabilities, but this neither justifies nor demands making those structures into a language acquisition device capable of storing and activating grammatical principles; (2) language acquisition is not separate from intelligence; it is one of our abilities that require intelligence, but whose structural impairment does not necessarily impair our other intelligent abilities.

4. Chomsky's Universal Grammar: A hopeless monster[21]

The idea of a Chomskyan-style universal grammar has been contested on linguistic, neurobiological and anthropological fronts. Studies in descriptive linguistics have shown that there is no universal set of principles determining language; it is diversity, rather than universals, that is found at almost every level of linguistic organization. In their target article, which summarizes decades of cross-linguistic work, Evans and Levinson (2009) show just how few and unprofound the universal characteristics of language are,[22] and how languages vary radically in sound, meaning and syntactic organization. Where there are significant recurrent patterns in organization, these are better explained as stable engineering solutions satisfying multiple design constraints, reflecting both cultural-historical factors and the constraints of human cognition. So that '... the great variability in how languages organize their word-classes dilutes the plausibility of the innatist UG position' (2009, 429; 435). Research on syntax have brought Dunn et al to conclude that there is no universal set of rules determining the evolution of language; rather, it is cultural evolution that is the primary determinant of linguistic structure, at least with respect to word order (2011, 79).

The notion of an innate structure of mind imposing 'universals' has also been rejected from a biological perspective. As Wolfram Hinzen affirms, there is no clue, empirically, about the type of rule that would be able to organize neuronal connections that enable language competence; there is no biology specific to language; no Universal Grammar rooted in the human genome (2012a, 636). This chimes with Christiansen and Chater's findings: 'a biologically determined UG is not evolutionarily viable' in that the processes of language change are much faster than processes of genetic change, so that language constitutes a 'moving target' both over time and across different human populations and cannot therefore provide a stable environment to which language genes could have adapted (2008, 489). And Terence Deacon abundantly demonstrates that Chomsky's scenario is unsupported by evolutionary anthropology which evidences a *gradual* adaptation of the human brain and vocal chords to the use of language rather than the sudden appearance of a language organ containing a complete set of parameters enabling all grammars[23] – Chomsky's 'Big Bang' theory.[24]

'Don't think, but look!' (PI 66), writes Wittgenstein. By this, he means that we should draw our accounts of human life from *life*, from what we *do* rather than from presuppositions often generated by false analogies that lead to false requirements. And what we do shows that language acquisition is not due to the activation of principles but to the acquisition of a technique, a know-how, an ability. Children are not mini-grammarians. They don't need to 'cognize' and apply the Location Principle or any grammatical principle to acquire language. They use words in the same way we play tennis, without knowing what the mechanics are. Stipulating a Principle Requirement creates a problem where none was there, and appealing to innateness fabricates a solution where none is needed. Rather than 'language growing in us' – as Chomsky would have it – it is we who physiologically, psychologically and socially *grow* into language.[25]

We can now move on to Wittgenstein, whose view of language development – in contrast to Chomsky's 'Big Bang' theory – seems to me ontogenetically and phylogenetically consistent and coherent.

5. Wittgenstein's social account of language acquisition

5.1 The primitivity of action: the deed, not the word

One of the important things Wittgenstein said about language is that it has its root in gesture – or, as he also put it, in 'action', and more precisely: 'reaction' or 'instinct': 'What we call meaning must be connected with the primitive language of gestures' (BT 24). By this, he means instinctive gestures and reactions which – first through evolution, then through enculturation – are replaced by words. This – Wittgenstein's 'primitivism' (Canfield 1997, 258) – prompted Michael Tomasello to realize that '[i]f we want to understand human communication, ... we cannot begin with language'; contrary to primatologist dogma, apes' *gestures*, not their vocalizations, are the precursors of human language (2008, 59; 53–5)[26].

When Wittgenstein writes that '[t]he study of language games is the study of primitive forms of language or languages' (BB 17), he does not, by this, mean words or symbols, but reactions:

> The origin and the primitive form of the language game is a reaction; only from this can more complicated forms develop.
> Language – I want to say – is a refinement. 'In the beginning was the deed.'
> CE 395

Language, then, is a refinement, or 'an extension', of our primitive behaviour;[27] it emerges from the *development* of some of our animal or natural reactions. Not just *any* natural reaction – not singular or idiosyncratic ones, like tics – but our *shared* natural reactions; what Wittgenstein calls 'the common behaviour of mankind' (PI 206): reactions such as crying when in pain or sad; smiling when glad; jumping when startled; gasping or screaming when afraid; but also reacting to someone's suffering. He writes: 'In its most primitive form [the language-game] is a reaction to somebody's cries and gestures, a reaction of sympathy or something of the sort' (CE 414).

These instinctive common reactions or action patterns are, Wittgenstein says, the *prototypes* of our modes of thought (RPP I, 916), of our concepts. And so, the basis for the development of language is constituted by a number of such distinct instinctive, behavioural patterns which John Canfield calls 'proto-language games' (1996, 128). Without these behavioural patterns, there would be no language.[28] This is the case phylogenetically as well as ontogenetically, for these natural configurations of behaviour – such as: '[t]he natural, untutored behaviour of one pre-linguistic hominid helping another it sees is hurt' – are part of the species' inheritance' (ibid.). So that ontogeny recapitulates phylogeny[29].

5.2 Training

In the *Investigations*, Wittgenstein writes that the primitive forms of language are those used by the child when it is learning to talk and that, here, 'the teaching of language is not explanation, but training' (PI 5). Why? For an obvious reason: in the learning of a first language, the initiate has only instinct and reactions but no language at her disposal, and so the learning of a native language will *have* to do with action or behaviour – language at first playing only a background music role. This is why language cannot take its impetus from explanation: 'Language did not emerge from some kind of ratiocination' (OC 475).

Language, then, is an extension of our patterned non-linguistic behaviour through training. On Wittgenstein's view, this should include at least one competent trainer – that is, a reasonably adept user of the language, endowed with enough pedagogic ability to mould or shape the child's responses to the training so that they end up in harmony with the norm.[30] Of course, 'training' here does not meant anything formal but rather the kind of repeated direct and indirect guidance that is effected through intersubjective interaction in various contexts. More formal teaching may – it does not always – come later.[31] But it is clear that for Wittgenstein, language acquisition is not a one-track affair: he rejects the Augustinian view of it as resulting from a mere nominalization process, and describes it in terms of habituation and enculturation.

So how is the child trained to go from proto-language games to language, from her instinctive reactions to language? '. . . how, asks Wittgenstein, is the connexion between the name and the thing set up?' – and he replies:

> This question is the same as: how does a human being learn the meaning of the names of sensations? – of the word 'pain', for example. Here is one possibility: words are connected with the primitive, the natural, expressions of the sensation

and used in their place. A child has hurt himself and he cries; and then adults talk to him and teach him exclamations and, later, sentences. They teach the child new pain-behaviour.

PI 244

So the *connection* between the name and the thing is not made by an act of ostension, not by merely hooking gestures on to their public referents, but by processes of drill or habituation that are similar to stimulus-response conditioning, but that must be supplemented by training *into the practice* in which those words are used.[32] Note: what the child is taught in learning to replace his primitive reactions with words is new *behaviour*; that is, in first picking up the linguistic expression, the child is not *describing* with it or *referring* with it, but still *reacting* with it.

Ostensive *teaching*, as opposed to mere ostensive *definition*, involves behavioural conditioning: the child is taught, through repetition and exercises, to utter certain words in certain contexts or situations. These drills are used to tap and channel the child's natural reactions. What we witness in these initial stages is not yet language, but 'processes resembling language' (PI 7); for a language is not the mere repetition of certain sounds in certain contexts and after certain prompts. Wittgenstein is not a behaviourist. Drill is not enough; beyond mere conditioning (cf. PI 6), a normative *attitude* towards utterances, towards how things are to be done, must be inculcated in the child so that it can learn to regulate itself.[33] And acquiring a normative attitude demands nothing less than being enculturated. It is thanks to her acquiring this normative attitude that the child is eventually able to go on, on her own; to proceed *from other-regulation to self-regulation* (Medina 2002, 165). Successful enculturation means the child can then judge for herself that in a particular instance a word or phrase makes sense, not by comparing it to a benchmark, context-free, use but on the basis of her experience of multiple language-games in which the word or phrase is employed. For Wittgenstein, the acquisition of language is the acquisition of a technique, skill or capacity, and capacities are flexible to individual and occasion; they allow for – and indeed, are basic to – productivity and creativity.

6. Technique: Wittgenstein's answer to the productivity problem

'To understand a language means to be master of a technique' (PI 199). That 'technique', I suggest, is Wittgenstein's answer to the nativist problem of productivity, which is how to account for our capacity to produce an unlimited number of novel utterances from the limited set of grammatical rules and the finite set of terms we acquire from experience. On Wittgenstein's view, we are we able to extend our limited acquired knowledge of language to new situations and contexts precisely because the teaching of language is not a teaching of principles but the transmission of a technique, which does not aim for total regulation, but for self-regulation.

It is criteria that determine whether a speaker is following a rule or using a word in accordance with the norm that is being inculcated. These criteria are public, not private; they can be transmitted to the child and invoked to guide and correct him in his attempts to use the words he is being taught. The child's various attempts are guided (encouraged/discouraged) until enough training allows her to grasp what *sorts of contexts* are propitious for the use of the word: semantic development involves 'becoming increasingly sensitive to how characteristics of different contexts constrain the words one can use' (Montgomery 2002, 373).[34] However, though constraint is necessary, there is no exhaustive determination of use but an indication of proper use (the use is *constrained, not shackled*), which allows for and explains creativity/productivity.

We might make an analogy here with a dog that is trained not to bite: the dog will not only not bite the people present at the training, but not bite in all similar contexts (e.g., unthreatening contexts). Or again, when the child is taught to open a door, she doesn't just learn to open *that* white, single panelled door which her mother is using to teach her, but all doors that she will come across in experience – whether they be white, black, double-panelled, glass and so on. This is where the teaching of a technique surpasses, say, ostensive definition. As Wittgenstein writes: 'Teaching which is not meant to apply to anything but the examples given is different from that which "*points beyond*" them'[35] (PI 208).

To suggest that we need a Language Acquisition Device, or the like, to explain how we can produce an unlimited number of new and correct sentences from limited input is like suggesting we need a Manoeuvre Acquisition Device to explain the potentially unlimited variety of manoeuvres that a cyclist is able to execute from the basic or limited training he has received (cf. Rorty 2004, 225). Wittgenstein's answer to the productivity problem is encapsulated in this passage: 'Yes, there is the great thing about language – that we can do what we haven't learnt' (LPP 28).

So, *contra* Chomsky, first-language acquisition is *essentially* social; it requires that at least one member of the linguistic community mould the child's primitive reactions and proto-language games into language-games, bringing the child, through a process of enculturation, to assimilate, conform to and apply the standards of correctness of its linguistic community. Acquiring language is like learning to walk: the child is stepped into language by an initiator and, after much hesitation and repeated faltering, with time, multifarious practice and repeated exposure, it disengages itself from its teacher's hold and is able, as it were, to run with the language.

7. Training is not enough

This may be a good time to bring up Chomsky's argument that while both human babies and animals can be trained, if they are exposed to exactly the same linguistic data, the human child will acquire language, but the kitten will not. For Chomsky, to suggest that language is *not* innate is to imply that no crucial and relevant internal nature differentiates a child from a rock or a rabbit; so that if we put a rock, a rabbit and a child in an English-speaking community, they should all be able to learn English (Chomsky 2000). It is in order to avoid coming to this conclusion, he says, that we must accept that the relevant capacity the child has but which the stone and rabbit lack is the 'language acquisition device' (LAD). Yet this, I suggest, is like using a hammer to crack an egg. We hardly need resort to a language acquisition device to mark a difference here – internal or otherwise – between humans and animals (to say nothing of rocks). Before resorting to something as *ad hoc* as a language organ to account for the difference, we might, for a start, evoke obvious, traceable physiological requirements such as the anatomical structures necessary for the vocalization of human speech that are lacking in rabbits and rocks. Or indeed as Elizabeth Bates does, to differences between human brains and, say, those of chimpanzees, but differences – she insists – that do not require us to postulate a language organ (1993, 8). However, the difference is not only physiological[36].

Rebecca Saxe, a cognitive scientist at MIT, argues that the key difference between apes and humans seems to be that we have *explicit teaching* while animals have only imitation. Chimps may use sticks as rudimentary tools, but they learn such skills through observation and mimicry as well as trial and error, rather than direct instruction. Humans learn through all of these, but teaching may be the signature skill of our species. Also, a part of teaching is 'triadic attention': being able to work out the coordination of my attention and the other person's attention on this third thing – the task I'm trying to teach. I have to pay attention to all three elements continuously. Finally, it seems like 'it's not just a cognitive capacity that's necessary for teaching; there's this other thing, which is *wanting to teach*. That may be even more critical. We need to understand that somebody else is unable to do what we're doing, and also have some reason, motivation, desire to help that person learn it. As Saxe says: 'That desire to teach seems to be really pervasive in humans and may be mysteriously missing in apes' (2008). Humans have both the passion and the mental skill to teach each other.

The inability of rabbits and stones to speak and teach goes some way in explaining why they don't acquire language and we do. But the fact that children *expect* (and like) to be taught also makes a vital difference, and this is visible in their capacity for attention. Though the learner's *triadic* attention is a development, attention for teaching appears before language kicks in. Apes can't get into that; although they do things together and coordinate their actions together, they have no *shared goals based on shared commitment*. Kids, on the other hand, have these naturally, almost immediately.

Another distinguishing feature of humans is what John Haugeland calls 'norm-hungriness' (2002, 22) – an expectation of norms that parents try to teach us. Haugeland claims the fundamental divide between humans and animals lies in our essential use of norms. Humans display a norm-susceptibility, and a deep 'norm-hungriness'; deep, both in that the desire is almost insatiable, and in that the norms are unique in their richness and complexity (ibid., 31).

8. Wittgenstein's universal grammar

I'd like to conclude this chapter by suggesting that we replace Chomsky's universal grammar with Wittgensteinian grammar. Inasmuch as the latter is all the grammar we require to possess a language, and inasmuch as its acquisition can only be achieved through enculturation, it makes an otiose monster out of Chomsky's hopeful monster.

As linguist Dan Everett (2012) says: 'universal grammar doesn't seem to work, there doesn't seem to be much evidence for that'; but what, he asks, can we put in its place? His answer is a Wittgensteinian one: 'A complex interplay of factors, of which culture, the values human beings share, plays a major role in structuring the way that we talk and the things that we talk about'. In view of the implausibility of Chomsky's UG,[37] Wolfram Hinzen seeks to rehabilitate universal grammar as internally linked to human nature, without that centrally involving notions of innateness, essence or modularity (2012b, 55). Gone is the idea of grammar as an autonomous module described by arbitrary formal rules; grammatical theory is a theory of the mode of thought that we find expressed in human language and that is manifest in human culture (2012a, 643). Hinzen's view of grammar seems apt to resonate with Wittgenstein's in that Wittgensteinian grammar is a description of the rules or bounds of sense that determine, and are embedded in, our use of language as a result of the evolution of languages in the various cultures of human life.

For Wittgenstein, there is no question that language depends on grammar; but Wittgensteinian grammar is a different animal from Chomsky's. Whereas Chomsky construes grammar as a set of arbitrary *principles* existing in advance of use or practice, for Wittgenstein, it is not principles, but rules or norms that are necessary to the existence of a language, and these do not pre-exist language but are inextricably bound up with its practice. As John Canfield puts it: 'The practice underlies the rule rather than vice-versa' (1975, 114), which is to say that grammatical rules merely express or *bring out* our *normative* use of words and expressions. In fact, rules of grammar, as Wittgenstein conceives them, are nothing like linguistic principles; they are garden-variety or ordinary expressions (reminders) of the norms that have been regulating our meaningful use of words (e.g., 'A bachelor is an unmarried man'; 'This(is what we call a table'; 'Red is darker than pink'; 'A rod has a length'). The child assimilates these norms as it assimilates the language – through guidance in (which may, but need not, involve explicit reminders of the norms), and exposure to, correct usage. As Peter Hacker puts it: 'Rules for the use of words are exhibited in human discourse, in explanations of meaning, in corrections of errors, in what counts as accepted usage' (2010, 29). Nothing more complicated than that.

Learning the meaning of a word is nothing but learning how it is used; that is, assimilating the *norms that govern its use* – what Wittgenstein calls its *grammar*. We could not speak of the number of people in a room if we did not have a norm- or rule-governed use of the words 'people', 'number' and 'room'. So that if I were to say that I have counted 30 people in the room, of whom two dogs and a cat, I would not be using the words 'people', 'dog' and 'cat' correctly. I would not be speaking grammatically. Grammatical norms determine what it makes sense for us to say also by excluding certain combinations of words from meaningful use[38].

The grammatical rules I have been describing are what we might call 'thin' and 'local' – and here, more precisely: 'linguistic': they are norms for the use of words, expressions, and numbers[39] ('2 + 2 = 4' is for Wittgenstein as much a rule of grammar as 'A rod has a length'). But Wittgenstein came to realize that many of our grammatical rules are 'thick' or 'reality-soaked': they are *conditioned* by empirical reality.[40] So, for example: 'The earth has existed for a long time'; 'Human beings have bodies'; 'If someone's head is cut off, he is dead and will never live again'; 'Babies cannot look after themselves'; 'Human beings are born, grow old and die; they need air, water and sleep; they usually smile or laugh when they're happy; cry when they're sad or in pain'.

Now of course Wittgenstein is well aware that these look like run-of-the mill empirical propositions, not expressions of rules of grammar. Yet he notices that these are propositions about which 'no doubt can exist if making judgments is to be possible at all', and so they do not, in fact, *function* as empirical propositions[41] but as *logical* propositions: they 'form the foundation of all operating with thoughts (with language)' (OC 401). Failing, in our language-games, to 'assume' the indubitability of such propositions would result in a failure to make sense: for an English speaker to ask, in a non-sci-fi context, whether 'human beings have bodies' would be as nonsensical as asking whether a 'rod has a length'. Either question would make us suspect, first, the speaker's proficiency in English and if that were ascertained, her sanity. Inasmuch, then, as our language-games are *logically* hinged on such putative 'propositions', Wittgenstein takes them to have a *grammatical* role ('logical' and 'grammatical' are synonymous for the later Wittgenstein). Such 'propositions' are in fact expressions of rules of grammar.

Their seemingly empirical nature is due to these rules of grammar being *conditioned* by 'very general facts of nature' appertaining to 'the natural history of human beings'[42] (PI 230, 415): 'it is characteristic of our language that the foundation on which it grows consists in steady ways of living, regular ways of acting' (CE 397). Their being conditioned by facts that unassailably pertain to the human form of life makes them *universal* rules of grammar – that is, laws of thought belonging to the 'scaffolding of thought' of any normal human being. They are the bounds of sense from which *any* human being must begin to make sense[43]. Such rules, I suggest, constitute alongside our more local grammars, a universal grammar.[44]

9. Conclusion

We have seen that Chomsky's UG faces multiple objections from multiple fronts – objections it cannot answer. This, however, has not managed to take the wind out of UG's sails.[45] Myths are difficult to debunk. For, if anything transpires from even a glance at Chomsky's position, it's that it does have the trappings of myth. On the other hand, Wittgenstein's conception of language acquisition – resulting as it does from observations so basic as to be incontestable – is of the order of 'perspicuous presentation'; it merely makes obvious the *familiar unseen*: 'We want to understand something that is already in plain view. For this is what we seem in some sense not to understand' (PI 89).

There is nothing mysterious, speculative or *ad hoc* about Wittgenstein's view of language acquisition: no positing of hidden principles lodged in the brain and requiring 'cognisance'; all that is needed is the (plain-to-see) ability to be initiated in and master the technique of language through enculturation. Any more detail than this must be left to empirical research, but of the non-mythopeic kind[46] – the kind, instead, that Ramscar and Yarlett are gesturing at here:

Language is ultimately a cultural capacity (Tomasello, 1999; Wittgenstein, 1953 [PI]); arguably, it is the capacity for culture that sets Homo sapiens apart from our closest neighbors. Understanding how the processes of imitation that appear to be key to the acquisition and establishment of cultural common ground interact with the processes that allow humans to exert more cognitive control over their responses, and thus achieve agency across the course of cognitive development, may ultimately result in a much deeper understanding of our capacity for, and the nature of, both language and culture.

2007, 952

Constancy of meaning, linguistic communication and expression are made possible by a grammar, but this grammar is not a set of innate linguistic principles biologically programmed in our brains in advance of all use, and enabling the inner growth of language. In contrast to Chomsky's grammar, there is nothing inexplicable about Wittgenstein's grammar. On his view, human grammar is internally related to human life and action – this is what his concept of the language-*game* conveys, as well as his often-reiterated conviction that 'at the beginning is the deed'. If universality is the motivating force behind nativism, there is in our shared natural history and in our shared instinctive reactions, universality enough. Our grammars are embedded in our use of language and conditioned by our forms of life; it is therefore in the 'stream of life' – and not in the human brain – that Wittgenstein rightly locates these grammars.

3

Words as Deeds

Wittgenstein's 'Spontaneous Utterances' and the Dissolution of the Explanatory Gap

Wittgenstein demystified the notion of 'observational self-knowledge'. He dislodged the long-standing conception that we have privileged access to our impressions, sensations and feelings through introspection, and more precisely eliminated *knowing* as the kind of awareness that normally characterizes our first-person present tense psychological statements. He was not thereby questioning our *awareness* of our emotions or sensations, but debunking the notion that we come to that awareness via any *epistemic* route. This makes the spontaneous linguistic articulation of our sensations and impressions nondescriptive. Not descriptions, but *expressions* that seem more akin to behaviour than to language. I suggest that Wittgenstein uncovered a new species of *speech acts*. Far from the *prearranged* consecration of words into performatives, utterances are deeds through their very *spontaneity*. This gives language a new aura: the aura of the *reflex action*. I argue, against Peter Hacker, that spontaneous utterances have the logical status of deeds. This has no reductive consequences in that I do not suggest that one category is reduced to another, but that the boundary between them is porous. This explodes the myth of an explanatory gap between the traditionally distinct categories of saying (or thinking) and doing, or of mind and body.

Since Descartes first put it in the machine, not many philosophers have attempted to get the ghost out. Based on the mechanics of the body, the idea is that whatever we think or do must have first been processed in some way. This, in itself, would be trivially acceptable if the process were not posited as explanatory. If, that is, it were a mere mechanical description of what happens in our bodies when we speak or move; a description having no significant link with *why* we speak or move – with our (particular) *reasons* for saying 'Good morning' or waving good-bye. But for many philosophers and neuropsychologists, our thinking and acting are not only *causally* dependent on some hardware, be it a neurological or functional (computer-like) framework, they are *generated* by it and reducible to it. The brain is not merely one of the vital organs without which we cannot live, and therefore think or act, it is – unlike the heart or the liver – the very source of our acting and thinking. Not simply a mechanical *enabler*, the brain is the *generator* of our wills, desires, intentions and actions. Of course the outside world has some impact on us (e.g., I see an apple), but in order for the body to react, this impact must be translated or transmuted into something that can trigger a move. A belief ('this is an apple') or will ('I want this apple') is therefore posited as the *reason* that *causes* the body to move (I reach out for the apple). But how can something as ethereal as a belief or a will activate something as physical as my hand and make it reach out for the apple? How can a mental state *cause* a muscle to contract? In an attempt to bridge this explanatory gap between the mind and the body, philosophers have sought to formalize or to naturalize our intentions, beliefs or thoughts. Like Searle and Fodor, they have vainly attempted to transform our intentions into efficient, physically empowered triggers that can move our tongues to speak and our hands to reach out; they have sought to transmute a ghostly belief or thought into some biological, formal or propositional form that could then supposedly activate the machine. According to such Ghost-in-the-Machine philosophers,[1] we think the thoughts we do and perform the acts we do *because* of some prior internal cognitive processing (that is, in some way, physical). Some spectral belief, will or intention must be there to preface what we say and trigger our moves.

In this chapter, I argue that spontaneous utterances are exemplary cases of expressions that are not the result of any cognitive process and that they are equivalent to deeds. This does not herald a behaviourist revival. It is not claimed that all words are reducible to acts, but that the case of spontaneous utterances evinces that there is no logical categorial gap between words and deeds, between mental states and behaviour, which would require a reductive transformation of one into the other. That is, the categories of speaking (or thinking) and doing are still alive and well, but they are porous.

1. Not a question of knowing

– *Do you feel like singing?* said Camier.
– *Not to my knowledge,* said Mercier.

From *Mercier and Camier* by Samuel Beckett

I often come upon tentative readers of Wittgenstein who tell me how, offended by his stabs at what can be called 'observational self-knowledge', they have turned away in disbelief: 'how can it be said I don't know I'm in pain!' What these readers fail to grasp is Wittgenstein's precision here: he is eliminating *knowing* as the kind of awareness that normally characterizes being in pain. His aim is not to invalidate *awareness* of one's pain, but to debunk the notion that one comes to that awareness via introspective observation, or via any epistemic route at all. We say we *know* something when we have acquired that information from observation, recollection, inference or research, but it is through none of these routes that I am aware of my own pain. In fact, I follow no route at all, for there is no gap between my pain and my awareness of it. I cannot be in pain without being aware of it. Moreover, the problem with *claiming to know* is that it is not infallible. I can be wrong about something I thought I knew, but I cannot make a mistake about being in pain. Even in cases of self-delusion, the (phantom) pain is felt.

The logical infallibility characteristic of one's awareness of being in pain is not therefore adequately described as a *knowledge* claim. This is true of many other first-person present tense uses of psychological verbs:

> '*I know* what I want, wish, believe, feel, ...' (and so on through all the psychological verbs) is either philosophers' nonsense, or at any rate *not* a judgement *a priori*.
>
> 'I know...' may mean 'I do not doubt...' but does not mean that the words 'I doubt...' are *senseless*, that doubt is logically excluded.
>
> One says 'I know' where one can also say 'I believe' or 'I suspect'; where one can find out.
>
> PI p. 221; first emphasis mine

Wittgenstein views first-person present tense psychological statements as *typically* nonepistemic expressions, most of which are more akin to behaviour than to propositions. They predominantly belong to our primitive, not to our sophisticated use of language. A 'that-clause' is not always a harbinger of propositional thought. We shall see that some articulations of so-called *propositional attitudes* are not really *propositional* at all: to say 'I believe that ....' or 'I hope that ...' is not always to adopt a *propositional* attitude. It is not only mental events such as pain that are not subjectible to propositional form, but some cases of belief, desire, expectation, intention etc. The deciding factor here is whether a deliverance is a *description* or an *expression*. And in some cases, deliverances of belief, desire, expectation, intention are just such expressions.

2. Descriptions vs expressions (or utterances)

For words do not all have the same function: some steer, some describe, others express.[2] As regards our first-person present tense psychological statements (e.g., 'I'm in pain', 'I hope he comes', 'I'm afraid'), they have traditionally been regarded as *descriptive:* the utterance 'I am in pain' thought to be a privileged and infallible description resulting from my introspection of my mental state of being in pain. Wittgenstein, however, perceived that our first-person psychological statements are, for the most part, not descriptions, but *expressions*:

> Surely one doesn't normally say 'I wish ...' on grounds of self-observation [*Selbstbeobachtung*], for this is merely an expression [*Äusserung*] of a wish. Nevertheless, you can sometimes perceive or discover a wish by observing your own reactions.
>
> RPP II, 3

Indeed, we sometimes discover how strongly we feel about something from the (to ourselves) surprising intensity of our spontaneous reaction; as for example, realizing, from one's own sharp rejoinder to a colleague, that we have surprisingly strong and clearcut feelings about how philosophy ought to be taught.[3] Wittgenstein did not then

– as is often assumed – rule out a descriptive or self-observing use of first-person psychological verbs, but he held it to be secondary to the expressive,[4] which is nondescriptive. He usually refers to the nondescriptive deliverances of our psychological states as 'utterances' (*Äusserungen*) or 'expressions' (*Ausdrücke*).[5]

To say that an expression is nondescriptive is to say that, in using it, the speaker does not *describe* anything (like an emotion or sensation that she allegedly has privileged, introspective, access to); she is not articulating an informative conclusion she has come to from self-observation, not issuing a proposition susceptible of falsification or verification. A nondescriptive expression *can* be informative, but it is not *based on* information. My spontaneous 'I want to die!' is nondescriptive in that it is not a propositional rendering of a desire I have observed in myself, but it may be news to my therapist, or to myself – *once I have uttered it*.

3. Spontaneity: The distinguishing feature

It is not always easy to distinguish between descriptive and expressive language-games. Indeed, the very same string of words may be either descriptive (a report) or expressive (a manifestation / occurrence) of a state of mind:

> When someone says 'I hope he'll come' – is this a *report* [*Bericht*] about his state of mind, or a *manifestation* [*Äusserung*] of his hope? – I can, for example, say it to myself. And surely I am not giving myself a report. It may be a sigh; but it need not.
>
> PI 585

> I say 'I am afraid'; someone else asks me: 'What was that? A cry of fear; or do you want to tell me how you feel; or is it a reflection on your present state?'
>
> PI, p. 187

The difference lies not in the words themselves, but in the circumstances of their pronouncement:

> The exclamation 'I'm longing to see him!' may be called an act [*Akt*] of expecting. But I can utter the same words as the result of self-observation [*Selbstbeobachtung*], and then they might mean: 'So, after all that has happened, I am still longing to see him.' The point is: what led up to these words?
>
> PI 586

What is the setting, the context, the origin of utterance? In expressive utterances, no reflection *leads up* to the words. They are uttered, as it were, *without a thought*. We can gather from Wittgenstein's numerous comparative analyses that the distinguishing feature between descriptive and nondescriptive uses of first-person present-tense psychological utterances is: *spontaneity*; a *spontaneous* deliverance being one that no reflection or self-observation has 'led up to'. *Spontaneous* expressions of pain do not describe our internal states, or at least they never *intend to*. There is no room where description can take place, no self-observing gap between the feeling or sensation and its spontaneous expression: 'For how can I go so far as to try to use language to get between pain and its expression [*Äusserung*]' (PI 245). In our *spontaneous* deliverances of desire, belief, sensation and emotion, the word is not a detached *report* of the pain or desire felt, not a *description*, but the *expression* of pain or desire. Spontaneous expressions are nondescriptive, unverified, unreasoned expressions. They are not due to introspection or self-observation: 'Does someone crying out 'Help!' want to describe how he is feeling? Nothing is further from his intentions than describing something' (LW I, 48).

Spontaneity, then, forms the dividing line between first-person present tense psychological *expressions* and *descriptions*. But *within* the category of spontaneous expressions, a further dichotomy must be made. Whilst no reasoning informs the use of *any* of our spontaneous utterances, some are emotionally (or sensationally) charged, and others emotionally (or sensationally) neutral. In *Insight and Illusion*, Hacker gives varied examples of spontaneous utterances (which he calls 'avowals'[6]):

> ... exclamations ('I'm so pleased'), cries of pain ('It hurts, it hurts!'), sighs of longing ('Oh, I do hope he'll come'), expressions of emotion ('I'm furious with you') or expectation ('I expect you to come'), avowals of thought or belief, expressions of desire ('I want a glass of wine') or preference ('I like claret') and so forth. . . .
>
> 1989, 298

These are all spontaneous utterances, but they are not all of the same nature. Rather than follow Hacker in distinguishing them according to their being or not 'expressions of *experiences*' (ibid.), I shall distinguish between *compulsive* and *neutral* spontaneous expressions.[7] *Compulsive* spontaneous utterances are compelled by, expressive of, and (as we shall see) sometimes also *part of,* active states of emotion and sensation.[8] These, *we can't help using*: 'Suppose I said: The expressions get their importance from the fact that they are not used coolly but that we can't help using them' (LPE 281). First, let's examine our less compulsive spontaneous utterances.

4. Neutral spontaneous utterances

Though they are spontaneous in that they are not the product of self-observation, description or reflection, some first-person psychological expressions do not compulsively spring from the heart, but soberly inform ('I like claret'), or demand ('I want a glass of wine'). Where the sole *raison d'être* of compulsive utterances is *expression,* and where their utterance is comparable to a reflex action, *neutral* spontaneous utterances are intentional: they are intentionally informative and require a third party. Spontaneous, but not compulsive, they do not resemble reflex actions. Still, like compulsive utterances, neutral utterances are not propositions insofar as they are not descriptions, not falsifiable conclusions of self-observation. It must be stressed that for some spontaneous utterances to be emotionally neutral does not mean that they are the product of reflection or self-observation. In no way are they descriptions.

Of course, there are many cases where our formulations of belief or preference *are* descriptive. Upon being asked whether or not he believes in an afterlife, someone who had not before given it much thought, will do some soul-searching to come to a conclusion. Or again, when questioned as to whether she prefers the wines of Bordeaux or Burgundy, someone who had never previously considered it, will hesitate and ponder before replying. In both these cases, replies will be first-person present-tense psychological deliverances (e.g., 'I guess I don't believe in an afterlife'; 'Come to think of it, I prefer Bordeaux – I tend to buy it more often than Burgundy'), but not of the spontaneous type. These are neither compulsive nor neutral *expressions,* but *cool* (*they* are 'used coolly'; cf. LPE 281 above) or reflective *descriptions*: statements resulting from thought, deliberation, reflection, and possibly intent on deceiving.

In contrast, someone well acquainted with wine, who has come to have a well-seasoned preference, need undergo no such precursory reflection. Her response will be automatic – which does not mean that she has never given the matter a thought, only that she did not do it, did not need to do it, *on this occasion*. Having for many years frequented the small, welcoming vineyards of Burgundy, familiarized myself with their warm, textured, dark-fruity, flowery flavours, built up a respectable collection of Vosne-Romanées and the like, and having comparatively sampled many a stern, majestic Bordeaux, I, upon being asked, express my predilection for Burgundy without hesitation or pondering. My expression of preference is as little due to reflection, introspection, and therefore as barred from the possibility of pretence as 'My name is Danièle'.

'I prefer Burgundy': this may be a spontaneous utterance or a pondered description. Circumstances, not appearance, determine the status of our words. Identical strings of words will form, in one context, a spontaneous utterance; in another, a report or description. Whereas *spontaneous* deliverances of what one believes or prefers are more likely to fall under the neutral category, spontaneous utterances of emotion or sensation are likely to of the compulsive variety.

5. Compulsive spontaneous utterances: words as verbal reactions

> '... sometimes it seemed as if speech came to me without any will of my own, and words were given to me that came out as the tears come, because our hearts are full and we can't help it.'
>
> From *Adam Bede* by George Eliot

When utterances are compulsive, it is as if we did not *use* words, rather they seem to come out – unprompted by ourselves – in a bang or a whimper:

> In this way I should like to say the words 'Oh, let him come!' are charged with my desire. And words can be wrung from us, – like a cry. Words can be hard to say: such, for example, as are used to effect a renunciation, or to confess a weakness. (Words are also deeds.)
>
> PI 546

Words are also deeds. This, then, not only alludes to the active aspect of language generally – to speak is to act – premised in speech-act theory; nor is it sufficiently covered by Wittgenstein's praxial[9] view of language – words are *used* and language in use is a language-*game* – rather, it points out a particularity of *some* words. If, generally, words are *also* deeds, specifically, some words are, in some contexts, *only* deeds. They do not *describe* a psychological state but are the *verbal* equivalent – and in cases of language acquisition: the verbal replacement – of the *nonverbal* expression of a psychological state: 'words are connected with the primitive, the natural, expressions [*Ausdruck*] of the sensation and used in their place' (PI 244). So that nonverbal expressions such as a *cry* of pain or despair, an *act* of desire or surrender can be used in the place of verbal ones, such as 'I am in pain', 'I grieve', 'Oh, let him come!', 'I want to die'. Indeed, as children, we acquire language by being taught to thus replace our nonverbal reactions with verbal ones:

> A child has hurt himself and he cries; and then adults talk to him and teach him exclamations and, later, sentences. They teach the child new pain-behaviour.
>
> PI 244

The word, exclamation or sentence assimilated as a replacement of the natural expression is itself behaviour. It is not a clearer, more eloquent *description* of the sensation, but constitutes an alternative *expression* of the sensation – an *alternate mode of behaviour*: 'the verbal expression [*Ausdruck*] of pain replaces crying and does not describe it' (PI 244). So that where we use words in the place of groans, this replacement does not *entail* a categorial change, but only a change of manner or manifestation. In emotion and sensation, where our original spontaneity has been least subject to the mutations of sophistication, the word, often *is* a deed, *nothing but* a deed:

> The exclamation 'I'm longing to see him!' may be called an *act* of expecting.
>
> PI 586; my emphasis

> The words 'I am happy' are a bit of the behaviour of joy.
>
> RPP I, 450

We must, however, take care not to confuse the deed or behaviour with the sensation itself. That some words are in some contexts categorially assimilable to behaviour does not make them identical to the sensation or feeling expressed. Peter Hacker does well to remind us that 'behaviour is not a sensation!' (1993, 262). And yet Wittgenstein *does* mention cases where we could not dissociate the behaviour from the sensation itself. It is sometimes possible to say that the behavioural expression is *part of* the feeling or sensation:

> For think of the sensations produced by physically shuddering: the words 'it makes me shiver' are themselves such a shuddering reaction; and if I hear and feel them as I utter them, this belongs among the rest of those sensations.
>
> PI p. 174

This is where the boundaries between word and deed dissolve; where language and behaviour melt into one another, become indistinguishable; where the word *is* behaviour, a reflex action.[10] Here, Wittgenstein has uncovered a new category of utterances, never before picked out by philosophy. Resembling Austin's *performatives* in that they are linguistic utterances whose grammatical determination as *acts* is dependent on context, they part company in their being independent of conventional procedure. Far from the prearranged or conventionally fixed consecration of words into performatives, utterances are deeds through their very spontaneity. This gives language, or a part of language, a new aura: the aura of the unpremeditated *act*, the reflex action.

The *compulsive* expression – whether the act of crying or that of saying 'I am in pain' – is in both cases a *reaction*, though the latter, a more complicated form of the reaction. It is not, that is, available to infants or animals. Not a translation or description resulting from my observation of my internal state, compulsive expressions are simply another version of the tears or the cry of agony – 'articulated crying' as Fogelin puts it (1987, 170).

6. The levelling of the linguistic and the nonlinguistic

Nonverbal expressions have traditionally been categorized as deeds; verbal ones as language[11], regardless of function. And yet it is precisely function, use and grammar, not appearance, that should determine categorial categories. In those cases where the linguistic expression *springs* from an emotion or sensation, in the manner of a moan or a groan, of a *cri de coeur*, the linguistic is *at par* with the nonlinguistic: my spontaneous 'It hurts!' is as much an *act* as my groaning or moving my finger away from the flame. Although a groan does not physically resemble a sentence, when both are spontaneously expressed their 'grammar' is fundamentally the same, and so a crucial rapprochement is wanting. We should assimilate spontaneous utterances to reactions, their linguistic aspect notwithstanding. This assimilation is rejected by Peter Hacker:

> It is important to emphasize that Wittgenstein was not *assimilating* avowals to the natural expression of 'inner states'. An avowal of pain is not *just like* a groan, and it would be as misleading to say that it has the same logical status as a groan as it is to assimilate it to description. For there are differences as well as similarities. An utterance (*Äusserung*) of pain, unlike a moan, is articulate; it is a linguistic expression consisting of words in grammatical combination. A sentence that can be used in a spontaneous avowal has other uses too. It can be embedded in the antecedent of a conditional, it has an intelligible negation, and there are tense transforms of such a sentence. These cases are not expressions or manifestations of inner states and must be treated differently.
>
> 1993, 90

Of course an avowal of pain is not *just* like a groan. It looks or sounds different: it is comprised of words, as opposed to mere sounds. And yet this should not lead to the conclusion that its logical status is different from that of a groan. It seems to me that, here, Hacker is guilty of the sort of confusion Wittgenstein was wariest of: conflating appearance and use. Identical appearance does not give words used in different contexts the same meaning, but neither does it give them the same logical status. That a sentence has, in *one* of its uses, the potential to be embedded in the antecedent of a conditional, or negated, should not presume on the logical status of its *other uses*. There is no infectious symmetry here. Granted, Hacker is not conflating two distinct uses of the same string of words: he is not saying that an avowal can be embedded in the antecedent of a conditional etc., but he is saying that the fact that in another use, it *can* be, affects the logical status of the avowal itself. It does not. The syntactic and propositional characteristics of the description do not overlap into the nondescriptive, nonreflective utterance, even when the latter is identical in appearance to the former. What applies to four words that make up a descriptive statement does not apply to four identical words when they are used as the spontaneous expression of a sensation. We must dismiss appearance as determining use, and accept that something that has the *appearance* of a sentence can be grammatically barred from sentential *use*: 'If you look at the use of what appears to be a statement you may find it is not a statement' (AWL 156). *Looking like* a statement does not condemn a string of words to the logical status of a description. The *descriptive* 'I'm in love' can be embedded in the antecedent of a conditional, put in the interrogative, negated etc., but the the nondescriptive one *cannot*. The nondescriptive phrase is grammatically equivalent to a sigh. And a sigh cannot be negated.

7. The new boundary line: spontaneous versus descriptive

Traditional focus on the linguistic aspect of spontaneous utterances has blinded us to their often *exclusively* praxial nature: their being the linguistic *equivalents* of acts, such as groaning or crying. Wittgenstein's point was that something's being couched in words does not *entail* a difference in nature with something that is not couched in words. Our spontaneous linguistic expressions are not (vertical) *derivations*, but (horizontal) *extensions* of our primitive, *spontaneous* language-games:

> Why should the wordless shudder be the *ground* of the verbal one?
>
> PI, p. 174; my emphasis

> The primitive reaction may have been a glance or a gesture, but it may also have been a word.
>
> PI, p. 218

> The primitive reaction could also be a verbal reaction.
>
> LWI 134

Using words, in some contexts, has no further resonance than making a 'natural sound' (RPP II, 176). Many of our first-person psychological statements have the grammatical status of behaviour. That they should be verbal does not entail that they are the product of reasoning, conceptualization or self-observation. As Norman Malcolm puts it: 'The learned verbal expressions of pain, or fright, are no more due to thinking or reasoning than is the unlearned preverbal behaviour' (1986, 148). There is a use of words which does not grammatically differ from nonlinguistic, indeed from animal, behaviour.

What Wittgenstein does not sufficiently make clear is that his analogy between words and deeds is not one between spontaneous words and *any* deed, but between spontaneous words and *spontaneous* deeds. For, to equate some strings of words with deeds or behaviour is not necessarily to remove them from the realm of premeditation or indeed, deception – a groan can be as intentionally deceptive as a statement: it can be used in the place of a word or a sentence as a response to a question, and that response can be the fruit of pretence. What *does* exclude both acts and words from the possibility of deception is their spontaneity, their not being, as Malcolm puts it, 'due to thinking or reasoning'. To say that some utterances are *spontaneous* is to say that they are not descriptions, and therefore *cannot* be lies. First-person psychological spontaneous expressions are the most reliable strings of words uttered by human beings. Again, Peter Hacker disagrees.

8. Spontaneous lies?

Reflecting on the spectrum he has drawn, which opposes '*Avowals and descriptions*',[12] Hacker admits that *all* avowals (be they, in his terms, *experiential* or not; in my terms, *compulsive* or *neutral*) are nondescriptive and not susceptible of mistake, but some, he believes, can nevertheless be lies:

> At this end of the spectrum the concept of *description* gets no grip, nor does that of *truth*. Of course, dissimulation and deceit are possible.
>
> 1989, 298

One wants to ask: how are deceit and dissimulation possible where truth gets no grip? Hacker's continuum is linguistic, and he also views it as propositional (1996, 181). Yet propositionality implies susceptibility to truth and falsity, and Hacker rightly insists that truth gets no grip at the 'avowal' end of the spectrum. So where does Hacker stand? In *Meaning and Mind* (1993), he reiterates the inapplicability of the concepts of truth, falsehood, mistake and description to avowals and again does not thereby eliminate the possibility of dissimulation and deception, but he is clearer as to which avowals are open to this possibility:

> The diversity is indefinitely large... But in all these cases the concept of *description* gets no grip. ... Indeed the concepts of truth and falsehood are typically out of place here, although *dissimulation and deception are possible in such contexts*, as indeed they are with groans, smiles, or laughs. Similarly, the more utterances approximate to exclamations, the less room there is for evaluating them as sincere or insincere; for this dimension of evaluation gets a firmer grip in relation to

articulate expression of one's inner life, confessions, and telling others how one feels or what one thinks.

1993, 93; last emphasis mine

Here, Hacker makes a distinction between avowals that are more linguistically articulate (i.e. that more resemble and are closer to the 'descriptions' end of the continuum), such as confessing – and there, sees room for dissimulation and pretence – and those, like exclamations, where he sees less room. Utterances are evaluated as open to dissimulation or insincerity the more linguistically articulate they are. And pretence can be logically excluded only in extreme, presumably nonlinguistic, cases: 'If someone is thrown into the flames, etc., it makes no sense to say "Maybe he is not in pain, but just pretending". There are circumstances in which one may say that there is no such thing as pretending' (1993, 264). But Wittgenstein's point is precisely that pretence is logically excluded not only in extreme, unambiguous cases such as someone being thrown in the flames, or a baby crying, but in *all* spontaneous utterances. They are all, *at par* with such obvious cases. It is their being spontaneous, not their being exclamations, that makes them logically impervious to pretence. It isn't the brevity of an expression or its apparent similarity to a nonverbal expression that makes an utterance spontaneous – a three year-old can say 'Ouch!' although her fall did not hurt, merely to get her mother's attention; conversely, a spontaneous outpouring of emotion can last a very articulate hour. The determining feature here is whether or not the expression is *spontaneous,* not whether or not it resembles a sentence.

9. There are confessions and there are confessions

A confession is not always sincere or spontaneous: it can be premeditated or the result of more or less elaborate preparations, such as Augustine, Rousseau or De Quincey put in their *Confessions*. We can speak of a false confession, such as a mother wanting to save her child and 'confessing' to a crime he committed; of a mistaken confession, such as someone confessing to a murder they thought they had committed (it was a set-up and the gun fired blanks); of a fictional confession, such as the *Confessions of Felix Krull: Confidence Man*. A confession can consist of two volumes, three pages, a single word, a nod or an eye movement. Whether it is a truthful or a deceptive confession has nothing to do with its appearance, but only with the circumstances of its pronouncement. The very same words (e.g., 'I did it!') can be used to formulate a premeditated or a spontaneous confession, a truthful or a deceptive confession. Rather than decide that not all cases of confessing are spontaneous avowals, Hacker places 'articulate expression of one's inner life, confessions, and telling others how one feels or what one thinks' en masse in the avowal end of the spectrum, and is then left having to account for cases of *deceptive* avowals. He does this by insisting that their being, by (his own) definition, spontaneous, nondescriptive, not susceptible of truth or falsity does not prevent some avowals from being lies. So that, on Hacker's view, a person can lie about something which she does not hold as either true or false. Granted, an avowal cannot be mistaken because it is not a description, but it can be insincere, contends Hacker:

> My confession of my thoughts may be inadequate, but not because I have made a mistake – rather because I have been untruthful or have held something crucial back, have exaggerated or understated.
>
> 1993, 95

Hacker believes that excluding the possibility of *mistake* sufficiently guarantees the nondescriptive status of 'avowals'. It does not. The possibility of *pretence* too must be excluded. For to lie about something is to make a consciously false *description*. And Hacker himself recognizes that 'in all these cases the concept of *description* gets no grip'. So how can he admit lies, which are false statements or descriptions, into the category of nondescriptive avowals? He does this by disconnecting lying from knowing:

> One will ... want to object: surely when I lie about my thoughts or feelings I *know* or am conscious that I am really thinking or feeling thus-and-so and not as I said? This is wrong, for the very phrase 'to know that I am lying' is misleading. One ... does not *find out* that one is lying. One does not 'know' that one is lying ... Of course I *know* later that I have lied, but not because I *knew* earlier, but because I *lied* earlier.
>
> 1989, 300

Inasmuch as, strictly speaking, knowing is justified true belief, Hacker is right to say that it is misleading to say we *know* we're lying; and this, for the same reason it is misleading to say we *know* we're in pain. There is, in the act of lying, as little room for justification or verification as there is in our feeling pain. There is, however, an awareness or consciousness about lying that Hacker seems to be neglecting here; and without which we would, by default, be lying unawares, as it were – spontaneously.[13] I suggest that we can cater to this neglect in two ways: the first is by replacing knowledge with a *noncognitive* type of assurance that would give pretence its needed basis: certainty. *Knowing* is not the only kind of assurance at our disposal, as Wittgenstein makes clear in *On Certainty*: there is a more basic, nonreflective, 'animal' assurance that underpins knowing.[14] This means that I don't have to 'know' something in order to make a false description of that thing. I don't *know* that I am in my room – rather I am indubitably 'certain' of it – but I can lie about it: I can pretend to someone on the phone that I'm at the office. The second way we can cater to Hacker's neglect is by understanding 'knowing' in a broader or looser sense than that implying justified true belief. This is probably how Wittgenstein, unlike Hacker, understands it in these passages which predate *On Certainty* and take lying to be internally connected to knowing:

> Our point is: the liar knows that he is telling an untruth. But we are not going to say it. It means nothing at all. The statement is grammatical.
>
> LPP 196

> Lying always consists in intention.
>
> LPP 211

Of course, there are premeditated, insincere confessions, but *they* are *not* avowals; they are cases where the concept of description *does* get a grip. Inasmuch as Hacker has placed 'confessions' at the end of the spectrum where 'the concept of *description* gets no grip', he has made them *ipso facto* immune to the possibility of *deception*. To evaluate a *spontaneous* confession as possibly deceitful is as much grammatical nonsense as to evaluate a *spontaneous* moan as possibly deceitful. In certain circumstances, it will be grammatical nonsense to think of *any* expression – be it a confession or a moan – as dissimulative:

> When I say that moaning is the expression of t[oothache], then under certain circ[umstance]s the possibility of it being the expression without the feeling behind it mustn't enter my game.
> *It is nonsense to say: the expression [Ausdruck] may always lie.*
> *The language games with expressions of feelings* (private experiences) *are based on games with expressions of which we don't say that they may lie.*
> LPE 245; my emphasis

It is nonsense to say that the expression may *always* lie. Whereas expressions in general can be deceitful, *spontaneous* expressions cannot/cannot be. They are the genuine item, the pretence-free basis which deception learns to imitate. There is no room for dissimulation in a spontaneous utterance because it is an unreasoned expression: 'How is a lie possible in a case where there is no justification?' (LPE 250). If an expression is spontaneous, it is *by definition* not mediated, and therefore cannot be contrived, deceitful, premeditated or manipulated: 'The expressions get their importance from the fact that they are not used coolly but that *we can't help using them*' (LPE 281; my emphasis). Sincerity is inherent in, *definitive* of, spontaneous utterances; and not, as Hacker seems to think, optional.

A spontaneous utterance is an uncontrolled movement, an impulsive act: 'the word which you *utter* is a reaction' (LPE 249; my emphasis). In the realm of the spontaneous, the utterance is itself the measure or criterion of sincerity; its mere occurrence guarantees its truthfulness.[15] Spontaneous utterances are not *propositions, descriptions* or *lies*. Some words are, in some contexts, nothing but *unknowing deeds*.

10. Nonpropositional attitudes

Words and deeds. Analogously: mind and body. To insist on the insurmountability of the distinction between words and deeds betrays a failure to let context rather than appearance determine use and status. Hacker's claim that because sentences (in their most common use) can be syntactically manipulated, they cannot (in *any* use) be the equivalent of deeds, denotes a conservative reluctance to relax traditional dichotomies. But Wittgenstein's philosophy, his contribution to our better understanding of ourselves, hinges on precisely such a relaxation, if not wholesale rejection, of our traditional dichotomies. A more perspicuous *rearrangement* of our concepts can only result from a *disturbance* of our dormant dichotomies, not a smug brandishing of them. The attenuation of word-deed or language-act dualism is crucial to the later Wittgenstein's philosophical enterprise: it is the very life-blood of his treatment of rules, hinge certainties (in *On Certainty*), and of course spontaneous utterances. To suggest that Wittgenstein could not have envisaged the possible equivalence of act and deed is not only to ignore his various injunctions to 'treat the word itself as a gesture' (PG 66), it is, more consequentially, to prevent him from solving or dissolving, one of our most persistent philosophical problems – that of the explanatory gap.

The mind-body problem can be approached from several angles. Ryle's bête noire was the category mistake of viewing mental phenomena as if they were ethereal versions of physical phenomena. Envisaging the mind as functioning in ways analogous to the body forces us to posit *inner causes* of our words and deeds. But because it is after all the realm of the mind that is in question, these causes cannot be outrightly mechanical, and so *reasons* take the place of mechanical *causes*. Beliefs, intentions and desires are posited as the mandatory reasons prompting what we say and do; the ghosts required to activate the machine. The really damaging consequence here is reductionism – *reducing* mental phenomena, such as thoughts, desires and beliefs to physical entities so as to invest them with some concrete efficacy. Attempts to reduce the mental to the physical are altogether misdirected. What needs be done is to deny the very existence of a gap: rather than strive to materialize ghosts, we should denounce their fictitiousness. In cautioning us against the overriding influence of mechanical pictures in our understanding of the mental, Ryle's intention was not to urge that we steer both categories well clear of each other, thereby deepening an alleged gap. Far from stressing a categorical categorial division between the mental and the physical, Ryle did more than his share to *dissipate* 'the hallowed contrast between Mind and Matter' (1949, 23).

Categories have their purpose, but they should serve not dominate. It was the tyranny of (Frege's) concepts with *sharp boundaries* that gave impetus to Wittgenstein's *concepts with blurred edges* (PI 71) and *family resemblance concepts* (PI 67). The intellectual craving for neat, hermetic compartments can blur, rather than clarify philosophical analysis. Some categories, like some concepts, should be made permeable if we are to get rid of explanatory gaps. We should have learned long ago, since Descartes proceeded to bridge the explanatory gap with the pineal gland, that relegating the body to one impermeable category and the mind to another will not do. We separate the mental (thought) and the physical (act) into incommensurable categories, but in fact what we call an act can manifest itself verbally (spontaneous utterances and, with added paraphernalia, performatives); and what we call thinking (believing, expecting, intending) need be nothing but a way of acting. Where propositionalists insist on logically prefacing our acts with a proposition or a thought, there need be only the act: *my standing up* need not be preceded by: 'I *believe* that my feet are still there'; *my cringing* need not be justified by 'I *expect* the dentist to hurt me as he approaches with his hypodermic needle'; *my opening the door* need not be prompted by 'I *intend* to go out'. The acts of standing, cringing and opening the door are not *prompted by* but *embody* or *manifest* or *enact* a belief, an expectation, an intention. Our beliefs, expectations and intentions are not always, as has traditionally been assumed, *propositional* attitudes. They can manifest themselves in *what we do*. This is Wittgenstein's late version of the saying-showing distinction:[16]

> ...we can see *from their actions* that [people] believe certain things definitely, whether they express this belief or not.
>
> OC 284; my emphasis

> If someone is looking for something and perhaps roots around in a certain place, he *shows* that he believes that what he is looking for is there.
>
> OC 288; my emphasis

To believe something may be equivalent to *acting in a certain way*. Belief can be expressed propositionally (*said*), but also nonpropositionally (*shown*) – in our acts. And if a belief, a desire, an expectation or an intention can come in the form of a *way of acting*, philosophers need no longer seek to give them some functional, biological or propositional form that will explain how they prompt behaviour. If beliefs and intentions sometimes *are* behaviour, there is no logical incompatibility in kind between our beliefs and our actions – and therefore no gap. This is not to say that there is no categorial difference between words and deeds, only that the categories are porous. Or as Wittgenstein put it:

> Different concepts touch here and run some way together. But you need not think that all lines are *circles*.
>
> PI, p. 192; my translation, emphasis as per the original

11. Conclusion

Just as our words are sometimes combined to form, in certain contexts, *descriptions* or falsifiable sentences – that is, propositions – they can also be combined to form nonmanipulable *expressions*, the logical equivalent of acts. Wittgenstein's assimilation of some words to deeds effects precisely that crucial blurring of categories which shows that there is no necessary gap between our thoughts and acts. Word and deed *cannot* be incommensurable if they are sometimes commensurable, of the same nature. If some words *are* deeds, then the incommensurability between words and acts, and between mind and body vanishes. If *some* cases obviate the need for an explanatory link, then it can no longer be *systematically* postulated that there is a feeling, sensation or thought or anything *behind* our words or our acts that prompts them in some mysterious way. In some cases, to say 'I want an apple' *is* to want an apple. And in those cases where the expression does not constitute *the whole* of the belief, feeling or desire, it can be seen as one of its *manifestations* rather than as its consequence – thereby eluding the need for justification. And where there is no need for justification, no explanatory gap occurs.

Recognizing the exclusively praxial character of some first-person psychological deliverances is part of a larger task: that of conjuring all ghosts out of the machine – which, it must be stressed, is not the same as saying that we have no inner life. It contributes to the general realization that what we say is not the result of an *inner, nonverbalized thought process*, and that *some* of what we say can be a primitive reaction – part of our nonreflective, animal behaviour.[17] The immediacy of spontaneous utterances, their similarity to reflexes, makes them exemplary instances of language not doing its traditional, representative act, but more radically enactive work. It is in such nonpropositional manifestations that language best shows itself as an *extension* of behaviour, which implies that, at some point, it must be of the same nature as behaviour – that somewhere, these concepts touch and run some way together. It is in this fringe area that one suddenly perceives language as as much part of our natural expression of ourselves as are our feelings and actions and reflexes. Glimpsing the nature of spontaneous utterances changes our perspective on the whole landscape of language. The sophistication our language is capable of should no longer blind us to its origins, to its intimate relatedness to the behaviour we share with animals. Animals need no ghostly proposition to prompt their actions. Why should we? The fact that we are capable of intricate thought does not make intricate thought essential to our every move.

Peter Hacker has greatly contributed to the clarification of Wittgenstein's attempts to get the ghost out of the machine. But his insistence that words are *never* (for that is what it comes to) assimilable to deeds, and that some of our most spontaneous (unreflective) expressions are propositions open to pretence, prevents the ghost from vanishing. Hacker does not go all the way with Wittgenstein. He draws back at the crucial point. He acknowledges the forays, recognizes the clarifications, the demaskings, some of the reclassifications and rearrangements, but not the upheaval, not the revolution itself. Hacker's reading of Wittgenstein is a conservative reading. His teetering on the brink prevents him from making the leap Wittgenstein made, and hinders our viewing the paradigm shift at hand.[18]

4

Literature as the Measure of our Lives

In her Nobel Prize acceptance speech, Toni Morrison said: 'We die. That may be the meaning of life. But we do language. That may be the measure of our lives.' In this chapter, I explore, with Wittgenstein, how world and language delimit each other, and particularly how the language of literature can be the measure of our lives only by exceeding language – that is, through enactment: by *showing*, through language and literary devices, what cannot be *said*.

'We die. That may be the meaning of life. But we do language. That may be the measure of our lives.' With these words, uttered in her Nobel Prize acceptance speech (1993), Toni Morrison may have captured the distinctive importance of language in the constitution and expression of human morality, sociality, psychology, science and art; but this is not to say that, as the Tractarian Wittgenstein had it, 'the limits of my language mean the limits of my world' (TLP 5.6). Whatever linguistic idealism may or may not have informed this Tractarian remark, the *later* Wittgenstein was no linguistic idealist: he did not share the view – as Bernard Williams (1981) would have us believe – that there is no reality independent of our conception of it.[1] Wittgenstein's groundbreaking realization is that we do not read off our concepts from nature – as if nature could even be in the business of offering concepts. Our concepts do not track a conceptual ghost line in reality but rather create an order in reality – an order conditioned, but not dictated, by reality. Wittgenstein does not therefore preclude the existence of a language-independent reality to which our language connects; only the connection is not due to our *discovering* tracks in nature but to *making* them. The connection is not a correspondentist or empirical one, but a grammatical one: 'The connection between "language and reality" is made by definitions of words, and these belong to grammar' (PG 97).

Nor does this grammatical or conceptual ordering preclude reality's impact on our ordering. Though we don't read off our concepts from nature, '[t]he rule we lay down is the one most strongly suggested by the facts of experience' (AWL 84). And so our concepts are closely interwoven – though not inferentially – with what is most fundamental in our way of living (LW II, 43–4). The later Wittgenstein well understood that language is rooted in and *conditioned* by the extra-linguistic; by natural *facts* which are fundamental or salient for us: 'very general facts of nature' such as the 'common behaviour of mankind' (PI, p. 56; PI 206). 'Indeed – he asks in *On Certainty* – doesn't it seem obvious that the *possibility* of a language-game is conditioned by certain facts?' (OC 617).

I have addressed in Chapter 1 the ways in which language is embedded in the extra-linguistic; what I would like to do in this chapter is explore how its being impacted by the extra-linguistic' – how its being 'reality-soaked' – makes language the vital and *autonomous* force that it is. I am *not* interested here in how we use language to describe and refer to the world, but rather in how we use language aesthetically to evoke what cannot be described or referred to veridically, and yet deeply generates or enhances understanding. Inasmuch as the most potent manifestations of language carrying life and conveying understanding are to be found in literature, I will use literature to help me flesh out how, in this non-referential and nonpropositional way, language is, immeasurably, 'the measure of our lives'.

The aim of the *Tractatus*, writes Wittgenstein in its Preface, is 'to draw a limit to thought, or rather – not to thought, but to the expression of thoughts'; and that, he adds, can only be done by drawing the limit in language.[2] We might also put it this way: the *Tractatus* aims to demarcate 'what can be said' from nonsense. That the limit of thought can only be drawn in language is not to say that the limit of thought coincides with that of language, for language exceeds 'what can be said'. Though the *Tractatus* narrows down what can be said or spoken about to a specific subgroup of propositions – the propositions of natural science (6.53) – language consists of far more than this. If what can be said, technically speaking, is narrowed down to what can be true or false – that is, to what is verifiable: empirical propositions – there is much that cannot be said but is nevertheless dependent on language for its expression. When, at the close of the book, Wittgenstein writes: 'What we cannot speak about we must pass over in silence' (TLP 7), he is alluding to 1) that which *can* be put into words, but is not strictly speaking sayable because not truth-evaluable; and 2) that which *cannot* be put into words but shows itself through the use of words. It is the latter ineffable that I am concerned with here: how some of the most acute and sensitive manifestations of 'the measure of our lives' depend on language, though they cannot be formulated.

1. Language 'is in order as it is' (PI 98)

Wittgenstein writes that the ethical and the aesthetic are not sayable (6.421). Our words will give us 'facts, facts, and facts but no Ethics' (LE 40). The 'mere description' of the facts of a murder, in all its physical and psychological detail, 'will contain nothing which we could call an *ethical* proposition. The murder will be on exactly the same level as any other event, for instance the falling of a stone' (LE 39; original emphasis). This is a version of the fact-value distinction. Value cannot be said because all that can be said is natural (or factual) meaning, and value is supernatural. This does not mean that value finds no expression; only that its expression is not, and should not be confused with, empirical or natural/factual expression. The ethical value of the murder cannot be *said* for there are no ethical propositions; it can only *show* itself *in* what is said: 'There are, indeed, things that cannot be put into words. They *make themselves manifest*' (6.522; original emphasis).

On the other hand, many of the things that *can* be put into words – e.g., tautologies (including propositions of logic) and contradictions – 'say nothing' (TLP 4.461, 5.43,

6.1, 6.11). And so language can be misleading in that what looks like it *is* saying something – simply because it doesn't *look* as if lacking sense, (e.g., the propositions of logic) – in fact does lack sense and says nothing (TLP 4.461)³. Indeed, Wittgenstein regularly complains about 'the misleading uniformity of language', from the *Tractatus* where he thanks Russell for 'showing that the apparent logical form of a proposition need not be its real one" (TLP 4.0031), to the *Blue Book* where he notes the confusion provoked by 'the outward similarity between a metaphysical proposition and an experiential one' (BB 55f). In *Philosophical Grammar*, he writes of 'the confusion caused by the form of word-language, which makes everything uniform' (PG 422); and in the *Investigations*:

> Of course, what confuses us is the uniform appearance of words when we hear them spoken or meet them in script and print. For their *application* is not presented to us so clearly. Especially when we are doing philosophy!
>
> PI 11; original emphasis

This is why the philosopher's task is '[t]he clarification of the use of language' aimed at dismantling the '[t]raps of language' (P 183/ BT 311). However, though the problems that arise through our misinterpreting the forms of our language go deep (PI 110), this cannot generate a desire for another language; it can only prompt the philosopher to alert us to instances of language going on holiday (PI 38) – as, for example, when philosophers say that radical 'doubt' is possible. Here, language goes on holiday because philosophers use the word 'doubt' in a way that transgresses its use in our ordinary language games and thereby confounds us; for, Wittgenstein reminds us, to speak of radical doubt is nonsense: 'A doubt that doubted everything would not be a doubt' (OC 450); 'Doubting and non-doubting behavior. There is the first only if there is the second' (OC 354). For, in order even to doubt we must at least be certain of the meaning of our words (see OC 370).⁴

In spite of his wariness about the misleading uniformity of language, Wittgenstein does not fall into what Ben Ware calls 'the modernist-linguistic impasse' (2015, 120). His acknowledgement of the 'traps' that come with the nature of language – and which are compounded by our inattention to context, our misleading reifications, our violations of grammar – in no way betrays a dissatisfaction with ordinary language. Quite the contrary, Wittgenstein finds it perfectly in order as it is – and this, from the *Tractatus* onward:

> In fact, all the propositions of our everyday language, just as they stand, are in perfect logical order.
>
> TLP 5.5563

> On the one hand it is clear that every sentence in our language 'is in order as it is'. That is to say, we are not *striving after* an ideal, as if our ordinary vague sentences had not yet got a quite unexceptionable sense, and a perfect language awaited construction by us. – On the other hand it seems clear that where there is sense there must be perfect order. – So there must be perfect order even in the vaguest sentence.
>
> PI 98 original emphasis

These remarks are all on the side of ordinary language: not only is it in no need of interference or improvement, it *cannot* be improved, for it is – even in its vaguest sentences – in 'perfect order'. However, that 'philosophy may in no way interfere with the actual use of language' (PI 124) does not mean that it should not correct *philosophical* use when it goes 'on holiday'. Conceptual elucidation is the philosopher's job:[5] she is responsible for discerning 'differences' in 'the misleading analogies in the use of language' (P 163), and so ought not to use concepts indiscriminately. Though Wittgenstein refuses to admonish or correct the ordinary use of language when prey to misleading analogies, the philosopher must be corrected:

> For when Moore says 'I know that that's a …' I want to reply 'you don't *know* anything!' – and yet I would not say that to anyone who was speaking without philosophical intention.
>
> OC 407; original emphasis

Here Wittgenstein inveighs against Moore for his carelessness; for the 'wrong use' he made of the proposition 'I know …'. (OC 178).

Wittgenstein himself struggled with language: 'Here I am inclined to fight windmills, because I cannot yet say the thing I really want to say' (OC 400). However, Wittgenstein's struggle with language[6] is not a struggle with the limitations of language; it is a struggle with thought, a philosophical struggle. Language is perfectly adequate; it is the philosopher who may not be: 'I do philosophy now like an old woman who is always mislaying something and having to look for it again: now her spectacles, now her keys' (OC 532). We should therefore take neither the incapacity of language to say 'the supernatural' (i.e. the aesthetic, the ethical or the mystical generally), nor the philosopher's struggle with language, to be indications of any shortcoming in language. In the latter case, the philosopher's struggle, though it involves a struggle with language, is not due to any failing on the part of language, but to the philosopher's difficulty in apprehending and perspicuously relaying 'something that already lies open to view and that becomes surveyable by a rearrangement' (PI 92). In the former case, it is simply that the *mode* of expression is not *saying*, but *showing*; language is perfectly adequate and indeed, where literature is concerned, essential to the evocation of the ineffable.

2. The language of literature: showing, not saying

For Wittgenstein, the significance of aesthetics lies in the artist's ability to present objects, not as they exist in the empirical world, but *sub specie aeternitatis*.[7] Literally this is 'from the point of view of eternity'; that is atemporally, or non-contingently; from outside the world. This can mean something as metaphysically loaded as 'from God's eye view' or more simply 'with detachment', whereas the 'usual way of looking at things sees objects … from the midst of them', the artist views them from outside', with aesthetic wonder ('*Künstlerische Wunder*') (NB 86). This means that she views them with the kind of *detachment* that contemplates not facts, but the fact of existence: 'Aesthetically, the miracle is that the world exists. That there is what there is' (NB 86).

The world the artist sees is not factually different from the world we ordinarily see, but it is her attitude to, and perspective of, that world that are different and transformative. For Wittgenstein, a kind of Gestalt switch takes place in artistic contemplation: where we 'usually' see 'the bare present image' as a 'worthless momentary picture in the whole temporal world', the artist in aesthetic wonder sees it as 'the true world among shadows' (NB 83). It is the same 'bare present' world for nothing has been added or removed from it, and yet an altogether different world, where the contingent and temporal fade out to allow the atemporal significance to emerge: '... only an artist can represent an individual thing as to make it appear to us like a work of art.... A work of art forces us – as one might say – to see it in the right perspective but, in the absence of art, the object is just a fragment of nature like any other' (CV 4–5).

And so the very same thing which had not otherwise made an impression on us will make one – indeed, the 'right' one – when presented from an artistic perspective. This brings to mind Wittgenstein's notion of a 'perspicuous presentation' – whereby something which had always been in plain view, and yet overlooked by us, when properly arranged (or *perspicuously presented*) is brought to our attention and strikes us significantly and as never before. There is something about the *artistic presentation* of a woman throwing herself under a train out of despair that a newspaper report of such an event cannot convey. Why is this? Many attempts have been made to explain it, but I find Wittgenstein's view (which he shares with F. R. Leavis) the most compelling. It's all in the term 'presentation' – to be contrasted with 'report'. If literature – the creative use of language – enables us to see in an event, a face or a gesture, a significance that the ordinary use of language is unable to evoke, it is because literature *presents* it so that we see it 'in the right perspective'; but also because literature does not try to *say* what cannot be said. Wittgenstein is right, all that really matters in human life cannot be put into words, but it can be intimated or presented *through* language – particularly the language of literature:

> The poem by Uhland is really magnificent. And this is how it is: if only you do not try to utter what is unutterable then *nothing* gets lost. But the unutterable will be – unutterably – *contained* in what has been uttered.
> EL 7; original emphasis

The poem does not make its point by what it literally says, but by what its words evoke or show – and *that* cannot be said. Wittgenstein's friend, Paul Engelmann, writes:

> The 'positive' achievement of Wittgenstein, which has so far met with complete incomprehension, is his pointing to *what is manifest in a proposition*. And what is manifest in it, a proposition cannot also state explicitly. The poet's sentences, for instance, achieve their effect not through what they say but through what is manifest in them, and the same holds for music, which also says nothing.
> EL 83; original emphasis

For Wittgenstein, literature – where words are used not naturalistically, but in a dance (CV 37) – is capable of showing the ethical. It is (non-paradoxically) not through *saying*, but only through *showing* that it can do this. I have elsewhere made a rapprochement between Wittgenstein's 'showing' or 'presenting' and Leavis's 'enactment' or 'presentment', of the ethical in literature;[8] here, I want to flesh out what it means for language to present or show something.

Here is Leavis, defining a reader's task: 'What we have to look for are the signs of something grasped and held, something presented in an ordering of words, not merely thought of or gestured towards' (Craig 2013). And Wittgenstein:

> We speak of understanding a sentence in the sense in which it can be replaced by another which says the same; but also in the sense in which it cannot be replaced by any other. (Any more than one musical theme can be replaced by another.)
>
> In the one case the thought in the sentence is something common to different sentences; in the other, something that is expressed only by these words in these positions. (Understanding a poem.)
>
> PI 531

Both Wittgenstein and Leavis are here acknowledging the inseparability of form and content in literature. Because the formal properties of a creative work essentially contribute to its meaning, attempting to prise apart meaning from its creative presentation will result in vacuous paraphrase. Garry Hagberg puts it well:

> The question what is the meaning of a work of art, where "meaning" caries an implicit analogy with language and where in turn language implies a fundamental separability of meaning from materials, is a question that ought to be treated with extreme caution.
>
> 1995, 74

'Art is a kind of expression. Good art is complete expression' (NB 19.9.16, 83), writes Wittgenstein. Complete, in that nothing can be changed without sacrificing the expression. Yes, as Engelmann is right to point out, language is incalculably necessary, but the expression is equally dependent on the form: '[p]oetry can produce a profound artistic effect *beyond* (but never without) the immediate effect of its language. It is true that it needs a rare and felicitous conjuncture to bring off that effect' (EL 84; original emphasis). Alluding to Wittgenstein's recitation 'with a shudder of awe' of Mörike's *Mozart's Journey to Prague*, Engelmann remarks:

> In the rare cases where the venture succeeds ... we are in the presence of sublime peaks of poetic language, and thus of verbal expression altogether. Here was one of the great passages in literature touching on Wittgenstein's most central language problem: that of the border of the unutterable and yet somehow expressible.
>
> EL 86

This border where the unutterable somehow gets expressed is where meaning is not uttered or said but shown. *Saying* is not enough because the aesthetic and the ethical are not expressible in literal or naturalistic terms. We are not here in the realm of the verifiable but of what Wittgenstein calls 'imponderable evidence' (LW I, 920–4): where the buzzing indeterminacy, spontaneity and irreducibility of human life[9] hinges on its basic regularity and predictability so that although it is impossible to 'put this indefiniteness, correctly and unfalsified, into words' (PI, p. 227), it is not impossible to *show* it.[10] We have here to do with imponderable evidence – evidence that cannot be demonstrated, but can be 'monstrated', as it were, or *shown*. Evidence that can only be apprehended non-discursively: through the blood, rather than the mind, would say D. H. Lawrence, for whom the novel, more than any other artistic medium, has this capacity for presentment or showing. Literature, and the novel in particular, gives us what philosophy, or any other discursive medium, cannot: 'a passionate, implicit morality, not didactic. A morality which changes the blood, rather than the mind. Changes the blood first. The mind follows later, in the wake' (1964, 162). The idea here is to deintellectualize the ethical, to get us to see it as an attitude, a way of being and acting; and to deintellectualize, too, ethical understanding: morality reaches the mind through the blood – that is, through the immediacy of the aesthetic which is another kind of 'perspicuous presentation': 'A poet's words can pierce us' (Z 155) in a way a philosopher's cannot. For it is in the inextricable interrelatedness of form and content that meaning is made manifest; this is done by language, which enacts rather than says: 'Shakespeare displays the dance of human passions, one might say. . . . But he displays it to us in a dance, not naturalistically' (CV 36–7).

For, meaning enacted in literature is grasped – as it is given – nondiscursively, with what Leavis calls 'irresistible immediacy' (1948, 204). The kind of grasp or understanding that requires no interpretation: we get the meaning or the point; we grasp it – the way we ordinarily grasp language, or the way we see an aspect emerging from a configuration, or the way we see emotion on a face. This is the *spontaneous, immediate intelligence* Christiane Chauviré recognizes as characterizing much of what Wittgenstein means by 'understanding':

> The relation of works of art or even musical phrases to the understanding we may have of them is not causal but internal, just as the relation of words that we read or hear in ordinary language is internal to our understanding of them. The drawback of interpretation is that it denotes an explicit verbal development that can engender others *ad infinitum*, each interpretation replacing the previous "as if we were content with one for the time being, until we thought of the next waiting immediately behind". And so, whether with regard to art or to rule-following, Wittgenstein reinstates spontaneous intelligence, immediate, silent at times, but always expressive.
>
> 2012, 338; my translation

Wittgenstein clearly articulates this kind of nonpropositional understanding prompted by music and literature: 'If a theme, a phrase, suddenly means something to you, you don't have to be able to explain it. Just *this* gesture has been made accessible to you' (Z 158; original emphasis); that is, you 'understand it'[11] (Z 159). We can be impacted by, or 'understand', the words of a poem, *directly*, which means without interpretation; for it speaks to us, writes Wittgenstein, '[t]he way music speaks. Do not forget that a poem, although it is composed in the language of information, is not used in the language-game of giving information' (Z 160). For there is meaning that can be explained and meaning that does not come out in an explanation (Z 156). I would now like to give an idea of how a novel can *show* us what I can only poorly explain.

3. The perspicuous presentations of literature

In *Madame Bovary*, Gustave Flaubert depicts the life and state of a woman prey to ennui. To say that she finds herself engulfed in 'a feeling of listlessness and dissatisfaction arising from a lack of occupation or excitement' (OED) would certainly summarize her state, but it would give you nothing of the texture of ennui or of the texture of Emma's life that is engulfed by it. Short of reading the novel, one cannot perceive and penetrate the ways in which ennui in turn builds up and corrodes Emma's feelings, moods, expectations and dreams; how it comprises the recurring cycle of the fabrication of and luxuriating in what Baudelaire calls the 'Ideal' and its slow, desperate consumption by the 'Spleen'. But perhaps these passages, albeit in translation, might give us a glimpse:

> [Charles] came home late – at ten o'clock, at midnight sometimes. Then he asked for something to eat, and as the servant had gone to bed, Emma waited on him. He took off his coat to dine more at his ease. He told her, one after the other, the people he had met, the villages where he had been, the prescriptions he had written, and, well pleased with himself, he finished the remainder of the boiled beef and onions, picked pieces off the cheese, munched an apple, emptied his water-bottle, and then went to bed, and lay on his back and snored. As he had been for a time accustomed to wear nightcaps, his handkerchief would not keep down over his ears, so that his hair in the morning was all tumbled pell-mell about his face and whitened with the feathers of the pillow, whose strings came untied during the night.
>
> ....
>
> She asked herself if by some other chance combination it would have not been possible to meet another man; and she tried to imagine what would have been these unrealised events, this different life, this unknown husband. All, surely, could not be like this one. He might have been handsome, witty, distinguished, attractive, such as, no doubt, her old companions of the convent had married. What were they doing now? In town, with the noise of the streets, the buzz of the theatres and the lights of the ballroom, they were living lives where the heart expands, the senses bourgeon out. But she – her life was cold as a garret whose dormer window looks on the north, and ennui, the silent spider, was weaving its web in the darkness in every corner of her heart.
>
> ....
>
> she was becoming more irritated with him. As he grew older his manner grew heavier; at dessert he cut the corks of the empty bottles; after eating he cleaned his teeth with his tongue; in taking soup he made a gurgling noise with every spoonful; and, as he was getting fatter, the puffed-out cheeks seemed to push the eyes, always small, up to the temples.

Sometimes Emma tucked the red borders of his under-vest unto his waistcoat, rearranged his cravat, and threw away the dirty gloves he was going to put on; and this was not, as he fancied, for himself; it was for herself, by a diffusion of egotism, of nervous irritation. Sometimes, too, she told him of what she had read, such as a passage in a novel, of a new play, or an anecdote of the "upper ten" that she had seen in a feuilleton; for, after all, Charles was something, an ever-open ear, and ever-ready approbation. She confided many a thing to her greyhound. She would have done so to the logs in the fireplace or to the pendulum of the clock.

At the bottom of her heart, however, she was waiting for something to happen. Like shipwrecked sailors, she turned despairing eyes upon the solitude of her life, seeking afar off some white sail in the mists of the horizon. She did not know what this chance would be, what wind would bring it her, towards what shore it would drive her, if it would be a shallop or a three-decker, laden with anguish or full of bliss to the portholes. But each morning, as she awoke, she hoped it would come that day; she listened to every sound, sprang up with a start, wondered that it did not come; then at sunset, always more saddened, she longed for the morrow.

Scenes such as these penetratingly *show* the effect of ennui, with all the colour, light and shadow that language is capable of. To that effect, nonpropositional devices are used, such as image, metaphor, symbolism, juxtaposition, tension, mood, tone, cadence, irony etc. It is through the internal connectedness – or 'subtle interrelatedness', as Lawrence puts it (1961, 528) – throughout the novel of these literary devices, as also of description, dialogue and action, that a nonpropositional, immediate, impact is made on us. As Leavis says: 'The duly responsive reader cannot but *see* what it is that he has in front of him' (1986, 63; original emphasis). And indeed we cannot but see the hopeless circularity that besets Emma's life through the novel as she perpetually fabricates an 'ideal' only to watch it dissolve into vacuity. And beyond the force of individual passages, it is their being woven together to bolster, echo, and resonate from each other that gives the novel that structured, penetrating, coherence which is not of a discursive or philosophical kind. It leaves us with, as Leavis puts it: the 'certitude' that we have 'taken possession of . . . perceptions, intuitions and realizations communicated with consummate delicacy' to us in the creative work of a great writer. 'Such certitude of possession is an ultimate; what could a proof, if proof were possible, add to it?' (1982, 192). This immediate, irresistible, grasp of what literature *shows* resembles the certainty Wittgenstein describes in *On Certainty*. A certainty whose objects we take hold of, the way we directly take hold of a towel 'without having doubts'; 'And yet this direct taking-hold corresponds to a *sureness*, not to a knowing' (OC 510–11). An immediate nonpropositional certainty; a certainty where mistake is 'logically excluded' (OC 194).

What great literature does is flesh out the density and texture of psychological and moral lives or experiences, thereby enhancing our understanding of what it means to be prey to ambition, remorse, alienation, jealousy, gnawing envy and so on. So that, having read *Macbeth* and seen with exceptional clarity how the killing, spurred by ambition, of an innocent person can infect a life to the point of no return, sowing unbearable remorse, near-madness and the will to die, we are indubitably more perspicuously acquainted with the psychological and moral complexions of ambition and murder. Or, in Dostoevsky's *Crime and Punishment*, having observed how a man persuades himself of the permissibility of unprovoked murder, we close the book a couple of hundred pages later having witnessed in irrefutable clarity what it is like to live the life of a murderer in its unrelenting existential reminders of the irreparability and consequences of a gratuitous act, and why it is not a life worth living. As also, having observed the vicissitudes of Emma Bovary's relentless aspirations, relentlessly crushed, we come to understand how an unquenchable thirst for the Ideal makes it impossible to see life in the every day.

In all these works, we live through the insidious, devastating, waste of a life. We are struck by the imponderable rightness of the narrative; its capturing, in wit-like acuity, what strikes us as not just *approximate*, but irrefutable. An irrefutability knitted in the intricate coherence of the whole work, so that, as Wittgenstein's certainty, what stands fast does so not on its own merit but because 'it is held fast by what lies around it' (OC 144). And that is the power of the *story*, or what Aristotle called, the plot, and Amélie Rorty 'a *structured* representation'.[12] It is the importance of this *structured* or artistic representation that the words 'not naturalistically' allude to in the following passage: 'Shakespeare displays the dance of human passions ... But he displays it to us in a dance, not naturalistically' (CV 36–7).

In *Madame Bovary*, Flaubert illuminates and extends our concept of boredom, showing how our mundane understanding of it as an occasional event cannot encompass the existential malady Emma is continually prey to. Flaubert's original depiction of it takes us to the extreme, though not uncommon, manifestation of what we would call 'boredom' and gives it more clarity and definition than, arguably, any other work preceding it.[13] And, of course, he does this through a struggle with language. Here is Maupassant's account of Flaubert's manner of composition:

> Possessed of an absolute belief that there exists but one way of expressing one thing, one word to call it by, one adjective to qualify, one verb to animate it, he gave himself to super-human labour for the discovery, in every phrase of that word, that verb, that epithet.
>
> 1884, 59

We may find excessive, even when applied to literature, Flaubert's alleged belief that there exists but one way of expressing one thing. Although, as we shall see, Flaubert would by no means be the exception here, it may perhaps be better to say, as Richard Beardsmore does, that the writer's goal is 'in some sense ... to get things right' (1971, 61). Or as we have seen Wittgenstein put it, to see things 'in the right perspective' (CV 4–5). But if Flaubert's concern is to get things right, one might ask 'what does "right" mean here?'. As suggested earlier, the answer would not be 'a veridical concordance with reality or with a principle', but rather something like 'you know it when you see it'. However, in striking our psychological and moral chords, a great novel attunes or enhances, not our knowledge, but our understanding. It does this by presenting things in such a way that we 'recognize' them as right, rather than 'discover' them to be right because we are not aliens reading the novel, but human beings ensconced in human ways of living and responsive to the common behaviour of mankind. The language used by the creative writer is rooted and soaked in psychological and moral 'promptings and potentialities' (1976, 26) – as Leavis puts it – that have been 'won or established in immemorial human living' (1975, 68). It is human life that resonates in language, and the reader – the attentive and sensitive reader – will be 'pierced' only by the right resonance – the one that coheres beyond (or rather beneath) explanation.

Flaubert had to wrestle with, and away from, the common conception of boredom to show us its existential face: ennui. Thanks to Flaubert, and other writers, we are now more or less fluent with that new or revised concept: able to recognize its difference from mere boredom. In English, we mark that difference by adopting the French word; in French, when writing, we either italicize the word or capitalize its initial letter; when speaking, we qualify it somehow – 'l'ennui existentiel' – or use a near equivalent – 'le spleen'. The word 'boredom' just won't do. However, what a creative writer does to our understanding is not always explicitly reflected by a change of word; and yet it behoves us to recognize it even where it is not thus flagged. Even when not signalled by a new word, the ongoing clarification and enrichment through writers of the concepts, virtues, vices that are most salient in our lives – love, ambition, jealousy, daughterliness, parenthood, friendship, sexuality, *joie de vivre*, faith, loyalty, deceit, war, depression, loss, death – are immense. Creative writing is a struggle with language in an effort to release from it an enhanced understanding of our basic and evolving humanness.

Wittgenstein well understood this power of literature. For reasons that will immediately be obvious, I cannot resist mentioning yet another occasion which testifies to that. In 1945, Malcolm wrote a letter to Wittgenstein in which he alludes to the war as a 'boredom'. This is Wittgenstein's reply:

> I want to say something about the war being a 'boredom'. If a boy said that school was an intense boredom, one might answer him that, if he could only get himself to learn what can really be learned there, he would not find it so boring. Now forgive me for saying that I can't help believing that an enormous lot can be learned about human beings in this war – if you keep your eyes open. And the better you are at thinking the more you'll get out of what you see. For thinking is a digestion. If I'm writing in a preaching tone I'm just an ass. But the fact remains that if you're bored a lot it means that your mental digestion isn't what it should be. I think that a good remedy for this is sometimes opening your eyes wider. Sometimes a book helps a little, e.g., Tolstoi's *Hadshi Murat* wouldn't be bad.
> Malcolm 1958, 41

And here the philosopher hands over to literature. As Wittgenstein writes: 'You cannot lead people to what is good: you can only lead them to some place or other. The good is outside the space of facts.' (CV 3). Well, literature leads us to some place or other, outside the space of facts, or what Wittgenstein calls 'natural meaning', to a space of stories. And, there, *shows* us, not THE Good, but ways we ought to live and not live. In my attempt to understand how literature measures our lives, I was led to the active role of language in literary creation. Our moral being, as so much else, is embedded in language, and this is perhaps why in the same way that great creative literature cannot get away with stylistic blunders, it cannot get away with moral ones either. It is internally connected, as Wittgenstein rightly thought, to ethics.

'What expresses *itself* in language, *we* cannot express by means of language' (TLP 4.121; original emphasis). There is in this sentence a hint of language transcending any individual voice; of our shared language as an autonomous and irresistible force. The next and final section acknowledges language as a force whose measurement of human life which, though emerging from human life, we do not control.

4. The irresistible force of language

Language is public property and so it has a force and a life of its own – the life of generations of reality-embedded, reality-soaked, use. It carries shared concepts, feelings, meanings, emotions and values, as well as density, precision and a huge array of descriptive potential that the gifted user of language needs to wrestle with and interrogate, rather than manipulate. And, of course, we know – as Leavis and Wittgenstein have, in their different ways, enabled us to – that language is not a mere vehicle for thought but the *sine qua non* enabler of thought. Here is Leavis:

> Without the English language waiting quick and ready for him, Lawrence couldn't have communicated his thought: that is obvious enough. But it is also the case that he couldn't have thought it. English as he found it was a product of an immemorial sui generis collaboration on the part of its speakers and writers. It is alive with promptings and potentialities, and the great creative writer shows his genius in the way he responds.
>
> 1976, 26

Because language is a collaborative achievement, in using it, we tap into a collective source of meaning – that 'apprehended totality of what, as registered in the language, has been won or established in immemorial human living' (1975, 68). And inasmuch as 'the fullest use of language is to be found in creative literature' (1982, 143), it is there that we find the fullest engagement with the precipitate of immemorial human living, with human values, the human psyche and the question of how to live. If the creative writer is going to render us to ourselves with any acuity and depth, it will be through her confrontation with, and abandonment to, language. It is in the act of creation, in her intense and unimpeded head-to-head with language, her strenuous delving into its resources and potency for expression, that the artist finds she is not totally in control. In the 'interplay – as Leavis puts it – between the living language and the creativity of individual genius' (1975, 49), the writer finds not only the source of creativity but also her own limits. Language has fight and mettle: as she measures herself against language, the writer finds that she is 'playing with elastic, indeed even flexible concepts. But this does not mean that they can be deformed *at will* and without offering resistance' (LW II, 24; original emphasis). Words cannot be manipulated without resistance; they can only be appealed to, interrogated and acquiesced to. This is not to say that the creative writer does not also transform the language, but that she cannot do so without first abandoning herself to its deep-lying embeddedness in the reality of human living and fighting the fight from which both writer and language come out triumphant. As Bernard Harrison splendidly puts it: 'The writer's occasional power to enlighten us comes, not from a special cognitive faculty, but rather from his power to ride the reality-gorged tiger of language' (ms 19).

Creative writers often speak of themselves as the passive receptacles of an inspiration beyond their control. They say that the creative flow takes over, leads them; many of them speak of *watching* the characters in their novel develop and take on a life of their own; of *discovering* their characters' personalities and intentions; of *following* the morality of the plot as it *emerges*. In his study of 'Creative Writers and Revision', David Calonne finds descriptions of 'inspiration' by writers to be fairly consistent: 'The writing seems to take place almost "against the writer's will" – it is "automatic" in a sense, or autonomous' (2006, 156). Although it is also clear that inspiration does not exclude perspiration – or, as Ionesco phrases it: 'spontaneous creation does not exclude the pursuit and consciousness of style' (2006, 155), the autonomy of language prevails in the following extracts from Calonne's study:

> ... in writing a draft, writers often speak of finding what they have to say in the process of trying to say it. They find their way to their true thoughts about a subject only through wrestling through the fierce struggle of putting words down on paper. In the search for expression, one finds out that to which one is really committed. And there is often great surprise for the writer as he/she discovers in the act of writing what lies dormant within the self.
>
> 2006, 144

> The author himself/ herself clearly often does not know where the trail will lead as they embark on a poem, play or novel.
>
> 2006, 173

> The writer is the caretaker of an indwelling genius, an inner daimon/demon which speaks in riddles like an oracle – speaks sometimes seemingly unintelligibly but in the pure language of the poetic unconscious.
>
> 2006, 156

'Not I, but the wind that blows through me', writes D. H. Lawrence.[14] Such accounts of inspiration have often been given a metaphysical or spiritual reading, but they needn't have. What is in play here is the autonomous force of *language*. Inspiration is the active participation of language in a writer's attempt to bring something to clarity, and yes it also involves perspiration: it is the mysterious welling-up and laborious harnessing through language of notions, feelings and fears that were hitherto unformed. It is only through language that the writer can achieve the perspicuous presentation of her unformed notions and perceptions in all of their subtle interrelatedness. As their testimonies make clear, writers feel that creation and revelation are brought about *in the process of* composition; as *resulting* from their immersion in, and struggle with, words. In an interview, Ernest Hemingway said: 'I rewrote the ending to *Farewell to*

Arms, the last page of it, thirty-nine times before I was satisfied.' When asked by the interviewer: 'Was there some technical problem there? What was it that had stumped you?' Hemingway replied: 'Getting the words right' (2006, 149). This struggle of the writer with language signals both the *potency* of language and its *autonomy*: language has, as it were, a life of its own.

The creative imagination is really creative; it doesn't stage the ethical but allows it to emerge from the artistic fabric. The morality is in the novel, not in the novelist: 'Never trust the artist. Trust the tale', writes Lawrence (1964, 8). This perhaps clarifies what Wittgenstein means by 'What expresses *itself* in language, *we* cannot express by means of language' (TLP 4.121; original emphasis). And so the important things don't get expressed by our *saying* them; it is when language is used in a creative way that the important things get expressed. This dovetails with what Leavis calls 'creative impersonality' (1986, 67). None of this is meant, as post-modernists have tried, to 'kill' the author: writers are the writers they are because of the individuals they are, but this has to include an acutely sensitive attention to, and engagement with, language.

The way literature enlightens us is not through *saying* but through *showing*. Of course words are used, but the insight they evoke is not of the propositional kind; it cannot be said. And so we conclude this journey in the realization that when we reach the power of language at its peak – in literature – we have simultaneously also returned to its limits. And yet those limits – literature's inability to *say* the most important things – should not blind us to its unlimited ability to *show* what can never be demonstrated, neither by the language of science nor by that of philosophy.[15]

Part Two

Mind

As we saw in the previous section, Wittgenstein insists that we not lose track of the spontaneous or nonreflective, or what he also calls the 'animal', in the human form of life. For Darwin, 'the difference in mind between man and the higher animals, great as it is, is one of degree and not of kind'. This is also Wittgenstein's view: 'I want to regard man here as an animal; as a primitive being to which one grants instinct but not ratiocination. As a creature in a primitive state. Any logic good enough for a primitive means of communication needs no apology from us. Language did not emerge from some kind of ratiocination' (OC 475). Wittgenstein sees the emergence of human language and mind as a seamless extension of instinctive or animal behaviour – both ontogenetically and phylogenetically. Rejecting the common picture of the mind as synonymous with, and inhabiting in, the brain, Wittgenstein thinks of it in terms of a person having and exercising certain dispositions and capacities which are enabled by, but not reducible to, the brain, and which have evolved from the dispositions and capacities of our nonhuman ancestors. The brain is no more a storage place for memories than it is a processor of thoughts. In this section, we shall see that Wittgenstein rotates our picture of the mind outwards and locates the mental primordially in ways of acting: '(And by "psychological" I don't mean "inner".)' (RPP II, 612)

5

From Deed to Word

Gapless and Kink-free Enactivism

In memoriam John V. Canfield (1934–2017)[1]

In their most recent book, *Evolving Enactivism: Basic Minds Meet Content* (2017), Dan Hutto and Eric Myin claim to give a complete and *gapless* naturalistic account of cognition, but it comes with a kink. The kink is that content-involving cognition has special properties found nowhere else in nature, making it the case that minds capable of contentful thought differ *in kind*, in this key respect, from more basic minds. Contra Hutto and Myin, I argue that content-involving practices are themselves simply a *further extension* of action and do not therefore warrant being called 'different in kind' or 'kinky'. With the help of Ludwig Wittgenstein and John V. Canfield, I show that Enactivism meets the challenge of explaining higher-level cognition; and, *contra* continuity sceptics, offers 'a philosophically cogent and empirically respectable account' of how human minds can emerge from nonhuman minds.

There are many versions of Enactivism, but what might be said to hold them together is 'the insight that the embedded and embodied activity of living beings provides the right model for understanding minds' (Hutto et al 2014). Enactivism is a view that favours 'the primacy of ways of acting over ways of thinking when it comes to understanding our basic psychological and epistemic situation' (Hutto 2014, 281). With Enactivism – particularly Dan Hutto and Eric Myin's Radical Enactivism – representational content is out of the picture in basic human cognition. Does this mean that Enactivism loses its grip when it comes to higher-level cognition? The problem is that the plausibility of the embodied and enactive nature of basic cognition – its being contentless, fundamentally interactive, dynamic and relational[2] – does not easily extend to forms of cognition involving language, representation, information, thought, logic and mathematics. Linguistic and mathematical capabilities constitute a challenge for the Enactivist approach because an explanation of these abilities requires us to move beyond dynamic interaction with the here-and-now environment. And so, as Hutto and Myin recognize, 'if it wants to become a full-blown alternative to representationalism, Enactivism … has to confront [the] challenge of explaining higher-level cognition' (2017, 7).

In fact the problem, as I understand it, is not only one of the *restricted* validity of Enactivism but of its validity *tout court*; for, inasmuch as language and mathematics are *symbolic*, and therefore content-involving, the question is how they could have emerged from, and how they can interact with, the basic, contentless forms of cognition endorsed by Enactivism. If there is no accounting for that, there is no place for Enactivism at all. For, what would be the use of positing the existence of basic cognition in humans if we can't see how it segues with our more sophisticated forms of cognition? And here, I take it, we must be able to show continuity – ontogenetically, phylogenetically and logically. The possibility for phylogenetic continuity is clearly rejected by what Doris Bar-On dubs 'continuity sceptics', according to whom:

> ... there can be no philosophically cogent or empirically respectable account of how human minds could emerge in a natural world populated with just nonhuman creatures of the sort we see around us. Few would deny that, biologically speaking, we 'came from' the beasts. But ... we must accept an unbridgeable gap in the natural history leading to the emergence of human minds[3]. ... Human mental and behavioral capacities as we now know them cannot be illuminated by seeing them as elaborations on the capacities of some nonhuman ancestors.
>
> 2013, 294

I disagree with this position. Like Wittgenstein – whose own radical enactivism is the hallmark of his thought and broke ground for current Enactivism (see Introduction in this volume) – I see language as fundamentally enactive, and the emergence of language as simply a seamless *extension* of action. An extension which, for generating novel or unprecedented possibilities, should not be considered incommensurable with, or different in kind from, its less sophisticated manifestations. As John Canfield writes:

> We are unique on this planet, no doubt; none of our fellow creatures could understand a *New Yorker* cartoon, for example, or die for an abstraction like *nation*. But our rise to that level of sophistication does not require ... an ontological difference between us and them.
>
> 2007, 77

This chapter strives to show that – contra continuity sceptics – there *is* a philosophically cogent and empirically respectable account of how human minds could emerge from nonhuman minds.

1. Evolving Enactivism – but there's the kink

The *continuity scepticism* challenge is taken up by Dan Hutto and Eric Myin in their most recent book, *Evolving Enactivism: Basic Minds Meet Content* (2017). Their aim is to 'provide a complete and gapless naturalistic account of cognition, right here, right now' (2017, 41). They claim they can do this by invoking the important, special, role played by sociocultural scaffolding. On their view, only minds that have mastered a certain, specialized kind of sociocultural practice involving public norms for the use of *symbols* can engage in content-involving thoughts and speech (2017, xix; 12; 134; 146). Because this enhanced cognitive repertoire appears to have occurred in full form only in the human lineage, they claim that 'minds capable of contentful thought differ *in kind*, in this key respect, from more basic minds' (2017, 134, 136; my emphasis). In acquiring the capacity for contentful cognition, the human animal does not lose its capacity for basic cognition, therefore retaining a commonality with other animals, but Hutto and Myin nevertheless take content-involving cognition to mark a distinction *in kind* not just between nonhuman animals and humans, but also within the human sphere (2017, 135–6).

This, they say, does not make their account gappy, for the social scaffolding responsible for contentful cognition does not imply an inexplicable gap in nature (2017, 146; see also Hutto and Satne (2015, 510)). What is crucial to their story about the natural origins of content, they argue, is that 'biological capacities gifted by evolution could have given rise to social learning, and ... there is nothing gappy about that (2017, 129). Biological continuity is thus safeguarded; yet, they affirm, in accord with Derek Penn and colleagues (2008, 110), that: 'Darwin was mistaken: the profound biological continuity between human and nonhuman animals[4] masks an equally profound functional discontinuity between the human and nonhuman mind' (2017, 134). So that Hutto and Myin are no continuity sceptics: they find no biological discontinuity in our acquisition of higher cognition but take our content-involving practices, because these are exclusive to human minds, to constitute a difference in kind between human and nonhuman minds: 'Content-involving minds have features and capacities that other, more basic minds lack: they stand apart. This difference can be thought to mark a difference in kind, not just degree, of mindedness' (2017, 134). They find appropriate to call this 'profound *functional* discontinuity' a 'kink'.

Though I agree with Hutto and Myin that 'content-involving cognition is *a special achievement*' (2017, 88; my emphasis), I do not agree that its purported exclusivity[5] in nature warrants considering it as 'different in kind' from non-content involving cognition. As they themselves insist, the sociocultural scaffolding that have enabled the emergence of this higher-level cognition does not imply an inexplicable gap in nature (2017, 146), so why attribute kinkiness to an achievement that results from a natural, seamless continuity? Why is what is only a *further development* not shared by others because of empirical conditions, get dubbed 'different in kind'? Why not instead think in terms of *arrested development* in other species, also due to empirical conditions? Hutto and Myin themselves suggest that there is no empirical obstacle to further development:

> As it happens, this appears only to have occurred in full form with construction of sociocultural cognitive niches in the human lineage. ... Should creatures with basic minds manage to master such practices, they would gain new cognitive capacities and become open to new possibilities for engaging with the world and other creatures.
>
> 2017, 134

And indeed, as we shall see, some nonhuman animals *are* capable of contentful behaviour. On one hand, then, Hutto and Myin think of contentful behaviour as an exception in nature; on the other, they say our evolutionary story is continuous, and were other species to follow the human route, they would achieve the same. But if the 'kink' merely refers to a point of evolutionary development which humans alone have reached, and not anything that is empirically or conceptually impossible for other species, is it a kink? The fact that only humans have been capable of extending action to the complexity required to achieve full-blown, syntactic language does not make this extension kinky; it makes it only *a further extension*.

It seems to me that, in spite of endorsing biological continuity, Hutto and Myin have fallen prey to the idea that the ability to use symbols constitutes a fundamental dividing line between human and nonhuman animal cognition[6] (as also between basic and nonbasic cognition). This calls to mind Terence Deacon. In *The Symbolic Species*, Deacon claims that for something to be called a 'language', even 'a simple language', it needs to be a form of symbolic representation; anything devoid of syntax or symbolism is merely 'a form of communication': to speak of 'animal language' is but to speak metaphorically. And so although Deacon's account of human brain and language evolution emphasizes the unbroken continuity between human and nonhuman *brains*, it also flags a singular *discontinuity* between human and nonhuman *minds* (1997, 13). On Deacon's view, language is the outward expression of an unusual mode of thought: symbolic representation – where 'symbolic thought does not come innately built in, but develops by internalizing the symbolic process that underlies language' (1997, 22). So that: 'Biologically, we are just another ape. Mentally, we are a new phylum of organisms. In these two seemingly incommensurate facts lies a conundrum that must be resolved before we have an adequate explanation of what it means to be human' (1997, 23). The acquisition of language is, for Deacon, 'a Rubicon that was crossed at a definite time and in a specific evolutionary context' (ibid.). But note that Deacon's definition of language as necessarily symbolic stacks the cards, and prevents gapless continuity from the get-go. The appeal of *inner* representations is difficult to shake off; but allowing *outer* representations to *define* language, or the human, may prove if not just as problematic, problematic enough. It seems to me that in endorsing the existence of a deep functional discontinuity or difference in kind between basic, contentless minds and nonbasic, content-involving minds, Hutto and Myin enter the representationalist camp – not less mined (and undermined) for containing external rather than internal representations.

2. No kink to mind

Hutto and Myin's kink sounds like Deacon's Rubicon. It reflects the view that divides animal *forms of communication* from language proper. On such a view, language essentially requires the manipulation of symbols – the possibility to go from basically expressive modes of communication to referential or representational modes of communication. For there to be a language – or for our ancestors to have crossed this Rubicon – they had to have mastered the ability to use sounds that hooked up with referents by representing them. This is a view which, it seems to me, ought *not* to be endorsed by Enactivism of any kind. It certainly doesn't square with Wittgenstein's enactivism.

For Wittgenstein, language is essentially linked to use, be it representational or otherwise. What gives our gestures or words meaning is their use – whether that use be as *expressive* as 'Ouch' when punched in the stomach or as *symbolic* as Caesar's thumb down for the poor bloke in the arena. And of course, use has all to do with our language-games and our forms of life. In the same way that 'the appeal to the inner as grounding or providing a full-blown 'referential' language must be rejected' (Canfield 2007, 34), so too must the view of referential language as something that transcends or goes beyond the scope of action be rejected. Rather, we must view 'language *tout court* [as] a set of customs in which words play a role' (2007, 34); language, that is, is nothing but 'custom-regulated action' (2007, 35).

As Wittgenstein shows, language is *inherently* enactive. This is not to say that there is no categorial difference between the concepts of language and action, but that the boundary between the two is porous.[7] The passage – be it phylogenetic or ontogenetic – from contentless to content-involving cognition, in *sometimes* involving language, does not involve something that is incommensurably different from action or behaviour. Not all action is linguistic, but language is fundamentally – that is, phylogenetically, ontogenetically and, indeed, logically, linked to action. This is obvious enough to see in animal languages, but the human use of language – as Wittgenstein has made clear – is nothing but the mastery of a *technique*, a *know-how*. However sophisticated the mastery may become – however sophisticated the symbols it involves – it remains a mastery; a matter of know-how, not of knowing that. Enactivism is not dislodged by the use of symbols, however complex. Hutto and Myin agree with this: 'Even when cognition involves content and inferential processes, the ultimate character of cognition remains enactive and dynamic (2017, 91). But then why insist that 'if it wants to become a full-blown alternative to representationalism, Enactivism ... has to confront [the] challenge of explaining higher-level cognition' (2017, 7)? The putative worry, mentioned at the beginning of this chapter, is that content is not enactive-friendly in that it goes beyond action – 'beyond interaction with the here-and-now environment' – and is therefore incommensurable with animal or basic cognition. But is an animal's wooing call not just as distant from the here-and-now environment as Marvell's 'To His Coy Mistress'? Is one not simply a more sophisticated call than the other – and so manifests a difference in degree, not in kind? There is as much anticipation, desire, hope, and sometimes even deceit, in the courtship calls of some animals as there are in those of humans. Take the fall field cricket; its less desirable smaller males produce courtship calls that dishonestly signal the body size of high-condition males in order to be more sexually attractive (Harrison et al 2013).

This example of animal interaction beyond the here-and-now environment also indicates that animals are capable of false representation. But this crosses Hutto and Myin's dividing line between animal and human cognition. For, on their view, forms of cognition are content-involving in that 'they represent the world in ways that can be true or false, accurate or inaccurate, and so on' (2017, xii), and this is thought to be a kinky departure from animal cognition. But is it? If animals are capable of deceit and the manipulation of attention and evidence, then according to Hutto and Myin's definition of content, there is room for content in animal communication and social practices. And of course the fall cricket is far from the only animal capable of deceit. As Whiten and Byrne (1988) have shown, all groups of monkeys and apes use deception, though the insight necessary to *plan* or *understand* deception seems restricted to great apes (Byrne 1995, 203). Examples of deception include: leading other animals towards or away from places; making them think that the agent has been hurt; concealing the excited glances that would reveal a hidden food, or concealing the food itself in the hand or under the body.

So misrepresentation does not require the use of symbols. Indeed, prelinguistic children often misrepresent their feelings and behaviour – sometimes concealing the latter, and exaggerating the former by forced crying. But nor is the use of symbols exclusive to humans. And by this, I don't only mean the use of symbols that humans have taught animals,[8] but the naturally-occurring arbitrary relationships between signified and signifier in some animal communication. A celebrated example being that of vervet monkeys (Seyfarth and Cheney, 1990; Cheney and Seyfarth 1996) who have been shown to use a 'bark', a 'cough' or a 'chutter' to communicate the presence, respectively, of a leopard, an eagle, or a snake.[9] As linguist James Hurford writes:

> There is nothing (as far as we know) inherently leopard-like in a bark, or inherently bark-like in a leopard. It seems more reasonable to grant that the vervets are using genuinely arbitrary symbols, than to assume that vervets perceive the world in ways radically different from our own, so that for them the relationships here are somehow iconic or causal. So some arbitrary symbolic behaviour can be found in nature. And in fact such very limited arbitrary symbol systems can be seen in many species, especially in their alarm calls. There is a vast difference *in degree* between the inventories of arbitrary symbols used by animals (up to about thirty distinct calls used by wild chimpanzees) and the vocabularies of human languages, which contain many tens of thousands of items.
>
> 2004, 553–4; my emphasis

And Hurford also argues that 'recursive thought could have existed in prelinguistic hominids, and that the key step to language was the innovative disposition to learn massive numbers of arbitrary symbols' (2004, abstract). If the human use of symbols differs from some uses of animal vocalizations and gestures only in quantity and degree or quality, the difference – Darwin was right to say – is not one of kind[10]. As Hurford adds: 'even qualitatively new features have precursors – they don't just come from nowhere' (2004, 2).

The kinds of practices enabling the emergence of symbols are continuous with those that are not thus enabling. That the *products* of those practices; *what our practices enable* – be they the wheel, spaceships or mathematics – are unprecedented in our evolution and (still) exclusive to human minds does not (*pace* continuity sceptics) cause a gap in the continuity of that evolution, and (*pace* Hutto and Myin) warrant regarding them as constituting a functional kink in that evolution. It is inasmuch as our *practices* are gradual and continuous that no gap is created, regardless of the novelty (or kinkiness) of what they enable.

Note that Hutto and Myin do find their own continuity story gappy in one respect: 'it can't fill in all the relevant details' (2017, 140). So I will now try – with the help of Wittgenstein and Canfield – to fill in some of those details.

3. Wittgenstein's Enactivism

One of the important things Wittgenstein said about language, and indeed meaning, is that it has its root in gesture – 'What we call meaning must be connected with the primitive language of gestures' (BT 24) – or, as he also put it, language is rooted in 'action', and more precisely: 'reaction' or 'instinct':

> The origin and the primitive form of the language game is a reaction; only from this can more complicated forms develop.
> Language – I want to say – is a refinement. 'In the beginning was the deed.'
>
> CE 395

Language, then, is a refinement, or 'an extension', of our primitive behaviour:

> Believing that someone is in pain, doubting whether he is, are so many natural kinds of behaviour towards other human beings; and our language is but an auxiliary to and extension of this behaviour. I mean: our language is an extension of the more primitive behaviour. (For our *language-game* **is** a piece of behaviour.)
>
> RPP I, 151

He makes this clear in *On Certainty*:

> I want to regard man here as an animal; as a primitive being to which one grants instinct but not ratiocination. As a creature in a primitive state. Any logic good enough for a primitive means of communication needs no apology from us. Language did not emerge from some kind of ratiocination.
>
> OC 475

That we can use reason does not mean that language emerged from the use of reason, or is dependent on reason. The very same 'logic' – or grammar – responsible for primitive language is responsible for ours. Wittgenstein conceives of language as rooted in our primitive actions and interactions – not in reason, and not in symbols.

Language, for him, is an extension of our primitive behaviour; it emerges from the *development* of some of our animal or natural reactions. Not just any natural reaction – not singular or idiosyncratic ones, like tics – but our *shared* natural reactions; what Wittgenstein calls 'the common behaviour of mankind' (PI 206): reactions such as crying when in pain or sad; smiling when glad; jumping when startled; gasping or screaming when afraid; reacting to someone's suffering. These instinctive common reactions or action patterns are, Wittgenstein says, the *prototypes* of our modes of thought (RPP I, 916); of our concepts. Without these behavioural patterns, there would be no language. These are the starting points of language: 'it is characteristic of our language that the foundation on which it grows consists in *steady ways of living, regular ways of acting*' (CE 397; my emphasis). Our acquiring concepts, such as pain, requires that we have appropriate, i.e. normal, human reactions: 'If a child looked radiant when it was hurt, and shrieked for no apparent reason, one couldn't teach him to use the word "pain"' (LPP 37).

So how is the child trained to go from proto-language games – that is, from her instinctive reactions – to language? How, for example, asks Wittgenstein, does a child learn the meaning of the word 'pain'? And he replies:

> Here is one possibility: words are connected with the primitive, the natural, expressions of the sensation and used in their place. A child has hurt himself and he cries; and then adults talk to him and teach him exclamations and, later, sentences. They teach the child new pain-behaviour.
>
> PI 244

So the connection between the name and the thing is not made by an act of ostension, not by merely hooking gestures on to their public referents, but by contextualized repetition in practice. As psychologist Derek Montgomery observes, if the carer repeatedly uses the verb 'want' while interpreting the infant's behaviour in certain contexts, it is 'reasonable to suspect that when the verb emerges in the child's lexicon it will be in familiar contexts such as [those] where the child has repeatedly heard it being used. The meaning of the term, like the meaning of the prelinguistic gesturing, is bound up in the role it plays within such contexts' (2002, 372). Note: what Wittgenstein says the child is taught in learning to replace his primitive reactions with words is new *behaviour*; that is, in first picking up the linguistic expression, the child is not *describing* with it or *referring* with it, but still *reacting* with it.

4. Canfield's elaboration: ontogeny

Wittgenstein's view that language is an extension of action is often mentioned, but not often fleshed out. John Canfield remedies this in his book: *Becoming Human* (2007). In keeping with Wittgenstein's prescription 'Don't think, but look', Canfield writes: 'To see what language is, examine – observe – language-*games*. To do that, begin by observing the simplest ones the child comes to master' (1995, 197). Canfield did just that from his philosopher's armchair, by keeping a diary of his daughter Zoe's acquisition of language.

Canfield draws a threefold classification of language or language-related phenomena which he finds implicit in what he calls Wittgenstein's 'philosophical anthropology'. These are:

1. 'proto language-game'
2. 'gestural stage' and
3. 'primitive language-game

His observation begins at the bedrock level of the development of language, constituted by the naturally-occurring *pre-symbolic interaction patterns* – which, as noted earlier, Wittgenstein calls the *prototypes* of our modes of thought (RPP I, 916). Canfield calls them *proto language-games*. They include nursing, giving things to the child, cleaning, dressing, hugging, responding to cries, playful two-person dealings such as tickling, or passing an object back and forth, accompanied by eye contact.[11] We are not yet here in the realm of language: the proto language-game precedes even the simplest use of symbols and gestures – remembering that a *gesture* is an *intentional* movement: 'a movement of part of the body, especially a hand or the head, to express an idea, meaning or feeling' (*Cambridge Dictionary*). The child is engaged in behaviour patterns basic to language; she is not using language:

> Both the before-language hominid and the pre-linguistic child engage naturally in certain behaviour patterns basic to speech. As regards the child, consider the acts and responses connected with request words. At the earliest stage the child simply cries when hungry, or cold, or wet, and so on. Then the mother responds, say by bringing it to her breast, whereupon the child does its part by suckling. Similarly, there is the interaction pattern of the child's reaching toward something, and the mother's response of handing it to the child. Such interactions arise naturally, without any drill or explicit instruction, between child and caretaker. They support the development of language, which could not arise without them.
>
> 2007, 37

Such interaction patterns – found in many animals – are rooted in our animal nature, in particular in our ability to anticipate and respond to one another's actions.

The next stage to language is through gesture. When a proto language-game is modified, emphasized or added to, in a way that brings it to the other's attention, it becomes what Canfield calls 'a natural gesture'. An example is when an infant turns an action – such as instinctively raising its arms when being picked up – into a gesture, by performing it in the absence of being picked up; that is, in the absence of the interactive behaviours normally preceding it. Franz Plooij speaks here of 'the development by human infants of an arm-raising gesture which at first appears in the infant's repertoire as a *passive response* to being picked up and later becomes an *active request* to be picked up' (1978, 117; my emphasis). And he finds this very same development occurring in primates:

> In order to groom [the infant's] side and armpits, [the chimpanzee mother] takes his arm and pulls it upwards. [Later] the infant ... adopt[s] this posture unaided while his mother grooms him.... At the age of 11 months an infant... came up to his mother, sat down in front of her and adopted this posture.... Almost predictably, his mother groomed him.
>
> ibid.

Canfield calls these '*natural* gestures' in that he sees them as biologically based, arising naturally, without being taught.

Another example of a spontaneous action developing into a natural gesture is a child reaching toward something she wants but can't get, and so makes an opening and closing motion with her outstretched hand. The mother's responding to the child by giving her the thing she wants will eventually lead to the child adopting that motion to deliberately 'ask' for what she wants. In both examples, the gestures function like signals; they constitute communicative acts: 'We would, I believe, have no trouble in saying that the child making the hand opening and closing gesture is communicating with its mother. The distance between that gesture and speech per se is small', writes Canfield (2007, 39).

Such 'natural gestures' are a stylized overlay upon the prior, naturally-existing interaction pattern. The third stage comprises the further stylization made when simple or one-word language-games develop from the proto-type or its gestural embellishment. This is the scenario sketched by Wittgenstein in PI 244: the child learns the meaning of the word 'pain' when it is connected by an adult to a natural expression of pain. We must beware not to think of this last stage as a mere nominalization process. The child's using the word 'up' doesn't result from a mere ostensive teaching of words, but from exposure to and habituation in a form of life. For the child to use the word 'up', it had to have been exposed to a variety of 'language-games', where the utterance of the word 'up' is interwoven with action – the child is lifted and lowered to the accompaniment of 'up we go ... down we go'; a bird is pointed to as being 'up on the tree'; she hears that her teddy bear is in her room 'upstairs' etc. Here, words, behaviour and context repeatedly and variously interact to inculcate in the child her native language. Wittgenstein's lesson is that language should be understood as the mastery, not of a calculus or principles, but of complex interlocking language-games.

In the simple language-game, the word replaces the gesture and takes over its function: telling the mother what the child wants. The child – having been previously coached – might say 'up' instead of gesturing with a look. The word/symbol is a more sophisticated development of the gesture in that its relationship to its function is purely conventional and arbitrary. Any other short and easily pronounceable word would have served the same purpose. We can see that it is a very small step – and not a leap – that the child takes from gesture into word-language; and far from evincing a 'profound functional discontinuity' between basic and nonbasic cognition or between animal and human cognition, it shows functional *continuity*: the word, or other symbol, replaces the gesture and takes over its function. As Stephen Cowley, glossing Canfield's Wittgensteinian account, notes: 'resembling as it does the gestural expression of pre-linguistic games, there is no deep puzzle about this new word-language' (2007, 279). I will let Canfield summarize:

> In being able to speak its intention the child manifests two linked abilities. The first is one shared with any number of animals – it is to evince the behaviour we call acting with an aim. It is to pursue a project. The second ability is, it seems, unique to humans, at least if we restrict the claim to animals in the wild. It is to speak a word or otherwise provide a symbol-token that indicates the end point of the project the person is in fact engaged upon.
>
> While this later ability is (with the earlier qualification) unique, it is but a small embellishment of a capability which is not unique – the talent of indicating one's

project by a natural gesture. The passage to speech does not cross some great ontological divide; there is no fundamental difference between us and other animals. In fact, captive chimpanzees can learn to 'express their intentions' in symbols. Here Wittgenstein, as opposed say to Chomsky, is a Darwinian.

2007, 41

5. Grammar: Enactive and embedded

What is important to note is that, in mastering different language-games – such as those involving the word 'up' – the child is mastering the *grammar* of the word; its use in the language. Wittgenstein's notion of grammar is not more complicated than this. Rules of grammar are simply expressions of the norms of sense that are socially generated and maintained; they grow out of, and with, our natural ways of acting and our socio-cultural practices. Grammar does not generate language; nor does it exist independently of language or action; it is embedded and enacted in what we say and do. The proper use of the word 'up' is manifested in our ways of acting and speaking. The child assimilates these norms as it assimilates the language – through guidance in and exposure to, correct usage. As Peter Hacker puts it: 'Rules for the use of words are exhibited in human discourse, in explanations of meaning, in corrections of errors, in what counts as accepted usage' (2010, 29). And the same can be said of numbers: 'Our children – writes Wittgenstein – are not only given practice in calculation but are also trained to adopt a particular attitude towards a mistake in calculating[12] [variant: '... towards a departure from the norm']' (RFM VII 61, p. 425) – that is, children are habituated into standards of correctness of the practice in question, and thereby formed to act and react in particular ways; they are thus trained to master a technique through the inculcation of a normative attitude.

The assimilation of rules – be they linguistic or mathematical – does not have the features of a *learning that*, but of a *learning how* – of a training or a conditioning. As varied as they may be, rules are assimilated with the aim of gaining a technique, a skill, a method, a way of acting (or refraining from acting, as in rules of social etiquette or games). Wittgenstein:

> A rule is best described as being like a garden path in which you are trained to walk, and which is convenient. You are taught arithmetic by a process of training, and this becomes one of the paths in which you walk.
>
> AWL 155

Calculating, using mathematical rules, are mechanical *activities*; like making *moves* that one was *trained* to perform. Wittgenstein compares rules of mathematics to *orders* or *commands* (RFM VII 40; V 13): 'The mathematical proposition says to me: Proceed like this!' (RFM VII 73); 'it determines ... lays down a path for us' (RFM IV 8). We do not come to a rule from reasoning, we *accept* a rule blindly (provided we want to play the game): 'When I obey a rule, I do not choose. I obey the rule *blindly*' (PI 219).

For Wittgenstein, 'the centre of gravity' of *our* mathematics lies '*entirely* in *doing*' (RFM IV 15). Equations are, like rules, *essentially* enactive: to *formulate* an equation, say '2 + 2 = 4', has, in heuristic contexts, the status of a deed, parallel to directing a child's first steps with one's hands; at other times, it is to *perform* an operation. And to *follow* a rule can be like reacting to a push. To follow a rule is not to make a judgement, but to *make a move*. Indeed, in the *Remarks on the Foundations of Mathematics*, Wittgenstein considers the dispensability of propositions in arithmetic, stressing the similarity of calculating to gestures, and of the teaching of arithmetic to a training:

> Might we not do arithmetic without having the idea of uttering arithmetical *propositions,* and without ever having been struck by the similarity between a multiplication and a proposition?
> Should we not shake our heads, though, when someone shewed us a multiplication done wrong, as we do when someone tells us it is raining, if it is not raining? – Yes; and here is a point of connection. But we also make gestures to stop our dog, e.g., when he behaves as we do not wish.
> We are used to saying '2 times 2 is 4', and the verb 'is' makes this into a proposition, and apparently establishes a close kinship with everything that we call a 'proposition'. Whereas it is a matter only of a very superficial relationship.
>
> RFM III 4

It should now be clear that Wittgenstein's account of the emergence and practice of language and mathematics is an enactive account. Language is simply an extension of an underlying action pattern, a way of acting; and we come to extend the scope of our ways of acting through grammar – that is, through a *normatively* generated and sanctioned use of words or symbols. The generating, sanctioning, transmitting and understanding of these symbols are all logically due to, or embedded in, action; that is, they are inherently enactive. The transmission of language is the transmission of an extension of action; of new ways of acting. Wittgenstein rightly stresses that in teaching a child to replace the natural expression of pain with the word 'pain', adults teach the child 'new pain-*behaviour*' (PI 244; my emphasis); that is, they also teach the child a new way of acting, a skill. For grasping a concept is not a matter of connecting a referent to a public symbol, but of acquiring a skill. It is thanks to her acquiring this skill, this normative *attitude*, that the child is eventually able to go on, on her own; to proceed *from other-regulation to self-regulation* (Medina 2002, 165). Successful enculturation means the child can judge for herself that in a particular instance a word or phrase makes sense, not by comparing it to a benchmark, context-free use but on the basis of her experience of multiple language-games in which the word or phrase is employed.

6. Content is not an inner growth

Language grows in sophistication not because of some language of thought that craves expression, but in tandem with the sophistication of our socio-cultural practices or customs. It isn't, as Lawrence Shapiro would have it, that 'language or its symbols acquire their meaning from meaningful thoughts – how could it be otherwise?' (2014, 217) – but rather that meaningful language or thought acquires its meaning from use – both synchronically and diachronically speaking. *Synchronically*, the meaning of a word or sentence is determined by its use or the context in which it is uttered; *diachronically*, meaning is conditioned by our 'ways of acting' and 'very general facts of nature'. As Wittgenstein writes: 'it is characteristic of our language that the foundation on which it grows consists in steady ways of living, regular ways of acting' (CE 397). That is to say: the very grammar of our language is conditioned by our ways of living. This is what I call the *reality-soaked* nature of grammar and concepts.[13] So, for example, the term (or concept) 'daughterliness' as *loving attention to the integrity of the daughter–parent relationship*, as also our acquisition of that term – are conditioned by, and embedded in, our forms of life, ways of acting, instinctive behaviour etc. We could not learn the proper use of that term without experiencing or at least being exposed to practices in which terms like 'daughter' 'father' 'mother' are used in the context of loving attention, respect etc. to individuals immediately related by blood or adoption. That is, we can't acquire the meaning of such a term as 'daughterliness' other than through some exposure to, or experience of, the phenomena that can give rise to such a term. We come to know what kinds of behaviour constitute or qualify as daughterly for having learned the term 'daughterly' by experiencing or otherwise being exposed to such behaviours.

So that what the adult does when teaching a child to replace the gesture with a word is, as Stephen Cowley nicely puts it, enable the child 'to align its behaviour with the grammar of [the word]', to 'attune to a bundle of local customs' (2007, 293). Once it is clear that words are symbols – that is, functionally continuous replacements for ways of acting and communicating that are *embedded in* these ways of acting, symbols cease to appear unnatural or unaccountably alien to our natural practices. To speak as do Hutto and Myin of 'the emergence of a special sort of normative sociocultural practice involving the use of public symbols' (2017, 146) is not to encounter a kink in our practices, but a natural and enactive extension of our practices.

Stepping into language is not a crossing into a brave new world, where suddenly, because the word (sometimes) replaces the deed, concepts have become incommensurable with our actions. Yes, our tools are more sophisticated than those of primates but they evolve from those, without a kink. Wittgenstein has no trouble tracing some of our concepts back to the apes, as in this passage:

> An ape who tears apart a cigarette, for example. We don't see an intelligent dog do such things. The mere act of turning an object all around and looking it over is a primitive root of doubt.
>
> RPP II, 345[14]

As for mathematics, it is, he writes, 'an anthropological phenomenon' (RFM p. 399).

7. Ontogeny recapitulates phylogeny

Canfield concedes that there is nothing new in the idea that speech grows from an earlier stage of gesture. What is new about the Wittgensteinian view he and I defend is the idea that there is no categorial difference between gestural and verbal communication, and that symbolic communication is not exclusive to either.[15] As Canfield succinctly puts it: 'Language is a set of customs in which words play a role' (2007, 70). The difference between our ancestors and other primates seems to be that only the former were able to further develop their communicative abilities from the rudimentary social life they shared with other primates: 'We are just animals, part of the natural world; clever ones that can be raised to a mastery of a whole complex of human customs – human ways of interacting including the deployment of words. But animals none the less' (2007, 77). Why the development went further for humans but not for chimpanzees is empirically a question for anthropology and primatology, but the philosopher too can offer answers. Canfield suggests that for material culture and societal organization to have influenced the development of language-customs

> ... [the] use of words must have had a point, and in the life of wild chimpanzees, where food is possessed only as long as it takes to eat it, and where tools are normally discarded after use, there is no, or extremely little, room for there to be such a point. But with the development of prized articles of material culture, and a societal practice that amounts to the honouring of ownership, a proto-language game of possession can emerge, and there may develop associated natural gestures, such as seizing back some object.... There would then be scope for the emergence of a word which, by replacing such a gesture, in such a context, makes a *claim* of possession, as opposed to simply taking [back].... It is easy to imagine how the mastery of various language-games could have facilitated cooperation among our hunter-gatherer ancestors.
>
> 2007, 72–3; my emphasis

This, at first blush, seems very close to Michael Tomasello, on whose account the evolution of intentionality into human-specific forms was due to the need for cooperation: 'Human beings ... are all about (or mostly about) cooperation. Human social life is much more cooperatively organized than that of other primates, and so ... it was these more complex forms of cooperative sociality that acted as the selective pressures that transformed great ape individual intentionality and thinking into human shared intentionality and thinking' (Tomasello 2014, 31). There is, however an added twist to Tomasello's account: it is poised on Theory of Mind: the ability to ascribe unobservable mental states to others. This ability is called a 'theory' in that mental states are (allegedly) inherently unobservable, and so the rightness of our ascriptions can never be verified; it can only be inferred. As Wittgenstein and Merleau-Ponty have argued, this theoretical presumption imposed on the possibility of intersubjective understanding is both superfluous and misleading.[16] Intersubjective understanding is wrongly taken to depend on 'mindreading', particularly as embodied and extended capabilities are sufficient to sustain social understanding and interaction[17] – or what John Michael calls 'interactionism' (2011, 560). And if mindreading is not what basically enables *humans* to interact with, and understand, one another, it should certainly not be pinned on our *nonhuman* ancestors[18].

Even as he affirms the importance of interaction and sociality for the transformation of individual into human-shared intentionality, Tomasello takes these to rely on individual meta-representations of others' mental states (2014, 94). It is here that – having gone a long way with Wittgenstein – he parts company with him: having advocated the enactive genesis of language, Tomasello cannot resist a complementary appeal to 'theory of mind'.[19] But the mentalist /representationalist seduction – rooted, at best, in a superfluous, unsubstantiated metaphysical assumption – must be resisted.

Not an easy task. Louise Barrett describes the kind of 'backward reasoning' that drives current evolutionary theory when it comes to phylogenetic language acquisition: it is assumed that 'language has to arise from a mentalizing mind (rather than certain aspects of the human mind being a consequence of language)'; that 'a certain kind of mindedness ['Theory-mindedness'] must be in place prior to language so that we can get to the forms of linguistic communication that are used to define our own species' (2018, 10–11). The possession of ToM goes hand in hand with the indexing of social intelligence to brain size – and more specifically to an enlarged neocortex size, taken to focus principally on the ability to 'use knowledge about other individuals behaviour – and perhaps mind-states – to predict and manipulate those individuals' behaviour' (Dunbar 2003, 167). As Barrett concludes: '... the ToM paradigm ... drives much of the social intelligence/brain hypothesis' (2018, 13), so that '[w]e do not begin with 'man as an animal', in Wittgenstein's words, but with a particular scientific construction of human mindedness, which we then extend far back into the evolutionary past', 'generating an overly intellectual view of what it means to be a competent and successful social primate' (2018, 10; 2). This retrospective attribution of ToM to our ancestors as, allegedly, the only way to justify the complexity that comes with social bonding and successful cooperation is profoundly amiss, for ToM should not even be applied to humans.[20] I suggest, however, that once rid of its ToM component, much good can be drawn from a hypothesis that puts social pressure and social intelligence at the helm of phylogenetic language acquisition. It's important that we retain the Bonding Theory when we get rid of the misleading ToM imposition.

And here I think Robin Dunbar's (1993) theory of 'vocal grooming' replacing manual grooming deserves renewed attention. It offers a plausible, thoroughly enactive-friendly, account of the evolutionary emergence of verbal language, which echoes Canfield's and Tomasello's emphasis on cooperation without importing the mentalistic picture.[21] Starting from the generally accepted view that the cohesion of primate groups is maintained by social grooming, Dunbar argues that, as group size increased in nonhuman primates, social cohesion could no longer be achieved through the usual *manual* grooming. Because they freed the hands and allowed for simultaneous foraging and other activities, and for multiple partners to be groomed at once, vocalizations or 'vocal grooming' came to replace it.[22] And so language evolved as a more efficient form of social grooming, 'enabling ancestral humans to maintain the cohesion of the unusually large groups demanded by the particular conditions they faced at the time'[23] (1993, 11). Dunbar sees human language as continuous with primate vocal communication, viewing the contact-calls used in many species of anthropoid primates as possible natural precursors for human language: 'Although these calls have traditionally been interpreted for maintaining contact during movement (hence their generic name), it has become clear that there may be more subtle layers of meaning to [them]' – as for example, vervet monkeys using them 'to comment on events or situations as they occur' (1993, 17). He considers the vocal signalling of vervet monkeys as an 'archetypal protolanguage', already incipiently speech-like. In his view, these monkeys are almost speaking when they emit 'quite arbitrary' sounds in referring to 'specific objects' (1996, 140). In fact, Dunbar suggests that grammar was present long before human language, being central to primate cognition including social intelligence. An objection made to Dunbar is that he has not addressed the problem of how 'meanings' came to be attached to previously content-free vocalizations,[24] but I would say that meaning was there all along (and, with it, grammar[25]) – it just didn't come in propositional form. And nor does it need to. As Wittgenstein has argued, meaning is not always propositional or truth-conditional. For example, what Wittgenstein calls 'spontaneous utterances' – spontaneous first-person present-tense psychological expressions (e.g., 'I'm afraid', 'I hope he comes', 'I'm in pain') are non-descriptive, nonepistemic expressions, akin to behaviour.[26]

We can view the passage from 'manual grooming' to 'vocal grooming' as the phylogenetic equivalent of the child's stepping from gesture into word. In both cases, the move seems functionally continuous. The use of words and symbols is a naturally coherent move to increase efficiency, proficiency, flexibility and density of expression and communication. The economy and manipulability of verbal language is such that it can rise to a level of sophistication of meaning that gesture alone could not reach, but as Wittgenstein reminds us, meaning is intrinsically connected to the primitive language of gestures (BT 24).

8. Conclusion

Given a Wittgensteinian account of the nature of language and its possible origins, it is not necessary to posit some representational gap or leap between nonhuman and human primates, or a content-involving kink demarking humans from the rest. The latter gives fodder to the view that explaining higher-level cognition is a challenge for Enactivism, but I hope to have shown that it isn't really. As to the former (continuity sceptics), accounts of the circumstances that enabled the move of some animals into word-language may be speculative, but those that consist in the postulation of ad hoc properties or entities such as inner representation systems or a language organ should, I suggest, come last and not first in the list of our plausible accounts. Where there is a simple, plausible story that will do, why – in the name of science or philosophy – convolute it? I hope to have at least made more plausible that, *pace* continuity sceptics, 'human mental and behavioral capacities as we now know them' can, indeed, 'be illuminated by seeing them as elaborations on the capacities of some nonhuman ancestors' (Bar-On, 2013). I don't see that the use of public symbols marks a gap between basic, contentless cognition and content-involving cognition, 'or even a 'challenge' that an enactivist account must face in explaining higher-level cognition (Hutto and Myin 2017, 7). As Canfield writes:

Our language has grown from a stage of primitive gesture communication found in many animals to full-fledged modern speech. There is now a difference of quality between our mode of communication and that of the other animals. But this difference of quality can be seen as arising from a difference in quantity. New language-games appear; old ones are refined and added to in various ways; speech customs proliferate and evolve. But in all this we do not supersede our basic animal nature.

2007, 77

The sophistication our language is capable of should not obfuscate its relatedness to its animal origins. It has been shown that most of what we believed set us apart from animals does not – animals have language; they use tools; they use symbols; they even share our Machiavellian intelligence; and – inasmuch as culture is defined as behaviour that is socially transmitted – they have culture: they cooperate and teach each other things. So if language, symbols, cooperation, tools, deceit and culture are not unique to humans, where's the kink? In the ability to look forward, suggest Seligman and Tierney in their book *Homo Prospectus* (2016). Only we, *human prospectus*, can anticipate what fellow humans will do in the *distant* future. Seligman and Tierney attribute this feature to our brain, but I would attribute it simply to the sophistication of our language – which explains why, as Wittgenstein noted, a dog can believe his master is at the door, but it can't believe his master will come home the day after tomorrow.[27] Dogs can anticipate alright – they can pine for the return of their master in the future; and sit in expectation at the door – but what they can't do is put a date on it. And, as I hope to have shown, that *we* can put a date on it is perfectly in keeping with Enactivism.

6

Wittgenstein and the Memory Debate

In this chapter, I survey the impact on neuropsychology of Wittgenstein's elucidations of memory. Wittgenstein discredited the storage and imprint models of memory, dissolved the conceptual link between memory and mental images or representations and, upholding the context-sensitivity of memory, made room for a family resemblance concept of memory, where remembering can also *amount to* doing or saying something. While neuropsychology is still *generally* under the spell of archival and physiological notions of memory, Wittgenstein's reconceptions can be seen at work in its leading-edge practitioners. However, neuroscientists, generally, find memory difficult to demarcate from other cognitive and noncognitive processes, and I suggest this is largely due to their considering automatic responses to be part of memory, termed *nondeclarative* or *implicit* memory. Taking my lead from Wittgenstein's *On Certainty*, I argue that there is only remembering where there is also some kind of *mnemonic effort* or *attention*, and therefore that so-called *implicit memory* is not memory at all, but a *basic, noncognitive certainty*.

1. Introduction

Explicit reference to Wittgenstein is made in the (neuro)psychological literature on memory, but perhaps not enough to warrant the claim which I want to make here, that his thought has infiltrated and decisively impacted the subject. And yet, to speak of Wittgenstein's contribution to the scientific concept of memory is to speak of a philosopher's elucidation, which is to say that even where the elucidation is not always or fully acknowledged, it can have unsettled the fundaments and reset the direction of research. It would take a separate study to fathom how philosophy does make such a mark on the (human) sciences, but in Wittgenstein's case, the mystery dissipates when we realize that his contribution is better measured in terms of a paradigm shift than by way of explicit recognition.[1] So that psychology can have changed course whilst not necessarily be aware of the source of change.[2]

Wittgenstein has produced this paradigm shift by shedding suspicion on, and hence destabilizing, Cartesian premises of thought and Platonic methods of thinking. He has achieved this through a demystification of 'the inner' and a correlated emphasis on action; a resistance to explanatory ghostly mental processes that themselves remain unexplained; and an unprecedentedly broad appeal to context or use in the determination of meaning, understanding, and memory. Because of Wittgenstein, physicalists and functionalists throughout the humanities and the sciences have had to abandon the quest for neat, unitary and closed concepts and accommodate the ineluctable input of broad context into their models – indeed, going as far as seeking to incorporate it *physiologically* in their models; as, for instance, Alan Parkin who claims that the diencephalic region may be 'crucial for enabling context to be incorporated into memory' (1999, 12). Neuroscientists have also started trading ontologically full-blown entities (e.g., the will, intention, expectation) for ways of acting; and biologically full-blown entities (e.g., memory) for capacities.

The immediate concern of this chapter is to show how Wittgenstein's rejection of the old models and his conceptual elucidation of memory have impacted on neuroscientific research and should continue to do so. As we shall see, neuroscientists are coming to the same conclusions about memory that Wittgenstein came to more than half a century ago. In that light, whether we choose to see Wittgenstein as having merely *anticipated* or actually *impacted* that research, his as yet unechoed thoughts on memory will seem all the more worthy of attention.

I begin, in the next two sections, by highlighting Wittgenstein's insights, which take the form both of questionings and of outright claims on memory. Section 4 offers a brief account of current neuroscientific conceptions of memory. In the fifth section, I underline the problem, perceived by some neuropsychologists, in calling *implicit* memory systems, memory systems at all. I then show how the noncognitive certainty depicted by Wittgenstein in *On Certainty* provides a revolutionary and viable alternative to so-called 'implicit memory'. In section 6, I conclude with a proposal that we not attribute to memory, or call mnemonic, any activity that requires no effort or attention. Section 7 briefly hints at the way forward.

2. Clearing the way: Memory traces and memory storage

In 1946–7, Wittgenstein wrote the following remark:

> I saw this man years ago: now I have seen him again, I recognize him, I remember his name. And why does there have to be a cause of this remembering in my nervous system? Why must something or other, whatever it may be, be stored-up there *in any form*? Why *must* a trace have been left behind? Why should there not be a psychological regularity to which *no* physiological regularity corresponds? If this upsets our concepts of causality then it is high time they were upset.
>
> RPP I, 905

It is remarks like this that have earned Wittgenstein the label: 'behaviourist' whilst also perpetuating the impression that he was on an exclusively deconstructive mission, not concerned with offering constructive alternatives to the myths he was debunking.[3] Certainly, Wittgenstein wants to alert us to the *possibility* that our conceptions of the mental are nothing but preconceptions: 'There is the idea that for memory the thing must be written in the brain. But need memory be like reading old writings?' (LPP 90); 'It is thus perfectly possible that certain psychological phenomena cannot be investigated physiologically, because physiologically nothing corresponds to them' (RPP I, 904); but his 'physiological agnosticism', as Michel ter Hark calls it (1995, 115), is not all-encompassing:

> No supposition seems to me more natural than that there is no process in the brain correlated with associating or with thinking; so that it would be impossible to read off thought-processes from brain-processes. I mean this: if I talk or write there is, I assume, a system of impulses going out from my brain and correlated with my spoken or written thoughts. But why should the *system* continue further in the direction of the centre? Why should this order not proceed, so to speak, out of chaos?
> RPP I, 903[4]

Wittgenstein's intention here – or ever – is not to reject a psychophysical correlation between the brain and our mental activities; on the contrary, he *assumes* such a correlation. What he does reject is a 'psycho-physical *parallelism*' (RPP I, 906); that is, an *isomorphic* correlation (as Köhler would have it) between brain processes and thoughts or memories:

> ... nothing seems more possible to me than that people someday will come to the definite opinion that there is no copy in either the physiological or the nervous systems which corresponds to a *particular* thought, or a *particular* idea, or memory.[5]
> LW I, 504; original emphasis

Wittgenstein is not denying that we need brain activity for thought, and in that limited sense, remembering *is* causally dependent on the brain – on brain structures in different brain areas and on synaptic modifications in these areas – but it does not follow that these structures are *representations* of particular memories, stored and encoded in the brain. We must beware of confusing brain processes with thought processes[6]:

> Even if we knew that a particular area of the brain is changed by hearing *God Save the King* and that destroying this part of the brain prevents one's remembering the occasion, there is no reason to think that the structure produced in the brain represents *God Save the King* better than *Rule, Brittania*.
> LPP 90

> Whatever the event does leave behind in the organism, *it* isn't the memory.
> RPP I, 220; original emphasis

What Wittgenstein is, in fact, rejecting is the representational theory of mind, which stipulates that we need to have *representations* in the brain in order to remember, think etc.[7] To think it can be possible 'to read off thought-processes from brain processes' (RPP I, 903) is to conflate brain reading with mind reading,[8] and retention with physical storage. But as Bennett and Hacker point out, although storage may sometimes imply retention, retention does not imply storage:

> Memory, being the retention of knowledge acquired, is the retention of an ability to just the extent that knowledge itself is an ability – but it is not the storage of an ability. One may acquire and retain an ability, but that does not imply storage. For there is no such thing as *storing* an ability, even though there is such a thing as retaining the neural structures that are causal conditions for the possession of an ability. ... To remember that p is to *possess* the information that p, but it is not to *store* or *contain* the information that p. One stores the information that p if, for example, one writes it down, and stores the inscription in a filing cabinet or computer which then contains it.
>
> 2003, 164–5

(I shall later argue that remembering that p is more than possessing the information that p.)

The brain, then, is a *mechanical* enabler, not the storehouse and codifier of our memories. Representationalism is the product of a misconstrued and mislocated causality. But as well as this *misleading* view of causality, which conflates causal conditions with causal representations, a *narrow* view of causality compounds our misconceptions of memory: we are loath to envisage a causation that is not physiological. We therefore not only mistakenly take the brain to be recording what we see in an isomorphic trace or 'engram',[9] we also see this trace as having an *activating* function: it acts as mediator and activator between the original event and our ability to call it to mind. So that every time someone remembered an event, besides representing it, the trace would also select, decode and activate the memory. In this mediating capacity, the trace would play, for memory, a role analogous to that attributed to the pineal gland in our interactions between mind and matter/brain.

But, to localize (rightly or wrongly) a process, capacity or faculty is not yet to explain it.[10] The notion of memory traces *seems* to explain the source of memory, but all it does is offer the semblance of a physiological grip on a seemingly mystifying faculty; and so, we are left with what Norman Malcolm calls 'an illusion of explanation' (1977, 102). Wittgenstein's diagnosis of the need to postulate a *physiological* mediator between mind and brain is that our conception of causality is too narrow to admit a causality between psychological phenomena which is not mediated physiologically without this implying a belief in a gaseous mental entity (cf. RPP I, 906). A trace is required because, as Malcolm puts it, '"action at a distance" is a repugnant idea' (1977, 178). But, in fact, asks Wittgenstein: 'Why should not the initial and terminal states of a system be connected by a natural law, which does not cover the intermediary state?' (RPP I, 909). That is, in cases like someone's excessive ambition causing their loneliness; or greed causing someone to become corrupt, no physiological connection obtains, though many psychological connections do (and *they* are not gaseous: we know that greed can move people to criminal thoughts and criminal behaviour). Similarly, no physiological traces link my last year's trip to Indonesia to the numerous recollections I have had of it since.

What, before Wittgenstein, is not envisaged, is that *we* make the connection. In fact, to suggest that the brain 'remembers' is to attribute to it an ability that only beings possess, and to commit what Bennett and Hacker call 'the mereological fallacy' – the fallacy of ascribing to a part of a creature (e.g., the brain) attributes that can logically only be ascribed to the creature as a whole (e.g., the human being).[11] Memory is an *ability*, and it is an ability that *beings* have, not traces or brains. For, writes Wittgenstein, 'even if [remembering] showed us scenes with hallucinatory clarity, still it takes remembering to tell us that this is past' (RPP II, 592); it is not 'some feature of our memory image that tells us the time to which it belongs' (LWII, 5). And, he goes on: 'if memory shows us the past, how does it show us that it is the past? It does *not* show us the past. Any more than our senses show us the present' (RPP II, 593). It 'takes remembering to tell us that *this is past*' (RPP II, 592; my emphasis), and remembering is done by a person.

It is in this Wittgensteinian vein that Gianfranco Dalla Barba argues that there are no such things as mental representations or memory engrams because there is no homunculus there to interpret them and to provide memory traces with their relationship to a past event. Dalla Barba contends that current theories of memory are based on a paradox – what he calls the *memory trace paradox*; and that they trade on what he refers to as the *fallacy of the homunculus* (2000, 138–9). He argues that any theory which bases the possibility of recollection on the preservation of an event inside a trace is prey to the misleading assumption that time can exist in things. But of course, things are not in themselves temporal; 'they acquire a temporal dimension only in the presence of a person who goes to the trouble of making them temporal' (ibid., 139).

The paradox fleshed out by Dalla Barba is that the past is seen to derive from present elements (traces). But how is this done? This is where the homunculus comes in. Inasmuch as for something to be called memory it must be 'correct' memory and not confabulation or false memory, recollection must result from certain selection and verification mechanisms of the memory trace that are not subjective (i.e. voluntary and conscious). But to accept the hypothesis of unconscious monitoring mechanisms is precisely to fall into the *homunculus fallacy*: 'the contradiction of postulating the existence of a type of *unconscious consciousness* – unconscious monitoring mechanisms endowed with intentionality that select, evaluate and reject false memories and provide *conscious consciousness* with only real memories' (ibid., 145). This is to attribute intentionality (i.e. conscious selection, decision, rejection) to an unconscious process. Nothing has been gained, since we find ourselves with an unconscious made up of the same elements as a conscious subject; and what we had invoked to *explain* conscious memory now itself requires an explanation (ibid., 146–7). What Dalla Barba has done here is flesh out the Wittgensteinian insight that remembering can only be done by a person.

The most pervasive conception of memory is that of a storage space in which representations of past events are stored. Here, writes Wittgenstein in the *Brown Book*, remembering is thought of as 'a peculiar state of the person's brain' (BB 118) paradigmatically resulting from a process of comparison of reality with a stored picture or representation (BB 85–6). Of course, we do sometimes have mental pictures that help us remember, and we do compare these with reality, but because such mental images sometimes exist, we think that remembering necessarily involves them (RPP I, 1050) and essentially consists in comparison and identification. But as early as 1933-4, Wittgenstein rejects this unitary model of memory. In the Ambrose Lectures, he writes:

> Different sorts of memories are to be distinguished. One kind passes in time, cinematographically. Another is like an image given all at once, but afar off. And we must not fail to take account of the kind of memory which consists in remembering a poem or tune rather than some event of the past. In these cases 'to remember it' means 'to be able to reproduce it'.
>
> AWL 56

There is no one conception, picture or metaphor that will render the multifarious ways in which we remember something and, more importantly, Wittgenstein unprecedently affirms that, in remembering, our behaviour – what we say and do – is just as important as what we 'see'; as, that is, any introspection or retrospection that might occur: 'The memory image and the memory words are on the *same* level' (RPP I, 1131).

3. Wittgenstein's lead: Memory as a *way of acting*

Whereas we are inclined to believe that saying or doing something cannot be all there is to memory – that it leaves out the essential feature of the mental process of memory and gives us only an accessory feature (cf. BB 86) – Wittgenstein stresses that 'memories ... in language are not mere threadbare representations of the real experiences'[12] (PG 131), but that words, as well as gestures, can *constitute* remembering. Remembering can *amount* to 'doing something' such as reciting a poem by heart or fetching someone's key for them; recognizing someone can *consist in* saying 'Hello!' to them in words, gestures, facial expressions, etc. (BB 165-6):

> Remembering, then, isn't at all the mental process that one imagines at first sight. If I say, rightly, "I remember it," the most *varied* things may happen; perhaps even just that I say it.
>
> PG 42

> If someone remembers his hope, on the whole he is not therefore remembering his behaviour, nor even necessarily his thoughts. He says ... that at that time he hoped.
>
> RPP I, 468

These hardly resemble mental consultations of mental archives.

Wittgenstein is not, however, suggesting that there can be no mental process of remembering. If you ask me when was the last time I had chocolate fondue, I'd have to stop and think about it, and so *there* would be a mental process of remembering. Nothing mysterious here; *I* would be doing the remembering, the deliberate calling to mind of certain moments in my past. What Wittgenstein rejects is only that 'peculiar' mental state or process which is thought to necessarily occur *along with or in advance of* the expressions (utterances, gestures etc.) of memory.[13] On Wittgenstein's view, we are warranted in speaking of a memory act if by it we do not mean a ghostly, amorphous mental event that *must* precede and cause an expression or act of recall:

> In remembering a poem we do not first [subconsciously] visualize the printed poem and then say it. We simply start off by saying it ...
>
> AWL 56

> What we deny is that the picture of the inner process gives us the correct idea of the use of the word 'to remember'.
>
> PI 305

Wittgenstein's major contribution to the elucidation of the concept of memory is his discrediting the picture of memory as information *storage* and replacing it with the idea that memory is nothing but an *ability* (which, of course, is – as are all our abilities – physiologically supported by the brain) and that, in some contexts, remembering *amounts* to *a way of acting*; that is to an act or expression which does not result from introspection or retrospection (e.g., BB 85). The input of context is essential here. What gives a gesture or an utterance their mnemonic status is not any property they may have, or any mental representations they are based on, but their *context*: it is context that makes an act (say, a smile or a nod) a memory act, rather than, say, an act of politeness. As Malcolm suggests: 'A smile and a greeting would reveal *recognition* in one context, but just *friendliness* in another' (1977, 53).

Since Wittgenstein, neuroscientific theory on memory has evolved, though not in choral unison. If 'scientists agree that the brain does not operate like a camera or a copying machine' (Schacter 1996, 40), most of them still speak of memory as stored and encoded[14] even as they also speak of it as an ability. Although, as we have seen, the science on memory is catching up with Wittgenstein's insights, Dalla Barba's revolutionary stride is not the norm. This is not to say that he is a maverick, but let's have a look at the mainstream, before going on to more Wittgenstein-inspired conceptions of memory.

4. Current neuroscientific conceptions of memory

4.1 The multiple systems approach: Classifications of memory

In neuropsychology, the notion of memory as a single faculty of the mind has mostly given way to a *multiple systems* or *structuralist* approach, where memory is no longer seen as stored in one memory system, but in different 'storage sites', corresponding to various memory systems.

A major distinction was drawn in 1972 by Endel Tulving between what he called *episodic* (or *autobiographical memory*)[15] and *semantic memory*. Episodic / *autobiographical* memory is memory for personally experienced events. It enables us to answer questions such as 'What did you have for breakfast?' or 'Where did you park your car?' and is associated with a qualitatively distinct consciousness or experiential awareness. *Semantic memory* comprises the general, basic, stable knowledge about the world and language that we share with our community, such as knowing the meaning of the word 'bottle', what a stop sign means, or what we do in a restaurant. Semantic memory is of things we recall without any sense of when we learned or experienced them.

Yet, classification between episodic / autobiographical and semantic memory has proved problematic. For one thing, 'semantic memory also forms the basis for a good deal of personal autobiographical knowledge' (Schacter 1996, 151); and for another, some items of allegedly *autobiographical* memory, such as telling someone your name, do not require *experiential awareness* at recall. In 1992, Alan Baddeley asked:

> If you tell me your name, is that a piece of autobiographical memory? If you remember a list of words I have just presented, is that autobiographical memory?
>
> 1992, 13

Finding it difficult to neatly distinguish between episodic and semantic memory, and finding also that these did not cover all types of memory, neuropsychologists effected a more comprehensive and viable division between *declarative* (or *cognitive* memory) – which subsumes both the episodic/autobiographical and semantic memory just mentioned – and nondeclarative (or *procedural* memory[16]). *Declarative memory*, also defined as a 'knowing that', is a memory for *facts and events* that can be consciously accessed (inspected) and verbalised (declared) irrespective – now – of whether they are autobiographical recollections or pieces of general knowledge (Parkin 1997, 20). It is sometimes also called 'explicit memory' (Squire 1999, 521). *Nondeclarative / procedural memory* is viewed as an *action* system or a know-how: its operations are expressed in performance and can occur independently of cognition; they do not require the kind of conscious awareness that characterizes other forms of memory (Tulving 1993, 286). Not consciously accessible or verbalized, nondeclarative memory is used in acquiring, retaining and performing cognitive, motor and perceptual skills (e.g., speaking your native language, riding a bicycle, recognizing faces); it is involved in training and the development of habits and is sometimes also called 'implicit memory' (Squire 1999, 521; 390).

Besides persistent problems of overlapping classifications, a more fundamental perplexity is plaguing neuroscientists. They are not always clear, consistent or sure about whether these classifications are meant to refer to biological parts of the brain, or are simply theoretical machinery: 'No one has much doubted the usefulness of the concept of episodic memory for classificatory ("bookkeeping") purposes, but there has been considerable resistance to the idea that it represents anything special in biological reality', writes Tulving (2005, 8). The considerable resistance he is referring to comes from (Neo-)functionalists, the new contenders in the memory arena. Countering the general assumption that memory systems refer to biologically real entities or structures, they claim that distinctions between memory systems are not based on a direct morphological analysis of the structure of memory, but are in fact derived from a *functional* or *task-based* analysis; and that this leads to a fundamental circularity in the explanation of memory. As this suggests, the new debate on memory is between multiple systems analysts (structuralists) and functionalists; unitarians are fading out of the picture.

4.2 Functionalism: memory as an *ability* and an *activity*

In spite of their name, (neo-)functionalists, are not to be associated with functionalism à la Fodor. For them, the major problem with system-based approaches is that these take memories to be concrete entities instantiated in a mental or neural representation. In this, multiple analysts miss the very nature of memory, because to see memory in a representation is to freeze in time and space what is in essence a fluid activity that is spread across both (Toth and Hunt's 1999, 256; 264):

> Like walking, memory is a dynamic event that exists only in its operation. [...] one could say that when we are not experiencing (or recollecting) a prior event, or otherwise being ('implicitly') influenced by that event, memory is, 'strictly speaking, non existent'[17].
>
> ibid., 257

Functionalists hold that memory is an ability that manifests itself *in action*: 'memory is not an abstracted copy or representation of some previous content but is simply the set of operations used in dealing with [an] event. *There is nothing else*' – (ibid., 263; my emphasis). As Ian Hunter, functionalist before his time, remarks: 'remembering is something a person *does*'; in testing someone's claim that they have an excellent memory, we do not observe anything which could be called a memory, but watch the person as he *does* something, namely repeat or try to repeat the page he has read: 'In short, we have concerned ourselves not with an object but with activity; not with his memory but with his activities of learning and remembering' (1957, 18; 13). This smacks of Wittgenstein's and Ryle's *de-reification* of intentional concepts, and of Wittgenstein's explicit rapprochement between memory and acting. Indeed, Norman Malcolm's book on memory – itself heavily indebted to Wittgenstein – is referenced in Toth and Hunt's paper.

Most neuroscientists now speak of memory as an ability. This *should* preclude – but unfortunately does not – their also regarding memory as stored; only functionalists seem to have rejected the notion and image of memory storage, and speak exclusively of memory as an ability or function, and its occurrences as activities or (trans)actions. On the functionalist view, then, memory is an ability which manifests itself as a *transaction* between a person and a context of recall, or 'retrieval environment' (Toth and Hunt, 263). Indeed, memory is seen as no longer definable outside a '*retrieval*' environment:

> When we say that memory reflects an interaction between a person and a retrieval environment, we mean quite literally that memory cannot be discussed in the abstract, outside of the context of retrieval cues and [...] the goals of the remember.
>
> ibid., 258

It seems, then, that Wittgenstein's deflation of representationalist accounts of memory and its correlated emphasis on the context-sensitivity, or indeed the contextuality or situatedness, of memory have informed theorists and prompted, in Toth and Hunt's words, 'the relocation of memory from something that exists "in" the person or brain to something that obtains in the interaction between the person (and their brain) and the environment in which acts of memory occur' (ibid., 257).

Far from the 'snapshot' account of memory, the functionalist approach defines memory as 'a doing' (ibid., 255). By this, it is often meant that memory is *situated* or *external*. I shall not here enter the buoyant and variegated field of embodied or embedded or extended mind, but one direction of research might be worth noting, in which memorization is viewed as imprinting-like learning *behavior* and where emphasis is laid on the role that an agent's morphodynamics and situatedness play in the generation of such behavior (Izquierdo-Torres and Harvey 2006). This is foreshadowed by Wittgenstein's insight that remembering is often *prompted by* or *embedded in* certain *acts*, as expressed in this passage from the *Lectures on Philosophical Psychology*: 'I draw a curve on paper when the man speaks; when I trace the curve again I can repeat the sentence; but the curve can't be read as a code' (LPP 90). Retracing the curve is here a necessary condition for recall, but Wittgenstein insists that it is not any representative nature the curve would have acquired that makes it thus necessary – 'the curve can't be read as a code'. Nor would Wittgenstein have agreed with extended mind theorists that such examples of situated and embodied memory are mere *cognitive scaffolding*, or that they are, as writes Andy Clark, 'best seen as alien but *complementary* to the brain's style of storage and computation' (1997, 220; original emphasis). For Wittgenstein, retracing the curve can be a *sufficient* condition for recall. In a similar passage, he adds: these jottings would 'not be a *rendering* of the text, not a translation, so to speak, in another symbolism. The text would not be *stored up* in the jottings. And why should it be stored up in our nervous system?' (RPP I, 908).

5. Implicit vs explicit memory

Although there remains today in the science of memory a great deal of interest in encoding and storage, the principal focus is now on retrieval (Tulving 2002, 271), and therefore on *use*. Memory is now often defined as 'the faculty to *use* any type of acquired information' (Dalla Barba, 2000, 138). *Explicit memory* is said to be at work when a person *intentionally or consciously* recollects something, whereas *implicit memory* refers to *the unintentional, nonconscious use of previously acquired information* (Schacter and Tulving 1994, 11–12). As noted earlier, implicit memory is sometimes used synonymously with procedural memory or know-how. It is claimed to be evolutionarily more primitive than explicit memory, and is attributed to animals and infants. It is thought to be at work in conceptual domains (e.g., accessing words) as well as perceptual ones (e.g., recognizing faces) (Schacter 1996, 189). And when past *experiences* unconsciously influence our perceptions, thoughts, and actions, such as riding a bicycle or playing the piano effortlessly, this is also said to be due to implicit memory (Schacter 1996, 5) – though we are warned not to confuse implicit memory with the Freudian unconscious (ibid. 190–1).

It is clear, then, that implicitness and absence of awareness do not prevent theorists from thinking it is a kind of *memory* that is here in question:

> As we have come to learn that memory is not one single thing, we've opened up a whole new world of implicit, nonconscious *memory* that underlies our abilities to carry out effortlessly such tasks as riding a bicycle or playing a piano, without having to direct each movement consciously every time we attempt the task.
>
> Schacter 1996, 5; my emphasis

But there are signs of worry. According to Roediger et al:

> ...the non-declarative memory systems begin stretching our usual notion of memory. If you get up from your chair to leave the room, do you 'remember' how to walk? When you reach down to tie your shoelaces, do you have to remember how? When you streak across the court to execute a forehand volley, do you have to remember how to do so? Using the word 'remember' seems strange in these contexts?
>
> 1999, 39

And Alan Baddeley wonders whether the whole range of implicit learning systems that have been contrasted to the episodic system 'should be referred to as *memory* systems at all, as they typically involve relatively automatic retrieval processes that are often not under the direct control of the subject' (1999, 516; original emphasis).

5.1 Reconceptualizing, from Wittgenstein

Baddeley's and Roediger's worry has not made waves. Neurologists still generally believe that 'we often remember information without being aware of it' (ibid., 17). Even Toth notes that 'any serious account of memory must acknowledge the dramatic difference that obtains between "memory with awareness" and "memory *without awareness*"' (2000, 245; my emphasis). In opposition to what is the default assumption in neuropsychology,[18] I want to suggest that without some kind of awareness, it isn't memory that we are talking about. This is *not* to say that memory necessitates awareness of the recollective experience (what Tulving calls autonoetic remembering). It *is* to say that to put under the banner of memory the mere *use* of knowledge acquired in the past is to, as it were, over-employ the concept of memory; to employ it merely because the knowledge in question was acquired *in the past*. With Wittgenstein's help, I now want to argue that being unconsciously or *implicitly* influenced by our experience of a prior event does not warrant speaking of memory, and that memory should only be evoked in cases of *attentive remembering, of effortful remembering, and of memorizing*.[19] So that what Ian Hunter refers to as 'that rapid, automatized and depersonalized recalling which is typical for material that, as we say, we know well' (1957, 31) is, on my view, not a recalling at all.

Baddeley's and Roediger's worry is that, *at the procedural level*, our usual notion of memory is being stretched. Wittgenstein would certainly share that worry. He would agree that we should, in nonpathological cases, no more call riding a bike a case of 'remembering' than we should call walking a case of 'remembering'. So that unless we are children learning, or adults relearning (after, say, a stroke), to walk or tie our shoelaces or ride a bike, these are all skills that we've acquired and perform without the use of memory. We do not, as normal adults, *remember* how to walk, tie our shoelaces, or ride a bike before or during our performance of these things. In such cases, we would not speak of memory, but of know-how, skill or capacity.

Wittgenstein's worry, however, would not be limited to the procedural level; he would protest that our usual notion of memory is being stretched across *all* the so-called memory systems, and that many manifestations of so-called declarative memory – semantic and autobiographical (or episodic) – should not be regarded as manifestations of memory at all. Throughout his work, Wittgenstein often excludes memory (or recognition) as necessarily prefacing our use of words and skills, and he generally regards memory as superfluous in most explanations. But more specifically in his last work, *On Certainty*, he logically excludes it – and in fact, any other epistemic process – from prefacing our assurance about any of our *basic beliefs* – such beliefs as are included by neuroscientists in semantic and autobiographical memory.

Put briefly, in *On Certainty* Wittgenstein takes our *basic* beliefs or certainties to be ungrounded, unjustified certainties: 'At the foundation of well-founded belief lies belief that is not founded' (OC 253). He compares these basic beliefs to 'hinges' on which the door of inquiry turns,[20] making them noncognitive certainties that logically underpin our cognitive inquiries. Some of these certainties are natural, instinctual or animal-like certainties (OC 359) that are never taught, or even articulated *as such* – that is, not articulated *qua certainties*; e.g., 'I have a body', 'I can move', 'I cannot walk *through* other people'. Such sentences are only artificial verbal renderings of what are in fact nonpropositional certainties: here, to be certain does not imply that one can formulate the sentences or even understand the words that compose them. A one-year-old child not yet in possession of language shows that she is endowed with such certainties by using her body, reacting to other people, avoiding people rather than attempting to walk through them etc.[21] Other hinges are *acquired*, but where hinges are acquired, assimilation is effected through some form of conditioning, not propositional learning. They are either *explicitly* acquired – e.g., through cultural *training* or educational *drill* (e.g., 'This is (what we call) the sky'), or they are *implicitly* assimilated – without any training or often no formulation at all – through something like *repeated exposure* (e.g., 'People sometimes lie'). So that, although we can put them into words for heuristic purposes, such as pedagogical training or philosophical discussion, these basic certainties are nonpropositional and ineffable *qua* certainties. They only show themselves *in* what we say and do.[22]

The next two sections aim to show that *some* of what neuropsychologists call semantic and autobiographical memories are in fact basic certainties that are not susceptible of recall in ordinary (e.g., nonpathological) circumstances. This is not to say that these certainties cannot be modified or rendered obsolete (and would then be susceptible of recall). If, say, it were decreed that the word 'table' would be replaced in

English usage by another word, we would unlearn the word 'table', such that in twenty years it may well require some effort to recall it. Hinges can be unhinged, but *as long as they are hinges*, they are not susceptible of recall – or forgetfulness: 'Suppose a man could not remember whether he had always had five fingers or two hands? Should we understand him? Could we be sure of understanding him?' (OC 157). Any 'forgetfulness' here, or even (genuine) hesitation, would be the sign of 'a mental disturbance, perhaps a transient one' (OC 71).[23]

5.2 'Semantic' hinges

What neuroscientists refer to as semantic memory comprises our general knowledge about the world, concepts, rules and language. This is covered first of all by Wittgenstein's *linguistic certainties*.[24] The trained assimilation of language produces an indubitable certainty about certain words:

> We say: if a child has mastered language – and hence its application – it must ... be able to attach the name of its colour to a white, black, red or blue object without the occurrence of any doubt.
>
> OC 522

And if there is no occurrence of doubt, this renders otiose the presence of remembering. Indeed, '[i]t is simply the normal case, to be incapable of mistake about the designation of certain things in one's mother tongue' (OC 630). *Certain things*, not all. What Wittgenstein is saying is that we cannot normally be mistaken or uncertain about the meaning of *our most basic words*. And here, the simplicity of Wittgenstein's examples is important; he uses words like 'table', 'chair', 'red' and 'blue' rather than 'funambulist' or 'perfunctory'. If I am a fluent speaker of English, I may hesitate, reflect or attempt recall before using words like 'funambulist' and 'perfunctory', but not before using words such as 'red' and 'table'. It is only at this basic level that Wittgenstein questions that our use of words involves memory:

> When I talk about this table, – am I *remembering* that this object is called a 'table'?
>
> PI 601; original emphasis

> Is it ever true that when I call a colour 'red' I serve myself of memory?? / make use of memory?
>
> LPE 220

Here, Wittgenstein outrightly questions the preconception that an act of memory *always* prefaces our use words (indeed, he wonders if it *ever* prefaces our use of some words). When as a child I first learned the use of the word 'table', I did make use of memory, but after years of repeated use and exposure, only a cognitive disorder could cause me to forget that this object is called a 'table'. Repetition has, as it were, *drilled it into me*: I no longer need, as I did when I first learned the word, to recall it each time; I utter it automatically, without a thought, the same way I get on a bicycle and start pedalling without having first to recall the technique I learned as a beginner. Once the technique is mastered – and this is not to say the mastery cannot break down or be deliberately modified – there is no question of appeal to memory. Our certainty in using such words is not due to the implicit, instantaneous recall of rules prior to each use; it is a thoughtless *know-how*:

> 'Understanding a word' may mean: *knowing* how it is used; *being able* to apply it.
> PG p. 47

> 'I can use the word "yellow"' is like 'I *know how* to move the king in chess'.
> PG p. 49; my emphasis

Wittgenstein's insight that the understanding of language, like that of a game, is not a knowledge of rules but more like the *mastery* of a calculus – an *ability*, in other words – came late to neuroscience on memory; only recently did performance on word identification come to be viewed as no longer reflecting semantic memory, but procedural memory (Toth and Hunt 1999, 259). All that now needs to be done, I suggest, is to stop regarding this know-how as any kind of *memory*.

The same goes for our *basic* general knowledge.[25] Although we may have once learned that human beings die or that they have brains, once these facts have been assimilated they are no longer (in normal circumstances) objects of recall, or of any cognitive process. This is also true of perceptual hinges:

> But when I say 'It tastes exactly like sugar', in an important sense no remembering takes place. So I do *not have grounds for* my judgement or my exclamation. If someone asks me: 'What do you mean by "sugar"?' – I shall indeed try to show him a lump of sugar. And if someone asks 'How do you know that sugar tastes like that?' I shall indeed answer him 'I've eaten sugar thousands of times' – but that is not a justification that I give myself.
> RPP II, 353

For this kind of certainty is *basic* (it has become basic through habituation) and therefore ungrounded – though others may demand grounds from us, *we* are not certain on the strength of any grounds (there is a first-/third-person asymmetry here). In unexceptional circumstances, we do not *remember* that this tastes like sugar or that this is a bottle or that what we do in restaurants is eat, drink etc. Our certainty about such things is as noncognitive and unjustified as a reflex action – which, again, is not to say that our certainty cannot be unlearned or modified, the same way our reflexes can be retrained[26].

5.3 'Autobiographical (Episodic)' Hinges

Similarly, for Wittgenstein, *basic* autobiographical facts are not objects of memory, but noncognitive certainties that constitute the ungrounded starting points of what it makes sense for an individual to say of herself[27]. In *On Certainty*, he writes:

For months I have lived at address A, I have read the name of the street and the number of the house countless times, have received countless letters here and given countless people the address. If I am wrong about it, the mistake is hardly less than if I were (wrongly) to believe I was writing Chinese and not German.

OC 70

Autobiographical certainties resemble *truths* which I *know*, but although, from a third-person perspective, these are truths which can be kn*own*, that is not how *I* relate to them. I do not have a cognitive rapport with my autobiographical certainties; they are not *derived* from reflection or *memory*.

If someone asks me what I have been doing in the last two hours, I answer him straight off and I don't read the answer off from an experience I am having. And yet one says that I *remembered*, and that this is a mental process.

RPP I, 105

One might also marvel that one can answer the question "What did you do this morning?" – without looking up historical traces of activity or the like. Yes; I answer, and wouldn't even know that this was only possible through a special mental process, remembering, if I were not told so.

RPP I, 106

For although one calls this 'remembering', it is no more remembering than the following is a case of recognizing: 'Asked "Did you recognize your desk when you entered your room this morning?" – I should no doubt say "Certainly!" And yet it would be misleading to say that an act of recognition had taken place' (PI 602).

Some *basic* autobiographical facts – for example, 'My name is Danièle', 'I live in London', 'I have no children', 'I speak French' – *cannot*, in normal circumstances, be the product of recall. That my automatic assurance of these facts is vulnerable to amnesia does not make them, in non-pathological circumstances, a product of memory, or even disposed to be recalled.[28]

What is it then that makes some autobiographical facts hinge certainties, and others not? Why is my having been to Paris a hinge for me, not susceptible of error or hesitation or recall (though, of course, details of my individual stays in Paris are thus susceptible), but not my having been, say, to Montelimar? Absence of hesitation, automaticity may be achieved through repetition or drill, but will be greatly assisted by a high degree of salience (proximity, familiarity, simplicity etc.). Paris has been salient in my life: I have lived, studied and lectured there; I regularly visit my Parisian friends and colleagues and have been several times to the Musée Guimet and the Louvre etc. But the fact that I can give a list of reasons for my certainty does not mean that I, myself, have come to this certainty from following a line of reasoning (again, first/third person asymmetry). As for Montelimar, I have often driven past it on my way to the south of France and remember the lure of its world-class nougat, but not whether it ever succeeded into making me swerve into the city.

Temporal and spatial proximity also contribute to hinge certainty: I may not be certain about which day last week I went to the theatre and may have to tax my memory to find out, but – all being otherwise well with me – I would have not a moment's hesitation about having been to the theatre an hour ago. I would no more hesitate or reflect here than I would to assert that I am not at the theatre right now or that I have often been to Paris. Any hesitation or forgetfulness here would translate not uncertainty, but some form of pathology.

6. Mnemonic effort and attention

I certainly agree with Jason Leboe (personal communication, 2007) that events in one's past determine our current success in engaging in virtually every thought and behaviour possible, but I do not find this reason enough to envisage every learned pattern of thought or behaviour as involving memory. The acquisition of these patterns may *have involved* memory at some point, and this may be ground enough to see them as *continuing* to be products of memory, but this is only trivial ground. To suggest that the degree of a current task's automaticity depends on how much experience has supported the performance of that task (and so the rapidity and efficiency of our current mental processes reflect the level of memory's contribution) is to say no more than that memory *has* played a role in the achievement of certainty, not that it continues to do so in the subsequent deployment of all our behaviour and thought.

Defining memory as 'the use of prior experience to guide current thought and behaviour' (Leboe 2007) or 'the faculty to *use* any type of acquired information' (Dalla Barba 2000, 138); and defining remembering as 'the use of knowledge retained' (Bennett and Hacker 2003, 156) suggests that we use memory for just about everything we think and do, making memory so pervasive a concept as to be useless or meaningless. I suggest inserting the single word 'attentive' to these definitions, making memory 'the *attentive* use of prior experience to guide current thought and behaviour', thereby precluding speaking of remembering where there is only automaticity. To speak of memory, there must also occur what I would call *mnemonic effort* or, at least, *mnemonic attention*.

Examples of mnemonic efforts are concentration, focus or, more elaborately, the little tricks we use in trying to remember a name (e.g., I suspect it starts with the letter 'B', and run through the whole gamut: BA, BE, BO... until the word springs to mind: 'Borden!'); or in trying to recall what we set out to do (e.g., returning to the spot where we first thought of it). But what about unprompted memories – where one remembers a situation or occurrence '*at a moment*' (RPP I, 837) – as when a mental picture of last night's family dinner, or a thought I had yesterday for this paper, spontaneously come to mind? Here, where no mnemonic effort is made, what we might call *mnemonic attention* is paid. That is, we *attend* to the mental picture of *last night's* dinner or *yesterday's* thought as something that is being, as it were, revisited – as opposed, say, to an imagined picture, or to a thought never before envisaged. Indeed, the idea that a picture of last night's dinner must have been stored if it is to be able to spring to mind weakens its hold when we think that *imagined* pictures can, as it were, 'come from nowhere'. We think that a memory picture must have been stored because we think of it as a 'reproduction' or replica, which therefore must in some way contain the original. But not only do we usually remember the original scene or event with very little detail; and indeed, often misremember it, the idea that an imprint of the original must be stored in order for the original to be 'reproduced' is based on a mechanistic picture of human abilities, and on grammatical confusions often prompted by words like 'storage' and 'retrieval'[29].

What neuroscientists have called implicit memory seems to me very close to what Wittgenstein has described in *On Certainty* as an attitudinal assurance that is either instinctual or automatic, and that should therefore be envisaged not as a product of memory (in any nontrivial sense), but more in terms of reflex action. To the objection voiced to me that this attempt to oust automatic linguistic and nonlinguistic behaviour from the realm of memory seems alien to the Wittgensteinian spirit, which tends to expand rather than restrict concepts, I would reply that Wittgenstein has expanded where expansion was needed (cf. section 3), and that he never meant family resemblance concepts to be a carte blanche for groupings of heterogeneous concepts. Rather than contribute to the homogenization of memory, I believe *On Certainty* shows differences to those who see memory everywhere.

7. The way forward

Wittgenstein helps us move away from the distorted picture of memory as the storage and retrieval of reified 'memories' towards a conception of memory as something that can be situated, contextualized, external and in action. My remembering something can be in the form of a mental picture, but it can also have the form of a gesture or a sentence. Remembering can amount to something I say or do. This helps discredit the picture of mental phenomena as essentially representations internal to the brain and sheds light on the mental as an ability whose manifestations can be as much in what we do as in what we think, but never in what our brain 'does' or 'thinks'.

Wittgenstein has influenced some current neuropsychological conceptions of memory, but the struggle is still uphill. Also, the notion of extended memory[30] – for better or for worse – owes something to Wittgenstein, but it is in the conception of exten*sive* memory proposed by Erik Myin and Karim Zahidi (2012)[31] that I believe Wittgenstein is best present. Dissatisfied with the notion of exten*ded* memory because it remains grounded in an internalist and representational view of memory (that is, extended memory presupposes an internal memory to extend from), Myin and Zahidi introduced the notion of 'exten*sive* memory', according to which remembering is 'a contextualized capacity' to make the past matter in current activities (2012, 115; Myin translation)[32]. Here, representations are *eliminated, not accommodated*. What is traditionally explained in terms of explicit representations is explained in terms of interactions. Memory is seen not as a matter of storing and retrieving representations, but as a particular way of interacting with the environment (ibid., 126).

In this chapter, I have focused on how Wittgenstein discredits the storage and imprint models of memory, dissolves the conceptual link between memory and mental images or representations, upholds the context-sensitivity of memory; and on how his work encourages us to stop treating *automatic* behaviour as behaviour that is (subconsciously) remembered. I have argued that what neuropsychologists have called nondeclarative, procedural or implicit memory is nothing but automatic or habitual ways of acting or speaking that are not reliant on memory, though of course they can initially have been (as when a child first tries to tie her shoe laces and seeks to remember what she is supposed to do). So that so-called 'implicit memory' is no memory at all. There's another cognitive layer pared away by Wittgenstein's razor.

When presenting my views on Wittgenstein and memory to neuropsychologists at the 5th International Conference on Memory,[33] I was delighted and relieved to find a receptive audience. Interestingly, however, the main question put to me was: if not engrams, what would neuropsychologists working on memory have to work with? Well, that's an odd question, for no evidence has ever been found for the existence of engrams (the engram is a hypothetical entity). Indeed, Fergus Craik had, in his inaugural plenary lecture, cautioned that: 'remembering is better thought of as an activity of mind and brain, akin to perceiving, and the 'search for the engram' is therefore doomed to failure'.[34] But there is also a positive answer here, and it is twofold: (1), Wittgenstein is not taking the brain away from neuropsychologists – he is merely adjusting the target, what it is they should be (and should not be) looking for in the brain; (2), there is *behaviour* to work on. If, as Craik stresses, remembering is an activity – let's also work on that.[35]

Now, one might object that Wittgenstein can say what he likes, but where's the evidence? As Jesse Prinz quips, enactive and embodied approaches are easier to 'sell than to prove' (2009, 419). Well, it is scientists, not philosophers, that base their claims on evidence. What philosophers do is work on more perspicuous *conceptual* presentations of how things are. And what Wittgenstein has done is show that we cannot make conceptual sense of engrams that work like people. But now let me return the question and ask scientists: where is *your* evidence? As Fergus Craik confirms, there is none. There are, of course, always new findings on the nature of the brain structures and mechanisms involved in learning and memory,[36] but there has never been found anything resembling an engram, no shadow of anything representational or encoded in the brain since Karl Lashley began his famous 'search for the engram' in the 1920s. So why insist we go representational in our accounts of the mind when even science is unable to demonstrate that that's the way to go? Why – when there are conceptually viable enactivist accounts of ourselves as mindful beings, and nothing resembling *or demanding* a realization of the mental in the brain – should we persist in a search that is, as Fergus Craik puts it, doomed to failure?[37]

7

Wittgenstein on Psychological Certainty

As is well known, Wittgenstein pointed out an asymmetry between first- and third-person psychological statements: the latter, unlike the former, involve observation or a claim to knowledge, and are therefore *constitutionally* open to uncertainty. In this chapter, I challenge this asymmetry by challenging the *constitutional* uncertainty of third-person psychological sentences, and argue that Wittgenstein did that too. There are cases where third-person psychological ascriptions (e.g., 'He is in pain'; 'She is terrified') are not susceptible of error. This logical psychological certainty, though occurring only in basic cases, is sufficient to rebut scepticism of other minds and invalidate the necessity of a 'theory of mind' (ToM) in our understanding of others.

1. Introduction

Wittgenstein gives approximately 300 examples of basic certainties in *On Certainty*, and we are well aware that these are but an infinitesimal sample of the innumerable basic certainties that underpin our everyday acting, thinking and speaking in the world. Examples of these are: 'My name is such and such' (OC 571); 'The person opposite me is my old friend so and so' (OC 613); 'I have never been on the moon' (OC 218); 'Cats don't grow on trees' (OC 282); 'I have a body' (OC 244); 'Here is a hand' (OC 9); 'My hands don't disappear when I'm not paying attention to them' (OC 153); 'I am a human being' (OC 4); 'The words composing this sentence are English' (OC 158).[1] There is, however, a specific subgroup of basic certainties (or what I call 'hinge certainties') that is hardly mentioned in *On Certainty*: these are *psychological* certainties.[2] These, Wittgenstein largely addresses in his writings and lectures on philosophical psychology, the final one of which – *Last Writings on the Philosophy of Psychology, vol. II* – is contemporaneous with the notes that make up *On Certainty*. The aim of this chapter is to follow the *third* Wittgenstein – that is the post-*Investigations* Wittgenstein[3] – in his attempt to grasp the nature of our psychological certainty. But note that the certainty in question here is psychological not in its nature, but in its objects: it is a certainty regarding things psychological. Indeed, I will argue that, on Wittgenstein's view, some *psychological* certainties – both first- and third-person – have a *logical* status.

As is well known, Wittgenstein pointed out an asymmetry between first- and third-person psychological statements:

> The salient thing [about the psychological verb] is the asymmetry; "I think", unlike "he thinks", has no verification.
>
> LPP 49

> The truth is: it makes sense to say about other people that they doubt whether I am in pain; but not to say it about myself.
>
> PI 246

The latter, unlike the former, involve observation or a claim to knowledge,[4] and are therefore *constitutionally* open to uncertainty. This chapter will challenge this asymmetry by challenging the *constitutional* uncertainty of third-person psychological sentences and argue that Wittgenstein ultimately also did.

I begin by suggesting that, on Wittgenstein's view, not all of our *third-person* psychological statements (e.g., 'She's unhappy'; 'He is in pain'; 'They're perplexed') are epistemic. Some are – they are conclusions drawn from inference – while others stem from a subjective assurance which, though not the result of an epistemic process such as inference, is not invulnerable to error in that it is a kind of *unreflective assumption* (e.g., I unreflectively assume that the voice saying 'Doors are closing' in the lift belongs to a person whereas it is computer generated). I then go on to show that, following relentless questioning and wavering, Wittgenstein concedes that some third-person nonepistemic psychological certainties are not merely subjective but (what he calls) objective; that is, they are logically indubitable (of the same order as 'I am in pain' or '2 x 2 = 4'). This puts in question Wittgenstein's affirmation of a first-/third-person asymmetry, but it also positively reinforces his rebuttal of other mind scepticism. I conclude with a response to objections about the legitimacy of calling an assurance that is *logical* (i.e., that does not have uncertainty or doubt on its flipside) a 'certainty', by suggesting that the flipside is to be found in pathological cases. To make my point, I focus on cases of *dyssemia* – a disability affecting nonverbal communication, whereby individuals cannot properly interpret the meaning of, and/or express meaning through, facial expressions, tone of voice, body movements, posture, gestures and so on. Such pathological cases constitute a foil to the default objective certainty with which we ordinarily grasp and express basic expressions.

2. Wittgenstein's 'objective certainty'

> With the word 'certain' we express complete conviction, the total absence of doubt, and thereby we seek to convince other people. That is *subjective* certainty. But when is something objectively certain? When a mistake is not possible. But what kind of possibility is that? Mustn't mistake be *logically* excluded?
>
> OC 194

What Wittgenstein calls 'objective certainty' differs from what is usually understood by 'objective certainty': it is neither a certainty à la Nagel grounded on mind- or human-independent objectivity, nor a certainty based on 'compelling grounds' (OC 270), and therefore indistinguishable from knowledge. What Wittgenstein understands by 'objective certainty' is *not* to be confused with knowledge;[5] it is a certainty in which mistake is 'logically', not *rationally*, excluded.[6]

Before specifically addressing our *psychological* objective or hinge certainties, I now give a brief description of our hinge certainties generally. On Wittgenstein's view, our basic or hinge certainties are not falsifiable propositions but unhesitating *attitudes* or *ways of acting*[7] that are reflex-like and that only show themselves, *qua* certainties, *in* what we do and *in* what we say. So, for instance, our certainty that neonates cannot care for themselves shows itself in our feeding and clothing them, and in our saying such things as 'I need a babysitter for tonight'. We sometimes formulate our basic certainties (e.g., the sentences: 'Human beings think', 'Neonates cannot pretend', 'We cannot feel another's pain'), but such *sentences* do not, qua basic certainties, constitute propositions or thoughts; they are mere formulations – mostly for heuristic reasons, such as philosophical analysis or pedagogical instruction – of certainties that are nothing but natural reflexes (e.g., 'I have a body') or acquired grammatical rules (e.g., 'This is (what we call) a hand'). What makes these *hinge* certainties is that they *logically* underpin our epistemic enquiries; which means, as Wittgenstein makes clear, that someone purporting to 'doubt' them could only: (1), be prey to a psychological disorder (e.g., OC 257; 155); (2), not be engaged in *real* doubt, but only in the behaviour of doubt[8] (OC 255); or (3), be prey to a linguistic misunderstanding (e.g., OC 526).

3. The pull in two directions

Before we begin investigating the nature of psychological certainties, I would like to suggest the existence, throughout Wittgenstein's philosophising, of a persistent pull in two directions: on one hand, his *reactive* and *revolutionary* resistance to sharp boundaries and closed concepts, to Platonic essences or Kantian schemata – a resistance that gives rise to family resemblance concepts, highlights the positive importance of indeterminacy of sense, and appeals to the notion of *imponderable* evidence – the stress being on 'imponderable' (see LW I, 920-4). Pulling against this reactive and revolutionary tendency, however, is a *reactionary* one which I want to draw attention to particularly because it is not sufficiently recognized. This reactionary pull is a constant gravitating back, on Wittgenstein's part, towards regularity, predictability, fixity and indubitability. It translates itself in the work as an urge to draw limits (e.g., to thought or sense, as in the *Tractatus*; see Preface); as a repeated appeal to *frames of reference*;[9] an acknowledgement of *foundations* (even 'unmoving' ones) – those of our language-games (e.g., OC 403), or of thought and action (e.g., OC 411), *scaffoldings* (of the world: TLP 6.124, or of our thoughts: OC 211), and *hard substrata* (of our concepts: RPP I, 600, or of all our enquiring and asserting: OC 162); a growing commitment to the idea that for the door of inquiry to turn, its hinges must *stay put* (OC 343); and a relentless urge to find that *stopping* place of inquiry, where one's justifications are exhausted, and where one's spade is turned (PI 217). This tendency is not limited to *On Certainty* – indeed, the drawing of limits to thought or sense is from the *Tractatus*, and the 'turned spade' image comes from the *Investigations*. It is also blatantly visible in the philosophy of psychology: in Wittgenstein's repeated and explicit attempts to *classify* psychological concepts (cf. RPP II, 148) and to trace *patterns* of life (LW I, 211); in his reminders that, though psychological judgement is by no means an exact science, *Menschenerkenntnis* can be learned from someone more 'expert' than oneself, and improved through experience;[10] and in the stress he also puts on *evidence* in 'imponderable evidence'. Two directions, then: one away from regularity and fixity; the other towards it. So that this same philosopher can say both that 'the application of a word is not everywhere bounded by rules' (PI 84) and that '[t]he rule-governed nature of our language permeates our life' (RC III, 303).

The pull both ways is particularly noticeable throughout the third Wittgenstein's questionings on psychological certainty. There is a constant vacillation and struggle between two imperatives that is well encapsulated in the notion of 'imponderable evidence': acknowledging and formulating the buzzing indeterminacy, spontaneity and irreducibility of human life,[11] whilst perspicuously assessing its basic regularity and predictability, as well as the certainty on which it is all hinged. For, that is what Wittgenstein – as he is unravelling the hurly-burly of our actions – keeps bumping into again and again: a fundamental, reliably human, 'constant repetition' (RPP II, 626); and a certainty which, without reason or justification, lies there as the given and necessary bedrock on which our uncertainties can battle. The pull both ways is then symptomatic of the *difficulty* Wittgenstein is experiencing in his attempts to describe our ways of thinking and acting, as well as of the *nature* of what he is attempting to describe. For, as Jean-Jacques Rosat puts it:

> The course of human life is made up of the interweaving of our feelings and ways of acting – pains, joys, hopes, ploys, etc. – and consists of nothing but their infinite repetition. This means that in order to rest assured in our judgements, we have at our disposal no support or reference other than this perpetually moving background, which obeys no general plan nor is determined by some global order. The manner in which human actions and passions are intertwined is more like something resembling chaos or hurly-burly. [... Yet] this background is not, for all that, pure diversity; regularities are also present. The actions and passions that make up the stream of life are always present in certain forms, in certain constantly recurring patterns. [...] Without this repetition, this mechanism, our concepts would have no grip.
>
> 2007, 200

There is an *indefiniteness* or *indeterminacy* essential to the kind of *repetition* in question; for it is a repetition that is embedded in life. And yet, as Wittgenstein takes the plunge, for philosophy, from the static, abstract, sovereign regularity of third realms into the stream of life, he realizes that the stream could not be one if it had no bedrock. But let us first see how Wittgenstein deals with the indeterminacy.

4. *Logical* indeterminacy and *constitutional* uncertainty

For Wittgenstein, the background of psychological judgements is a pattern in highly complicated filigree (RPP II, 642). Human behaviour is not everywhere uniform or predictable, and so the concepts that capture that behaviour are accordingly indeterminate. This indeterminacy shows itself above all 'in two prominent aspects of human life: i) the irregularity of human physiognomy; ii) the unpredictability of human behaviour' (ter Hark, 1990, 149). Our form of life is such that there is not only one, or even a handful of 'occasions' that we might call 'grief', but innumerable ones that are interwoven with a thousand other patterns (cf. LW I, 966). And this is so for *all* our psychological concepts, because the 'natural foundation' for the way they are formed 'is the complex nature and the variety of human contingencies' (RPP II, 614). As a result the concepts themselves lack determinacy and have a kind of elasticity. Where Wittgenstein's agenda is to capture the natural indeterminacy in our psychological concepts and judgements – 'I do not want to reduce unsharpness to sharpness; but to capture unsharpness conceptually' (MS 1367, 64) – most philosophers attempt to tame or reduce the indeterminacy; that is, to simplify, formalize or schematize it[12]. But, as Wittgenstein suggests, any attempt to give our psychological concepts fixed limits, to reduce or restrain the variety, would not be an attempt to draw *our* concepts (cf. RPP II, 615). It is then to be expected that such indeterminacy of sense should result in uncertainty of judgement:

> Concepts with fixed limits would demand a uniformity of behaviour. But what happens is that where I am *certain*, someone else is uncertain. And that is a fact of nature.
>
> RPP II, 683

Still, Wittgenstein cautions us against seeing the uncertainty in our psychological judgements as the inevitable result of the *hidden nature of mind* or of a temporary blindness due to our not (yet) having the right epistemic tools at our disposal; rather, he says, it is an *objective* uncertainty, and he calls it (or rather, he calls the certainty regarding this uncertainty) *constitutional*[13]:

> 'To be sure, this uncertainty isn't always subjective, but sometimes *objective*.' (But what does that mean?)
>
> LW I, 887

> 'Objective uncertainty' is an indefiniteness *in the nature of the game,* in the admissible evidence.
>
> LW I, 888; last emphasis mine

> The uncertainty of the ascription 'He's got a pain' might be called a 'constitutional certainty'.
>
> RPP I, 141[14]

Our psychological judgements are uncertain or indeterminate because our psychological concepts are indeterminate; and our psychological concepts are indeterminate because human behaviour is indeterminate. So that, unlike *subjective* uncertainty, *psychological* uncertainty, is *not* due to an epistemic shortcoming that can be remedied, say, by getting closer to the evidence; it is an *essential* feature of our psychological concepts[15]. This means that, unlike most of our physical concepts, our psychological ones could seek precision only at the cost of betraying the very nature of their object: 'unforeseeability must be *an* essential property of the mental. Just like the endless multiplicity of expression' (LW II, 65).

Wittgenstein does not view psychological indeterminacy as a vice of psychological concepts or as pervasive: 'We are playing with elastic, indeed even flexible concepts. But this does not mean that they can be deformed *at will* and without offering resistance, and are therefore *unusable*' (LW II, 24). In fact, Wittgenstein's depiction of psychological indeterminacy is everywhere bounded – not by rules, but by certain *regularities*.[16] And, although our psychological language-games are elastic, they are not so elastic as to lack a hard core, or what ter Hark calls 'a solid centre of meaning'. In his analysis of individual psychological concepts, such as 'willing' or 'expecting', writes ter Hark:

> ...Wittgenstein, as a philosopher, does draw sharp lines and boundaries. In this way he shows that psychological concepts within language-games have a solid centre of meaning. Although he is convinced that these concepts too show a certain elasticity at their edges, since they are embedded in forms of life, this does not mean that their meaning cannot be clearly defined within certain limits.
>
> 1990, 153

As Wittgenstein notes, 'here there are simple and more complicated cases; and that is important for the concept' (LW I, 967) – indeed, for it is the simple cases that give the concept its solid centre, its unambiguous core. Though the margin is elastic, though '[s]ufficient evidence passes over into insufficient without a borderline' (RPP II, 614), there is a core of sufficient evidence provided by the simple cases; so that where the evidence for real laughter is insufficient, it is not so insufficient as to be evidence for the opposite[17]. Similarly, if '[s]omebody gets burned and cries out; only in very rare circumstances would his behaviour be called "pretence"' (LW I, 967).

And so our uncertainty, however *constitutional*, turns out, for all that, not to be pervasive. Because of the overlapping of our concepts, our judgement often 'fluctuates' (LW I, 953); but not always:

> The *uncertainty* whether someone else... is an (essential) trait of all these language-games. But this does not mean that everyone is hopelessly in doubt about what other people feel.
>
> LW I, 877

Recognizing the extent of 'psychological indeterminacy' does not blind Wittgenstein to the possibility of psychological certainty. Although he admits that '[t]here is no clear border separating sufficient from insufficient evidence', he goes on to say: 'And yet, there is evidence here' (LW I, 952). He calls this evidence *imponderable* (LW I 921). It is evidence that does not have the character of proof such as might be presented in a court of law, but that includes such things as 'subtleties of tone, of glance, of gesture' (LW I, 936). Still, the indeterminate nature of the evidence does not preclude it from being evidence:

> That an actor can represent grief shows the uncertainty of evidence, but that he can represent *grief* also shows the reality of evidence.
>
> LW II, 67

That *an actor* can represent grief shows that we can be tricked into believing that someone is grieving when they are in fact not grieving; but that he *can* do this; that he knows what gestures, what posture, what tone to adopt in order for us to believe he (his character) is grieving – indeed, to the extent that some of us shed tears of compassion for him – shows the *reality* of the evidence. As Wittgenstein writes: '"That seems genuine" only makes sense if there is a "That is genuine"' (LW II, 86). Our emotionally engaging in something that is not real but only pretence or 'make-believe' is due precisely to the fact that there is something that we consider 'the real thing' that can be imitated. And it is, as Wittgenstein affirms, in the power of great art to capture it[18]:

> I can recognize a genuine loving look, distinguish it from a pretended one. And yet there is no way in which I can describe it to someone else. If we had a great painter here, he might conceivably represent a genuine and a simulated look in pictures [...].
>
> LW I, 937

And here, it is important to distinguish, with Wittgenstein, between our *right* to treat something as evidence, and our inability to spell out (to more than 'full detail') the evidence that it is:

> Haven't I the *right* to be convinced that he is not pretending to me? – And can't I convince someone else of my right?
>
> RPP II, 589

> If I tell him in full detail how my friend behaved, will he have any reasonable doubt as to the genuineness of my friend's feelings?
> Does anyone doubt the genuineness of Lear's feelings?
>
> RPP II, 590

That the evidence is not clear cut (that the reasons for the certainty cannot be specified (cf. RPP II, 654)) does not make it less compelling:

> If it is said, 'Evidence can only make it probable that expressions of emotions are genuine', this does *not* mean that instead of complete certainty we have just a more or less confident conjecture.
>
> RPP II, 684

That the evidence is indeterminate does not make the certainty half-hearted; indeed, affirms Wittgenstein, imponderable evidence is sufficient to make one *completely certain*. But what does Wittgenstein mean here by 'complete certainty'? Are we in the realm of *subjective* certainty, where we might be *completely certain* – that is, convinced – and still be wrong? Or have we moved to the realm of *objective* certainty, where indubitability is not psychological or epistemic, but *logical*? Put another way, have we moved from asking: '*Does* anyone doubt the genuineness of Lear's feelings?' to: '*Can* anyone doubt the genuineness of Lear's feelings?'. If we have, then Wittgenstein must have given up the idea of a *constitutional* uncertainty as regards third-person psychological judgements.

5. Kinds of psychological certainty

5.1 Kinds of *objective* psychological certainty

In Table 1 (opposite), I list the different kinds of psychological certainties that I take Wittgenstein to treat as *objective*. I will consider unproblematic the inclusion here of (C): sentences that resemble empirical descriptions or generalizations, but are in fact grammatical elucidations, either of (i) individual psychological concepts – what Wittgenstein also calls 'conceptual stipulations'[19] – of say, being grateful, regretting, pretending; or, of (ii) what look more like anthropological generalizations, but are in fact also grammatical.[20] I will also consider unproblematic the inclusion of (A): first-person psychological certainties that are not descriptions[21]. But what about the inclusion of (B): some third-person psychological certainties? If, as I will suggest, this should also be seen as unproblematic, there must be less asymmetry between first- and third-person psychological ascriptions than Wittgenstein originally believed.

5.2 Third-person *subjective* psychological certainty

We grasp psychological phenomena, in most cases, without inference or indeed with no epistemic process taking place at all – immediately:

> [...] We do not see facial contortions and *make the inference* that he is feeling joy, grief, boredom. We describe a face immediately as sad, radiant, bored, even when we are unable to give any other description of the features. – Grief, one would like to say, is personified in the face. This is essential to what we call 'emotion'.
>
> RPP II, 570

In most cases, we do not infer from someone's behaviour that he is sad or angry. We will not ask ourselves whether a driver shouting insults in the direction of a car that is blocking traffic, repeatedly pounding on his horn, eyes glaring and nose flaring, is sad or angry. We *assume* he is angry and either stay out of his way or try to calm him down. In most cases, we *read* or *see* the emotion in someone's behaviour or expression; we do not *infer* it:[22]

> In general I do not surmise fear in him – I *see* it. I do not feel that I am deducing the probable existence of something inside from something outside; rather it is as if the human face were in a way translucent and that I were seeing it not in reflected light but rather in its own.
>
> RPP II, 170

Table 1 Kinds of Objective Psychological Certainties

	'And everything descriptive of a language-game is part of logic' (OC 56)		
(A) First-Person	(B) Third-Person	(C) Conceptual Elucidations	
		i) Of individual concepts / verbs	ii) anthropo-logical …
			'The basic concepts are interwoven so closely with what is most fundamental in our way of living that they are therefore unassailable.' (LW II, 43–4).
		EXAMPLES	
'I am in pain'	'He is in pain' (e.g. of someone falling into the flames and crying out (LPE 287), or of someone badly wounded and in dreadful pain (LW I, 964))	'We cannot feel another's pain.' (LPP 155) 'A man can pretend to be unconscious; but *conscious*?' (RPP I, 931)	'Human beings feel pain' 'Human beings sometimes think.' (RPP II 29) 'We can't talk about the joy and sorrow, etc. of fish.' (RPP II 29)
'I am a human being / I have a mind'	'He is a human being' (of someone towards whom we have 'eine *Einstellung zur Seele*' – an attitude towards a soul (PI, p.178))	'Neither is the newborn child capable of being malicious, friendly, or thankful. Thankfulness is only possible if there is already a complicated pattern of behaviour.' (LW I 942) 'A child learns to walk, to crawl, to play. It does not learn to play voluntarily and involuntarily.' (RPP II, 269) 'Anyone who regrets something thinks about it.' (RPP II, 306)	'… a table or a stone don't have any motives.' (RPP I, 631) 'We don't say of a table and chair that they think; neither do we say this of a plant, a fish, and hardly of a dog; only of human beings. And not even of all human beings.' (RPP II, 192) 'An animal cannot point to a thing that interests it.' (LW II, 41)

Inasmuch as no epistemic process is taking place, the assumption is not a case of knowing, but of nonepistemic certainty. In reaction to his objector's claim that we can never be certain about what someone else is feeling (because it is hidden from us), Wittgenstein often insists that in fact, we *are* certain:

> Every day we hear one man saying of another that he is in pain, is sad, is merry, etc. without a trace of doubt, and we relatively seldom hear that he does not know what is going on in the other. In this way, then, the uncertainty is not so bad.
>
> RPP I, 138

But this uncertainty – that is 'not so bad' – makes room for a *subjective*, not an *objective* certainty. Granted, there is, in ordinary and simple cases, no *trace* of doubt, but this does not mean that doubt is logically excluded. Unlike the case of first-person certainties, here 'know' does *not* mean that the expression of uncertainty is senseless (see PI 247). We may be certain that someone is happy, sad or bored, but in some cases, we could be wrong; in many cases, the certainty is subjective; it is a mere *assumption*.[23]

5.3 Third-person *objective* psychological certainty

Note here, with Rosat (2007), that the reason we can be mistaken in the *subjective* cases is not necessarily because there has been dissimulation, and certainly not because emotions are inner and therefore hidden, but simply because we are not always able to discern what is in front of our eyes; perhaps an emotion is too enmeshed with other emotions or too complex to detach itself distinctly from the background; or perhaps it is a variant too unlike the typical pattern for us to correctly identify it – or, as ter Hark puts it: 'If the inner seems concealed, this is not because it is hidden by the outer, but because the *outer* is hidden' (1990 144). But, of course, there is also the possibility that the person is simulating an emotion. Indeed, the nature of the beast is such that we *are* capable of dissembling. Yet, what Wittgenstein also says (contra radical scepticism) is that we can't always be had, precisely because dissembling is *not* always a possibility. To the question: 'Is it thoughtlessness not to keep the *possibility* of pretence in mind?' (RPP II, 591), Wittgenstein's answer is clear:

> Dissimulation is *nothing* but a particular case; we can regard behaviour as dissimulation only under particular circumstances.
>
> LW I, 252

> The concept 'dissimulation' has to do with the cases of dissimulation; therefore with very specific occurrences and specific situations in human life. And here I mean external occurrences, not inner ones, etc.
>
> Therefore it isn't possible for all behaviour, under all circumstances, to be dissimulation.
>
> LW I, 253

If dissimulation is not a universal or systematic possibility, nor can doubt be universal or systematic.[24] It is at this conceptual point that Wittgenstein passes from subjective to objective certainty; that is, to cases, where we *could not* be mistaken because there is no *logical* room for mistake, even in the case of third-person psychological certainties:

> If we see someone falling into the flames and crying out, do we say to ourselves: 'there are of course two cases: ...'? Or if I see you here before me do I distinguish? Do you? *You can't!* That we do in certain cases, doesn't show that we do in all cases.
> LPE 287; my emphasis

> Just try – in a real case – to doubt someone else's fear or pain.
> PI 303

> If I see someone writhing in pain with evident cause I do not think, all the same, his feelings are hidden from me.
> LW II, 22

> 'I can only guess at someone else's feelings' – does that really make sense when you see him badly wounded, for instance, and in dreadful pain?
> LW I, 964

> Need I be less certain that someone is suffering pain than that 12 x 12 = 144?
> LW II, 92

> 'I am *certain* that he's in pain.' – What does that mean? How does one use it? What is the expression of certainty in behaviour, what *makes* us certain?
> Not a proof. That is, what makes me certain doesn't make someone else certain. *But the discrepancy has its limits.*
> LW II, 21; last emphasis mine

If the discrepancy has its limits, this means that there *are* cases where what makes me certain *does* also make someone else certain. In *Last Writings*, volume II, Wittgenstein is making his way from believing that 'There is no such agreement over the question whether an expression of feeling is simulated or genuine' (LW II, 24) to believing the opposite:

> In an extremely complicated way the outer signs sometimes mean *unambiguously*, sometimes without certainty: pain, pretence and several other things.
> LW II, 59; my emphasis

And, moreover, to believing that the certainty is of a logical kind:

> There is an *unmistakable* expression of joy and its opposite.
> Under these circumstances one *knows*[25] that he is in pain, or that he isn't; under those, one is uncertain.
> LW II, 32; emphasis in the original

Yet there *are* cases where only a lunatic could take the expression of pain, for instance, as sham.

LW II, 33; emphasis in the original

In the first place, "I cannot know [*wissen*] his feelings" does *not* mean: ... as opposed to *mine*. In the second place, it does not mean: I can never be completely sure [*ganz sicher*] of his feelings.

LW II, 89; emphasis in the original

The last passage indicates that the problem is now no longer to determine whether or not certainty can be objective – it *can* be – but to stress that objective certainty should not be confused with knowing. Here, in the penultimate passage of *Last Writings* II, Wittgenstein distinguishes between the logical (and physical) impossibility of *knowing* what is going on in someone's mind, and the fact that we *can be*, and indeed often are, *certain* about what is going on in someone's mind:

> Is the impossibility of knowing [*wissen*] what goes on in someone else physical or logical? [...]
>
> The logical impossibility lies in the lack of exact rules of evidence. (Therefore we sometimes express ourselves in this way: "We may always be wrong; we can never be certain; what we observe can *still* be pretence."...) [...]
>
> *But of course it isn't true that we are never certain [sicher] about the mental processes in someone else. In countless cases we are.*

LW II, 94; my emphasis of last sentence

It is impossible to *know* what goes on in someone else, for knowledge requires justification, and here there are no 'exact rules of evidence' – the only 'evidence' is *imponderable*. But that there is no exact evidence does not mean that we cannot be *certain* about what is going on in someone else – and 'in countless cases we are'.[26] Knowledge, no; certainty, yes. That Wittgenstein isn't here alluding to mere *subjective* certainty is made clear by the sentence being a direct response to his objector's allusion to the ever-lurking possibility of error: 'We may *always* be wrong; we can *never* be certain.' It would seem then, that at the close of his last writings on philosophical psychology – and we should note here that the passage is dated 'April 15 1951', and that the last dated passage of *On Certainty* is '27 April 1951' – Wittgenstein is no longer saying that uncertainty is a *constitutional* or *essential* trait of our psychological ascriptions. He has come to see that, in some cases, we *are* as *objectively* certain about 'He is in pain' as about 'I am in pain'.

6. *Einstellung zur Seele*: Objective certainty as an attitude

Our certainty about people around us being human beings, capable of thinking, suffering, pretending, is not subjective, but objective. And on a more individual level, doubting whether my neighbour of ten years is a human being, or whether the retired businessman I have just had a conversation with on the train has a mind, would not result in any suspicion about *them,* but only about my sanity. As mentioned earlier, objective certainty is not the product of an attentive or conscious attitude towards a hypothesis, but manifests itself as an unhesitating attitude – an *Einstellung*.[27] And indeed, this nonintellectual certainty, this *Einstellung*, is best seen in our treatment of 'other minds':

> My attitude towards him is an attitude towards a soul [*eine Einstellung zur Seele*]. I am not of the *opinion* that he has a soul.
>
> PI, p.178

As Wittgenstein uses '*Einstellung*', writes Peter Winch:

> There is no question here of an attitude which I can adopt or abandon at will. My *Einstellung* […] is a condition I am in vis-à-vis other human beings without choosing to be so.
>
> 1980–1, 149–50

And Winch goes on to say that, by using this expression, Wittgenstein 'is obviously emphasizing the *instinctive* character of the phenomena he is interested in' (ibid., 150), and its not involving having certain quasi-theoretical beliefs about other people (ibid., 147). Like that of instinctive and habitual actions, the manifestation of this certainty involves no degree of choice, but also no degree of attention. On the contrary, the presence of attention would be a sure sign that the certainty in question is *not* a hinge certainty.

It might be objected then that the logical nature of this certainty should preclude it from being called a certainty at all. That is, it would only make sense to speak of behaviour as non-doubting or certain if that behaviour could conceivably be replaced by a doubt or an expression of uncertainty. This is a valid objection – precisely the kind of objection made by Wittgenstein to our claiming to 'know' in cases where we couldn't *not* know: 'I can't be said to know that I have toothache if I can't be said not to know that I have toothache' (LPE 287). Similarly here, can I be said to be 'certain' if I can't be said not to be certain?

7. Can we speak of certainty here at all?

Where indubitability is, as in the case of objective certainty, logical – that is, where it is *not* the result of verification, but stems from something's not being susceptible of doubt (and therefore of verification and falsification) *at all*, is it not idle to speak of certainty? Olli Lagerspetz refuses to call something 'certainty' that does not admit of the logical possibility of the absence of that certainty; for certainty to be worthy of the name, there must coexist the possibility of doubting.[28] On his view, to call 'certainty' something that is logically impervious to uncertainty must be *tautologous* (cf. 1998, 161). This, of course, does not mean that being *actually* certain requires envisaging the possibility of not being certain or doubting; all that is required, says Lagerspetz, is an 'outside' perspective from which one can imaginably suggest uncertainty or doubt (1998, 133).

This 'outside perspective' is, I suggest, provided by pathological cases. Where Lagerspetz speaks of the breakdown of the natural order as *unimaginable,* and that therefore to speak of *trusting* it (or being certain of it) would be superfluous or 'tautologous', he fails to envisage cases where the natural order, or the normal order, *does* break down. So that the obverse of objective or logical 'certainty' would not be a logical uncertainty or doubt, but lies in the absence or breakdown of objective certainty – that is, as Wittgenstein repeatedly points out, in pathology, aberration, dementia, alienation: (e.g., OC 71; 155; 257; 281, 674).

Where, in normal cases, human beings are objectively – that is: effortlessly, noninferentially and indubitably – certain of themselves and others having a mind, some autistic individuals are unable to intuitively attribute mental states to self and others[29]; they suffer from what psychologists call an impaired 'Theory of Mind'[30] – or what is also called 'mind-blindness' (Frith and Happé 1999, 1, 7). An autistic child, for example, must be explicitly trained into what others intuitively possess or unproblematically acquire, like the use of the self-referential pronouns 'I' and 'me', and the attribution of emotions or sensations, even pain, to other than themselves. Unlike normal individuals, autistic individuals must *work at* such things as self-consciousness, introspection, and belief attribution; what is ordinarily automatic and thoughtless requires from them thought, anticipation, considered effort and explicit training. This effort is most apparent in individuals with high-functioning autism or Asperger syndrome who manage to arrive at belief attribution and self-consciousness, but only by 'a slow and painstaking learning process (ibid. 2). And in spite of all effort, the understanding of mental states developed by these individuals remains rather different from the effortless, automatic, intuitive grasp of the normal pre-schooler (ibid. 7). This 'mind-blindness' betrays a psychological *struggling* about many aspects of self and others, where normally there is a comfortable *certainty*. Accounts from patients of Asperger syndrome invariably relate the difficulty of what normally *comes naturally*:

> Autism makes me hear other people's words but be unable to know what the words mean. Or autism lets me speak my own words without knowing what I am saying or even thinking.
>
> ibid. 15

> It was ages before I realised that people speaking might be demanding my attention ... you have to work so hard in order to understand speech ... trying to speak is quite an effort.
>
> ibid.

In many delusional beliefs also, we find the pathological exceptions that confirm the rule: for instance, the conviction that thoughts are constantly being inserted into our brain (psychiatrically identified as the Delusion of Thought Insertion), or that we are dead (the Cotard Delusion).[31] Normal, ineffable, recessive certainty about our fellow humans having thoughts, feelings, desires, beliefs; about our being alive and not dead, *can* and *does* break down, or can be altogether absent. There *is* an 'outside' possibility of the absence, betrayal or breakdown of objective certainty, and so objective certainty *does*, however recessively, deserve its name.

Delusional beliefs and autistic behaviour attest, then, to the breakdown or absence of some first-person and third-person basic certainties, but there exists a less familiar disability that has struck me as particularly apposite here. It is called *dyssemia,* a term coined in 1992 by psychopathologists Stephen Nowicki and Marshall Duke, to refer to a 'nonverbal social communication deficit' which manifests itself as a 'difficulty (*dys*) in using nonverbal signs or signals (*semes*)' (1992, 18):

> By nonverbal signs we mean all human responses that are not words (either spoken or written) but convey meaning, especially emotional meaning. Nonverbal behaviours include facial expressions, tone and inflection of voice (paralanguage), body movements and posture (sometimes called kinesics), gestures and touching, use of personal space (proxemics), and rhythm and use of time (chronemics).
>
> 2002, 5

In much the same way that dyslexics have difficulty with the written word, *dyssemics* 'cannot understand or 'read' the quieter messages of others' (ibid., 19). For example, a dyssemic child will misread a happy face as an angry one and as a result will return a smile with a frown or glare. Reading faces accurately is only half the story; if the child is affected with *expressive* as well as *receptive* dyssemia, she will also be unable to produce facial expressions that reveal her true feelings: she will unknowingly put on an angry face where she means to smile; or indeed, have a 'negative resting face' – our resting face being the expression we show when we are emotionally in neutral – so that the child looks permanently *intensely* angry. The problem may also be one of *modulation*: a person may be unable to smile in moderation; if he tries to smile, he has to laugh out loud (ibid., 88). Duke and Nowicki photographed dyssemic children who had been asked to make facial expressions reflecting *various feelings*; all the photographs turned out to look essentially *the same*. The children were unaware of it, but they were using *the same facial expressions* to communicate *different emotions* (ibid., 87).

Besides *facial* dyssemias, there are *gestural* and *postural dyssemias*, where for example words are paired with a gesture of opposite meaning, or a slouching-resting posture is adopted though the person is highly interested in what is being said. There are also *spacial or territorial dyssemias*, where individuals unknowingly infringe or violate other people's space: for example, a dyssemic individual will move up to within an inch of another person's nose to speak to them, or choose the seat next to the only other person in an empty theatre, or get into an elevator last and stand facing and looking straight at the people already there, rather than, say, turn around to face the door, or look at the changing floor numbers.

One easily imagines the reactions to these socially inept behaviours: a dyssemic girl who looks angry when she thinks she looks happy will prompt a negative response. And of course these predictable reactions only highlight the existence of solid and unmistakable norms or expectations. That, as the authors write: 'other children *cannot help but* respond to her as if she were upset" (ibid., 12; my emphasis) says as much about the pathology as about the normality. The majority of normal children, when presented with clear-cut, basic, unambiguous (cf. LW II, 59) samples of facial expressions – what Wittgenstein would call the 'simple cases' (LW I, 967) – and asked to identify them, have no trouble doing so.[32] So that Nowicki and Duke are convinced that 'although the grammar of the nonverbal language is unwritten, there are still rules for its use': *'residual rules'* – these are the nonverbal rules for any given situation, and they are only noticed when they are broken.[33] Dyssemia, then, provides us with the pathological flipside to an otherwise default certainty regarding *basic* facial expressions, gestures, postures etc.

The point here is not to eradicate indeterminacy, but to recognize that there are *basic* regularities in the 'hurly burly of human action' (Z 567), and that these are what shape our psychological bedrock or psychological grammar. This, without losing sight of the fact that 'simple language-games [...] are *poles* of a description, not the groundfloor of a theory' (RPP I, 633; my emphasis). So that, *pace* Lagerspetz, we, as philosophers and psychologists, do have a need for 'the language of certainty'. The concept of objective certainty is needed for when the 'residual rules' are violated, to explain the exceptional, cases[34]. As Wittgenstein writes:

> After all, there could be someone who had serious, hopeless doubts about others. But how would he act? (Like a lunatic.)
>
> LW I, 248

8. Scepticism about other minds

Whereas, as we shall see in the Epistemology section of this volume, *On Certainty* focuses on defeating external world scepticism,[35] in his philosophical psychology, Wittgenstein can be said to rebut scepticism about other minds. In both cases, he rebuts the sceptic by showing that knowledge is our secondary, not our primary, assurance; and it vitally rests on a nonepistemic certainty that is *logically* invulnerable to doubt. This gives us a version of Wittgenstein's rebuttal of other-mind scepticism that is more robust than Michel ter Hark's. As ter Hark sees it, first–third person asymmetry allows us to confound the sceptic's *comparative* argument that first-person knowledge is superior to, because more immediate than, third-person knowledge by replying that there is no question of knowledge *at all* in the first-person: we do not 'know' ourselves directly or indirectly[36], and therefore the comparison is otiose (cf. 1990, 129). What I am suggesting is a stronger, more positive, rebuttal of scepticism, resulting from Wittgenstein's realization that some third-person psychological certainties are as *logical* or *indubitable* as some first-person certainties; that I *am* as *logically certain* of others having a mind as I am of having a mind myself. Our certainty about other minds is an *Einstellung zur Seele*. Not a *knowing* at all, but a condition for knowledge; or as Winch says, a *condition* I am in vis-à-vis other human beings. Moreover, the insight that, in some cases, we *are* logically certain of what someone else is feeling makes the positing of a default theory of mind otiose.

There are (fictional or pathological) contexts in which a human being comes to know that others have minds, but in normal circumstances, we do not come to know such things. Our belief in other minds is not a hypothetical belief, but an instinctive, nonepistemic attitude; not resulting from inference, it is not open to falsity or mistake. It may be open to pathological failure, but then this, as we have seen, is only the exception that confirms the rule.

Part Three

Epistemology

Having, in the Investigations, *put the 'animal' back in language, Wittgenstein allows the 'animal' to surface in epistemology – making clear, for philosophy at large and not only epistemology, that just as thought is not prefaced by yet more thought, neither is knowledge fundamentally underpinned by yet more knowledge: 'I know my way about in a room: that is, without needing a moment's reflection, I can find the door, open and shut it, use any piece of furniture, I don't have to look for the table, the books, the chest of drawers or think what can be done with them. That I know my way around will come out in the freedom with which I move about in the room. It will also be manifested in an absence of astonishment or doubt. Now what answer am I to make to the question: whether this knowing-one's-way-around-in-this-room is a state of mind?' (RPP I, 295). Wittgenstein shows that the ultimate ground of knowledge does not consist of judgments or propositions, but of our animal or unreflective actions and reactions that evolve into content-laden thought and action. We do not go from proposition to deed, but vice-versa: from a non-reflective grasp to a sophisticated one; from doing to judging and thinking. In this section, we see how Wittgenstein veers us away from our 'propositional presumption', a symptom of our intellectualizing propensity, which misleads us into seriously envisaging an illogical/impossible radical scepticism and an illogical/impossible radical relativism. As he does away with propositional knowledge at the foundation of thought, Wittgenstein dissolves the possibility of radical doubt; and as he makes clear that our epistemic assurances are not ultimately founded on judgments but on 'the common behaviour of mankind', he dissolves the possibility of radical relativism.*

8

Wittgenstein on Knowledge and Certainty

In *On Certainty*, Wittgenstein subverts the traditional picture of basic beliefs. They are not indubitable or self-justified propositions, but animal certainties. With the word 'animal', he does not mean to reduce these basic certainties to brute impressions or to intuitions, but to say that they are nonreflective and nonpropositional. So that what philosophers like Descartes and Moore put forward as propositions susceptible of falsification and thereby of scepticism are in fact heuristic formulations of certainties whose status is logical or grammatical, and whose only occurrence *qua* certainty is in action – that is: in what we say (e.g., 'I'll wash my hands') and in what we do (e.g., we wash our hands). So that although they often look like empirical conclusions, our basic certainties do not constitute objects of knowledge but rather the ungrounded, necessary, nonpropositional basis of knowledge. This chapter delineates Wittgenstein's route to this conclusion, while countering the epistemic and/or propositional readings of 'hinge propositions' put forward by Michael Williams, Crispin Wright, Annalisa Coliva and Duncan Pritchard. It is argued that only a nonepistemic and nonpropositional reading of hinge certainty allows it to solve epistemology's core problem: the infinite regress of justification.

Wittgenstein's last notes were posthumously entitled *On Certainty*. They constitute his attempt, prompted by G. E. Moore's 'Proof of an External World', to understand the nature of our basic assurance – our assurance about such things as 'Human beings are born and die', 'The earth has existed long before I was born', 'I am standing here', 'I have a body', 'Here is a hand'.[1] As he develops his thought, Wittgenstein employs and considers several options besides 'certainty', but what he rules out from the outset is that this assurance is a *knowing*: 'If you do know that *here is one hand*, we'll grant you all the rest' (OC 1). Of course, he does not leave it there; much of *On Certainty* is devoted to fleshing out the distinction between certainty and knowledge.

1. Certainty vs knowledge

In seeking to describe a certainty that he cannot prove and that nevertheless seems to him the most indubitable of all, Moore (1939) refers to it as 'knowledge' because that is to him the concept that expresses the greatest degree of conviction on our epistemic continuum. Wittgenstein agrees that these objects of Moore's assurance are those of our most unquestionable beliefs, but disagrees that the certainty in question is of an epistemic nature; he believes this assurance to be of a more foundational breed than knowing:

> When I say 'how do I know?' I do not mean that I have the least *doubt* of it. What we have here is a foundation for all my action. But it seems to me that it is wrongly expressed by the words 'I know'.
>
> OC 414

Why does Wittgenstein not take this certainty to be a knowing? Because he adheres to the standard view of knowledge as justified true belief:

> One says 'I know' when one is ready to give compelling grounds. 'I know' relates to a possibility of demonstrating the truth.
>
> OC 243

> If Moore says he knows the earth existed etc., most of us will grant him that it has existed all that time, and also believe him when he says he is convinced of it. But has he also got the right ground for his conviction? For if not, then after all he doesn't know.
>
> OC 91

For Wittgenstein, our certainty that the earth existed long before we were born cannot be said to be *justified*, for it was never *verified*: 'I did not get my picture of the world by satisfying myself of its correctness; nor do I have it because I am satisfied of its correctness' (OC 94). In fact, unlike the objects of our *knowledge*, we have probably never even thought about many of the objects of our basic certainty:

> I believe that I had great-grandparents, that the people who gave themselves out as my parents really were my parents, etc. This belief may never have been expressed; even the thought that it was so, never thought.
>
> OC 159

Of course, we can formulate our certainty of these truisms, and this is what Moore does, but he mistakes these formulations for *epistemic claims*. This is where Wittgenstein corrects him. He takes Moore to task for confusing knowledge with the nonepistemic brand of conviction that logically underlies it, and he drives a categorial wedge between them: '"Knowledge" and "certainty" belong to different *categories*' (OC 308). In doing this, Wittgenstein breaks with the traditional presupposition in epistemology that we *know* our basic beliefs. On his view, beliefs are not necessarily propositional attitudes, and basic belief is described as a nonpropositional attitude: a belief *in*, not a belief *that*; a trust or taking-hold (e.g., OC 150; 509–11). As we shall see, this is not incompatible with taking them to be expressions of rules of grammar.

But in spite of Wittgenstein's categorial distinction, some commentators of *On Certainty* insist on seeing the certainty that underpins our knowledge as itself knowledge. As Michael Williams puts it: 'Knowledge . . . emerges out of prior knowledge'

(2001, 176). To concede that this does not require that the prior knowledge be individually generated but can be 'a shared and socially transmitted accomplishment'[2] (ibid.) does not take away from its conceptual link to truth and (ultimate) justification. Moreover, though Williams acknowledges a default background and a pragmatic component of this background, on his view, our 'bedrock certainties' are unavoidably propositional. For, he asks, how could our basic beliefs *not* be propositional, if they are to generate our nonbasic beliefs:

> However basic knowledge is understood, it must be capable of standing in logical relations to whatever judgements rest on it. For example, it must be capable of being consistent or inconsistent with them. But this means that even basic knowledge must involve propositional content....
>
> 2001, 97

But the message of *On Certainty* is precisely that knowledge does not have to be at the basis of knowledge. For Wittgenstein, underpinning knowledge are *not* default justified propositions that must be susceptible of justification *on demand* but, as we shall see, nonpropositional certainties – certainties 'in action' or ways of acting – which can nevertheless be expressed verbally, and whose conceptual analysis uncovers their function as unjustifiable *rules of grammar*. (Note: the fact that they can be expressed verbally does not imply they would have propositional content, for expressions of rules have no propositional content.) Hence basic certainties stand to our nonbasic beliefs, not as propositional beliefs stand to other propositional beliefs, but as rules of grammar stand to propositional beliefs. Knowledge need not emerge from knowledge: 'For why should the language-game rest on some kind of knowledge?' (OC 477).

To say that our basic certainties, or 'hinge certainties', or 'hinges', as I shall interchangeably call them[3] (following OC 341: 'the *questions* that we raise and our *doubts* depend on the fact that some propositions are exempt from doubt, are as it were like hinges on which those turn') underpin knowledge is not to say that knowledge is all they underpin. As Wittgenstein writes: they 'form the foundation of *all* operating with thoughts (with language)' (OC 401; my emphasis), of our language games (OC 403) – which means that they are as much the basis of our false beliefs as of our true ones. Our basic certainties make up our world picture, which Wittgenstein refers to as a 'mythology' (OC 95), not in the sense that it is a mystifying picture, but in the sense that it is a picture that is not *grounded* in – that is, *justified by* – science (knowledge).

The nonepistemic nature of hinge certainties is ascertained by the logical absence of justification and verification as regards our assurance of them.[4] This shall now be fleshed out in an examination of the other features shared by hinge certainties that further preclude their being knowledge claims.

2. The necessary features of hinge (basic) certainty

Wittgenstein's deliberations in *On Certainty* bring him to see that our basic certainties share the following conceptual features; they are *all*:

- *nonepistemic*: they are not known; not justified
- *indubitable*: doubt and mistake are *logically* meaningless as regards them
- *foundational*: they are the unfounded foundation of thought
- *nonempirical*: they are not conclusions derived from experience
- *grammatical*: they are rules of grammar
- *nonpropositional*: they are not propositions
- *ineffable*: they are, qua certainties, ineffable
- *enacted*: they can only *show* themselves *in* what we say and do

Having discussed the first feature, I now turn to the others.

3. *Indubitability*: doubt and mistake are logically meaningless

'There are cases where doubt is unreasonable, but others where it seems logically impossible' (OC 454), writes Wittgenstein. Our hinge certainties are not objects of subjective or psychological conviction, but of logical conviction: 'I cannot doubt this proposition *without giving up all judgement*'[5] (OC 494; my emphasis). Doubt here is tantamount to having lost the bounds of sense: 'If someone said to me that he doubted whether he had a body I should like him to be a half-wit' (OC 257).

Nor is it possible to be *mistaken* about a hinge certainty: if I believed that I am sitting in my room when I am not or that my biological parents are wolves, it isn't my possibly being mistaken that would be under investigation, but my sanity, or, at any rate, my knowledge of English. A mistake results from negligence, fatigue or ignorance. We cannot say of someone who believes that cats grow on trees, or that the world does not exist, that he is 'mistaken':

> In certain circumstances a man cannot make a *mistake*. ('Can' is here used logically, and the proposition does not mean that a man cannot say anything false in those circumstances.) If Moore were to pronounce the opposite of those propositions which he declares certain, we should not just not share his opinion: we should regard him as demented.
>
> OC 155

In thus *logically* closing the door to doubt and mistake as regards our hinge certainties, Wittgenstein closes the door to universal scepticism, and thereby also to the *contextualism* Michael Williams attributes to him (1991, 26). On Williams' neo-Humean reading,[6] Wittgenstein believes sceptical doubt to have no bearing in the pragmatic air of ordinary life, but to be legitimate and serious in the context of philosophical reflection. But this is a misreading: for Wittgenstein, the Cartesian demon is *never* a plausible threat; he has no more grip in the philosophical study than he does in our ordinary life. According to Wittgenstein, there can be *no context* in which our hinge certainties can be doubted or justified, for their indubitability is *conceptual*, not *contextual*. It isn't a *hinge* that can be doubted in some contexts and not in others; but a hinge can *never* be doubted whereas the *doppelgänger* of a hinge can be,[7] and this misleads Williams into thinking the hinge itself can, in some contexts, be doubted. An example of an empirical *doppelgänger* of our normally basic certainty of having two hands is the proposition 'I have two hands" uttered by someone able to make sure from removing the bandages that were concealing his wounded hands (OC 123).

What may have given Williams the impression that Wittgenstein adheres to contextualism is the difference he marks in *On Certainty* between the use of 'I know ...' in ordinary life and its use in philosophical discourse:

> What I am aiming at is also found in the difference between the casual observation 'I know that that's a ...', as it might be used in ordinary life, and the same utterance when a philosopher makes it.
>
> OC 406

But Wittgenstein suggests we treat these knowledge claims differently not because he thinks we *know* our basic certainties in ordinary life and not in the philosopher's study, but because Moore's being a philosopher ought to constrain him to use 'I know ...' with technical precision; that is, exclusively in cases of true justified belief.[8] This cannot be demanded of the ordinary person, however: we cannot and should not expect her to use 'I know ...' only when she means 'justified true belief' by it. As is well known, Wittgenstein refuses to admonish or correct our *ordinary* use of language, but the *philosopher* must be made accountable:

> So if I say to someone 'I *know* that that's a tree', it is as if I told him 'that is a tree; you can absolutely rely on it; there is no doubt about it'. And a philosopher could only use this statement to show that this form of speech is actually used. But if his use of it is not to be merely an observation about English grammar, he must give the circumstances in which this expression functions.
>
> OC 433

> For when Moore says 'I know that that's a ...' I want to reply 'you don't *know* anything!' – and yet I would not say that to anyone who was speaking without philosophical intention.
>
> OC 407; original emphasis

And so, according to Wittgenstein, a non-philosopher may say: 'I know ...' in cases where a philosopher may not, but this does not imply that the non-philosopher *knows* where the philosopher does not.

It isn't, as Williams claims, that sceptical doubts are *unnatural doubts* (1991, 2), and therefore sustainable only in the artificial or unnatural conditions of philosophical reflexion, but that they are *not doubts at all*. Williams seems not to have noted that, in *On Certainty*, Wittgenstein elucidates the concept of doubt in two ways: he shows that universal doubt is impossible and that not everything that has the *appearance* of doubt *is* doubt:

> If someone said that he doubted the existence of his hands, kept looking at them from all sides, tried to make sure it wasn't 'all done by mirrors', etc., we should not be sure whether we ought to call that doubting. We might describe his way of behaving as like the behaviour of doubt, but his game would not be ours.
>
> OC 255

In some cases, what looks like doubt is only *doubt behaviour*. Of course, where doubt has no rational motivation or justification, it may have (pathological) *causes* (OC 74), but normal doubt must have *reasons*. It isn't enough to *say* or *imagine* we doubt: genuine doubt, like suspicion, must have *grounds* (OC 322, 458). If Williams thinks sceptical doubt possible, it is because – like Moore and most philosophers since Descartes – he takes the mere *articulation* of doubt for doubt:[9] 'One gives oneself a false picture of *doubt*' (OC 249).

Wittgenstein's recognition that the sceptic's doubt is only doubt behaviour is spurred by his realization that it is hinged on the very certainties it dismisses. For, were she not hinged on some certainties, the sceptic could not even formulate her doubt:

> If I wanted to doubt whether or not this was my hand, how could I avoid doubting whether the word 'hand' has any meaning? So that is something I seem to *know* after all.
>
> OC 369

> But more correctly: The fact that I use the word 'hand' and all the other words in my sentence without a second thought, indeed that I should stand before the abyss if I wanted so much as to try doubting their meanings – shews that absence of doubt belongs to the essence of the language-game, that the question 'How do I know ...' drags out the language-game, or else does away with it.
>
> OC 370

Its being essential to our making sense means that this certainty underpins all our questions and doubts (OC 341), including the sceptic's (attempted) universal doubt, thereby invalidating it. At 'the foundation of all operating with thoughts (with language)' (OC 401) is an essential certainty, a certainty endorsed every time a doubt (towards it) is formulated. What we have here is a knock-down objection to universal scepticism.

Although Hume may be seen to have progressed from Descartes when he admits that sceptical doubt is not sustainable in ordinary life,[10] it takes Wittgenstein to recognize that universal doubt is not sustainable at all, inside the study or out – and this, not for pragmatic but for conceptual reasons: 'A doubt that doubted everything would not be a doubt' (OC 450); 'If you tried to doubt everything you would not get as far as doubting anything. The game of doubting itself presupposes certainty' (OC 115). Wittgenstein has demystified sceptical doubt; he has shown that the sceptic is only under an *illusion of doubt* (OC 19).

Basic certainty, as depicted by Wittgenstein and as it operates in our life, cannot be subsumed under 'knowledge', for it has no truck with truth or justification. To say that hinges are logically indubitable is not to say that they are *necessarily true*. There is no question of truth or falsity in the bedrock: 'If the true is what is grounded, then the ground is not *true,* nor yet false' (OC 205). The indubitability of our hinge certainties does not result from our having confirmed them, but stems from their not being susceptible of confirmation or falsification at all. Hinges are *logically* impervious to doubt. At some point, justification and doubt lose their sense; where the spade turns, there is the ungrounded ground where 'justification comes to an end' (OC 192).

4. *Foundational*: hinge certainties are the unfounded foundation of thought

In spite of the abundance of foundational images and remarks, commentators have denied the presence of foundationalism in *On Certainty*[11] on the grounds that basic certainties, as depicted by Wittgenstein, lack some of the traditional features of foundational beliefs. But, as previously mentioned, Wittgenstein's hinge certainties have their place in a foundationalist structure as the grammatical underpinnings of our beliefs. That is a *modification* of foundationalism, not the absence of it.

There can be no mistaking Wittgenstein's foundationalism; it is both explicitly stated – 'At the foundation of well-founded belief is belief that is not founded' (OC 253); 'What we have here is a foundation for all my action' (OC 414); 'the matter-of-course foundation for ... research' (OC 167) – and repeatedly illustrated: our basic certainties are said to be like the 'substratum of all [our] enquiring and asserting' (OC 162), 'the rock bottom of my convictions' (OC 248).[12] What is also clear is that their ungrounded or unjustified nature is not a pragmatic but a logical feature of hinges: 'it belongs to the *logic* of our scientific investigations that certain things are *in deed* not doubted' (OC 342; first emphasis mine). In fact, Wittgenstein explicitly denies that absence of justification as regards basic beliefs might be due to practical considerations: 'But it isn't that the situation is like this: We just *can't* investigate everything, and for that reason we are forced to rest content with assumption' (OC 343; original emphasis). He is unequivocal in declaring that 'the end [i.e., our basic belief] is not an ungrounded presupposition (OC 110) and that he does not want 'to regard this certainty ... as something akin to hastiness or superficiality' (OC 358).

For Wittgenstein, it isn't, as Williams suggests, that the justificatory process need not *actually* occur (though grounds must be produced on demand), or that it need not be self-conscious (2001, 35), but that hinge certainty is groundless by nature: 'I want to conceive it as something that lies beyond being justified or unjustified' (OC 359). If our certainty stems, or could stem, from justification, it is not a *hinge* certainty: 'I did not get my picture of the world by satisfying myself of its correctness' (OC 94).

Crispin Wright holds a view in substance not very different from that of Williams. He accepts the groundlessness of what he calls 'hinge propositions' while at the same time upholding (what he takes to be) their rational nature. He seeks to do this by thinning down the type of rationality at work here. Wright argues that absence of justification does not imply absence of a warrant to believe; there is 'a type of rational warrant which one does not have to do any specific evidential work to earn'; this nonevidential or 'unearned warrant' or 'warrant for nothing', he also calls 'entitlement'

(2004a, 174). It is an 'entitlement to trust' and trust, though not as robust as belief proper when it comes to rationality, 'is not per se irrational'; Wright still finds enough reason in trust: 'Entitlement is rational trust' (2004a; 194). How rational? The prevailing answer seems to be: that our forming basic beliefs 'falls short of the ideals of our reason' does not prevent it from being rational; we accept strategic entitlement in order to avoid *cognitive paralysis* (2004b, 50), and so there is still rational merit here. By now, however, it has become clear that the rationality in question is pragmatic, and not properly cognitive or epistemic; that the substance of Wright's argument lies in pragmatism, and so the same objections apply to him as to Williams (above). A more recent attempt at adulterating reason without emasculating it completely is Wright's suggestion that 'basic judgements' are made 'for *no reason that can be captured via the modus ponens model*' rather than 'made for *no reason at all*' (2007, 499). However, having rightly rejected John McDowell's account of reasons furnished by experience as inadequate, Wright does not then offer an account of his own, therefore making no advance on his attempt to dilute Wittgenstein's groundless certainty into a certainty with *some* grounds (reasons) – of the pragmatic kind. Pace Williams and Wright, for Wittgenstein, basic certainty is where reasons or justifications come to an end, full stop. His is a logical, not a pragmatic, account of some things having to hold fast for us if we are to speak and act sensically.

That hinge certainties lack some of the features of foundational beliefs as traditionally conceived should not prevent them from being foundational. In fact it is precisely their differing from the rest of our beliefs in being nonpropositional and nonepistemic that makes for the success of Wittgenstein's foundationalism. It is the realization that what we have traditionally taken to be propositional beliefs, rationally posited or arrived at, are in fact ungrounded or logical ways of acting that allows Wittgenstein to put a stop to the regress of justification.

5. *Nonempirical*: hinge certainties are not conclusions derived from experience

If our hinge certainties are not arrived at by reasoning, they are not arrived at by induction either. In *Philosophical Investigations*, Wittgenstein asks:

> 'The certainty that the fire will burn me is based on induction.' Does that mean that I argue to myself: 'Fire has always burned me, so it will happen now too?' Or is the previous experience the *cause* of my certainty, not its ground?
>
> PI 325

And in *On Certainty*, he replies:

> The squirrel does not infer by induction that it is going to need stores next winter as well. And no more do we need a law of induction to justify our actions or our predictions.
>
> OC 87

Of course, many natural phenomena are unquestionably predictable – e.g., that human beings are born and die, that mountains don't spring up in a day. On an empirical reading, our basic certainties are rational conclusions that we come to (tacitly or not) from having observed such regularities. Wittgenstein opposes this: 'No, experience is not the ground for our game of judging. Nor is its outstanding success' (OC 131). But to say that our certainties are not *grounded* (that is, *justified*) by regularity of experience and recurrent success is not to rule out *all* impact of experience on our certainty. Recurrent experience and success sometimes do contribute to our certainty, but they do so non-inferentially and non-inductively; that is, through *conditioning*,[13] not reasoning – 'Indeed, doesn't it seem obvious that the possibility of a language-game is *conditioned* by certain facts?' (OC 617). This is what Wittgenstein means when he speaks of experience as a *cause* rather than a *ground*: 'This game proves its worth. That may be the cause of its being played, but it is not the ground' (OC 474).

We think we come to the basic certainty that 'Human beings need nourishment' in the same way we come to a conclusion from reasoning. This confusion is due to our assuming that some reasoning must always take place for certainty to occur: 'Normal thought envelops even our basic judgements with a rhetoric of reasons', notes Wright (2007, 140). But Wittgenstein insists that although we do invariably invoke (an implicit) reasoning to explain our most basic beliefs, in fact no such reasoning takes place: we do not arrive 'at the conviction by following a line of thought' (OC 103; 84). Our hinge certainty is not rational but a-rational, animal: 'I want to conceive it as something that lies beyond being justified or unjustified; as it were, as something animal' (OC 359). Whether it starts out as instinctive (e.g., our certainty of having a body) or is the result of conditioning (e.g., 'This is (what we call) a table'), hinge certainty is best described as an involuntary reaction, and not as a thought:

> It is just like directly taking hold of something, as I take hold of my towel without having doubts.
>
> OC 510

> And yet this direct taking-hold corresponds to a *sureness*, not to a knowing.
>
> OC 511

Hinge certainty is not the result of judgement; that is the province of knowledge. Knowledge is *rationally grounded* in reality, in nature, in experience: 'Whether *I know* something depends on whether the evidence backs me up or contradicts me. For to say one knows one has a pain means nothing' (OC 504). And in the same way that it is nonsensical to say 'I *know* I have a pain' as if I had discovered it by observation, it is nonsensical to claim that 'I *know* I exist' or 'I *know* external objects exist' for the same reason.

That our hinges cannot be the result of verification does not mean that *some* of them (e.g., 'I speak French') could not be verified and confirmed by someone other than ourselves; it is simply that our own certainty is not grounded on any reasoning or verification, be it our own or someone else's. My certainty that I speak French, that I exist, that I am sitting at my desk, or that human beings need nourishment to exist is as logical and unreasoned as '2 + 2 = 4'. It is a certainty that is not *justified* by reality (thereby guaranteeing the autonomy of grammar), but *logically* underpins all I can say or doubt about reality. In order for our words and deeds to make sense, we must take as starting points such regularities as 'Human beings need nourishment'; what Wittgenstein has understood is that these are not empirical, but *logical* (or grammatical) starting points.

6. *Grammatical*: hinge certainties are rules of grammar

Passages in *On Certainty* point out a peculiarity of Moore-type certainties, such as 'There exists at present a living human body, which is *my* body', 'This body was born at a certain time in the past' (1925, 33). They look like empirical propositions, but what they express is indubitable, nonhypothetical. In fact, we can say of them what we say of mathematical sentences: 'Dispute about other things; *this* is immovable – it is like a hinge on which your dispute can turn' (OC 655).

Wittgenstein asks himself whether Moore-type certainties might be a kind of hybrid, but this possibility does not pass muster. It is not that rule and empirical proposition merge into one another (OC 309), but that what *looks like* an empirical proposition is not always one. Here again, as is so common in our philosophical speculations, we are misled by *form*:

> That is, we are interested in the fact that about certain empirical propositions no doubt can exist if making judgements is to be possible at all. Or again: I am inclined to believe that not everything that has the form of an empirical proposition *is* one.
>
> OC 308

Wittgenstein's view is that Moore-type propositions, though they have the form of empirical propositions, are in fact rules of grammar:

> So one might grant that Moore was right, if he is interpreted like this: a proposition saying that here is a physical object may have the same logical status as one saying that here is a red patch.
>
> OC 53

> When Moore says he *knows* such and such, he is really enumerating a lot of empirical propositions which we affirm without special testing; propositions, that is, which have a peculiar logical role in the system of our empirical propositions.
>
> OC 136

'A peculiar logical role': in other words, a grammatical role. As Wright puts it: 'the unwavering – dogmatic – confidence we repose in these propositions ... attaches to them in their role as in effect rules' (2004a, 35–6). But what Wright does not see is that inasmuch as hinge certainties are rules, they cannot be propositions, empirical or otherwise. This is not a mere technical point: the non-propositionality of basic certainties is one with their being 'animal'. And if for Wright: 'There is no animal in epistemology!' (Kirchberg 2003, Q&A), Wittgenstein has no qualms about saying that he wants to conceive of certainty as 'something animal' (OC 358–9).

7. *Nonpropositionality*: hinge certainties are not propositions

It can be argued that for Wittgenstein, for a sentence to be a proposition, it must be susceptible of truth or falsity.[14] Inasmuch as a rule is neither true nor false,[15] rules are not propositions. Hinge certainties being grammatical rules, and therefore neither true nor false (OC 205), are not propositions: '... the ground is not *true* nor yet false' (OC 205). Indeed, one passage in *On Certainty* leaves no doubt as to the nonpropositionality of our fundamental certainties: 'the end is not certain propositions' striking us immediately as true' (OC 204). So why does Wittgenstein, in other passages, refer to our fundamental beliefs as 'propositions'? The inconsistency is partly[16] justified by the fact that the nonpropositionality of hinges is not immediately clear to Wittgenstein in *On Certainty*, and so out of philosophical habit and in reference to Moore's 'propositions', he calls these certainties 'propositions'. Of all the insights Wittgenstein comes to in *On Certainty*, basic beliefs being ways of acting (and not propositions striking us as true) is the most groundbreaking, and must therefore have been the most difficult to come to. He does, however, come to it here:

> Giving grounds, however, justifying the evidence, comes to an end; – but the end is not certain propositions striking us immediately as true, i.e. it is not a kind of *seeing* on our part; it is our *acting*, which lies at the bottom of the language-game.
>
> OC 204

While Annalisa Coliva and Duncan Pritchard both agree that hinge certainty is nonepistemic, they find my nonpropositional reading of hinges problematic. This seems to reflect the general resistance of epistemologists in admitting the 'animal' into their midst. Here is Coliva:

> I ... think that Wittgenstein's definitive view on the nature of certainty wasn't that it is of an animal, non-propositional nature. But, of course, there is no denying that, at least at places, he also talked of this kind of certainty. Hence, the question is: how do the propositional and the non-propositional account of certainty go together, if they do?
>
> 2010, 172–3

Coliva's way of reconciling the two is to see hinges as judgements (and therefore propositions) that have a normative role (and therefore nonpropositional; they are, like rules, exempt from doubt) (2010, 80). This is not the view, explicitly voiced by Wittgenstein, that the same sentence can at one time express a judgement and at another a rule of testing (OC 98), but that a 'hinge proposition' is both at once:

'"Here is my hand", "The Earth has existed for a very long time", "My name is AC" ... play a normative role, while also being judgements'. This, claims Coliva,

> ... can be evinced from the fact that they constitutively contribute to the determination of what would count as, for instance, normal conditions of perception, evidence for or against historical or geological empirical judgements, normal conditions of human functioning and so on.
>
> 2010, 142

But I fail to see how this makes them judgements. If I appeal to '2+ 2 = 4' or 'This is (what we call) red' or 'Human beings die' as 'evidence' (say to a child, a non-English speaker or an alien), I am not appealing to a judgement[17].

Pritchard also finds the nonpropositional reading of hinges problematic, particularly because of what is known in the literature as 'the closure principle'. This is how he succinctly puts it:

> The key difficulty facing the non-propositional reading is to see how it ultimately amounts to anything more than simply embracing a mystery.... How could one recognise that a certain historical event (e.g., the battle of Austerlitz) took place at such-and-such a date, and that this entails that the universe has been around for more than 5 min, and yet not adopt a positive propositional attitude (e.g., belief, or something similar) to the entailed proposition?
>
> 2012, 266

I see no mystery here. I would reply that 'The universe has been around for more than 5 minutes' is not an 'entailed proposition' at all but a formulation of the certainty on which recognizing that the Battle of Austerlitz took place in 1805 is hinged. It may look like an entailment, but is only an apparent or otiose entailment. We have not deduced the certainty that the universe has been around for more than five minutes from recognizing that the battle of Austerlitz took place in 1805, for that certainty logically *underpinned* that recognition. The claim that the Battle of Austerlitz took place in 1805 could not be meaningfully formulated were it not for the underlying certainty that the universe has existed for more than five minutes. However, rather than the latter, Pritchard chooses to place an *über hinge* as the underlying certainty. What is this, and why do that?

Pritchard agrees that at the basis of of our rational practices is an arational, nonpropositional commitment, but he must reconcile this with what he takes to be the entailment of 'hinge *propositions*'. He does this by suggesting we think of 'hinge propositions' as

> ... in effect just *exemplifying a general hinge conviction that we are not fundamentally in error in our beliefs about the world*. That general conviction, however, need not take the form of a commitment to any particular proposition, even though it might manifest itself in various commitments to specific propositions which exemplify that general conviction.
>
> 2011, 282; my emphasis

So that the general conviction, which he calls an '*über* hinge commitment' (2012, 267) provides the needed nonpropositional basis, while the *specific* hinge commitments take the form of (entailed) propositions. This is how we get the essential nonpropositionality as well as the putatively required propositionality. The hinge *proposition* 'The universe has been around for more than five minutes' would then be the entailed expression of the nonpropositional *über*-hinge commitment that one is not radically and fundamentally mistaken in one's beliefs.

My first remark here is that Pritchard's *über*-hinge commitment – 'We are not fundamentally in error in our beliefs about the world' – seems to be a *reification* of an aspect of hinge certainty or of a hinge certainty. If, as Pritchard writes (above), the general conviction need not take the form of a commitment to any particular proposition, how does an *über*-hinge commitment manifest itself before it gets codified? Is it a kind of general trust without an object? Are we hinge-committed to nothing before the general hinge commitment gets individualized? This sounds like a general force distributed amongst occurrences, and smacks of the metaphysical. The kind of picture (e.g., of the will) Wittgenstein tried to wean us away from.

On my reading, hinge certainties are nonepistemic, nonpropositional, unjustified certainties that can only manifest themselves as ways of acting. These ways of acting in the certainty of *x*, can be philosophically rendered as grammatical rules or as nonpropositional beliefs or beliefs-*in*, and this applies to all our hinges. Putting these certainties into words for the benefit of philosophical elucidation is a mere heuristic aid; it no more makes our certainties into propositions than the alleged codifications of a general hinge commitment does.

On Pritchard's view, rejecting the closure principle puts the nonpropositional reading in a quandary 'given that we do seem very able to formulate the propositions expressed in hinge commitments, and recognise their logical relationships to other propositions which we rationally believe and know' (2012, 269). But the fact that we are able to formulate our hinge commitments should not lure us into thinking that this evinces their propositionality; as to the logical relationship between hinges and propositions, it is that between rules and propositions. And it is precisely their being rules that makes hinges *logically* ineffable in the language-game.

8. *Ineffability*: hinge certainties are *logically* ineffable

Articulating a hinge certainty in the language-game does not result in a display of certainty, but in a display of nonsense. It is perceived as queer (OC 553); incomprehensible (OC 347); a joke (OC 463); a sign of madness (OC 467); or a piece of philosophy (OC 553, 347, 463, 467). This is because grammatical rules are *nonsense*:[18] they *have* no sense they *determine* sense. 'This rod has a length' is, on Wittgenstein's view, as nonsensical as 'This rod has no length': the latter is nonsense in that it contravenes a rule of grammar; the other in that it *expresses* a rule of grammar (PG 129). This explains why he writes '"There are physical objects" is nonsense' (OC 35). It is nonsense because it expresses a hinge certainty and a hinge certainty functions like a grammatical rule.

To utter a hinge in the flow of ordinary discourse is to utter nonsense; it is to utter a rule where no rule is needed. If I were to say to the cloakroom attendant as I hand him my token: 'This is a token', he would look at me perplexed. Why am I saying this? 'The background is lacking for it to be information' (OC 461); the information the attendant requires in order to retrieve my coat is what the number on the token is. *That this is a token* is the ineffable hinge upon which his looking for the number on the token – and eventually my coat – revolves. Our shared certainty that 'this is a token' can only *show* itself in our normal *transaction* with the token; it cannot *qua certainty* be meaningfully *said*. To utter a basic certainty *within* the language-game invariably *arrests* the game[19]. Conversely, think of the fluidity of the game poised on its invisible hinges: I hand the attendant my token, he glances at the number on it and fetches my coat. Our foundational certainty is operative only *in action*, not in words.

We might be tempted to think that the ineffability of hinge certainties in the language-game makes them mere Gricean implicatures, those 'bizarre things we "should not say" [but which] would, for all that, be true', as Charles Travis puts it (1997, 95). But it is precisely this reference to truth – as also the implicatures' conceptual link with intentionality, knowledge and inference – that preclude any nontrivial rapprochement between them and hinges.[20] To say that hinge certainties are ineffable is not merely to point out the superfluity of articulating the obvious; it is to stress their logical unsayability. For Wittgenstein, sayability is internally linked to meaning and use:

> Just as the words 'I am here' have a meaning only in certain contexts, and not when I *say* them to someone who is sitting in front of me and sees me clearly, – and not because they are superfluous, but because their meaning is not *determined* by the situation, yet stands in need of such determination.
>
> OC 348; first emphasis mine

In certain contexts, the words 'I am here' *are* sayable (say, in a game of blind man's buff where a child lets his playmate know: 'I am here'); in other contexts, where the same words serve neither to inform, nor to express or describe, they are useless, and therefore meaningless: *they say nothing*.[21] It is important, however, not to confuse the relevance of context here with Michael Williams's *contextualism*. As we saw earlier, for Wittgenstein, our hinge certainties are *conceptually*, not *contextually*, nonepistemic and indubitable: if something is susceptible to doubt, it is not a hinge certainty (though it may look like one).

Basic certainty is a kind of nonpropositional, inarticulate, animal trust in certain things: 'I want to regard man here as an animal; as a primitive being to which one grants instinct but not ratiocination' (OC 475). Moore and Wittgenstein have given some of our certainties articulation. This is important in that it allows us to individuate and elucidate the objects of our basic certainty, but it can also be misleading: it can give the impression that our basic beliefs are propositional, epistemic and intellectual. We must remember that formulating and elucidating our animal certainty does *not* make it into an intellectual or propositional certainty.[22] Our hinge certainty is animal through and through. We can verbalize it, but the verbalization of a hinge certainty is never an *occurrence* of hinge certainty. As G. H. von Wright puts it: 'the fragments of a world-picture underlying the uses of language are not originally and strictly *propositions* at all. The pre-knowledge is not propositional knowledge. But if this foundation is not propositional, what then *is* it? It is, one could say, a *praxis*' (1982, 178). Our hinge certainty manifests itself exclusively *in action*. It is, as we shall see, a *logic in action*.

9. Enacted: hinge certainties can only *show* themselves *in* what we say and do

As Wittgenstein writes: 'it is our *acting*, which lies at the bottom of the language-game' (OC 204). Indeed Moore's *saying* 'I know that "here is a hand"' conveyed no certainty that was not already *visible* in his speaking about his hand, in his ostensibly *showing* it to his audience, or simply in his unselfconsciously *using* it. In the same way, our certainty that 'Tables, chairs, pots and pans do not think' shows itself in our *treating* them as unthinking, inanimate objects. Our hinge certainty that 'There are physical objects' shows itself in our *reaching out* to pick a flower, but not a thought. Hinges are grammatical rules, whose only manifestation *qua* hinge certainty is in action:

> That is to say, it belongs to the logic of our scientific investigations that certain things are *in deed* not doubted.
>
> OC 342

In deed [*in der Tat*], certain things are not doubted. Logic is embedded in our practices – in our *deeds*: 'Children do not learn that books exist, that armchairs, exist, etc., etc., – they learn to *fetch* books, *sit* in armchairs, etc., etc.' (OC 476; my emphasis). Our life, *our deeds,* show that we do not, *cannot* doubt some things if we are to proceed to doubt and knowledge.

With *On Certainty* we come to see that basic beliefs are not propositional beliefs that lie dormant in some belief-box tacitly informing our more sophisticated thoughts. The hinge belief verbalized as: 'I have a body' is a disposition of a living creature that manifests itself in her *acting in the certainty of having a body*. When asleep or unconscious, this belief remains a disposition, but becomes occurrent in any normal use she makes of her body[23] – e.g., in her eating, running, her *not* attempting to walk through walls as if she were a disembodied ghost. The occurrence of certainty resembles an instinctive reaction, not a tacit belief. My hinge certainty that 'I have a body' is much the same as a lion's instinctive certainty of having a body. In both cases, the certainty manifests itself in acting embodied; in my case, however, it can also manifest itself *in* the verbal references I make to my body, as when I say 'I lost weight'. Similarly:

> Doesn't "I know that that's a hand", in Moore's sense, mean the same, or more or less the same, as: I can make statements like "I have a pain in this hand" or "this hand is weaker than the other" or "I once broke this hand", and countless others, in language-games where a doubt as to the existence of this hand does not come in.
>
> OC 371

Their being ineffable does not prevent our hinges from showing themselves *in* what we say, but here too, certainty is beyond being justified or unjustified – in every case, something animal (OC 359).

10. A striated bedrock: A taxonomy of hinges

All our hinge certainties share certain features, which we have just examined. But they don't all share them in the same way. All hinges are foundational, but some are *universally* so, others only *locally* so. All our certainties are unfounded, but some because they are instinctive, others because their acquisition is effected through training or repeated exposure. But whatever their origin – whether they were or not inculcated as rules of grammar – all our hinges function as rules of grammar: they *condition* meaning. Being rules, they cannot be falsified but some can be abandoned, become obsolete, while others cannot (their rejection would 'drag everything with it and plunge it into chaos' (OC 613)). So that its uniform conceptual nature notwithstanding, the bedrock is stratified. The following taxonomy is not Wittgenstein's; it aims to harness the variegated examples of hinges used in *On Certainty* into a more manageable, and more perspicuous, presentation[24]:

1) **linguistic hinges**: e.g.: '2 + 2 = 4', 'What the colour of human blood is called', 'What is called "a slab" / "a pillar"', 'Which colour is meant by the word blue', 'This colour is called blue / green (in English)', 'The words composing this sentence are English', 'A is a physical object' (OC 455, 340, 565, 545, 126, 624, 158, 36).

2) **personal hinges**: e.g.: 'For months I have lived at address A', 'I am now sitting in a chair', 'I am in England', 'I have never been in Bulgaria / Asia Minor', 'I have never been on the moon', 'I have just had lunch', 'The person opposite me is my old friend so and so' (OC 70, 552–3, 421, 269, 419, 111, 659, 613).

3) **local hinges**: e.g.: 'There is an island, Australia', 'No one was ever on the moon', 'It isn't possible to get to the moon', 'The earth is round', 'Trains normally arrive in a railway station' (OC 159, 106, 106, 291, 339).

4) **universal hinges**: e.g.: 'The earth exists', 'There are physical objects', 'Things don't systematically disappear when we're not looking', 'If someone's head is cut off, the person will be dead and not live again', 'Trees do not gradually change into men and men into trees', 'I am a human being', 'I have forbears' (OC 209, 35–6, 234, 274, 513, 159, 234).

The grammatical status of the first subset is obvious; they are what Wittgenstein, before *On Certainty* and after the *Tractatus*, calls 'grammatical rules'. These are not themselves an object of analysis in *On Certainty*, but are mentioned as a benchmark against which the more problematic grammatical or logical nature of the other three types of hinges is measured.[25] So as to distinguish them from the generic group of *grammatical* rules, I have called them *linguistic hinges*. The certainties that make up the second group have to do with our individual lives; those of the third group belong, or have belonged, to the world picture of a community of people at a given time: (e.g., 'The earth is flat', 'The earth is round'; 'Human beings cannot go to the moon'; 'Human beings can go to the moon'). Some of these hinges (e.g., 'Human beings can go to the moon') have an empirical origin, but it is not as empirical propositions that they have fused into the foundations.[26] Other hinges (e.g., 'Human beings cannot go to the moon) have been ousted from bedrock (as rules that have become obsolete). But not all hinges are susceptible of expulsion; it is impossible to dislodge from the foundations of thought hinges such as 'Human beings have been to the moon'. The fourth group is made up of *universal* hinges; these are certainties which are foundational for all normal human beings.

The last three sets of hinges – which can be referred to as: 'nonlinguistic hinges' – might not appear to be plausible candidates for the role of grammatical rules, but we must remember that status is not determined by appearance but by use, and that for Wittgenstein 'What belongs to grammar are all the conditions (the method) necessary ... for the understanding (of the sense)' (PG 88). Our hinge certainties are all part of this 'method':

> I should like to say: Moore does not *know* what he asserts he knows, but it stands fast for him, as also for me; regarding it as absolutely solid is part of our *method* of doubt and enquiry.
>
> OC 151

11. Conclusion

Far from devaluing knowing, Wittgenstein reaffirms its role in our epistemic practices, but he also makes two major adjustments: first, he removes knowledge from its position as the most fundamental of our assurances; and second, he points out the erroneous conflation of knowing and claiming to know that results from our impression that the latter, when done in earnest and in the appropriate circumstances, guarantees knowledge (OC 21). In the position traditionally held by knowledge, Wittgenstein places certainty – a certainty that is both animal and logical. By this he means that its indubitability, though essential to our making sense, is not the result of thought and can only manifest itself as a way of acting.

The sceptic may then claim partial victory in Wittgenstein's affirmation that we don't *know* that external objects exist or that we are not brains in vats; but the more radical victory is on the side of certainty: 'That is to say, it belongs to the logic of our scientific investigations that certain things are *in deed* not doubted' (OC 342). With this, Wittgenstein recognizes that the real certainty that underpins our questions and investigations – in fact, all that we say and do, our language-games, generally – is an enacted, not a propositional certainty:

> But is it wrong to say: 'A child that has mastered a language-game must *know* certain things'?
>
> If instead of that one said 'must be *able to do* certain things', that would be a pleonasm, yet this is just what I want to counter the first sentence with.
>
> OC 534

And with this, Wittgenstein's enactivism impacts epistemology.

I have attempted in this chapter to elucidate Wittgenstein's account of hinge certainty by fleshing out the features that define it. Other commentators have, in their own accounts, left out some of these features: hinge certainty has been deemed epistemic but not justified; nonepistemic but not animal; unreasoned but not arational; arational but propositional; nonpropositional but not completely; and so on. These come down to two main difficulties: it is difficult for epistemologists to give up the idea that knowledge is our fundamental form of conviction. This would mean, as Pritchard puts it, 'granting that an awful lot of what we take ourselves to know is in fact unknown' (2012, 268–9). But that is psychologically repugnant for philosophers to say they don't 'know' that the earth exists, etc., is a psychological, not a logical difficulty (for our more fundamental certainty is there to make scepticism logically nonsensical). Once this is crossed, the next real barrier is nonpropositionality. Propositionality is difficult for the epistemologist to give up because its absence makes room for the 'animal' in epistemology; with nonpropositionality, we seem to give up our grip on the rational. But what *On Certainty* shows us is that our distrust of the arational (the animal) and our reliance on propositions are excessive. It is only by realizing that putting ways of acting into propositions is an artificial intellectualization designed to harness the animal, that we can take, as Wittgenstein did, the uncompromisingly revolutionary step to stop the regress of justification.

9

Too Cavellian a Wittgenstein

Wittgenstein's Certainty, Cavell's Scepticism

This chapter argues that Stanley Cavell's Modernist Wittgenstein is an overly Cavellian Wittgenstein. Wittgenstein's philosophy is not, as Cavell claims, permeated with a nostalgia for metaphysics, a dissatisfaction with language and criteria, an ineluctable scepticism – all prompting existential devastation and angst. I argue that Cavell reads his own preoccupations into Wittgenstein and this prevents him from seeing that, for example, Wittgenstein's certainty logically dismisses scepticism. Cavell's Wittgenstein is still a groundbreaking philosopher, but seen through Cavell's modernist glass darkly, his philosophy breeds disappointment, alienation and scepticism where it in fact sows enlightenment, community and certainty.

Modernism is notably difficult to circumscribe and, therefore, whether or not Wittgenstein is a Modernist will be equally so. If modernism is broadly defined as a dissatisfaction with the past or present mostly due to a crisis of representation, a case can be made for Wittgenstein's modernism. But modernism is more pointedly characterized as also including a distrust of language (its reliability or adequacy) along with a will, penetrated by a rejection of certainty, to overcome scepticism. For some commentators of Wittgenstein, notably Stanley Cavell, these traits also characterize Wittgenstein's philosophy. I will argue, mostly contra Cavell, that they do not. This would preclude Wittgenstein – both early and late – from being a modernist in any but a broad, vague sense.

My aim in this chapter is to show that Cavell's Modernist Wittgenstein is too Cavellian. Wittgenstein's philosophy is not – as Cavell claims it is – permeated with: (1) a nostalgia for metaphysics; (2) a dissatisfaction with language and criteria; (3) an ineluctable scepticism; all prompting (4) Existential devastation and angst. I will not deal with these themes seriatim but rather allow them to occur naturally in the course of the argument. I will conclude that Cavell reads his own preoccupations into Wittgenstein and that this prevents him from seeing that Wittgenstein's certainty logically dismisses scepticism. Cavell's Wittgenstein is still a groundbreaking philosopher, but seen through Cavell's modernist glass darkly, his philosophy breeds disappointment, alienation and scepticism where it in fact sows enlightenment, community and certainty.

Before examining what Cavell has to say about the Wittgenstein of the *Investigations*, I will briefly argue that the early Wittgenstein's view of language is not as bleak as it is often made out to be.

1. Tractarian language and silence

Dissatisfaction with language is characteristic of Modernism, something Ben Ware confirms in his recent book *Dialectic of the Ladder: Wittgenstein, the* Tractatus *and Modernism*:

> Modernism's deepest loneliness is rooted in its feeling of dissatisfaction with everyday or ordinary language. This dissatisfaction finds itself expressed in a number of different and often radically contradictory ways. On the one hand, we find a number of key modernist writers attempting to emancipate, to clarify, or to purify language, because, as they see it, language is being blocked, denatured or contaminated by the modern world. On the other hand, we find many writers preoccupied with the acute failure of language in the face of modern experience; and we thus see in their work a turning towards the themes of ineffability and science. Both of these trends ... perceive everyday language to be fundamentally inadequate.
>
> 2015, 119–20

Ware finds that '[n]umerous attempts have been made to locate the *Tractatus* somewhere on this modernist-linguistic spectrum. In addition to the "limits of language" readings ..., exegetes have interpreted the work as striving towards the ideal of "linguistic purity" or as attempting to express the "disenchantment of language, its systematic failure to put experience into words"' (2015, 120).

I agree with Anat Matar that the *Tractatus* is expressive of the crisis of representation and the demise of eternal metaphysical and ethical truths, but I do not see it as revealing the depths of the hubris embedded in the Western conception of language in its affirmation that all philosophers can do is demonstrate the failure to formulate meaningful philosophical propositions (2006, Chapter 1). Somewhat related to this view is the *reductively therapeutic* (henceforth, referred to simply as '*Therapeutic*') reading of Wittgenstein.[1]

The upshot of the *Therapeutic* reading is that it leaves (and says Wittgenstein leaves) nothing positive in its wake; at least, nothing but dissolution: the dissolution of images or views. Granted, therapy aims to change our attitude – rightly curing philosophers from a metaphysico-scientific tendency to theorize and explain, leaving us with a relatively untendentious attitude to the world – but the last thing the *Therapeutic* philosopher hopes we get from this is a new view.[2] As David Stern succinctly puts it: 'On [the Cavell / Therapeutic] reading, the aim of Wittgenstein's dialogues is not to lead his reader to any philosophical view, neither an idealised, frictionless theory of language, nor a pragmatic theory of ordinary language, but rather to help us through such ways of speaking and looking' (1996, 444). But the *Therapeutic* reading fails to grasp that there is a difference between a tendentious view and a perspicuous one, and that Wittgenstein *does* want to give us the latter. As Brian McGuinness writes: 'The therapy is not just a catharsis: there is an element of seeing the world aright at the end' (2012, 267).

It is a commonplace to think of the *Tractatus* as silencing us. Yet listen: 'What we cannot speak about we must pass over in silence' (TLP 7). Does 'what we cannot speak about' or 'being passed over in silence' mean: not being susceptible of expression at all? Of course not. For 'speaking' here has a specific, narrow definition which does not exclude other kinds of expression. What we *can* speak about, what *can* be said, Wittgenstein tells us, are the propositions of natural science (6.53). That is, what can be true or false; what is verifiable: empirical propositions. What, on the other hand, cannot be said is what can neither be confirmed nor refuted by experience. This is why the propositions of logic say nothing (5.43); and why the ethical and the aesthetic are not sayable (6.421). Our words will give us 'facts, facts, and facts but no Ethics' (LE 40). The 'mere description' of the facts of a murder, in all its physical and psychological detail, 'will contain nothing which we could call an *ethical* proposition. The murder will be on exactly the same level as any other event, for instance the falling of a stone' (LE 39). This is a version of the fact–value distinction. Value cannot be said because all that can be said is natural (or factual) meaning, and value is supernatural. This does not mean that value finds no expression; only that its expression is not, and should not be confused with, empirical or natural/factual expression. The ethical value of the murder cannot be *said* for there are no ethical propositions; it can only *show* itself *in* what is said.

In 'On Heidegger on Being and Dread', written in 1929 (the same year as the *Lecture on Ethics*), Wittgenstein writes:

> Man feels the urge to run up against the limits of language. Think for example of the astonishment that anything at all exists. This astonishment cannot be expressed in the form of a question, and there is also no answer whatsoever. Anything we might say is *a priori* bound to be nonsense. Nevertheless we do run up against the limits of language.... This running-up against the limits of language is *ethics*.
>
> WVC 68

Here again, the tendency is to think of the 'limits of language' as an ineptitude of language, and of nonsense as gibberish. The former is a misreading of Wittgenstein, and the latter a reductive reading. In this passage, the human urge to collide with the limits of language – that is with the ineffable and the nonsensical – is the urge, discouraged by Wittgenstein in the *Tractatus*, to say something where nothing can be said. But this, in keeping with earlier remarks in the book, should be taken to mean: not to treat as an empirical proposition (i.e. to *say*) something which is not an empirical proposition; as for instance, treating the astonishment that anything at all exists as an empirical proposition, as something that can be a claim (a question), rather than as something that underpins all questions and cannot itself be questioned. I do not hear, in the above passage, Wittgenstein expressing his frustration with the expressive or descriptive potential of language, but only his warning that a category mistake is being made in our urge to treat the logical as empirical; to mistake the unquestionable (of which the ethical and the logical are part) for empirical propositions.

What is ineffable is of great value to Wittgenstein, from beginning to end. It is a mistake on the part of the *Therapeutes* to have sought to minimize its importance and to disparage what they called 'Ineffabilists' – philosophers who, like Peter Hacker, see some nonsense as 'illuminating' – for 'chickening out'; for not being 'resolute' enough to recognize that all nonsense is 'plain nonsense', i.e., gibberish. They reduced all nonsense to gibberish in spite of such passages in the *Tractatus*[3] as:

> There are, indeed, things that cannot be put into words. They make themselves manifest. They are what is mystical.
> 6.522

> My propositions serve as elucidations in the following way: anyone who understands me eventually recognizes them as nonsensical....
> 6.54

To read Wittgenstein here as rejecting his own philosophical remarks is to fail to see that there are multifarious ways for something to be nonsense, and that they are not all derogatory.[4] Such a reductive interpretation is due to a default derogatory understanding of nonsense, an understanding singled out by the *Therapeutic* reading of *nonsense* as uniquely and necessarily gibberish, and of *ineffability* (and the related distinction between saying and showing) as something Wittgenstein is merely parodying. The latter in spite of such clear pronouncements by Wittgenstein as that 'the unutterable will be – unutterably – *contained* in what has been uttered' (EL 7), and testimony by Engelmann that 'Wittgenstein passionately believes that all that really matters in human life is precisely what, in his view, we must be silent about'[5] (EL 97). Language remains essential even where it only stages, rather than articulates, meaning – as in literature, where language is used to create the context necessary for the important unutterable to show itself[6]. For Wittgenstein, silence is not always a muting of meaning but often a manifestation (showing) of meaning.

The first Wittgenstein is not a sceptic about language. In seeking to explain what he means by absolute or ethical value, he says that the experience *par excellence* that would describe it is that of 'wonder at the existence of the world' – a wonder that cannot be *said* and is nonsensical because only empirical propositions have sense and can be said (TLP 6.53): 'it is nonsense to say that I wonder at the existence of the world, because I cannot imagine it not existing' (LE 41-2). There is no linguistic scepticism here. The sensicality of language is affirmed when it comes to empirical propositions; and when it comes to ethics, aesthetics, mysticism, their meaning cannot be said but can be shown in the use of language, as for example, in literature[7].

Wittgenstein came to add many tools to the linguistic toolbox, but I do not see him ever retracting his position on the ineffable nature of ethics, aesthetics and the mystical; and, indeed, he adds certainty to the list of the important ineffable.[8] These are not instances of language going on holiday, but cases where language is wrongly taken to be empirically *saying* because 'man feels the urge to run up against the limits of language' – the urge, that is, to see truth and falsity in what are logico-grammatical limits, *bounds of sense*. There is, then, no dissatisfaction with language on the part of the early Wittgenstein, but only an attempt at a more perspicuous ordering, or presentation, of language. What about the later Wittgenstein?

2. The estrangement of the ordinary

For Wittgenstein, 'the method of philosophy' is 'the perspicuous presentation of grammatical/linguistic facts' (P 171); indeed, the 'concept of a perspicuous presentation is of fundamental significance for us. It earmarks the form of account we give, the way we look at things' (PI 122). A 'perspicuous presentation' requires that the philosopher look with renewed attention at that which, in ordinary life, we no longer see for having it constantly before our eyes. The philosophical gaze at the ordinary must be sufficiently distanced or naive (rid of prejudice) so as to perceive the ordinary as unfamiliar or strange – that is *estranged* – and proceed to a more perspicuous vision and presentation of it. But, unlike Cavell, I don't see that Wittgenstein finds the ordinary *uncanny* or the sought-after strangeness *worrisome*.[9] In a 2002 interview in French, Cavell says about the Freudian notion of 'inquiétante étrangeté' that it is 'also present in Wittgenstein, slightly differently, but present':

> What happens in Wittgenstein? In the activity of our life, we are in the middle of an activity of language: we speak, we buy, we do things, and all of a sudden we stop in order to realize that we do not understand what we are doing. And then, as we reflect on that, we do not understand what we are in the middle of saying. And so it is in this series of stages that there is for me in Wittgenstein an experience very similar to that of the uncanny.
>
> 2002a; my translation

I must say I have no idea where Cavell finds this problematization of the ordinary in Wittgenstein other than in the distanciation or estrangement which I spoke of just now and which is not at all worrying, but sought after and positive. Cavell goes as far as to say that '[t]he everyday is what we cannot but aspire to, since it appears to us as lost to us' (1986, 107), but this seems to me an exalted formulation of the fact that Wittgenstein sees the ordinary as rendered opaque by familiarity. Wittgenstein is merely saying that the quotidian loses its vitality and clarity because it is always in front of our eyes and we no longer pay attention to it. There is in Wittgenstein a sense in which the ordinary is *lost* and then *recovered* or *rediscovered* but only in the banal sense of our having to recover, as adults – and more specifically as philosophers – the lost primitive or naive perception of reality we had as children. This does not imply that Wittgenstein perceives the ordinary as perpetually lost, as lost to scepticism, and us as consequently *homeless*. There is no sense, in Wittgenstein, of *homelessness* or *exile* from the world; no *anguish*, upon our return, at not finding the ordinary exactly as we left it, and so of our perceiving it as *uncanny* (1986, 100), as, upon each return, the 'invasion of a familiar by another familiar' (2002a; my translation). It seems to me that here

Cavell has applied his modernist stamp on Wittgenstein. Granted, Wittgenstein wants to make the ordinary an object of reflexion, but not because he finds it threatened by scepticism (1986, 114). Cavell is wrong to say that 'the *Investigations* ... is written in continuous response to the threat of skepticism' (1986, 106) – even where he associates such scepticism with a distrust of language.[10]

3. Language is in order as it is

No doubt, Wittgenstein's remark 'Philosophy is a battle against the bewitchment of our intelligence by means of language' (PI 109) contributed to Cavell finding in PI a suspicion of language that would have led Wittgenstein to scepticism

> It seems to me that the originality of the *Investigations* is a function of the originality of its response to skepticism, one that undertakes not to deny skepticism's power (on the contrary) but to diagnose the source (or say the possibility) of that power, to ask ... what it is about human language that allows us, even invites us, to repudiate its everyday functioning, to find it wanting.
>
> 1986, 106–07

We'll come back to scepticism; what I first want to question is the idea that Wittgenstein finds, or suggests we should find, ordinary language 'wanting'.

There is no question that Wittgenstein complains, throughout his work, about the potentially confusing nature of ordinary language: he notes its misleading uniformity in the *Tractatus,* where he thanks Russell for 'showing that the apparent logical form of a proposition need not be its real one' (TLP 4.0031); remarks in the *Blue Book* on the confusion provoked by 'the outward similarity between a metaphysical proposition and an experiential one' (BB 55f); and cautions us in the *Investigations* that we can be confused by 'the uniform appearance of words when we hear them spoken or meet them in script and print. For their *application* is not presented to us so clearly' (PI 11). And finally in *Remarks on Colour*[11] and *On Certainty,* he notes that it is easy to take a sentence that has only the *form* of an empirical proposition for an empirical proposition, whilst adding that in such cases we can always count on the function of the sentence to decide. Once we consider function, many sentences that resemble empirical propositions reveal themselves as rules of grammar.[12]

The outward similarity in language causes 'deep disquietudes' (PI 111) in that a simile can be absorbed in the forms of our language and mislead us (PI 112), but these disquietudes do not prompt in Wittgenstein the desire for a more transparent language. He finds language perfectly in order as it is, and says so clearly in the *Tractatus,*[13] as well as in the *Investigations*:

> On the one hand it is clear that every sentence in our language 'is in order as it is'. That is to say, we are not *striving after* an ideal, as if our ordinary vague sentences had not yet got a quite unexceptionable sense, and a perfect language awaited construction by us. – On the other hand it seems clear that where there is sense

there must be perfect order. – So there must be perfect order even in the vaguest sentence.

PI 98

In light of this, is Cavell entitled to say that the originality of the *Investigations* lies in its diagnosis of scepticism as an interrogation of what it is 'about human language that allows us, even invites us, to repudiate its everyday functioning, to find it wanting' (1986, 107)? I think not. The problem does not stem from language, but from our inattention to differences and our propensity to over-extend our concepts.[14] And correction is at the philosopher's fingertips: all she needs to do is 'not to be misled by the appearance of a sentence and to investigate its application in the language-game' (Z 247), thereby 'clarify[ing] our use of language' in order to avoid 'the misleading analogies in our use of language' (P 163). It is therefore a problem that has its solution, and not a problem that leads to scepticism. The confusion produced by language is neither inevitable nor omnipresent, and the philosopher intervenes only where language seems to have gone on holiday:

> The confusions which occupy us arise when language is like an engine idling, not when it is doing work.
>
> PI 132

> We are interested in language only insofar as it gives us trouble. I only describe the actual use of a word if this is necessary to remove some trouble we want to get rid of. Sometimes I describe its use if you have forgotten it. Sometimes I have to lay down new rules because new rules are less liable to produce confusion or because we have perhaps not thought of looking at the language we have in this light.
>
> AWL 97

So the philosopher's task is to 'remind' us of the grammar of our language, or indeed to *create new rules of grammar*. The latter would be propitious not only in the case of philosophers, but also cognitive scientists, needing to be weaned away from such misleading pictures or habits of thought as those that conflate mind and brain. A new grammatical rule here might be: 'The brain is not the mind.' The philosopher's task, then, is to put order in our concepts, to rearrange them:

> The philosophical problem is an awareness of disorder in our concepts, and can be solved by ordering them.
>
> BT 309

I don't see Wittgenstein here finding in ordinary language a strangeness so worrisome that it leads him to scepticism.[15] The *solution* to the disorder *sometimes* caused by language is, he insists, at the philosopher's reach.

Cavell well understands that 'Wittgenstein's motive ... is to put the human animal back into language and therewith back into philosophy', but he qualifies this by adding that Wittgenstein 'never underestimated the power of the motive to reject the human: nothing could be more human' (1979, 207). The will to reject the human is what we might call the metaphysical impulse. Cavell is right to say that Wittgenstein does not underestimate its force, but he is less right to think that the *Investigations* captures the disappointment felt by humans in dropping from metaphysical heights to the inadequacy of all too human criteria. Cavell seems to succumb here to a nostalgia for the metaphysical which leads him to scepticism, but he is wrong to believe that Wittgenstein shares both the nostalgia and the scepticism.

Wittgenstein is not disappointed by ordinary language or its functioning; he does not hanker after the fixity of sense, as Cavell thinks he does, because he does not believe in the fixity of sense, and because for him sense is not lost for being dependent on use. On Cavell's view, Wittgenstein sees the power of the metaphysical impulse to be such that it induces our exile from world and word, and this in perpetuity; whereas, in fact, Wittgenstein sees the metaphysical impulse as a corrigible straying, and the strayed metaphysician's repatriation to the rough ground as possible and even possibly definitive in that it only requires the dismantling of the linguistic trap that led to the straying in the first place. For Wittgenstein, bringing 'words back from their metaphysical to their everyday use' (PI 116) is indeed rediscovering criteria, but this doesn't lead, as it does for Cavell, to discovering the truth of scepticism.

In hankering after a metaphysics he does not in fact believe in, Cavell resembles Nietzsche's *Gay Science* nihilist who admonishes atheists (himself included) for having killed God. The fact that God never existed does not prevent or diminish his nostalgia, which is fuelled by the negativity of scepticism in a non-metaphysical world. For Cavell, falling from the metaphysical fixity of meaning to the rough ground where meaning depends on agreement or criteria leaves meaning open to the disagreement and instability that make scepticism ineluctable; for, criteria are not 'serious contenders in the battle to turn aside skepticism' (1979, 7). And to think that Wittgenstein believes otherwise is, says Cavell, to misunderstand him:

> If the fact that we share, or have established, criteria is the condition under which we can think and communicate in language, then scepticism is a *natural* possibility of that condition; it reveals most perfectly the standing threat to thought and communication, that they are only human, nothing more than natural to us. One misses the drive of Wittgenstein if one is not ... sufficiently open to the threat of scepticism (i.e. to the skeptic in oneself); or if one takes Wittgenstein ... to deny the truth of scepticism.
>
> 1979, 47

4. The disappointment with criteria

Cavell insists on the disappointment that criteria cause us[16] and denies that they can refute scepticism or that Wittgenstein thought they could (1979, 329):

> ... the major claim I make in the *Claim of Reason* about Wittgenstein's idea of a criterion, namely that while criteria provide conditions of (shared) speech they do not provide an answer to sceptical doubt. I express this by saying that criteria are

disappointing, taking them to express, even to begin to account for, the human disappointment with human knowledge.

1988, 87

Cavell sees Wittgenstein's notion of criteria as generative of scepticism towards language and knowledge. The natural or communitarian condition of language – the fact that meaning and knowledge are dependent on criteria – makes language constitutionally open to the sceptical threat in that criteria are too weak to prevent imitation and deception, and therefore mistake. But this alarmist (to put it mildly) interpretation of the second Wittgenstein overlooks the explicit message of the third Wittgenstein – as much in the *Writings* and *Remarks on the Philosophy of Psychology* as in *On Certainty* – which is that imitation and deception (and therefore the possibility of mistake) are only possible because deployed on a basis of certainty: 'That an actor can represent grief shows the uncertainty of evidence, but that he can represent *grief* also shows the reality of evidence' (LW II, 67). The very possibility of uncertainty or doubt depends on a backdrop of certainty: 'Doubt itself rests only on what is beyond doubt' (OC 519), and so 'the *questions* that we raise and our *doubts* depend on the fact that some propositions are exempt from doubt' (OC 341). Contra the sceptic, Wittgenstein maintains that we cannot always be deceived because deception or dissimulation is *not* always possible. To the question 'Is it thoughtlessness not to keep the *possibility* of pretence in mind?' (RPP II, 591), Wittgenstein's answer is clear:

> Dissimulation is *nothing* but a particular case; we can regard behaviour as dissimulation only under particular circumstances.
>
> LW I, 252

If deception is not a universal or systematic possibility, neither is doubt, and therefore scepticism is not sustainable. There are, on Wittgenstein's view, cases where we *cannot* be mistaken for there is no logical place for mistake; and this is so even in cases of third-person psychological 'judgements': 'Just try – in a real case – to doubt someone else's fear or pain' (PI 303). And he goes as far as to acknowledge that our certainty about some psychological behaviour is of a logical kind:

> There is an *unmistakable* expression of joy and its opposite.
> ... there *are* cases where only a lunatic could take the expression of pain, for instance, as sham.
>
> LW II, 32–3; emphasis in the original

> ... it isn't true that we are never certain about the mental processes in someone else. In countless cases we are.[17]
>
> LW II, 94

Where Cavell (much like the sceptic) thinks that where there is agreement, disagreement is always possible, Wittgenstein affirms that, even in cases of third-person psychological judgements, 'discrepancy has its limits' (LW II, 21) – in some cases, disagreement can only be pathological.

Though he acknowledges Wittgenstein's affirmation that human beings agree in the language they use (PI 241), Cavell thinks that this agreement is insufficient to ensure meaning or communication:

> We begin to feel, or ought to, that maybe *language* (and understanding, and knowledge) rests upon very shaky foundations – a thin net over an abyss. ... whether or not our words will go on meaning what they do depends upon whether other people find it worth their while to continue to understand us ...
>
> 1979, 178–9

Cavell fears that the dependency of meaning on context, without the underpinning of rules or universals, makes projection and understanding terrifyingly precarious:

> We learn and we teach certain words in certain contexts, and then we are expected, and expect others, to be able to project them into further contexts. Nothing insures that this projection will take place (in particular, not the grasping of universals nor the grasping of books of rules), just as nothing insures that we will make, and understand, the same projections. That on the whole we do is a matter of our sharing routes of interest and feeling, modes of response, senses of humor and of significance and of fulfillment, of what is outrageous, of what is similar to what else, what a rebuke, what forgiveness, of when an utterance is an assertion, when an appeal, when an explanation – all the whirl of organism Wittgenstein calls 'forms of life.' Human speech and activity, sanity and community, rest upon nothing more, but nothing less, than this. It is a vision as simple as it is difficult, and as difficult as it is (and because it is) terrifying.[18]
>
> 2002b, 52; see also 1979 192

Terrifying in that criteria are insufficient to guarantee meaning and ward off scepticism. But this is, I believe, to diminish the importance of language as mastery of a technique (PI 199). On Wittgenstein's view, we are able to project our limited acquired knowledge of language to new situations and contexts precisely because the teaching of language is the transmission of a technique; this, by definition, does not aim for total regulation but for self-regulation and regulation by others. It is criteria that determine whether a speaker is using a word in accordance with the norm that is being inculcated. These criteria are public, not private; and although constraint is necessary, there is no exhaustive determination of use,[19] which allows for and explains the creativity or productivity of language. This is where the teaching of a technique surpasses, say, ostensive definition. As Wittgenstein writes:

> Teaching which is not meant to apply to anything but the examples given is different from that which *'points beyond'* them.[20]
>
> PI 208

To claim that without the grasping of universals or the grasping of books of rules, language is on shaky grounds is to play Chomsky's game. Wittgenstein's answer to

Chomsky would be that technique suffices to regulate use: 'Yes, there is the great thing about language – that we can do what we haven't learnt' (LPP 28). Acquiring language is like learning to walk: the child is stepped into language by an initiator and, after much hesitation and repeated faltering, it disengages itself from its teacher's hold and is able, as it were, to run with the language. The acquisition and use of language do of course involve some hesitation and uncertainty, but let us not confuse that with scepticism. It is Cavell's vision of language as 'a thin net over an abyss' which makes the 'flat repudiation' of scepticism impossible (1979, 192), but that is a vision he should not attribute to Wittgenstein.

Cavell has a profound mistrust of language which he believes Wittgenstein shares. This is what he says in a 2012 conversation with Paul Standish:

> ...there is a dimension of anxiety, of threat, in human conversation and confrontation that the *Investigations* seems to me responsive to; ... this couldn't be so if the possibility of scepticism were not incessantly on its mind ... Wittgenstein gives a portrait of the modern subject that contains issues of diversity and anxiety and sickness and torment. Those are the things that I found in the *Investigations* at the beginning that dissociated my responses from those of virtually all my friends who were reading the work. They took away the pain and solace from the book, which for me was exactly to miss its dark side – its treatment, its recognition of the possibility, even sometimes I say the necessity, of scepticism. I felt this to be ... fundamental to meaning, to speech, to the inherent risk in speech.
>
> 2012, 156

This vision of PI seems to me, as it did to Cavell's friends back then, foreign to PI. It projects a sombre picture of devastation and alienation where I, and most readers, have found community, coherence, sharing, teaching and communication – with errors along the way of course, but these are exceptions that confirm the rule. The rule being that – accidents notwithstanding – traffic flows, and it does so fundamentally, ubiquitously: we can count on it. The *Investigations* have taught me that it is in language, coupled with behaviour, of course, and not 'in the head', that lies my cohesion to the human form of life; and I remain baffled by the idea that what struck Cavell about language in PI are disappointment, distrust and even vacuity:

> The silence in which philosophy begins is the recognition of my lostness to myself, something Wittgenstein's text figures as the emptiness of my words, my craving or insistence upon their emptiness, upon wanting them to do what human words cannot do. I read this disappointment with words as a function of the human wish to deny responsibility for speech.... (Wittgenstein describes the work of philosophy as having to turn our search around, as if reality is behind us), that I have said what there is for me to say, that this ground gained from discontent is all the ground I have, that I am exposed in my finitude, without justification. ('Justifications come to an end' is a way Wittgenstein says it.)
>
> 2001, 353

5. *Certainty* versus sceptical *acknowledgement*

I owe *The Claim of Reason* an initial phenomenological grasp of the Wittgensteinian revolution that no other commentator gave me, but its gloomy, modernist gloss of the *Investigations* is profoundly misleading. And having delved into *On Certainty*, I was convinced that Cavell had either forgotten to read it[21] or had misread it. For to think that for Wittgenstein, the end of justification means the beginning of scepticism, is to understand the opposite of what Wittgenstein means. For Wittgenstein, to be 'without justification' (as when 'justifications come to an end') does not mean to be vulnerable, or exposed in our finitude, but rather: *in*vulnerable. When 'justifications come to an end', it is not that we are at our wits' end but that we have reached the hard rock of certainty: 'If I have exhausted the justifications I have reached bedrock, and my spade is turned' (PI 217). Far from being an epistemic lack, failing or limitation – something that would allow the sceptic to triumph – the absence of justification or grounds (groundlessness) as depicted by Wittgenstein is descriptive of a certainty so robust, so anchored, so unquestionable, that it is not built on the back of justification,[22] but constitutes the logical (i.e. indubitable and necessary) base on which justification, as well as knowledge, must be hinged.[23] Cavell is wrong to think that, for Wittgenstein, the end of justification produces the vertigo of scepticism – on the contrary, it signals the triumph of certainty.[24]

Cavell claims that 'in Wittgenstein's work as in skepticism, the human disappointment with human knowledge seems to take over the whole subject' (1979, 44), but this is to misrepresent Wittgenstein's view of knowledge. Wittgenstein is not 'disappointed' by knowledge; he wants to remind us of its rightful place in our epistemic practices. Throughout his work, he shows that we often say or think we know where we oughtn't to, as when our believing, acting or feeling is neither a justified true belief nor the result of one (e.g., 'I know I'm in pain'). In *On Certainty*, he focuses on this problem, reminding us that knowledge is by definition *grounded* and that, therefore, when Moore speaks of knowledge where there is no logical room for justification, he is making a category mistake (OC 308):

> If Moore says he knows the earth existed etc., most of us will grant him that it has existed all that time, and also believe him when he says he is convinced of it. But has he also got the right *ground* for his conviction? For if not, then after all he doesn't *know*.
>
> OC 91; see also 483–4

The ungrounded nature of Moore's certainty precludes it from being a knowing. This reminder does not smack of alarm or disappointment, but of precision. Wittgenstein is clarifying where knowledge has its place (as justified true belief) and where it does not (Moore-type conviction) and should instead be classed as the most basic of our assurances, which he calls 'certainty'. It is this precision which seems to elude Cavell: he does not see that Wittgenstein makes a categorial distinction between knowledge and certainty,[25] and so conflates them. Not recognizing the place of certainty in Wittgenstein's work, he thinks that in saying that Moore does not know what he asserts he knows, Wittgenstein is acquiescing to the truth of scepticism which Cavell interprets thus: our relation to the existence of the world is not one of *knowing with certainty* but the deeper one of *accepting* or *acknowledging*:

> The answer [to skepticism] does not consist in denying the conclusion of skepticism but in reconceiving its truth. It is true that *we do not know the existence of the world with certainty*; our relation to its existence is deeper – one in which it is accepted, that is to say, received. My favorite way of putting this is to say that existence is to be acknowledged.
>
> 1981, 133; my emphasis

It is clear from this passage that Cavell has not grasped the categorial difference Wittgenstein makes between knowledge and certainty, but there is something in what he says. It is true that, for Wittgenstein, our relation to the existence of the world is something deeper and more immediate than knowing, but is it of a nature similar to Cavell's *acknowledgement / acceptance*?

> . . . we think scepticism must mean that we cannot know the world exists, and hence that perhaps there isn't one . . . . Whereas what scepticism suggests is that since we cannot know the world exists, its presentness to us cannot be a function of knowing. The world is to be *accepted*; as the presentness of other minds is not to be known, but acknowledged. But what is this 'acceptance', which caves in at a doubt?
>
> 2002b, 324

Cavell's reconceiving the truth of scepticism amounts to replacing knowing with acknowledging/accepting; but, however deep and immediate, there is a fissure in Cavell's *acknowledgement/acceptance* which distances it from Wittgenstein's *certainty*: it is susceptible of *avoidance* – indeed 'it caves in at a doubt' – and this is because its nature is psychological,[26] unlike Wittgenstein's *certainty* which is logical:

> I should like to say: Moore does not *know* what he asserts he knows, but it stands fast for him, as also for me; regarding it as absolutely solid is part of our *method* of doubt and inquiry.
>
> OC 151

In fact, the logical nature of Wittgenstein's certainty is such that: 'If Moore were to pronounce the opposite of those propositions which he declares certain, we should not just not share his opinion: we should regard him as demented' (OC 155). Such certainties as the world or other minds existing are not merely *acknowledged*, to be later revisited by doubt; they are *logical* underpinnings of thought. It is such certainties that prevent scepticism from so much as getting off the ground. Cavell is right: it is a mistake to want to stave off scepticism with knowledge, but wrong to think that what replaces knowledge here is *acknowledgement*. Cavell's misunderstanding of Wittgenstein's *certainty* prevents him from seeing that it is categorially distinct from knowledge and that, with it, Wittgenstein unequivocally refutes scepticism.

As Paul Standish rightly remarks: 'Cavell does not accept the received view of Wittgenstein's later work as providing a *refutation* of the sceptic .... In place of the epistemologist's reading of the *Philosophical Investigations* as a refutation of scepticism, Cavell finds in this text a testament to the existential truth in scepticism' (2007, 76–7). That is, Cavell sees scepticism as a human condition: we must learn to live with the clash between our continual temptations to conquer scepticism and our awareness that it can never be conquered. 'I live my scepticism', writes Cavell (1979, 437), because dismissing it would be to dismiss the important existential consciousness of the precariousness of human knowledge, identity and communication.[27]

As I have tried to show, Cavell's reading of Wittgenstein here is a misreading. For Wittgenstein, scepticism is *not* an important, ineluctable truth of the human condition; it is the product of a misunderstanding of our epistemic situation – a misunderstanding that is resolvable, once and for all. All that needs be done is to recognize that scepticism is conceptually untenable: 'If you tried to doubt everything you would not get as far as doubting anything. The game of doubting itself presupposes certainty' (OC 115). For Wittgenstein, scepticism is the result of grammatical confusion: the confusion between knowing and certainty; once the confusion is clarified, scepticism dissolves. Cavell wants to make scepticism an existential condition and therefore remains caught in its net. The problem is that he also tries to entangle Wittgenstein in that net. But Cavell's notion of scepticism is as foreign to Wittgenstein as the existential hell that he thinks also permeates his work:

> ... the human existence that is portrayed in *Philosophical Investigations*, as I see it, is one of continuous compromise with restlessness, disorientation, phantasms of loneliness and devastation, dotted with assertions of emptiness that defeat sociability as they seek it.
>
> 2005, 161

I ask myself: what was Cavell reading? And the only answer I can come up with is that Cavell was reading Cavell into Wittgenstein.[28]

10

Fighting Relativism

Wittgenstein and Kuhn

As Ilham Dilman puts it: 'language is the source of the system we find in nature.' There is no conception of reality independent of language. There are at least three problems with this – Kuhn's and Wittgenstein's – way of thinking: (1) the problem of incommensurability; (2) the problem of idealism – in the case of Kuhn and Wittgenstein, a linguistic idealism; (3) the problem of conceptual relativism. In this chapter, I argue that 'incommensurability' is a non-problem. I then defend Kuhn and Wittgenstein against the charge of linguistic idealism by showing that and how, on their view, our concepts attach to reality. Finally, I deflate the charge of conceptual relativism by arguing that although they reject the existence of an objective basis lying outside all human conceptual frameworks and world-pictures, neither Wittgenstein nor Kuhn endorses an acceptance of all conceptual schemes. In conclusion, however, we shall see that only Wittgenstein finds the stopping-place of relativism – in his (soft brand of) naturalism.

There are at least as many Kuhns as there are Wittgensteins – and, on my count, that makes three.[1] I have made no effort, in this chapter, to keep track of the changes in Kuhn's thought, helping myself simply to what I considered he did best. It is worth noting, however, that some commentators feel that Kuhn became too Wittgensteinian for his own good, particularly when he claimed that carving the world scientifically at its joints is not a matter of discovering already-existing joints, but of language supplying the joints.[2] This is of course frowned upon by scientists and other empiricists who believe that there is a good and a bad way to carve nature at its joints, and all one needs to do to find the right way is to observe the world properly[3]. This is the position of scientific realism, which Kuhn sums up here:

> Boyd [...] presupposes that nature has only one and only one set of joints to which the evolving terminology of science comes closer and closer with time [...] the thrust of his metaphor is ontological; the world to which Boyd refers is the one real world, still unknown but toward which science proceeds by successive approximation.
>
> 2000, 205, 207

Wittgenstein and Kuhn believed there are no joints already in the world; but that we, human beings, make them up. As Wittgenstein writes: 'One thinks that one is tracing the outline of a thing's nature over and over again, and one is merely tracing round the frame through which we look at it' (PI 114). This, however, is not to say that the world is an invention or construction of the creatures that inhabit it, but that languages – not the world – are responsible for the frame, our concepts: 'Creatures born into [the world] must take it as they find it', writes Kuhn: 'it is entirely solid: not in the least respectful of an observer's wishes and desires; quite capable of providing decisive evidence against invented hypotheses which fail to match its behaviour' (2000, 10). There *is* a language-independent world; it is the world about which we speak; the world our languages cut up. What there is *not* is a *conception* of the world independent of language; and inasmuch as there are different languages, there will be different conceptions of the world: 'languages cut up the world in different ways' (ibid., 164).

Having eliminated from our concern the extreme or absolute idealism which takes the world itself to be a human creation, we can focus on the kind of idealism which *should* concern us: that which results from the claim that our language does not follow, or attempt to follow, an existing (if inconspicuous) outline in the world which it is science's business to render more conspicuous; language is itself responsible for the outline. There are at least three problems with this way of thinking:

1. if our accounts of the world are relative to the language in which they are couched, how do different linguistic communities understand each other's respective accounts? The problem here is that allegedly resulting from **incommensurability**;
2. if our accounts of the world are nothing but linguistic projections, how do they attach to the world at all? This is the problem of *idealism* – in the case of Kuhn and Wittgenstein, it would be an 'idealism with a linguistic turn' or what has been called **linguistic idealism**;
3. if there is no neutral, language-independent way of depicting the world, to which our linguistic accounts can refer or appeal to for correction or guidance, *anything goes* – however a particular culture sees fit to describe the world cannot be gainsaid, becomes a benchmark in its own right. There will be as many so-called 'objective' accounts as there are languages. And here we face the problem of **conceptual relativism**.

I'll address these problems in turn.

1. Incommensurability, not incommunicability

For Kuhn and Wittgenstein, there is no objectivity in the Nagelian sense – that is, no 'view from nowhere'.[4] For a view from nowhere requires the absence of a place from which to view, and without a place, there can be no viewer either, and thus no *view*. This isn't to say there would be nothing there, but that it cannot be called a view, a perspective. Removing the perspective is precisely the point of Nagel's image, for a *perceived* reality is necessarily a distorted reality,[5] and the ensuing account of reality will be equally distorted, or subjective. So that, in their quest for an objective basis for knowledge, philosophers have sought to eliminate not so much the viewer – for that would defeat the epistemic enterprise altogether – but the viewer's input into the account: they have sought as impersonal an account as possible. This has meant looking for a basic language or 'brute data vocabulary' consisting of words attached to the world in ways that are unproblematic and independent of theory – a language which would provide a 'common measure' or neutral, mind-*independent* description of the world against which to evaluate our scientific, mind-*dependent* descriptions and theories. For both Kuhn and Wittgenstein, this philosopher's quest for such a language is of no avail.[6] As Kuhn writes:

> The heavens of the Greeks were irreducibly different from ours.... the difference is rooted in conceptual vocabulary. [It cannot] be bridged by description in a brute data, behavioural vocabulary.... No more in the natural than in the human sciences is there some neutral, culture-independent, set of categories within which the population – whether of objects or of actions – can be described.
>
> 2000, 220; see also 162

What we are left with then is a view, necessarily, from somewhere. And that somewhere, for linguistic creatures, is language. As Putnam says: 'We have no other place to stand but within our own language' (1995, 54); and in Kuhn's words: 'we have no access to a neutral sublinguistic means of reporting' (2000, 164). The essential theory-ladenness of language,[7] Kuhn argues, is responsible for incommensurability; that is: for the absence of a common, neutral language in which our theories could be fully expressed, and which could therefore be used in a point-by-point comparison between them (2000, 189). This, however, does not imply that different languages are *utterly* impenetrable to each other; nor does it imply that they are incomparable[8] or have nothing at all in common. The one thing they do *not* have in common is a neutral language from which they might all have emerged or to which they might all refer.[9]

Incommensurability precludes total translatability, but that does not prevent intelligibility, communication, comparability or learnability. Anything lost in translation can be approximated via interpretation, hermeneutics or paraphrase (2000, 45); indeed 'anything that can be said in one language can, with imagination and effort, be *understood* by a speaker of another' (2000, 61). So, Kuhn does not think that incommunication is 'ever total or beyond recourse' (2000, 124); there *is* communication between schemes – certainly, sufficient communication for a member of one scheme to realize *that* the other scheme is different and, often, precisely *where*. We *can* know that the heavens of the Greeks were irreducibly different from ours, in the same way we know that the ancient Greek concept of happiness (*eudaimonia*) was different from ours; we can know this because although their concepts of the heavens and of happiness 'cut across ours', as Wittgenstein would put it (Z 379), the rest of the language is sufficiently transparent, sufficiently close to ours, for us to get the drift. In comparative judgements, notes Kuhn, shared beliefs serve as a platform from which unshared or alien beliefs can be distinguished and evaluated (cf. 2000, 96), though not necessarily *thoroughly* understood or translatable.

For Kuhn, then, two scientific systems are neither wholly opaque, nor fully translatable into one another. As to Wittgenstein, his holding that there are different conceptions of reality in different languages and cultures does not prevent him from asserting that we can and do imaginatively or empathically enter into alien practices, and what is more, that we can see *sense* in them, even where we could hardly see *ourselves* in them (e.g., OC 594–5; Z 368–9; 383–90). On Kuhn and Wittgenstein's view, then, although our conceptual schemes are internally related to our languages, there is sufficient overlap between languages to allow for non-trivial communication, comparison and understanding (cf. OC 524). But if what is sought is something like a Gadamerian 'fusion of horizons', then more is needed; according to both Kuhn and Wittgenstein, something like a 'conversion' must be effected – a conversion, in that a whole world picture would have to be assimilated (OC 92; 1996, 151; 2000, 175), and for that to occur, there must be *participation* in the *practice* or *practices* of the other (OC 315; 2000, 54). So that when Wittgenstein writes that in combatting the man who 'instead of the physicist' consults an oracle, he would give reasons as far as they go, but that '[a]t the end of reasons comes *persuasion*' (OC 612), there is no suggestion here of an abandonment of position or communication, but of a maintenance of position in another, more fundamental, mode of communication.

2. No linguistic idealism

Now that we have ascertained the possibility of communication across conceptual schemes, we are better equipped to ward off conceptual relativism. But first we should try and clarify Wittgenstein and Kuhn's view of the relationship between world and language. For both thinkers, there is no such thing in nature as an outline, a system or a concept; nature is conceptually unmarked; nature simply *is*. The system does not reside in the nature of things, writes Wittgenstein (Z 357). It is we who, with our language, cut paths or inroads of salience and understanding – concepts – that allow us to harness the wild, the contingent, in ways that make and govern sense for us. Wittgenstein takes this harnessing to be not metaphysical, but grammatical or conceptual.[10] At the *conceptual* basis of our confrontation with experience are not bare particulars, but grammar: 'grammar is a preparation for description' (MWL 72), and it is *grammar* that tells us what *kind* of object anything is (PI 373). *As linguistic beings*, we come to experience and grapple the world *always already* with language, and there is no getting out of language to compare or measure our system / outline / beliefs against bare particulars.

Kuhn believed that 'a lexical taxonomy of some sort must be in place before description of the world can begin' (2000, 92), and it is this 'lexicon' which – like Kantian categories, though not fixed – constrains any description of experience. He rejects the idea that we attach or learn to attach scientific concepts to the world by strict correspondence, and claims that *paradigms* or *exemplars* are determined by our drawing *similarities* (or resemblances) and *patterns* from concrete examples that we are exposed to.[11]

So that, for both thinkers, it is *what we say* counts as 'real' or 'similar' and what does not that determines whether the experience is 'real' or 'illusory'; 'similar' or 'different'.[12]

The multifarious distinctions we make between what is real and what is not; what is similar and what is not; the systems of classification that enable us to speak of empirical reality in terms of 'real' or 'illusory', 'good' or 'bad', 'same' or 'different', 'high' or 'low', 'true' or 'false', *belong to language* (grammar),[13] not to the world. It is our language, then, that determines the world's conceptual outline. But '[i]s there some reality lying behind the notation, which shapes its grammar?' (PI 562), asks Wittgenstein. And his answer is: yes.

3. How nature makes herself audible

Granted, what we make of the solid, biological niche we find ourselves in, is internal to our language; as soon as we begin to reflect on the world as we find it, it becomes a world of *our making*; however, this conceptual outline is not disconnected from the world. Language does not operate in a vacuum. The empirical world has its word to say; it is not a silent partner:

> ... but has nature nothing to say here? Indeed she has – but she makes herself audible in another way.
> 'You'll surely run up against existence and non-existence somewhere!' But that means against facts, not concepts.
>
> Z 364

Facts, not concepts, he stresses.[14] The formation of our concepts must be impacted by existence, by nature, but this impact does not come in the form of *concepts* in nature (such as, purportedly, 'gravity'); it comes in the form of *facts* of nature:

> What we have to mention in order to explain the significance, I mean the importance, of a concept, are often extremely general facts of nature: such facts as are hardly ever mentioned because of their great generality.
>
> PI 56 – bottom note

'Indeed, doesn't it seem obvious that the possibility of a language-game is conditioned by certain facts?' (OC 617); that 'very general facts of nature' are 'favourable' to the formation of certain concepts[15] (Z 352)? Facts such as human beings experience pain; have the visual apparatus they do; cannot fly unaided; or that mountains don't spring up in half an hour and apples fall from trees. His acknowledgement of such 'basic facts' – the 'basic worldly dough', as Paul Boghossian calls it (2006, 35), on which our classifications can get to work – estranges the later Wittgenstein from fact-constructivism[16]. For Wittgenstein, such basic contingent facts inform our classifications – and were those facts different, so would our concepts be:

> It is a fact of experience that human beings alter their concepts, exchange them for others when they learn new facts; when in this way what was formerly important to them becomes unimportant, and *vice versa*.[17]
>
> Z 352

While this acknowledgement of the rootedness of our concepts in the world puts Wittgenstein outside the idealist camp, it does not thereby place him in the Realist camp (realist, here, with a capital 'R'). Our conceptualization of the world is made, not found, and so the 'realism' that is operative here cannot be of a strict correspondence kind. The difference is subtle, but crucial. Wittgenstein writes: 'The rule we lay down is the one most strongly suggested by the facts of experience' (AWL 84) – *suggested, not dictated*; and so the autonomy of grammar is, in spite of nature's input, maintained: although what gives a rule its importance are the facts of daily experience a 'rule *qua* rule is detached; it stands as it were alone in its glory' (RFM 357). Though nature provides the basic dough, it is we who cut it up into concepts; we are not *answerable* to nature for these concepts but to ourselves, to our epistemic endeavours and successes. A concept may be inadequate – it may fail to cohere with our other concepts or fail to enable the desired predictions – and we may need to change it. Gravity is not something we have observed; it is a concept we have formulated in an effort to order specific empirical events – events that we *have* observed; and the concept of 'gravity' is not *internally* linked to such events: we may find that what we have defined as 'gravity' is better defined by a new concept. To think that this inadequacy is due merely to our epistemic deficiency is to think that the right concepts are in nature, waiting to be discovered; but Kuhn and Wittgenstein would reply that nature has no concepts for nature has no language. Concepts are linguistic constructs and, as such, internal to language. Though nature has its impact, it is through *our* rules and *our* concepts that she 'makes herself audible'.[18]

We don't read off our concepts from nature, but this doesn't mean that these have no basis at all in nature. However, nature's connection to our concepts is not to be thought of in terms of correspondence, isomorphism, derivation, inference or justification: 'What is laid down depends on facts, *but is not made true or false by them*' (AWL 162, my emphasis). For, what is laid down – our grammar – is not susceptible of truth or falsity; it is a way of classifying reality, not a truth-evaluable description of it. There is no truthful correspondence between our concepts and the world, but there is a live connection:

> Would it be correct to say our concepts reflect our life?
> They stand in the middle of it.
>
> LWPP II, 72

Our concepts are immersed in our life, intertwined with it in a dynamic interaction: the fabric of our life provides the milieu in which our concepts are formed; in turn, our concepts order the fabric of life. And so the only sense we *find* in nature is the sense we *put* in nature, although that sense is necessarily influenced by that nature.

Kuhn, like Wittgenstein, sees a give-and-take between our paradigms and the world; or what he calls an 'accommodation of language and experience' (2000, 207), so that the changes or 'alterations in the way scientific terms attach to nature are not ... purely formal or purely linguistic. On the contrary, they come about in response to *pressures* generated by observation or experiment, and they result in more effective ways of dealing with some aspects of some natural phenomena' (2000, 204; my emphasis).

There is then nothing idealistic in saying that our account of reality is language dependent because: (1) it leaves room for a language-*in*dependent reality – that about which we speak and think; and (2) the fact that our concepts (our grammar) are not *veridically grounded* in experience does not mean that they are totally divorced from or impervious to it. Our concepts are not *empty*, but how they are informed by the world is not how realists and empiricists think they are; that is, they are not rationally linked to a veridical, absolute account, though they may be rooted, and certainly they have their life, in the natural conditions in which human beings are ensconced. The difficulty in making that difference clear is, I think, encapsulated in this sentence of Wittgenstein's: 'Not empiricism and yet realism in philosophy, that is the hardest thing' (RFM VI, 23, 325). The hardest thing for a philosopher is to show that not everything that is of the world, and not everything that is *experienced*, is *empirical*.

It is our concepts, our grammar, that lie at the foundation of knowledge, but these are impacted by what exists outside language. Kuhn and Wittgenstein share this view, and this is what prevents them from being any kind of idealist. We have seen that the view that our conceptual schemes are embedded in language neither implies that reality is our construct nor that we are not in touch with reality, but does it preclude objectivity? Are we doomed to conceptual relativism? I think not.

3. No conceptual relativism

The tendency is to think that if there is no theory-free account of reality in which our various accounts are anchored and to which they might appeal for comparison, justification or verification, any evaluation of schemes can only ever involve a comparison between schemes. Our evolving schemes would not therefore take us closer to the truth; they would simply be *other* schemes, other world-pictures (cf. 1996, 118). If relativism is defined as

(1) the view that there are no absolute truths about the world,

then Kuhn and Wittgenstein *are* relativists – the notion of 'absolute truths' being decisive[19]. Both reject the existence of a language-independent benchmark or 'true' concepts towards which our ordinary concepts are thought to strive.[20] But relativism can also be defined as

(2) the claim that any theory is as true / acceptable / good as the other; or

(3) the claim that there is no objective, universal basis to knowledge claims.

I will argue that while neither Wittgenstein nor Kuhn can be charged with (2), only Wittgenstein can steer clear of (3); on his view, there *is* a universally objective basis to knowledge claims – where 'universally' means 'humanly', not 'super-humanly'; not across 'all possible worlds', but across all forms of human life.

3.1 Kuhn and Wittgenstein against theory equivalence

Neither Wittgenstein nor Kuhn believes that any theory is as true/acceptable/good as the other. As we have seen, Kuhn thinks that incommensurability does not prevent intelligibility, but nor does intelligibility entail acceptability: semantic understanding does not eliminate the clash between paradigms. For Kuhn, we cannot accept an alien point of view as true, but only appreciate it.[21] Kuhn has no problem applying the label 'truth' intra-theoretically; he agrees with Popper that each historical theory was believed true in its time but later abandoned as false, and that the later theory was the better of the two 'as a tool for the practice of normal science': 'One scientific theory is not as good as another for doing what scientists normally do. In that sense, I am not a relativist' (2000, 160).

Similarly, although Wittgenstein's appreciation of other cultures is deep (as evidenced in his *Remarks on Frazer*), his *inability* – and by implication ours – to treat some beliefs as right or acceptable and some behaviours as human or normal is also clear. In *On Certainty*, he often calls people who do not share our basic certainties 'mad' or 'demented' (OC 217, 420; 155): 'If someone said to me that he doubted whether he had a body, I should take him to be a half-wit' (OC 257); and that includes philosophers: 'If Moore were to pronounce the opposite of those propositions which he declares certain, we should not just not share his opinion: we should regard him as demented' (OC 155). And in the following passage, theory equivalence is ruled out:

> We all believe that it isn't possible to get to the moon; but there might be people who believe that that is possible and that it sometimes happens. We say: these people do not know a lot that we know. And, let them be never so sure of their belief – they are wrong and we know it.
>
> If we compare our system of knowledge with theirs then theirs is evidently the poorer one by far.[22]
>
> OC 286

As to there being an objective, universal basis to knowledge claims, as earlier suggested, where objectivity is defined in absolutist, human-independent terms, Kuhn and Wittgenstein would both have to be seen as relativists. But on a more down-to-earth version of objectivity – which would be *objectivity, humanly speaking*[23] – Wittgenstein and Kuhn would be deemed relativists only if they denied the existence of a foundation upon which all *human* knowledge logically rests. Here, Kuhn parts company with Wittgenstein in that he considers objectivity to be culture-linked.

3.2 Wittgenstein: the human form of life as the stopping-place of relativism

Although Kuhn comes very close to Kant's transcendentalism when he speaks of the shared taxonomic categories that must be in place before description of the world can begin as 'a particular operating mode of a mental module prerequisite to having beliefs, a mode that at once supplies and bounds the set of beliefs it is possible to conceive', taking some such taxonomic module to be prelinguistic and possessed by animals

(2000, 94), he makes clear that the position he is developing is an evolutionary one. His, as he writes, is 'a sort of post-Darwinian Kantianism', with the difference that 'lexical categories, unlike their Kantian forebears, can and do change, both with time and with the passage from one community to another', with their lexical structures overlapping in major ways so as to enable communication between communities (2000, 104). So that Kuhnian categories differ from Kantian categories in that they are lexical and in that they are not fixed: 'I am a Kantian with movable categories' (2000, 264), he writes.

As for Wittgenstein, he speaks in *On Certainty* of the bedrock of our thoughts as consisting 'partly of sand, which now in one place now in another gets washed away, or deposited', but also 'partly of hard rock subject to *no alteration*' (OC 99; my emphasis). This means that some of our basic certainties 'underlie *all* questions and *all* thinking' (OC 415; my emphasis); such certainties as 'I have a body', 'The world exists' or 'Human beings express feelings' are examples. So that were we to meet a tribe of people brought up from early youth to give no expression of feeling of any kind, we could not see these people as human:

> 'These men would have nothing human about them.' Why? – We could not possibly make ourselves understood to them. Not even as we can to a dog. We could not find our feet with them.
>
> Z 390

That humans express feeling is part of the 'substratum' of human thought (OC 161); it is one of those 'universal certainties', as I have called them,[24] that logically or grammatically underpin anything any normal human being can say or think about her peers. Universal certainties are conditioned by *universally basic* facts of nature. Such facts importantly include what Wittgenstein calls 'the common behaviour of mankind': e.g., we are creatures who are born and will die; have the potential of evolving from infanthood to adulthood; require nourishment, air, sleep; inhabit and interact in a world peopled by other beings; (excepting pathological cases) acquire and use language, have and express feelings and emotions.[25] These facts logically condition the concepts or grammar of all normal human beings. Indeed, Wittgenstein writes that this 'common behaviour of mankind is the system of reference by means of which we interpret an unknown language' (PI 206) – by which he means any *human* language. What we have here, then, is the system of reference that marks the stopping-place of relativism.

Whereas difference, pluralism, and disagreement thrive in *the various forms of human life*, there is no pluralism, but only unquestionable unity as regards our *one human form of life*.[26] It is our universally shared form of life that informs Wittgenstein's realism by constituting the system of reference which logically underpins any meaningful account of ourselves and our world. It logically (grammatically) rules out a thoroughgoing relativism by ensuring that there are some things about which we, humans, cannot disagree if we are to make sense. To use one of Wittgenstein's examples: we cannot cut off someone's head and expect them to go on living (OC 274) – not in 'real life' anyway. And the fact that we can conceive of it – say, in fictional contexts, or in our magical or religious forms of human life – does not make it a real possibility in our human form of life. A brief look at the *Remarks on Frazer* will help illustrate this point.

As is clear from the *Remarks*, Wittgenstein is a relativist as far as religion and magic are concerned, but not where science or knowledge are concerned. Though a tribe's 'magic' may seem to contradict our universal certainties, Wittgenstein is clear that it does not *in fact* do so:[27]

> The same savage, who stabs the picture of his enemy apparently in order to kill him, *really* builds his hut out of wood and carves his arrow skilfully and not in effigy.
>
> GB 125; my italics

That is, he knows what *really* will kill his enemy, and what will act as protection in case that fails: a skilfully carved arrow and a hut built out of wood (GB 125). Contrary to what Frazer alleges, the human beings he calls 'savages' do not have 'a completely false (even insane) idea of the course of nature ... Only their *magic* is different' (GB 141).

Having denounced Frazer's interpretation of magic as 'essentially false physics' (GB 129), Wittgenstein wants to underline that magic cohabits with science in the lives of the 'savages' (as it does in twentieth-century societies) without their being confused about the two. Indeed, Frazer's belief that they confuse the two makes him, writes Wittgenstein, 'much more savage than most of his savages, for they are not as far removed from the understanding of a spiritual matter as a twentieth-century Englishman' (GB 131):

> The nonsense here is that Frazer represents these people as if they had a completely false (even insane) idea of the course of nature, whereas they only possess a peculiar interpretation of the phenomena. That is, if they were to write it down, their knowledge of nature would not differ *fundamentally* from ours. Only their *magic* is different.
>
> GB 141

To Wittgenstein's consternation, 'Frazer would be capable of believing that a savage dies because of an error' (GB 131). That is to say, Frazer would be capable of believing that, say, the women in the Trobriand Islands called *Yoyova* or flying witches, who are believed to have the capacity to fly, *really* believe they can fly. But of course they don't believe this, and that is why they have fire-flies do it for them[28]. Were a *Yoyova* to actually attempt to fly off a cliff, it wouldn't be the 'savage' in her but the deluded person who acted: her attempting to fly off a cliff would not be an error but a pathological act. What Wittgenstein says of the Rain King in the following passage also applies to the flying witch:

> It is, of course, not so that the people believe that the ruler has these powers, *and the ruler knows very well that he doesn't have them, or can only fail to know if he is an imbecile or a fool*. But the notion of his power is, of course, adapted in such a way that it can harmonize with experience – the people's as well as his own. That some hypocrisy thereby plays a role is true only insofar as it generally lies close at hand with most things people do.
>
> GB 139; my emphasis

Some hypocrisy but mostly, as he will say, symbolism. In any case, Wittgenstein is clear that there is no confusion between ritual and scientific belief. As regards the Rain King in Africa to whom the people pray when the rainy period comes, he writes: 'But surely that means that they do not really believe that he can make it rain, otherwise they would do it in the dry periods of the year' (GB 137).

Their magic notwithstanding, the 'savages' share our basic acceptance of the 'very general facts of nature' and the 'common behaviour of mankind'. When it comes to their basic beliefs and ordinary ways of acting, their magic does not trump their science, but vice versa: 'If the adoption of a child proceeds in such a way that the mother draws it from under her clothes, it is surely insane to believe that an *error* is present and that she believes she has given birth to the child' (GB 125). The mother cannot be in error because, magical rituals notwithstanding, she never believed she was in fact giving birth to the child. The adoption ritual is something she may believe *in*, not something she believes *that*. Or better, it is simply something symbolic.[29] As Wittgenstein insists, magic is not based on opinion but on symbolism.[30]

The 'savages' have science as well as magic, as do we.[31] It is not their magic that we should compare with our science, but their science that we should compare with our science (e.g., how they build their huts and carve their arrows) and, here, there is a better or worse way of doing things that they could learn from us, or us from them.[32] There is then only one benchmark when it comes to science. Wittgenstein would share Kuhn's anti-relativistic view of scientific progress – progress not in terms of truth but in evolutionary and praxial terms – as increasing fitness over time, where fitness means consonance with the state of the art as defined by the global scientific community.

The point is that magic – when it does not slide into madness – never overrides science. What ritual calls for is one thing – it has its role and its impact – but it does not trump the universal bedrock of human thought. Such certainties as 'Human beings can't fly unaided' or 'Human beings feel and express pain' (pathologies excepted) are part of the objective, universal foundation of knowledge claims – that to which Wittgenstein refers when, to the question 'Could a legislator abolish the concept of pain?', he replies: 'The basic concepts are interwoven so closely with what is most fundamental in our way of living that they are therefore unassailable.'

4. Objectivity, humanly speaking

Gertrude Conway calls Wittgenstein's position an *objectivism without absolutism*: the absence of absolutism doesn't mean that objectivity is lost, but that it is *conditional* on our human form of life – 'species-relative', as it were (1989, 94, 141–42). Yet rather than speak of Wittgenstein's notion of objectivity as 'species-relative', and given the puzzling nature of the notion of a *human or mind-independent* objectivity, I suggest we no longer think of the latter as the benchmark of objectivity and refer to it as 'absolutism', while using the notion of 'objectivity' to refer exclusively to *objectivity, humanly speaking*. In brief, I oppose the chimera of a superhuman, supernatural, imperturbable absolute logical necessity which, by dint of being applicable to all possible worlds, makes a farce of ours – forcing us, as it does, to consider evil geniuses, brains in vats, and zombies as real possibilities in our world. Logical necessity is not less compelling or objective for being specifically human. It is *objective, humanly speaking*. And this is the only objectivity we ought to appeal to if we want to stop being philosophically distracted by zombies or, more generally speaking, 'the illusion of possibility'.[33]

11

Beyond Hacker's Wittgenstein

In 'Wittgenstein on Grammar, Theses and Dogmatism', Peter Hacker addresses what he takes to be misconceptions of Wittgenstein's philosophy with respect to: (1), the periodization of his thought and to what should properly be counted as part of his work; (2), his conception of grammar since the Big Typescript (1929-33); and (3), his conception of philosophy as grammatical investigation. I argue that Hacker's restrictive conception of what ought to be considered part of Wittgenstein's philosophy and his conservative view of Wittgensteinian grammar are unjustified and prevent him from appreciating the revolutionary importance of *On Certainty* for epistemology. Finally, while agreeing that Wittgenstein views philosophy as grammatical elucidation, I suggest some reasons for the resistance this view has generated.

In 'Wittgenstein on Grammar, Theses and Dogmatism', Peter Hacker deals with three of the 'many misunderstandings, misrepresentations and misinterpretations of Wittgenstein's philosophy' (2012, 1); the first of which concerns 'the periodisation of Wittgenstein's thought'; the second, the supposition that what Wittgenstein called 'grammar' in PI differed fundamentally from, and was more limited than, his conception of it when he was writing the *Big Typescript*; the third, the claim that what Wittgenstein took to be grammatical statements are in fact dogmatisms, theories or doctrines inconsistent with his meta-philosophical remarks in PI. I address each of these concerns seriatim.

1. The 'periodisation' of Wittgenstein's thought

> A party game much indulged in by many philosophers studying Wittgenstein's works is 'Counting Wittgensteins'. The operative question is 'How many Wittgensteins are there?' – and the winner is the one who can find the most. This game should be shunned, for it breeds confusions.
>
> 2012, 1–2

This derisory remark is no doubt aimed in part at the idea I put forward several years ago, of a 'third Wittgenstein'.[1] Far from originating in a party game, the idea of a *third* Wittgenstein was rooted in the conviction that Wittgenstein's philosophy did not only consist of two distinct phases, each with its own masterpiece,[2] but of three phases, each with its own masterpiece. Granted, the third phase was not as radical a departure from the second because it was not due to a recantation, but there was after PI not only sufficiently different material and methodology to warrant flagging, but a neglected masterpiece that *needed* flagging: *On Certainty*. Aware of the unprecedented achievement of *On Certainty*, and finding also in the various writings and lectures on the philosophy of psychology not just more of PI, but new insights and achievements, I felt there was a need to prompt others to go beyond what was beginning to sound like arrested development with PI, and explore the rich terrain of the post-*Investigations* works[3].

However, as far as Peter Hacker is concerned:

> Wittgenstein wrote only two books – both masterpieces – which are fundamentally different from each other. All the other books published under his name are unfinished or discarded writings. One can speak of an early philosophy and of a later philosophy. There is no 'middle philosophy' or indeed 'last philosophy', since he produced no works between the *Tractatus* and the *Investigations*, and no works after the *Investigations*.
>
> 2012, 2

Now this last sentence sounds incredible: Hacker seems to be saying that because what Wittgenstein produced in these periods is in the form of unpublished remarks or notes, it should not be counted as part of his philosophy or of his works. This would prevent Wittgenstein's remarks on the foundation of mathematics; all of the writings, remarks and lectures on philosophical psychology; the notes that make up *On Certainty* – and much more besides – from being counted as part of Wittgenstein's philosophy. Hacker continues:

> After 1946, most of his writings (1900 pages) concern the philosophy of psychology. It seems he intended to produce a book on this subject too. The remainder of his fragmentary writings are on colour and on knowledge and certainty. There is no reason to suppose that these were intended to form a book of any kind.
>
> 2012, 3

But what of that? Why should an author's intention (or lack of it) to publish something decisively impact on our judgement of it as significantly belonging to the corpus of his work? And why, particularly in this case, should intention to publish be indicative of the importance of any of Wittgenstein's writings, when – as we know – he had decided not to publish PI itself?[4] Finally, and crucially, what does it matter whether or not Wittgenstein intended to form a book from his writings on knowledge and certainty, if what these writings do form is a masterpiece?

Some philosophers have no trouble writing and publishing their thoughts. There are, however, philosophers for whom writing is a problem – what they do best is teach. And then there are others who can write abundantly, but for whom publishing is a problem, perhaps even a major psychological block. Here is what Ray Monk has to say about Wittgenstein's 'fastidiousness about publication' (1991, 319):

Wittgenstein had a peculiarly laborious method of editing his work. He began by writing remarks into small notebooks. He then selected what he considered to be the best of these remarks and wrote them out, perhaps in a different order, into large manuscript volumes. From these he made a further selection which he dictated to a typist. The resultant typescript was then used as the basis for a further selection, sometimes by cutting it up and rearranging it – and then the whole process was started again. Though this process continued for more than twenty years, it never culminated in an arrangement with which Wittgenstein was fully satisfied, and so his literary executors have had to publish either what they consider to be the most satisfactory of the various manuscripts and typescripts (*Philosophical Remarks, Philosophical Investigations, Remarks on the Philosophy of Psychology*), or a selection from them (or rearrangement of them) made by the executors themselves (*Philosophical Grammar, Remarks on the Foundations of Mathematics, Culture and Value, Zettel*). These we now know as the works of the later Wittgenstein, though in truth not one of them can be regarded as a completed work.

1991, 319

Note in passing that *On Certainty* is not even mentioned, which is symptomatic of the attitude towards it at the time Monk was writing this (1991). But to return to our point: on the kind of record described by Monk here – where even the publication of *Philosophical Investigations* is not the product of an authorial decision – it seems hardly fitting for Hacker to speak of all books published under Wittgenstein's name, with the exception of TLP and PI – as 'unfinished or discarded writings' (2012, 2). Not only does this rubric seem much too clinical and short-sighted to subsume the remarkable writings in question, it should technically also include *Philosophical Investigations*. For – as Monk rightly indicates and others clearly state – PI is also 'unfinished writings',[5] which on Hacker's own criteria makes one wonder why he accords it the privileged status of being one of the only two 'books' Wittgenstein wrote.

The point here is that when philosophers obsessively 'fastidious' about publication, as Wittgenstein obviously was, leave behind thousands of unpublished pages, there is no reason not to consider those pages – particularly those that manifest philosophical genius – as part and parcel of their philosophy. Indeed, to make discriminations which exclude those written pages from intrinsically belonging to that philosopher's work because he had not explicitly (as far as we know) intended them for publication seems to me a bureaucratic, short-sighted and prejudicial exercise. Of course, had those pages contained mediocre thoughts or repetitive drafts unequal to the published works or to those intended for publication, there would be no issue here[6], but the 1,900 pages that Wittgenstein wrote after PI make up some of the best philosophical work ever written. Had we only those pages – had the *Tractatus* and *Philosophical Investigations* not been written – Wittgenstein would still have to be counted as a philosophical genius. To evaluate those pages properly – to decide whether they should be deemed as belonging to Wittgenstein's 'philosophy' or as meriting the qualification 'masterpiece' – one must look to their content, not to the author's intention or satisfaction with them. The Intentional Fallacy holds for philosophy too, and Hacker commits it here.

The criterion is not whether Wittgenstein intended to form books from his notes, but whether or not these notes do form what can be considered a genuine and original contribution to philosophy. This, Hacker seems not to think – particularly as concerns *On Certainty*:

> We can ... speak (cautiously) of the unfinished projects, e.g. of a book on the philosophy of mathematics and another on the philosophy of psychology. And we can speak of the late notes on certainty and explore the extent to which they modify conceptions advanced in the *Investigations*.
>
> 2012, 1–2

But *pace* Hacker, the 'late notes on certainty' far more than modify conceptions advanced in the *Investigations*; they directly and relentlessly tackle one of the most persistent problems in epistemology: the nature of basic beliefs. And they do so, as G. H. von Wright suggests, in a way 'which makes them almost unique' in Wittgenstein's corpus:

> During the last year and a half of his life, Wittgenstein wrote almost exclusively about knowledge and certainty. These writings possess a thematic unity which makes them almost unique in Wittgenstein's whole literary output. . . . Considering that the remarks constitute a first, unrevised manuscript they seem to me remarkably accomplished both in form and content.
>
> 1982, 166

Indeed, the only other work that can vie with the thematic unity of the notes that make up *On Certainty* is the *Tractatus*. *On Certainty* is neither a compilation of passages written over a twenty-year span, as is the case with *Philosophical Investigations*, nor a compilation effected in the main by someone other than Wittgenstein, as are *Remarks on the Foundations of Mathematics* or *Zettel*.[7] The notes that make up *On Certainty* constitute an uncharacteristically intense and focused treatment of a topic over a period of eighteen months. This is presumably why the editors, G. E. M. Anscombe and G. H. von Wright, had no qualms about calling it a 'work':

> It seemed appropriate to publish this *work* by itself. It is not a selection; Wittgenstein marked it off in his notebooks as a separate topic, which he apparently took up at four separate periods during this eighteen months. It constitutes a single sustained treatment of the topic.
>
> OC Preface, my emphasis

By the standards of all his writing – including *Philosophical Investigations* – *On Certainty* unquestionably qualifies as one of Wittgenstein's *works*. This much, however, must be conceded: it is a work *in progress*. But then again, one can say that about all of Wittgenstein's 'works', with the exception of the *Tractatus*. However, *On Certainty* is a work in progress which – like PI – also has the characteristics of an extraordinary *accomplishment*.

And so to the question of how *On Certainty* can be considered Wittgenstein's third masterpiece if it isn't even a 'work', the immediate reply is that *On Certainty* is much more of a work in conventional terms than PI is: it is thematically more homogenous, concentrated and contiguous than PI; and most of it written (and dated) within eighteen months.[8] But the more compelling reply is that the proof is in the pudding: the notes that make up *On Certainty* revolutionize the concept of basic beliefs and dissolve scepticism, making them a corrective, not only to Moore but also to Descartes, Hume, and all of epistemology.[9]

On Certainty shows Wittgenstein to have solved the problem he set out to solve – the problem that occupied Moore and plagued epistemology – that of the foundation of knowledge. Wittgenstein's revolutionary insight in *On Certainty* is that what philosophers have traditionally called 'basic beliefs' – those beliefs that all knowledge must ultimately be based on – cannot, on pain of infinite regress, themselves be based on further propositional beliefs. He comes to see that basic beliefs are really animal or unreflective ways of acting which, once formulated (e.g., by philosophers), look like (empirical) propositions. It is this misleading appearance that leads philosophers to believe that at the foundation of thought is yet more thought. Yet though they may often *look like* empirical conclusions, our basic certainties constitute the ungrounded, nonpropositional underpinning of knowledge, not its object. In thus situating the foundation of knowledge in nonreflective certainties that manifest themselves as ways of acting, Wittgenstein has found the place where justification comes to an end, and solved the regress problem of basic beliefs – and, in passing, shown the logical impossibility of hyperbolic scepticism. I believe that this is a groundbreaking achievement for philosophy – worthy of calling *On Certainty* Wittgenstein's 'third masterpiece'.

It also puts paid to the idea that *On Certainty* merely modifies conceptions advanced in the *Investigations*. This is not to say that Wittgenstein had never previously broached any of the questions addressed in *On Certainty*; but seeds are buried potentiality, not deployed thoughts and full-blown conclusions brought to the light of day by the power and resistance of argument. The intellectual struggle and flagged solutions that occur *within On Certainty* testify to the fact that any seeds sown prior to it had until then been left untended and unproductive – sterile. It took Norman Malcolm's prompting to get Wittgenstein going in 1949 and producing what was to become *On Certainty*. I quote from my Introduction to *The Third Wittgenstein Conference*:

> The idea that Wittgenstein produced nothing philosophically new, and indeed nothing momentous, after PI is precisely what I wanted to counter with the idea of a third Wittgenstein. To say that the post-*Investigations* works are just more of the same is to say that we could do without *On Certainty*; that it achieves nothing, substantially, that PI (or CE) hadn't achieved. But where, in the *Investigations*, is the problem of basic beliefs handled and put to rest; where is scepticism of the external world dissolved; where is the problem of doubt tackled and the 'false picture of doubt' (OC 249) laid bare with such formidable clarity; where is knowledge so firmly put in its place – in short, where is Wittgenstein's epistemology, if not in *On Certainty*?
>
> 2009, 559

The masterpiece constituted by the notes on certainty – whether intended or not – provides sufficient novelty to merit distinction from the earlier corpus. Put briefly: these notes provide a solution to the problem of basic beliefs – the *Philosophical Investigations* do not.

To say, as does Hacker, that it is 'misleading to speak of "the Middle Wittgenstein" or "the second, third, fourth or fifth) Wittgenstein". There is only one Wittgenstein' (2012, 3) is, in a sense, a truism – of course, there is only one man, one philosopher whose name is 'Ludwig Wittgenstein' and who lived from 1889–1951, etc. But the division into early/late, first/second Wittgenstein had been of immense value to the field in its attempts to come to terms with a tense and difficult philosopher of genius: it underlined a major shift in his thought. In the same way, it is not at all misleading – and indeed a facilitating and clarifying tool – to refer to early/first Kuhn or Baker and late/second Kuhn or Baker to indicate a (more or less radical) change in position. Although there is no radical philosophical repositioning between PI and post-PI, as there had been between TLP and PI, it is also true that, as von Wright suggests, 'Wittgenstein's writings from 1946 onwards represent in certain ways departures in *new* directions' (1982, 136).

My objective in demarcating a third Wittgenstein after over fifty years of scholarship on his output was to draw attention to what had been neglected in a near-exclusive focus on the *Tractatus* and the *Investigations*. I believe I speak for most Wittgenstein scholars in saying that Peter Hacker is in the stratosphere of Wittgenstein scholarship. He is certainly among the thinkers to whom I am most indebted for my understanding of Wittgenstein. But when even one of Wittgenstein's greatest proponents refuses to consider the post-*Investigations* writings – and OC in particular – as a fully fledged, invaluable, part of his philosophy, this confirms the need to call attention to a 'third Wittgenstein'. Hacker's position on this notwithstanding, I have found his rendering of that motivation as indulging in a party game competition unnecessarily cavalier. What is important here, however, is that the increase in publications, conferences, seminars, theses – and indeed workshops (summer or otherwise) – devoted to *On Certainty* these last several years may be due, at least in part, to the motivation, I still powerfully feel, to draw attention to the third Wittgenstein.

2. On grammar

2.1 Hacker's understanding of grammar

Hacker argues that, contrary to what is sometimes alleged, there is no *fundamental* change in his concept of grammar from the time Wittgenstein wrote the Big Typescript (1929–33) to when he started working on PI in 1936. If anything, in PI, 'far from abandoning the salient features of the concept of grammar that he hammered out in the early thirties, Wittgenstein elaborated it further' (p. 11). I can only agree with Hacker here, and indeed would add that Wittgenstein elaborated it *even further* in *On Certainty* and *Remarks on Colour*. But on this latter point, Hacker would not agree with me. And I suggest this disagreement would stem from his restricted and restrictive understanding of what Wittgenstein takes to be rules of grammar, which limited understanding I believe to be also responsible for Hacker's inability to recognize the importance of *On Certainty*.

For Wittgenstein:

> What belongs to grammar are all the conditions (the method) necessary for comparing the proposition with reality. That is, all the conditions necessary for the understanding (of the sense).
>
> PG, p. 88

or, as he also puts it in BT:

> The only thing that doesn't belong to grammar is what makes a proposition true or false. That's the only thing grammar is not concerned with. Everything that's required for comparing the proposition with the facts belongs to grammar. That is, all the requirements for understanding. (All the requirements for sense.)
>
> BT 42, p. 38

Now, Hacker's summary of this passage is:

> Grammar, qua *object* of grammatical investigations, consists of sense-determining rules of language. What belongs to grammar in this sense is everything required for determination of meaning, for comparing a proposition with reality – hence for understanding (BT 42).
>
> 2012, 5

This would be perfectly acceptable if the idea, inserted by Hacker here, of Wittgensteinian grammar consisting of 'sense-determining rules of language' did not flag an overly conservative understanding of Wittgensteinian grammar. Wittgenstein is emphatically liberal as to what can count as belonging to grammar: *all* the conditions (the method) necessary for the understanding (of the sense) (PG, p. 88); 'The only thing that doesn't belong to grammar is what makes a proposition true or false. That's the only thing grammar is not concerned with' (BT 42, p. 38). And of course we know, as does Peter Hacker, that in PI Wittgenstein included objects such as samples and tables as part of grammar (or, as he sometimes puts it: as 'part of language' or 'belonging to language'):

> We can put it like this: This sample is an instrument of the language used in ascriptions of colour. In this language-game it is not something that is represented, but is a means of representation.... What looks as if it *had* to exist, is part of the language. It is a paradigm in our language-game; something with which comparison is made.... this ... is ... an observation concerning our language-game – our method of representation.
>
> PI 50

We could 'call such a table the expression of a rule of the language-game' (PI 53). However, Wittgenstein's liberality as to what he will count as belonging to 'grammar' or 'language' does not stop here:

> I will count *any fact* whose obtaining is a presupposition of a proposition's making sense as belonging *to language*.[10]
>
> PR 45; first emphasis mine

And just as is the case for tables and samples, there is no reason why such 'facts' should not also be called 'expressions of rules of language'. Indeed, Wittgenstein speaks of 'facts' as grammatically underpinning our concepts in Part II of the *Investigations*[11]:

> What we have to mention in order to explain the significance, I mean the importance, of a concept, are often extremely general facts of nature: such facts as are hardly ever mentioned because of their great generality.
>
> PI, p. 56 – bottom note

> If the formation of concepts [var. in RPP I, 46: 'the structures of concepts'] can be explained by facts of nature, should we not be interested, not in grammar, but rather in that in nature which is the basis of grammar? – Our interest certainly *includes* the correspondence between concepts var. in RPP I, 46: '*our grammar*'] and very general facts of nature. (Such facts as mostly do not strike us because of their generality.)
>
> PI 230, xii; final emphasis mine

Here, then, Wittgenstein speaks of the correspondence between the structures of concepts – that is, our grammatical rules – our grammar – and very general facts of nature. The latter *condition* our concepts,[12] which means that they noninferentially or nonratiocinatively influence them: 'The rule we lay down is the one most strongly suggested by the facts of experience' (AWL 84). So that paradigmatic facts, such as human beings are normally susceptible to pain, are indeed at the basis of some of our grammatical rules, but the correspondence between these facts and our grammar is not a rational or deliberate one.[13] Some of the 'structures' of the concept of pain can be expressed in grammatical rules such as: 'Human beings are normally susceptible to pain'; 'Tables and chairs don't feel pain'; 'There is psychological as well as physical pain', etc. Thus far, Hacker might well agree that such sentences are expressions of fact-conditioned grammatical rules, inasmuch as they underpin or determine our use of the concept 'pain'; but he refuses to consider 'The world has existed for many years' as the expression of a rule of grammar conditioned by a very general fact of nature, on the grounds that it neither determines concepts nor inference rules:

> It is true that we can, in certain cases, transform an empirical proposition into a rule or norm of representation by resolving to hold it rigid. (But 'The world has existed for many years', which we could not abandon without destroying the web of our beliefs, is nevertheless not a rule, since its role is not to determine concepts or inference rules.)
>
> 1996a, 215

But where is such a restriction of the role of grammar made by Wittgenstein? For Hacker, the sense-determination of a rule of grammar is limited to concepts or inference rules; whereas for Wittgenstein, 'Rules of Grammar Determine Meaning' (BT 184) or sense; where the determination of sense is nowhere said to be limited to concepts or inference rules. In fact, as he writes: 'I [...] endeavour to emphasize the *diversity* of grammatical rules' (WVC 188; original emphasis). Hacker is not as liberal as Wittgenstein in what he counts as 'rules of language'. On Hacker's understanding, rules of grammar are merely rules for the correct use of *words*: 'Grammatical propositions or remarks are expressions of rules for the use of the constituent words' (2012, 8); whereas for Wittgenstein, they are certainly that, but not only that: they are also bounds of sense which are less specifically word- or concept-focused.[14] But this becomes clearer in *On Certainty*.

2.2 On 'hinges' as grammatical rules

Wittgenstein's view of grammar is much broader than Hacker takes it to be. After PI, Wittgenstein no longer considers grammar as merely rules for the use of constituent words. Many 'hinge certainties' contemplated by Wittgenstein in *On Certainty* are (like 'The world has existed for many years') not determinant of concepts or inference rules; they are expressions of 'facts' – some, very general, some not[15] – whose obtaining is presupposed in our making sense (PR 45). That is, though they look like empirical propositions, they are nonratiocinated certainties that underpin our making sense: e.g., 'I am called L.W.' (OC 470); 'I come from such and such a city' (OC 67); 'I live at address A' (OC 70); 'I have just had lunch /eaten' (OC 659); 'I have never been in Asia Minor' (OC 419); 'I have never been on the moon' (OC 111); 'The earth existed long before my birth' (OC 301); 'Every human being has a brain' (OC 159); 'My body has never disappeared and reappeared again after an interval' (OC 101); 'There is a cupboard in the room and it is still a cupboard when I see it later on, and not a stage set' (OC 472); 'Chess pieces don't change places of themselves' (OC 346); 'The stability of things is the norm, which is then subject to alterations' (OC 473).

Now, Hacker does himself recognize that it is possible for some empirical propositions to become rules of grammar:

> It is true that we can, in certain cases, transform an empirical proposition into a rule or norm of representation *by resolving to hold it rigid*.... It was an empirical discovery that acids are proton donors, but this proposition was transformed into a rule: a scientist no longer calls something 'an acid' unless it is a proton donor, and if it is a proton donor, then it is to be called 'an acid', even if it has no effect on litmus paper. The proposition that acids are proton donors (like '25 x 25 = 625') has been 'withdrawn from being checked by experience, but now serves as a paradigm for judging experience' (cf. RFM 325).
>
> 1996a, 215; my emphasis

And in the 2012 paper, he again reminds us:

> One of the most important remarks on grammar and necessity in RFM is: to accept a proposition as unshakably certain means to use it as a grammatical rule – it is this that removes the uncertainty of it (RFM 170).
>
> 2012, 11

Well, this should compel Hacker to acknowledge the grammaticality of *On Certainty*'s 'hinge propositions' – aren't they propositions that we 'hold fast' (OC 225) or that 'stand fast' (OC 235) for us: 'I should like to say: Moore does not *know* what he asserts he knows, but it stands fast for him, as also for me; regarding it as absolutely solid is part of our *method*[16] of doubt and inquiry' (OC 151)? But here again Hacker refuses to accord grammaticality to those 'propositions' that Wittgenstein describes as unshakably certain, such as 'The world has existed for many years', preferring instead to see *On Certainty* as problematic. A footnote to the passage above reads:

> It is noteworthy that when he started reflecting on Moore's peculiar propositions, he noted that it is not only grammatical propositions (rules for the uses of words) that are thus removed from possible doubt but also *empirical propositions of the world picture. Hence the problems of* On Certainty.
>
> 2012, 11n7; my emphasis

But *what* problems of *On Certainty*? The reply can only be: Hacker's problems. The veil Wittgenstein lifted is still down for Hacker, who refuses to accept Wittgenstein's coming to see that our holding fast to such *apparent* empirical propositions as 'The world has existed for many years' is a grammatical holding fast. It is one of those instances where holding a proposition as unshakably certain means to use it as a grammatical rule.

Rather than entertain this possibility, Hacker simply assumes hinge or *Weltbild* propositions to be empirical propositions, but is puzzled by their non-bipolar nature. For on Wittgenstein's bipolar view of the proposition, for something to be a proposition, it must be capable of being true *and* of being false; and as Hacker admits, hinge propositions cannot be false; they are indubitable, not negatable. So how can they be empirical propositions? Hacker's answer to this is that: finding hinge propositions to constitute exceptions to his principle of bipolarity,[17] Wittgenstein must have repudiated bipolarity as definitive of propositionality. The problem is: not only is there no textual evidence for Wittgenstein's abandoning bipolarity[18], even had he opted for the less stringent *bivalence*, this would make hinge certainties 'true empirical propositions' which Wittgenstein explicitly says there are not: 'If the true is what is grounded, then the ground is not *true* nor yet false' (OC 205). So the problem, for Hacker, remains.

It is only because Hacker insists on seeing hinge certainties as indubitable empirical propositions that he is forced to view them as problematic for Wittgenstein; whereas the unproblematic and consistent reason for the logical impossibility of negating hinge or *Weltbild* 'propositions' is simply that they are rules of grammar; and rules of grammar are neither true nor false (OC 205, 94). So that to say, in our human form of life: 'The world has existed for many years'; 'Human beings cannot fly unaided', 'Cars do not grow on trees' or 'Babies cannot take care of themselves' is not to utter true empirical propositions but to formulate bounds of sense whose negation does not result in false empirical propositions but in nonsense.

Hacker's refusal to consider the grammaticality of hinge certainties is due to his narrow view of grammatical rules as *exclusively* 'rules for the uses of words' (2012, 11n7) and not as more versatile bounds of sense[19]. If, as he quotes Wittgenstein (2012, 5), 'What belongs to grammar ... is *everything* required for determination of meaning'

(BT 42; my emphasis), why does Hacker not allow that rules of grammar can also be, as Wittgenstein affirms in *On Certainty*, part of our method of doubt and inquiry (OC 151); rules that underpin our world-picture (OC 95)? Moreover, in the course of his deliberations in OC, Wittgenstein asks: 'Is it that rule and empirical proposition merge into one another?' (OC 309) – which explicitly shows him contemplating treating Moore-type certainties as rules of grammar. He also asserts that Moore-type propositions are not empirical propositions at all, though they have the form of empirical propositions (OC 96); that they are *rules* of testing (OC 98); that Moore's 'I know' is the confused expression of a grammatical certainty: ' "I know" is here a *logical* insight' (OC 59; original emphasis), and that

> When Moore says he *knows* such and such, he is really enumerating a lot of empirical propositions which we affirm without special testing; propositions, that is, which have a peculiar logical role in the system of our empirical propositions.
>
> OC 136

Wittgenstein doesn't come much clearer than this. Also when he writes that 'To accept a proposition as unshakably certain ... means to use it as a grammatical rule' (RFM 81), this gives us leave to consider as grammatical not only, as Hacker concedes:

(1) propositions such as 'acids are proton donors' – because *we have resolved* to hold them rigid; *but also*
(2) 'propositions' such as 'The world has existed for many years' and 'Human beings have walked on the moon' that, *by dint of conditioning and/or repeated exposure*[20], have become rigid 'norms of representation'[21]; *as well as*
(3) personal certainties (such as 'I am sitting at my desk typing these words'; 'I have a body'; 'I speak French') whose indubitability is 'animal' and which I *cannot but* hold rigid – that is, hold as grammatical – if I am to speak and act logically.[22]

Pace Hacker, 'The world has existed for many years' – though it does not determine concepts or inference rules – is a bound of sense or 'a preparation for a description' (MWL 72) in the same way that '2 +2 = 4' or 'Tables and chairs don't feel pain' are. Now, the fact that some hinge certainties look like empirical propositions should not mislead us; we have been there before and, indeed, guided by Peter Hacker:

> Putative metaphysical propositions have the form of empirical propositions.
>
> 1989, 196

> [The metaphysician's] claims look like claims about the character of objects in the world. They have the form of empirical claims ...
>
> 1989, 200

But this is precisely how Wittgenstein describes Moore-type hinge certainties in *On Certainty*: they 'have the form of empirical propositions' but are not empirical propositions. Granted, these certainties are not putative *metaphysical* propositions that appear to describe the *necessary* features of the world, but they are putative *empirical* propositions that appear to describe the *contingent* features of the world. And therein lies some of the novelty of *On Certainty*.

On Certainty is continuous with all of Wittgenstein's earlier writings – including the *Tractatus* – in that it comes at the end of a long, unbroken attempt to elucidate the grammar of our language-games, to demarcate grammar from language *in use*.[23] Baker and Hacker have superbly elucidated the second Wittgenstein's unmasking of the grammatical nature of metaphysical or super-empirical propositions; what sets *On Certainty* apart is its further perspicuous distinction between some 'empirical' propositions and others ('Our "empirical propositions" do not form a homogenous mass' (OC 213)): some apparently *empirical and contingent* propositions being in fact nothing but expressions of grammatical rules. The importance of this realization is that it leads to the unprecedented insight that basic beliefs – though they look like humdrum empirical and contingent propositions – are in fact ways of acting which, when conceptually elucidated, can be seen to function as rules of grammar: they underlie all thinking (OC 401). So that the hinge certainty 'The earth has existed for many years' underpins all thought and action, but not as a proposition that strikes us immediately as true; rather as a way of acting that underpins what we do (e.g., we research the age of the earth) and what we say (e.g., we speak of the earth in the past tense):

> Giving grounds, however, justifying the evidence, comes to an end; – but the end is not certain propositions striking us immediately as true, i.e. it is not a kind of *seeing* on our part; it is our *acting*, which lies at the bottom of the language-game.
>
> OC 204[24]

The nonpropositional nature of basic beliefs puts a stop to the regress that has plagued epistemology: we no longer need to posit untenable self-justifying propositions at the basis of knowledge. In taking hinges to be true empirical propositions, Peter Hacker fails to acknowledge the ground-breaking insight that our basic certainties are *ways of acting*, and not 'certain propositions striking us as true' (OC 204). If all Wittgenstein were doing in OC was to claim that our basic beliefs are true empirical propositions, why bother? He would be merely repeating what philosophers before him have been saying for centuries, all the while deploring an unsolvable infinite regress. Why not rather appreciate that Wittgenstein has stopped the regress?

So while I agree with Hacker that there is no *fundamental* change in the salient features of Wittgenstein's conception of grammar, I find there is an *extension* of grammar in the third Wittgenstein – an extension of revolutionary magnitude for epistemology.

3. Philosophical theses

Hacker's third core argument is 'that there is no *fundamental* change in 1937, or indeed later, in the salient features of Wittgenstein's conception of … philosophy as a grammatical investigation, or of philosophical problems as *au fond* grammatical ones' (12). He opposes the supposition by some interpreters that Wittgenstein's grammatical propositions, observations and remarks are (i) theses, (ii) theories or hypotheses, or (iii) opinions, and (iv) that they are dogmatic (14). Here, I am substantially in agreement with Peter Hacker, but would like to attempt a clarification of Wittgenstein's position and suggest some reasons for the confusion.

Now, of course, there is no question that grammatical propositions, observations and remarks are not theses, theories, hypotheses or opinions. What must be asked is whether Wittgenstein's philosophical remarks are indeed grammatical remarks. Take sentences such as these:

> For a large class of cases ... the meaning of a word is its use in the language.
>
> PI 43

> Words are also deeds.
>
> PI 546

> The *truth* of certain empirical propositions belongs to our frame of reference.
>
> OC 83

> At the foundation of well-founded belief lies belief that is not founded.
>
> OC 253

They seem to be genuine theses; that is: statements that may be true or false and that are susceptible of agreement or disagreement.[25] Yet what of Wittgenstein's alleged claim that philosophy does not advance theses? Let us read it in context:

> Philosophy simply puts everything before us, and neither explains nor deduces anything. – Since everything lies open to view there is nothing to explain. For *what is hidden*, for example, *is of no interest to us*.
> One might also give the name "philosophy" to what is possible *before* all new discoveries and inventions.
>
> PI 126; my emphasis

> The work of the philosopher consists in assembling reminders for a particular purpose.
>
> PI 127

> If one tried to advance *theses* in philosophy, it would never be possible to debate them, because everyone would agree to them.
>
> PI 128

> *The aspects of things that are most important for us are hidden* because of their simplicity and familiarity. (One is unable to notice something – because it is always before one's eyes.) The real foundations of his enquiry do not strike a man at all.

Unless *that* fact has at some time struck him. – And this means: we fail to be struck by what, once seen, is most striking and most powerful.

PI 129; first emphasis mine

Note the apparent contradiction between: 'what is hidden . . . is of no interest to us' (PI 126) and 'The aspects of things that are most important for us are hidden' (PI 129).

Taken in context, PI 128 – 'If one tried to advance *theses* in philosophy, it would never be possible to debate them, because everyone would agree to them' – can be said to be merely emphasizing the point Wittgenstein was making in PI 126 and will continue to make in PI 129, namely the nonhermeneutic and uncontroversial aspect of philosophical endeavour and its elucidations. At 129, Wittgenstein writes: although 'the aspects of things that are most important for us are hidden', they are so 'because of their simplicity and familiarity'. How so? Take, for example, a pile of books that has been sitting in a corner of a room for months; it has so become part of the scenery that we no longer notice its presence. The books are not *really* hidden; they are in plain view, but because we don't notice them, they might as well be hidden; they are inconspicuous. This is then how the aspects of things that are most important to us can be non-paradoxically both hidden and 'in plain view'. And it is once brought forward by the philosopher's *perspicuous presentation* that we can 'be struck by what, once seen, is most striking and most powerful' (PI 129).

So the work of the Wittgensteinian philosopher[26] consists in 'assembling reminders for a particular purpose' – that is, it consists in reminding us of something which in a sense 'we have always known' (PI 109) because it was open to view,[27] but which we hadn't noticed because of its familiarity or simplicity (that is, its basicness). As, for example, in accounting for how language works, philosophers had failed to notice the essential and omnipresent contribution of context to meaning; in accounting for how we follow rules, they did not notice the essential contribution of training and exposure; and in saying 'I know "here is a hand"', G. E. Moore failed to notice the animal (or nonepistemic) certainty underpinning his epistemic affirmation.

One cannot refute 'meaning is use' in the way one might refute the Big Bang theory as a cosmological explanation of the early development of the universe. There is something irrefutable about: 'For a *large* class of cases . . . the meaning of a word is its use in the language' (PI 43), or – as Wittgenstein puts it in *On Certainty*: 'A meaning of a word is a kind of employment of it' (OC 61). And yet, philosophers before Wittgenstein were not aware of this internal relationship between meaning and use; they did not 'notice' how meaning really works, but made false assumptions about it. It took Wittgenstein to remind us, to make a perspicuous description of how meaning works. Wittgenstein did not invent anything; and he would probably more correctly be said to have 'uncovered' rather than 'discovered' something; and yet his reminders shed *new* light by rearranging things in an *unprecedented* way. This is how a philosopher's reminders, presentations or descriptions can contribute to a better understanding of ourselves. What philosophy does, then, on Wittgenstein's view, is highlight aspects of the obvious via rearrangement and comparison ('seeing connexions') so as to remind us of, to bring us to acknowledge or recognise, the previously unrecognised *obvious*. Unlike science, philosophy's solutions do not involve giving new information (PI 109) in the sense of making new discoveries, but this is not to say that philosophy is not going to bring something to light.

That said, one wants to add: a description, however perspicuous, is still a description – and therefore susceptible of mistake. Granted, there is something irrefutable – 'grammatical' – about Wittgenstein's reminders, and yet they are constantly being (putatively) 'refuted' or 'questioned', 'debated' or ignored; indeed, some of them may not in fact be all that perspicuous. It may be countered that the dissenters are speaking nonsense, not seeing things aright, not discerning the logical/grammatical in what appears to be a hypothesis or a thesis or a theory. And this is where the Wittgensteinian philosopher can be taxed with dogmatism. Why should a philosopher's reminders have the status of grammatical remarks and thereby be indubitable? And if it is (rightly) objected that, qua *grammatical* reminders, they may be susceptible of rejection, but not of doubt, does this preclude their being theoretical or hypothetical in some sense of those terms? If, as Dan Hutto suggests, perspicuous presentations are like maps (2007, 301), then they are not theories. I can draw a map of the London underground network, and get a couple of stations wrong. This doesn't make the faulty map a faulty theory, but a wrong description.[28] And yet isn't a theory nothing but a proposed description?[29]

In the *Remarks on the Philosophy of Psychology*, Wittgenstein is in the business of classification, and says so explicitly (RPP II 63, 148). We find him classifying psychological concepts like emotions and sensations according to certain characteristics like localization and duration. He is doing this because he believes it can cast light on 'the correct treatment' of these phenomena (RPP II 311), which alone can bring understanding. But in order not to 'put the phenomenon in the wrong drawer' (RPP I, 380), in order to get 'the right-fitting classification', one must 'know one's way about among the concepts of "psychological phenomena"... That is to say: one has got to *master* the kinships and differences of the concepts' (RPP I, 1054). But mastery is difficult; it is possible – even for Wittgenstein – to put a phenomenon in the wrong drawer. Inasmuch as philosophers can produce ill-fitting classifications, their presentations are in principle rejectable. Also, in order to know one's way about the concepts one is elucidating and to make a perspicuous presentation of them, one must *observe* how words are used and how this use is impacted by our form of life. For, remember, there is also 'looking around' in philosophy. Indeed, Wittgenstein specifically urges us: 'Don't think but look!' (PI 66).

Take Wittgenstein's remarks that language and meaning have their root in action (reaction, gesture, behaviour):

> The origin and the primitive form of the language game is a reaction; only from this can more complicated forms develop.
> Language – I want to say – is a refinement. 'In the beginning was the deed.'
> CE 395; CV p. 31

> What we call meaning must be connected with the primitive language of gestures (pointing-language).
> BT 24

In order to say that 'In the beginning was the deed' and mean this as a grammatical remark, even the Wittgensteinian philosopher has looked, and not just thought. Though the remark is not the result of empirical research, conceptual elucidation demands observation; it cannot be performed *ex nihilo*: 'Words have meaning only in the stream of life' (PI 913). And, indeed some grammatical remarks (e.g., 'What we call meaning must be connected with the primitive language of gestures (pointing-language))' seem to require more in-depth observation than others.

Is it, then, that conceptual elucidation is not categorially different from scientific conclusion in that it also requires observation, albeit only of the armchair variety? I think not, and the difference lies in the nature of the observation. 'Look, don't think!' is not only a rejoinder to look, but an enjoinder to look *without thinking*. That is, to give as candid or naive a description as possible; a description unencumbered by speculation, theory or explanation. Philosophical description differs from scientific theorizing in that it only describes, it only presents (though as perspicuously as possible); it does not offer an explanation or a theory that goes beyond, or beneath, the observation. Realism, not empiricism in philosophy, that *is* the hardest thing![30]

What Wittgenstein is doing in the various passages that state or suggest that philosophy is not in the business of making discoveries, advancing theses or formulating theories is demarcating the business of philosophy from that of science. It is science, not philosophy, that makes *new discoveries*, advances groundbreaking *theses* and propounds original *theories*; and there is a *categorial* difference between what philosophy does and what science does. This is not to say that there is no interaction between them, only that there is no *continuum* between them: science and philosophy are not separated by a difference of *degree* – as Quine and most philosophers of mind today would have it – but by a difference of *category*.

The obscurities of philosophy are not of the same order as those of science, and therefore nor will its elucidations be. Philosophical obscurity results from the 'misleading appearances', the bewitchments of language. Unlike the sciences, there is no discovery to be made in philosophy for the simple reason that philosophy already has all it needs at its disposal in order to carry out its business of conceptual elucidation: it has language and the stream of life in which language flows:

> What I want to oppose here is the false idea that we could hit upon something that today we do not see, that we can *discover* something entirely new. That is a mistake. In truth, we already have everything; in fact it is *present*, so that we do not have to wait for anything. We move within the realm of something already there, the grammar of our accustomed language.
>
> WVC, 182–3

But even the visible has its obscurity, and so language can be misleading: for one thing, its uniform appearance masks its multifarious uses, obscuring those uses. Just as it is difficult to see that first-person utterances such as 'That hurts!' are not always descriptions, but often non-truth evaluable expressions that do not differ from 'Ouch' or a groan. So that a sentence is sometimes equivalent to a gesture.[31] This is difficult to see because we do not think of sentences as gestures, but also because in some contexts, that same sentence will not have the function of a gesture but of a description – say to a doctor. Language can be misleading because its various functions are inconspicuous or hidden: a sentence does not carry its use on its sleeve, as it were. And so it is the philosopher's aim '...not to be misled by the appearance of a sentence and to investigate its application in the language-game' (Z 247). But also the figurativeness, the metaphorical flexibility of language can lead us astray. We talk about the brain *sending messages* to our legs, or our memories being *stored* in our brain, and such ways of talking, though perfectly legitimate, encourage us to think of the brain as an agent in its own right, and memories as encoded entities. They encourage us, philosophers particularly, to *posit* mysterious processes and entities, where in fact none are there; and this is when philosophy theorizes:

> When does one have the thought: the possible movements of a machine are already there in it in some mysterious way? – Well, when one is doing philosophy. And what leads us into thinking that? The kind of way in which we talk about machines. We say, for example, that a machine *has* (possesses) such-and-such possibilities of movement; we speak of the ideally rigid machine which *can* only move in such-and-such a way. – What is this *possibility* of movement? ... The possibility of a movement is, rather, supposed to be like a shadow of the movement itself. But do you know of such a shadow? ... (See how high the seas of language run here!) The waves subside as soon as we ask ourselves: how do we use the phrase "possibility of movement" when we are talking about a given machine? – But then where did our queer ideas come from? ... We mind about the kind of expressions we use concerning these things; we do not understand them, however, but misinterpret them. When we do philosophy we are like savages, primitive people, who hear the expressions of civilized men, put a false interpretation on them, and then draw the queerest conclusions from it.
>
> PI 194

In a paper entitled 'The Use of "theory" in philosophy', Oswald Hanfling reminds us that there are several senses of 'theory', and one of these may well apply to Wittgenstein's 'reminders':

> And what is wrong with describing Wittgenstein's 'reminders' themselves as theories, as some commentators have done? Thus, one might speak of his theories of first-person knowledge, family resemblances, meaning and use, the nature of mathematics, and what it is to follow a rule. It is true that there is no need to introduce the word 'theory' here ... Nevertheless, the description of his views as 'theories' would be in accordance with an established usage [of the term].
>
> 2004, 187

Hanfling suggests that Wittgenstein's sense of 'theory' can best be understood in terms of his rejection of 'what is hidden' in favour of what 'lies open to view' (PI 126). And here we come back to the seeming contradiction between the hidden that *is* of interest to us and that which isn't. The hidden that Wittgenstein *rejects* is not the hidden that is merely masked by language and can be brought to light by a perspicuous presentation; rather: it is some hidden entity or process, that is *posited* (2004, 192) – like the 'possibility of movement' reified in PI 194, or as in when we speak of obeying a rule, we posit the rule as an inner mental state or abstract entity which somehow 'contains' all of its possible applications. Positing entities and processes is the kind of theorizing that science and metaphysics do but philosophy should not do. This is how I understand Wittgenstein's remarks to differ from theories and theses.

I have stressed the Wittgensteinian philosopher's *observation* of the world in her conceptual elucidations because of the tendency to understand and transmit Wittgenstein's philosophy as a purely linguistic endeavour, out of touch with the world. Wittgenstein is too often regarded as a linguistic idealist; and this is not only wrong, it also alienates him from the rest of philosophy. For Wittgenstein, philosophy has to do not only with language but with the world. This is because language itself has to do with the world. And so, to speak of conceptual elucidation is also to speak of the elucidation of our form of life. When Wittgenstein elucidates what it is to remember, he does not only elucidate our use of the words 'remembering' or 'memory'. Elucidating memory requires looking at our behaviour and practices and arguing from these observations that our understanding of memory had better go one way and not the other; had better not, and indeed need not, involve notions of representations and encoded traces, but rather more of what we *do* when we remember.[32] Perhaps, then, it might make more strategic sense – in discussion with non-Wittgensteinians or scientists – to speak of Wittgenstein's 'social theory of language acquisition' than to speak of his '(hopefully) perspicuous presentation of language acquisition'.

And then, there is also the problem that Wittgensteinian philosophers are themselves involved in disagreement about Wittgenstein's grammatical remarks. Peter Hacker does not agree that basic certainties are rules of grammar, so he thinks I am making a wrong claim or that I am wrong to believe this is a conceptual remark, and that I am in the throes of conceptual confusion. I, on the other hand, believe that this is as much a grammatical remark as he takes 'Meaning is use' to be. And therefore, that I – propped on Wittgenstein's shoulders – am offering a conceptual elucidation of our traditional conception of basic beliefs. But this is where grammatical remarks begin to look like claims and hypotheses. Although philosophers advance conceptual elucidations and not hypotheses, they can be wrong in the elucidations they are advancing, and this makes their advances look hypothetical.

Wittgenstein has an extensive body of work on the philosophy of mind, but it does not cohabit with science or scientific method. Which is not to say that Wittgenstein was dismissive of science, or indeed of the philosopher's awareness of scientific research and progress.[33] And in the other direction, Wittgenstein sees philosophy as impacting science – indeed, possibly giving it new direction through a more perspicuous presentation of concepts. Indeed, Wittgenstein's view of philosophy and the practice of philosophy are *not* – as has been too often suggested – all about dissolution and deconstruction, but also about problem-tackling and solution-finding and indeed the offering of a new order to replace the conceptual disorder found in philosophy, but also in the sciences. He clarifies this in his *Remarks on the Philosophy of Psychology*:

What is it ... that a conceptual investigation does? Does it belong in the natural history of human concepts? – Well, natural history, we say, describes plants and beasts. But might it not be that plants had been described in full detail, and then for the first time someone realized the analogies in their structure, analogies which had never been seen before? And so, that he establishes a new order among these descriptions. He says, e.g., 'compare this part, not with this one, but rather with that' ... and in so doing he is not necessarily speaking of *derivation*; nonetheless the new arrangement *might* also give a new direction to scientific investigation. He is saying 'Look at it like *this*' – and that may have advantages and consequences of various kinds.

RPP I, 950

And so – far from entitling her to be a mere under-labourer to science, the philosopher's conceptual elucidation may go as far as giving scientific investigation its new direction. And here, I cannot but applaud Hacker and the extraordinary contribution he has made in taking Wittgenstein's conceptual elucidations beyond philosophy to science:

The task of philosophy is to resolve or dissolve philosophical problems. These are a priori conceptual problems.... This requires a perspicuous representation of the problematic concepts that illuminates the problems at hand. [Philosophy's] proper vocation ... is not armchair science. It is categorially distinct from science, both in its methods and its results. The a priori methods of respectable philosophy are wholly distinct from the experimental and hypothetico-deductive methods of the natural sciences, and the results of philosophy logically antecede the empirical discoveries of science. They cannot licitly conflict with the truth of scientific theories – but they may, and sometimes should, demonstrate their lack of sense. *One* task of philosophy is to set straight the conceptual confusions and incoherences of scientific theories. For philosophy is neither the Queen of the sciences nor their conceptual scullery-maid, but rather a tribunal before which scientific theory may be arraigned when it trespasses beyond the bounds of sense.

2007b, 143[34]

Notes

Introduction

1. For those who don't know Leavis, he is considered by many – myself included – the best literary critic of our time. He and Wittgenstein met at Cambridge.
2. Leavis (1982), 129, 134, 144.
3. On my justification for calling notes that were posthumously assembled and published a 'work', see Chapter 11, 'Beyond Hacker's Wittgenstein', in this volume.
4. Following the hinge metaphor in this passage: ' the *questions* that we raise and our *doubts* depend on the fact that some propositions are exempt from doubt, are as it were like hinges on which those turn' (OC 341). I return to hinge certainty in section 5 of this chapter, 'Certainty in action'; for a more extensive description, see Chapter 8, 'Wittgenstein on Knowledge and Certainty', in this volume.
5. On the single human form of life and the innumerable forms of human life, see Moyal-Sharrock (2015).
6. Aristotle was the only philosopher, to my knowledge, to have thus considered the mind before Wittgenstein. For Aristotle, the soul (*psuchē*) is a set of capacities (or functions), and *mind* (*nous*) is one of them. But unlike all the other capacities or faculties (e.g., sight, smell), the mind has no corresponding bodily organ (e.g., the brain). This, however, does not mean that Aristotle thinks the mind is not 'embodied' – that we could think, hope, expect, desire, will etc. without having a body, or that the body plays no role in our thinking, hoping, etc.: on the contrary, he claims there is no separating the mind from the body. This is his *hylomorphism*. Aristotle is then the first philosopher to envisage, and indeed, champion the notion of *embodied mind*.
7. Particularly in Chapter 3, 'Words as Deeds', and Chapter 6, 'Wittgenstein on Memory'.
8. It is this sense of explanation – the scientific sense – that, when practised by philosophers, Wittgenstein counters. Of course, not all explanation (*pace* strong explanatory scientism of the kind upheld by Stephen Hawking) is scientific (e.g., the explanation of a word's meaning), and Wittgenstein often alludes to a thinner sense of explanation which amounts to a re-description. This is related, but only partly, to what he refers to as 'further descriptions' rather than explanation, as what is called for, say in aesthetics, ethics and philosophy (MWL 106). On this, see Cioffi (1998; 2007) and Schroeder (1993).
9. TLP 2.18: 'logical form, i.e. the form of reality.'
10. I use these terms more or less interchangeably, as Wittgenstein often does. For what Wittgenstein means by 'grammar', see Chapter 1, 'Wittgenstein's Grammar: Through Thick and Thin', and Chapter 11, 'Beyond Hacker's Wittgenstein', in this volume.
11. 'The work of the philosopher consists in assembling reminders for a particular purpose' (PI 127). Wittgenstein speaks of 'reminders' here to contrast with 'new information' (PI 109). The philosopher is not in the business of informing us of something new, but of reminding us of what is always before our eyes though we don't see it, either because it is too familiar (like a stack of newspapers that's been in a

corner of the room for weeks) or because we have been led astray by the misuse of language.
12. On this, see Chapter 1, 'Wittgenstein's Grammar: Through Thick and Thin', and Chapter 10, 'Fighting Relativism', in this volume.
13. What Wittgenstein means by 'realism' here is not what is meant in the current philosophical usage of the term (i.e., physicalism), but in the use resurrected for philosophy by Cora Diamond in *The Realistic Spirit* (1991); realism as having to do with reality, with our life.
14. On this, see Chapter 3, 'Words as Deeds', in this volume, which rebukes physicalism for its view of the brain as not simply a mechanical enabler, but the generator of our wills, desires, intentions and actions.
15. See especially Chapter 6, 'Wittgenstein on Memory', in this volume.
16. Or that 'brains attach meaning to minds' (1990, 26). The article heading reads: 'Is the Brain's Mind a Computer Program? No. A program merely manipulates symbols, whereas a brain attaches meaning to them'. How is that done? The answer we get is never much more than mere reiteration: '... the mind imposes intentionality on sounds and marks, thereby conferring meanings upon them and, in so doing, relating them to reality' (1990, 139).
17. I am inspired, here, by Avrum Stroll's excellent 'Reflections on Water' (in his *Sketches of Landscape: Philosophy by Example* (Cambridge, MA: MIT Press, 1998), 37–73).
18. On action or behaviour as the phylogenetic, ontogenetic and logical origin of thought and language, see, respectively, Chapter 5, 'From Deed to Word: Gapless and Kink-free Enactivism'; Chapter 2, 'Universal Grammar: Wittgenstein versus Chomsky'; and Chapter 3, 'Words as Deeds' in this volume.
19. My first paper at the International Wittgenstein Symposium in Kirchberg in 1997 (before I'd ever heard the term 'enactivism') was entitled 'The enacted nature of basic beliefs'. I was taken to task by my audience for using the word 'enacted' as suggesting that there was something (inner) there, preceding the enactment, that was going to be enacted. So, I dropped the word, but I shouldn't have been so quickly discouraged. The word needn't be, and indeed hasn't been, thus understood. Wittgenstein is an enactivist through and through. I have resumed use of the term 'enactive' and its cognates in my work.
20. I prefer this expression to the more current '4E cognition' (embodied, embedded, enactive and extended) which still accords too much to the brain in sometimes seeing the relation between brain and mind as *contentfully* dynamic and complementary. This is particularly the case with the 'extended mind' approach, which Hutto, Kirchhoff and Myin (2014) have argued would be better replaced by an '*extensive* enactivism'. This explains my use of the term 'extensiveness' rather than 'extended mind'.
21. As opposed to, more narrowly, the movement founded by Varela, Thompson and Rosch (1991).
22. We must, however, acknowledge a direct line of 'action' from Aristotle to Wittgenstein: 'Back to the rough ground!' – away from the lifeless abstractness of Plato and metaphysics to concepts having meaning in the stream of life. I cannot say more on Aristotle here, but on the reality-soaked nature of concepts, see Chapter 1, 'Wittgenstein's Grammar: Through Thick and Thin', in this volume.
23. Of course, Wittgenstein's Razor is not exactly Occam's, but the underlying idea is the same: using parsimony, simplicity, and making the fewest assumptions in our descriptions (Occam would probably say 'explanations'); preferring 'the *simplest* law that can be reconciled with our experiences' (TLP 6.363).

24 Peter Hacker: '... behaviourism was right about *some* matters.... Where it was wrong was to suppose that the mental is *reducible* to behaviour and dispositions to behave. Ontological behaviourism (Watson and Skinner) was right to emphasize that language learning is based on training, and that it presupposes common behavioural reactions and responses.... It was correct to conceive of understanding in terms of abilities and dispositions, rather than as a hidden mental state or process. But the behaviourists were sorely mistaken to suppose that the mental is a fiction. One can think and feel without showing it, and one can exhibit thoughts and feelings without having them. Avowals of experience are indeed a form of behaviour, but what they avow is not behaviour' (2013, 21).

25 Hume, for one, was incensed by the speculative metaphysics of his predecessors – 'entirely hypothetical', depending 'more upon Invention than Experience' (1932, 3.6) – engaged in a reform of philosophy: waging 'war' on 'abstruse philosophy and metaphysical jargon that gets mixed up with popular superstition' and replacing them with 'accurate and valid reasoning' (1748, 5).

26 Certainly, Hume did not underestimate it: 'the chief obstacle ... to our improvement in the moral or metaphysical sciences is the obscurity of the ideas, and ambiguity of the terms' (1748, 45).

27 See Gennaro (n.d.).

28 Indeed, in its attempts to find the ghost in the machine, philosophical neuromania has even found its way to the *Scientific American* in the guise of 'experimental philosophy': 'Some philosophers today' – reads the headline in that journal – 'are doing more than thinking deeply. They are also conducting scientific experiments relating to the nature of free will and of good and evil' (Knobe 2011, 39). The article is entitled 'Experimental Philosophy: Thoughts Become the New Lab Rats', indicating that the thought experiments conducted by philosophers these days tend to emphasize the 'experiment' rather than the 'thought'.

29 Because they are so deeply built in to the way we speak. Moreover, though it is the philosopher's task to engage, and engage other philosophers, in conceptual elucidation, Wittgenstein is clear: 'Philosophy may in no way interfere with the actual use of language' (PI 124).

30 See Tejedor (2017).

31 There is no space here to give an account of the impact of Wittgenstein's own philosophy on the sciences, as well as other disciplines – e.g., psychology, neuropsychology, child development, sociology, anthropology, primatology, linguistics, language acquisition, sciences of education, gender studies, law, religion, literature, art. However, in several chapters of this volume, I use his insights to dissolve or shed light on some of the confusions that crucially hamper these disciplines, with Chapters 2, 5 and 6 focusing on what Wittgenstein brings to research on language acquisition, phylogenetic (evolutionary) development, and memory.

32 See especially Chapter 2, 'Universal Grammar: Wittgenstein versus Chomsky'; Chapter 5, 'From Deed to Word: Gapless and Kink-free Enactivism'; Chapter 6, 'Wittgenstein on Memory'; Chapter 7, 'Wittgenstein on Psychological Certainty'.

33 Noted, for example, by Garry Gutting: 'Almost every article that appears in *The Stone* provokes some comments from readers challenging the very idea that philosophy has anything relevant to say to non-philosophers. There are, in particular, complaints that philosophy is an irrelevant "ivory-tower" exercise, useless to any except those interested in logic-chopping for its own sake' (2012).

34 For a focused account of 'hinge certainty', see Chapter 8, 'Wittgenstein on Knowledge and Certainty', in this volume.
35 Although, due to the self-standing nature of the original papers that make up the book, the journey will inevitably include some repetition.
36 On this, see Chapter 11, 'Beyond Hacker's Wittgenstein'.
37 See Coliva and Moyal-Sharrock (eds) (2016).
38 I am immensely grateful to Ian Ground and Constantine Sandis for their probing comments and enriching exchanges which have contributed to this Introduction.

1 Wittgenstein's Grammar

1 I borrow the term 'reality-soaked' from Bernard Harrison, who uses it to speak of a 'reality-soaked language' (1991, 58).
2 An expression I coined to denote the post-*Investigations* corpus. I flesh out my motivation for this in Chapter 11, 'Beyond Hacker's Wittgenstein' in this volume, and in Moyal-Sharrock (ed.), *The Third Wittgenstein: The Post-Investigations Works* (London: Routledge, 2004).
3 Though I say more about 'patterns of life' and 'hinge certainties' below, these notions are fleshed out in Chapter 7, 'Wittgenstein on Psychological Certainty' and Chapter 8, 'Wittgenstein on Knowledge and Certainty' respectively.
4 For my present purpose, it is not necessary to mark the distinction made in the *Tractatus* between 'nonsense' and 'senseless', which dissolves in the later Wittgenstein.
5 See Moyal-Sharrock (2007b) for a detailed argument.
6 See *The New Wittgenstein*, eds A. Crary and R. Read (London: Routledge, 2000) *passim* in which so-called 'Ineffabilists' (philosophers who, like Peter Hacker, view some nonsense in the *Tractatus* as 'illuminating') are rebuked for 'chickening out', for not being 'resolute' enough to recognize that Wittgenstein viewed all nonsense as 'plain nonsense'; i.e., gibberish.
7 Ethics, aesthetics and the mystical 'cannot be put into words' (TLP 6.421; 6.522).
8 '... what can be said; i.e. propositions of natural science – i.e. something that has nothing to do with philosophy' (TLP 6.53).
9 Note also Wittgenstein's acknowledgment, in a letter to Fricker, that the important part of the *Tractatus* was the silent part: 'My work consists of two parts: the one presented here plus all that I have *not* written. And it is precisely this second part that is the important one.' (EL 143)
10 See also PI 23.
11 For a discussion of the presence of the saying/showing dichotomy as late as *On Certainty*, see Moyal-Sharrock (2007a), 94–7, and passim.
12 For further discussion on the ineffability of basic certainty, see Chapter 8, 'Wittgenstein on Knowledge and Certainty', in this volume; and Moyal-Sharrock (2007a) 65–71; 94–9.
13 Note that I will be using the terms 'reality', 'nature' and 'the world' interchangeably to refer to unconceptualized or raw reality – what Wittgenstein refers to as the 'reality lying behind the notation' (PI 562); where I mean a conceptualized world or reality, I will speak of 'my world', 'our world' or 'human reality'.
14 He saw logical questions as grammatical in that they, too, determine sense.
15 For further discussion, see Moyal-Sharrock (2016a).

16 For example: 'How can I be taught to recognize these patterns [in the weave of life]? I am shown simple examples, and then complicated ones of both kinds. It is almost the way I learn to distinguish the styles of two composers' (LW II, 42–3); 'When he first learns the names of colours – what is taught him? Well, he learns e.g. to call out "red" on seeing something red. – But is that the right description; or ought it to have gone: "He learns to call 'red' *what we too* call 'red'"? – Both descriptions are right. . . . What I teach him however must be a *capacity*. So he *can* now bring something red at an order; or arrange objects according to colour' (Z 421); 'As children we learn concepts and what one does with them simultaneously' (LW II, 43).

17 As Wittgenstein makes clear: 'We do not see facial contortions and *make the inference* that he is feeling joy, grief, boredom. We describe a face immediately as sad, radiant, bored, even when we are unable to give any other description of the features. – Grief, one would like to say, is personified in the face. This is essential to what we call 'emotion'. (RPP II, 570)

18 The mind is often *directly observable*, thus obviating the need for a Theory of Mind to attribute mental states – thoughts, perceptions, desires, intentions, feelings – to others. The notion of the mind as 'something inner', accessible only to oneself, has been seriously undermined by Wittgenstein. For an excellent discussion, see Vaaja (2013).

19 'Grammar is not accountable to any reality. It is grammatical rules that determine meaning (constitute it) and so they themselves are not answerable to any meaning and to that extent are arbitrary' (PG 184).

20 Note that although one of Wittgenstein's most persistent philosophical concerns is to make the distinction ever clearer between grammar and the use of language (BT 38), he does not always mark that distinction in his use of 'language' and 'grammar'. Where he is more preoccupied with distinguishing word and world rather than grammar from propositions, he often speaks of language where he means grammar (e.g., 'If I want to tell someone what colour some material is to be, I send him a sample, and obviously this sample belongs to language' (PR 38)); or speaks of them quasi-interchangeably (e.g., 'The calculus is as it were autonomous. – Language must speak for itself' (PG 63)). But the distinction between language and grammar remains a logical distinction: grammatical rules *govern* our use of language; they are not language but are essential to language; make language possible.

21 These – 'grammar' and 'concepts' – are often used interchangeably by Wittgenstein. A conceptual elucidation is a grammatical elucidation.

22 See Malcolm: 'The notes for 1930–1932, edited by Desmond Lee, exhibit at first a striking continuity with the *Tractatus*: language consists of propositions; a proposition is a picture of reality; a proposition must have the same logical multiplicity as the fact which it describes; thought must have the logical form of reality. But new concerns soon appear. What is the relation of the logical grammar of language to reality? The application of grammar to reality is not shown by the grammar; a picture does not contain its own application. "In all language," Wittgenstein says, "there is a bridge between the sign and its application. No one can make this for us; we have to bridge the gap ourselves. No explanation ever saves the jump, because any further explanation will itself need a jump." Can grammar be justified? Can we say why we use just these rules of grammar and not other ones? Is the logic of our language to be justified on the ground that it fits the nature of reality? No. "Our justification could only take the form of saying 'As reality is so and so, the rules must be such and such.' But this presupposes that I could say 'If reality were otherwise, then the rules of grammar would be otherwise.' But

in order to describe a reality in which grammar was otherwise I would have to use the very combinations which grammar forbids. The rules of grammar distinguish sense and nonsense and if I use the forbidden combinations I talk nonsense.' (1980 online).
23 PI Part II (1946–9) is roughly contemporaneous with RPP I (1946–7).
24 With the help of fertility goddesses.
25 '[A child] doesn't learn *at all* that that mountain has existed for a long time: that is, the question whether it is so doesn't arise at all. It swallows this consequence down, so to speak, together with *what* it learns' (OC 143). 237. 'If I say "an hour ago this table didn't exist" I probably meant that it was only made later on. ... If I say "this mountain didn't exist half an hour ago", that is such a strange statement that it is not clear what I mean' (OC 237).
26 For more detailed discussion, see Moyal-Sharrock (2007a).
27 Wittgenstein uses the German word *Muster*, which can be translated both as *model* or *pattern*.
28 There are also culture-bound, or 'locally' thick grammars – conditioned by the different forms of human life. For more on the distinction between the one human form of life and the innumerable forms of human life, see Moyal-Sharrock (2015).
29 To consider the thick rules that are reality-soaked but not strictly speaking *experiential* (e.g., 'Napoleon existed' (cf. OC 185)) as part of the 'grammaticalization of experience', we would need to either understand the term 'experience' in this phrase in a broad (culture-inclusive) sense, or say that not all of thick grammar is part of Wittgenstein's grammaticalization of experience. I would opt for the first.
30 See note 20.
31 'If I want to tell someone what colour some material is to be, I send him a sample, and obviously this sample belongs to language; and equally the memory or image of a colour that I conjure by a word, belongs to language' (PR 38). 'We can put it like this: This sample is an instrument of the language used in ascriptions of colour. In this language-game it is not something that is represented, but is a means of representation. ... And to say "If it did not *exist*, it could have no name" is to say as much and as little as: if this thing did not exist, we could not use it in our language-game. – What looks as if it *had* to exist, is part of the language. It is a paradigm in our language-game; something with which comparison is made. And this may be an important observation; but it is none the less an observation concerning our language-game – our method of representation' (PI 50). Although Wittgenstein speaks of samples as being part of, or belonging to, 'language', strictly speaking, he means to 'grammar' (see note 20).
32 David Lewis sees 'the mere possibility' that a person might switch bodies as real or serious enough to require refutation (1971, 47).
33 And, I would add, nothing more time-wasting for scientists to engage in experiments to try and (dis)prove philosophers' time-wasting thought experiments: http://www.pbs.org/wgbh/nova/next/physics/physicists-confirm-that-were-not-living-in-a-computer-simulation/.

2 Universal Grammar

1 Professor of philosophy at the University of Kent, Laurence Goldstein's work on Wittgenstein includes a book, *Clear and Queer Thinking: Wittgenstein's Development and His Relevance to Modern Thought* (1999), and articles such as 'What does "experiencing meaning" mean?' (in *The Third Wittgenstein*, 2004), and 'Wittgenstein

and Situation Comedy' (*Philosophia,* 2009). See his edited collection *Brevity* (Oxford University Press, 2013). Laurence was advisory editor for the 2005 *Monist* issue on the Philosophy of Humor. He was keenly interested in language acquisition, designed apparatus for teaching syllogistic to blind students and wrote a series of texts for teaching English to Chinese children.

2   It is worth noting that Chomsky has developed and revised his approach over the years – particularly reformulating his Principles and Parameters approach on the basis of his more minimalist program (Chomsky 1995), but while these changes have affected specialist theoretical and computationalist linguistics approaches, they have not fundamentally altered his nativist position whose core assumptions have remained constant (see Tomalin 2012, 334–7). Upon considering this chapter for republication, I looked in vain for anything in it that would no longer cohere with Chomsky's current view, which he has summarized at various venues in the past few years – as, for example, in his lectio magistralis, entitled 'The minimalist program and language acquisition', delivered on the occasion of his PhD honoris causa in Neuroscience at the International School for Advanced Studies (SISSA) in Trieste on 17 September 2012 (Chomsky (2012).

3   In fact, nativists recognize that not all principles occur in every language, but claim that this does not prevent that principle from being universal as long as the principle is *not broken*. Indeed a principle can be claimed universal on the basis of its occurrence in a single language: 'In what sense can a universal that does not occur in every language still be universal? Japanese does not *break* any of the requirements of syntactic movement; it does not need locality for question movement because question movement itself does not occur. Its absence from some aspect of a given language does not prove it is not universal. Provided that the universal is found in some human language, it does not have to be present in all languages'; '. . . it is not necessary for a universal principle to occur in dozens of languages. . . . it can be claimed to be universal on evidence from one language alone; 'I have not hesitated to propose a general principle of linguistic structure on the basis of observations of a single language' (Chomsky 1980b, 48), (Cook and Newson 2007, 21; 23).

4   Chomsky is no longer concerned by the degeneracy of the data, but only its poverty or meagreness. The poverty of stimulus argument now focuses on the poverty of language addressed to children (the fact that it does not contain the right kind of syntactic evidence) rather than on the degeneracy of the data (the fact that it is not always completely well-formed). This change is due to research on speech addressed to children which showed that it was highly regular, and so the data are arguably not as degenerate as was earlier thought. Newport et al (1977) found that only 1 out of 1,500 utterances addressed to children was ungrammatical (Cook and Newson, 2007, 192–3).

5   UG is 'the sum total of all the immutable principles that heredity builds into the language organ. These principles cover grammar, speech sounds, and meaning' (Chomsky 1983); they are the finite, invariant, genetically-innate set of principles common to all languages 'by which the child can infer, on the basis of the limited data available in the environment, the full grammatical capacity which we think of as a mature speaker's knowledge of a language' (Anderson and Lightfoot 2000, 6). UG is part of the LAD, an innate biologically-endowed language faculty. The LAD is also known as the 'initial state' of the language faculty – the state we are born with; we have learned English (i.e. the language faculty reaches its 'mature state') when, by being exposed to it, we have learned the lexicon and set the parameters for English.

6   Chomsky revised his Principles and Parameters (P&P) Theory in his Minimalist Program; however, it remains that 'UG provides a fixed system of principles and a

finite array of finitely valued parameters' (1995, 170). Parameters are language-specific, binary parameters that can be set in various ways. An example of a parameter is 'the head parameter', whereby a particular language consistently has the heads on the same side of the complements in all its phrases, whether head-first or head-last. So, for instance, English is head-first: *in the house*: preposition head-first before the complement; *killed the man*: verb head-first before the complement. Japanese is head-last. 'It may be that the values of parameters are set to defaults at birth, but that these can be changed across a small range of values by certain linguistic experiences' (Green and Vervaecke 1997).

7 Bishop (2014) objects: 'The problem is then to explain how children get from this abstract knowledge to the specific language they are learning. The field became encumbered by creative but highly implausible theories, most notably the parameter-setting account [see note 6], which conceptualised language acquisition as a process of "setting a switch" for a number of innately-determined parameters'. I would, however, begin by objecting to the 'abstract knowledge'.

8 Anderson and Lightfoot: 'the trigger experience, which varies from person to person ... consists of an unorganized and fairly haphazard set of utterances, of the kind that any child hears' (2000, 14).

9 Chomsky affirms having once said that 'the child has a repertoire of concepts as part of its biological endowment and simply has to learn that a particular concept is realized in a particular way in the language' and adds that '[w]hen you read the huge Oxford English Dictionary ..., you may think that you are getting the definition of a word but you're not. All you are getting is a few hints and then your innate knowledge is filling in all the details and you end up knowing what the word means' (Chomsky 2000). Cook and Newson (2007) speak of a 'computational system' in the human mind which bridges meanings to sequences of sounds in one direction and sequences of sounds to meanings in the other. The lexicon is allegedly represented in the mind and the computational system relies on this mental lexicon.

10 This paragraph is a faithful rendering of Anderson and Lightfoot (2000), 11.

11 For fleshed-out arguments on this, see Hutto and Myin (2013), Glock (2013) and Hacker (2007a). Hacker: 'It is common among psychologists and cognitive neuroscientists to speak of internal representations in the brain. In so far as 'representation' signifies no more than a causal correlate in the brain of an external stimulus, this is innocuous. But it is evident that all too frequently it is meant to signify a *symbolic* representation. And it makes no sense to speak of semantic (symbolic) representations in the brain ... [f]or such representations are determined by conventions' (2007a, 20–1).

12 Studies in language development find that children use a wide variety of cues, including syntactic, semantic, and prosodic information, to learn language structure (Bates and MacWhinney, 1989). Bishop (2014): 'Current statistical learning accounts allow us to ... study the process of language learning. Instead of assuming that children start with knowledge of linguistic categories, categories are abstracted from statistical regularities in the input (see Special Issue 3, *Journal of Child Language* 2010, vol. 37). The units of analysis thus change as the child develops expertise. And, consistent with the earlier writings of Bates and MacWhinney (1989), children's language is facilitated by the presence of correlated cues in the input, e.g., prosodic and phonological cues in combination with semantic context. In sharp contrast to the idea that syntax is learned by a separate modular system divorced from other information, recent research emphasises that the young language learner uses different sources of information together. Modularity emerges as development proceeds.'

13 Whereas the Chomskyan explanation here is that the regularity of such errors, and the fact that they are not based upon what the child hears, demonstrate that they are derived from the Universal Grammar. The child allegedly works through from the simplest possibilities offered by the UG to the more complex, until his own grammar is the same as the grammar of the mother-tongue. But even if we were to grant Chomsky the occurrence of such cerebral gymnastics, how does he explain that many children go on making mistakes of this kind into adulthood? I heard a man laughing at his companion who had just used the word 'sped' rather than 'speeded' (both are right), claiming that there's no such word. And how many of us are ever sure about when to use 'hung' or 'hanged'? It is bodies like the Académie Française, not UG, that legislate as to what is grammatically legitimate, and what changes are accepted, though it has a reactive rather than generative role – the evolution of language being mostly the spontaneous upshot of language users. As Ramscar, Dye and McCauley have found: 'children's overregularization errors both arise and resolve themselves as a consequence of the distribution of error in the linguistic environment, and . . . far from presenting a logical puzzle for learning, they are inevitable consequences of it' (2013, 760).

14 Ramscar and Yarlett (2007) and Ramscar, Dye and McCauley (2013) show the importance of expectation and error-driven learning processes in language acquisition. For example, when children erroneously expect an ungrammatical form that then never occurs, the repeated absence of fulfilment serves as a kind of implicit negative feedback which encourages them to correct their errors over time.

15 MacWhinney (1993) shows that language acquisition includes a 'rich armory of learning mechanisms' – including expressive and receptive monitoring, alongside competition, conservatism, complex, indirect and overt negative evidence, and cue construction – indicating that 'the logical problem of language learning is easily solved, and that there is really no logical problem of language acquisition at all'.

16 Moerk (1994) conducted a meta-analysis of 40 studies and found substantial evidence that corrections do indeed play a role, and that they are not only abundant but contingent on the mistakes of the child. Schoneberger (2010) cites findings that evidence (both positive and negative) available in the linguistic environment provides adequate constraints when learning a language. For example, children are provided positive evidence (a) when their grammatically correct utterances are directly reinforced by adults; (b) when their grammatically correct utterances are indirectly reinforced by adults by means of automatic reinforcement; and (c) when adults provide grammatically correct exemplars. Further, they are provided direct negative evidence when their grammatically incorrect utterances result in corrective feedback as well as indirect negative evidence by usually not being exposed to grammatically incorrect utterances. They also cite evidence to support the claim that reinforcement promotes language acquisition during naturally occurring parent–child verbal interactions.

17 There are of course many well-documented examples of this, such as changes in the grammar of Old English to that of Chaucer's Middle English.

18 Pidgins are basic or proto-languages developed as a means of communication by adults who do not share a common language. They are syntactically impoverished languages, characterized by reduced syntax and vocabulary, no fixed order of words and considerable variation from one speaker to another. However, a pidgin can evolve into a creole, which is a full-blown language. The argument here is that inasmuch as a full-blown language can be developed from an impoverished linguistic environment

(with only vocabulary, but not grammatical principles drawn from a pidgin inasmuch as pidgins do not possess such principles in the first place), principles must be innate.

19 The transition occurs progressively. It is only in the second generation that pidgin is established, by speakers who have retained some of their native language. It is this stable and developed form of pidgin, constructed by the second generation, which gives birth to creole. The Hudson-Kam and Newport (2009) experiments mentioned earlier also suggest that creole languages do not support a universal grammar. In a pidgin situation (as also in the real-life situation of a deaf child whose parents were disfluent signers), children systematize the language they hear based on the probability and frequency of forms, and not on the basis of a universal grammar.

20 I cannot expand on this here, but the literature is abundant – the cases of Victor and Genie being the most notable. In Genie's case, psychological and physical trauma was caused by her father who physically punished her if she made any sounds (Curtiss et al 1997, 127). As for Victor, he presented insensitivity to any feelings except joy and anger (e.g., he never cried; his eyes were without expression); he was virtually insensitive to noise and his sensitivity to temperature was different from the norm (e.g., he did not react to boiling water); he was unable to distinguish between a painting and an object in relief, and could not undertake mundane tasks like opening a door. See Singleton and Ryan (2004) against the validity of feral cases in support of the SLI hypothesis.

21 A wink at what biologists call a 'hopeful monster' theory, described by Deacon as 'the evolutionary theorist's counterpart to divine intervention, in which a freak mutation just happens to produce a radically different and serendipitously better-equipped organism. The single most influential "hopeful monster" theory of human language evolution was offered by the linguist Noam Chomsky' (1997, 35).

22 Views that espouse some universality don't need to appeal to nativism: Christiansen and Chater (2008) hold a non-formal conception of universals in which these emerge.

23 This is echoed by Christiansen and Chater (2008), whose research finds that it is non-linguistic constraints that have shaped language to the brain, and given rise to statistical tendencies in language structure and use. The question is not 'Why is the brain so well suited to learning language?', but 'Why is language so well suited to being learned by the brain?' Following Darwin, they argue that 'it is useful metaphorically to view languages as 'organisms' – that is, highly complex systems of interconnected constraints – that have evolved in a symbiotic relationship with humans' (2008, 490).

24 This view of the sudden appearance of language as a kind of evolutionary accident where humans, to the exclusion of all other animals, were somehow accidentally blessed with a fully functioning prefabricated language organ (see Chomsky 1988) has been found to be, Green and Vervaecke (1997) concede, hardly plausible. However, they retort: 'ironically, ... the *real* Big Bang theory is, as far as we now know, true! A substantial critique of the implausibility of 'catastrophic' or 'big bang' theories of brain evolution to account for humans' unique linguistic capacity can be found in Deacon (1997).

25 Chomsky is averse to saying that language acquisition is a learning at all; it is, to him, more akin to *growing* than to learning: 'In certain fundamental respects we do not really learn language; rather grammar grows in the mind' (1980a, 134); 'language development really ought to be called language growth because the language organ grows like any other body organ' (1983). Cook and Newson: 'Acquisition of language is, to Chomsky, learning in a peculiar sense: ... it is not like learning to ride a bicycle, where practice develops and adapts existing skills. Instead it is internal development in response to vital, but comparatively trivial, experience from outside' (2007, 185).

26 For an aperçu of Wittgenstein's impact in the field of language acquisition, see Nelson (2009).
27 'Being sure that someone is in pain, doubting whether he is, and so on, are so many natural, instinctive kinds of behaviour towards other human beings, and our language is merely an auxiliary to, and further extension of, this relation. Our language-game is an extension of primitive behaviour' (Z 545). 'What, however, is the word "primitive" meant to say here? Presumably, that the mode of behaviour is *pre-linguistic*: that a language-game is based *on it*: that it is the prototype of a mode of thought and not the result of thought' (RPP I, 916). Wittgenstein speaks of *primitive* or *animal* behaviour in the phylogenetic as well as the ontogenetic sense. Here is an illustration of the phylogenetic primitivity of our concepts: '(An ape who tears apart a cigarette, for example. We don't see an intelligent dog do such things. The mere act of turning an object all around and looking it over is a primitive root of doubt' (RPP II, 345).
28 Wittgenstein: 'it is characteristic of our language that the foundation on which it grows consists in *steady ways of living, regular ways of acting*' (CE 397; my emphasis). Our acquiring concepts, such as pain, requires that we have appropriate (i.e. normal) human reactions: 'If a child looked radiant when it was hurt, and shrieked for no apparent reason, one couldn't teach him to use the word "pain"' (LPP 37).
29 See Chapter 5, 'From Deed to Word' in this volume.
30 On Philippe Narboux' view, training is a necessary but insufficient condition for the learning of a *native* language whereas *second-language* acquisition doesn't require it, and can rely on nothing other than ostensive definition because it relies on previous training (2004, 136).
31 Once the child has some language, there will be more explanatory teaching, and perhaps the odd transmission of some linguistic principles (though not usually of the 'clitic' sort). Wittgenstein talks about teaching as well as training: (e.g., Z 318 & 186).
32 See Medina (2002), 173. As psychologist Derek Montgomery also observes, if the carer repeatedly uses the verb 'want' while interpreting the infant's behaviour in certain contexts, it is 'reasonable to suspect that when the verb emerges in the child's lexicon it will be in familiar contexts such as [those] where the child has repeatedly heard it being used. The meaning of the term, like the meaning of the prelinguistic gesturing, is bound up in the role it plays within such contexts' (2002, 372).
33 'Our children are not only given practice in calculation but are also trained to adopt a particular attitude towards a mistake in calculating [variant: '... towards a departure from the norm']' (RFM VII 61, p. 425) – that is, children are habituated into standards of correctness of the practice in question, and thereby formed to act and react in particular ways; they are thus trained to master a technique.
34 For Chomsky, in contrast, our words are informed by the brain; they get their meaning from internal meanings (which are abstract mental representations), and it is the brain that communicates meaning: the human mind bridges the gap between external sounds and internal meanings (which are abstract mental representations) via a 'computational system' that relates meanings to sequences of sounds in one direction and sequences of sounds to meanings in the mind in the other. The mind changes the representation of language used by the computational system into the general concepts used by the mind, called 'the conceptual-intentional system', i.e. *moon* is connected to the concept of 'earth's satellite'. Going in the opposite direction, while speaking the mind has to convert the concepts into linguistic representation for the computational system, i.e. 'earth's satellite' is converted into *moon*. (Cook and Newson 2007, 6). In contrast to this mentalist view, for Wittgenstein (echoed here by

Montgomery), it is in social practices that the meaning of words and the standards for their use are established. Meaning, as Wittgenstein says, is 'in use' – out there – not in the head, not in some mental repository.

35 Wittgenstein's rule-following argument shows precisely that generating new sentences is nothing but an instance of knowing how to go on, 'how to extend the speech that [we] have into new contexts' (Bruner 1983, 39). As H.-J. Glock notes, the early Wittgenstein's was also concerned with what is now known as the problem of 'the creativity of language': the number of propositions being indefinite although the number of words is finite (NL 98; TLP 4.02, 4.027 etc.) (1996, 298).

36 Actually, the deeper confusion here is that unless we assume that language is innate, exposure to English would have to result in the child, the rabbit and the rock learning English. As Wittgenstein said, 'If a lion could talk, we wouldn't be able to understand it' (PI 223), for he wouldn't – couldn't – speak 'human'. Learning human speak (e.g., English) – takes enculturation in a human form of life, and that presupposes shared behavioural reactions and responses. I won't even bother about the rock ...

37 Hinzen: '... controversies about UG abound and the enterprise is widely rejected as ill-conceived and unfounded' (2012a, 335n).

38 Wittgenstein does not think his conception of grammar contrasts with the grammarian's; he insists that 'any explanation of the use of language' is 'grammar' (MWL 69). On his view, 'A rod has no length' is as ungrammatical as 'A rod length has'; but as he concedes (to Moore), the former violation of grammar is of interest only to the philosopher (ibid.), whereas syntax – albeit also part of grammar – is not the part philosophers are interested in. Wittgenstein leaves it to grammarians to bring out the syntactic aspect of use. Grammarians and philosophers may find it of interest to map grammatical rules, but this does not make the apprehension of rules as such relevant to language acquisition. In picking up the correct syntactico-semantic use of language – its grammar – the child is not picking up rules as such, but simply, to repeat: correct use.

39 I am generalizing for simplicity's sake. For a more nuanced view of Wittgenstein's conception of grammatical rules, see Chapter 1, 'Wittgenstein's Grammar: Through Thick and Thin' in this volume.

40 See Chapter 1, 'Wittgenstein's Grammar: Through Thick and Thin'.

41 'That is, we are interested in the fact that about certain empirical propositions no doubt can exist if making judgments is to be possible at all. Or again: I am inclined to believe that not everything that has the form of an empirical proposition *is* one.' (OC 308)

42 Note: *conditioned*, not *justified* by facts or *inferred* from them. This is what precludes their being empirical propositions. Rules are not empirically or epistemically grounded in reality, though they may be 'caused' by reality (OC 131, 429, 474). This is why Wittgenstein writes: 'The rule we lay down is the one most strongly *suggested* by the facts of experience' (AWL 84). For clarification regarding the nonempirical nature of 'thick' rules of grammar, see Chapter 1, 'Wittgenstein's Grammar: Through Thick and Thin' in this volume.

43 Some people may hold beliefs that seem to violate – and so could not condition – universal rules of grammar. For example, in the Trobriand Islands, some women, called *Yoyova* or flying witches, are believed to have the capacity to fly. It is, however, also (accommodatingly) believed that they either leave their bodies behind when they do this, or have doubles in the form of fire-flies and so on do it for them (Young, 207). The universal rule of grammar: 'Human beings cannot fly unaided' is therefore not

actually transgressed. Any attempt to ignore or transgress it *in action* – such as a *yoyova* attempting to *actually* fly off a cliff (without 'leaving her body behind') – must be seen as pathological. For any local certainty that seems to violate a universal rule of grammar, such accommodating measures will always be found. There is no *normal* transgression of a universal rule. To genuinely think or act on the basis of such rules of thought as 'I can fly unaided' or 'Only I exist' is a pathological problem, not a doxastic option.

44 They are conditioned by 'extremely general facts of nature – such facts as are hardly ever mentioned because of their great generality' (PI 56) – including the 'common behaviour of mankind' – behaviours such as breathing, eating, walking, hoping, dying, speaking, thinking, giving orders, asking questions, telling stories, having a chat. It is this common behaviour that constitutes the universal 'system of reference' which conditions what might be called, though in obvious contrast to Chomsky, the 'universal grammar' of mankind – that grammar by means of which any human being can understand a foreign language (PI 206).

45 As Vyvyen Evans testifies, Chomsky's views are 'established fact in many of the linguistics textbooks currently in use in many of the stellar universities throughout the English-speaking world. I was trained using these textbooks, and they are still compulsory reading for today's undergraduate and graduate students – tomorrow's researchers, educators and language professionals – even at the university where I teach and work. University students are regularly told that there is a Universal Grammar, that language is innate, that language is incommensurable with non-human communication systems, and that all languages are essentially English-like' (2014, 19–20).

46 That it is necessary to have a well-functioning brain to achieve language acquisition does not make the brain the locus of language acquisition – or part of it, a 'language organ'. The brain is a mere mechanical enabler: its proper functioning is necessary to our acquiring and using language in the same way it is necessary to our ability to walk or digest – without it implying the existence of walking and digestion organs in the brain.

3 Words as Deeds

1 The well-known expression 'ghost in the machine' is Gilbert Ryle's. It appears in his *Concept of Mind* (1949) in the form: 'the dogma of the Ghost in the Machine', denounced as the 'Cartesian category-mistake' of representing minds as ghosts harnessed to machines (21). Though Ryle designates this as 'Descartes' myth', he acknowledges its origin in Platonic and Aristotelian theories of the intellect as well as in theological doctrines of the soul (24).

2 Cf. PI 23, but this tripartite division of the function of language is due to Karl Bühler (1934), confirming Kevin Mulligan's thesis that 'Bühler finds a system in what Wittgenstein presents as part of the inexhaustible variety of language' (1997, 209). Bühler speaks of 'representation' rather than 'description'.

3 I owe this example to James Hill.

4 Cf. RPP I, 693. As Michel ter Hark notes, the first-person *descriptive* language-game is less often played and more demanding than the *expressive* one (1990, 114). A language-game for which I suggest we adopt 'self-observation' [*Selbstbeobachtung*] (PI 586) to avoid the inner voyeurism suggested by 'introspection', or Wittgenstein's overly

technical reference to 'functional states' (RPP I, 61). Such self-observation seldom reaches that expressed by D. H. Lawrence: 'myself has watched myself' (Letters 1.39).

5 See respectively OC 510 and RPP I, 572. Wittgenstein does not consistently use these terms in this way.

6 Hacker repeatedly refers to avowals as 'spontaneous'; see (1993) 86, 89, 90, 92 etc.

7 I am not using the term 'compulsive' in its specialized, psychopathological connotation of obsessional, neurotic behaviour, of a person's acting *against* her wishes, but rather as alluding to behaviour that occurs not *in accordance with* one's wishes or thoughts, that is not rationally but emotionally driven; coming, as it were, *from the guts*. I want to relate the feature of these expressions that both Wittgenstein (LPE 281) and George Eliot (see epigram to Section 5 in this chapter) characterize in terms of: we *can't help* using them, and of which Eliot specifically writes that they 'come *without any will* of my own' (my emphasis) – not *against* her will. Other terms I have envisaged have proved more equivocal. For example, 'reflexive' (means both 'of the nature of reflex' and 'of the nature of reflection').

8 As opposed to such 'passive' states of feeling as sensory impressions and kinaesthetic sensations.

9 For want of an adjectival and adverbial cognate of 'action', I once used the term 'pragmatism' – though in a broad sense – to denote Wittgenstein's emphasis on action, and was discouraged from doing so because of unwarranted association with pragmatic philosophy. Disinclined to use the term 'actional', I have opted for 'praxial' instead.

10 That language is based on convention does not make some of our uses of it less automatic. Our language has been, for the most part, *drilled* into us, and in ordinary use, we use basic words (*table, rain, people, flower, street* etc.) habitually, without precursory reflection, hesitation or recall.

11 The notable exceptions to such categorization being Adolf Reinach (1883–1917) and J. L. Austin. The inclusion of nonlinguistic fields in language was effected precisely by Karl Bühler.

12 A section heading in (1989), 297 and a chapter heading in (1993). Hacker consistently uses 'avowal' to denote nondescriptive *linguistic* expressions. Elsewhere, the spectrum is said to be composed of 'sentences' (1993, 92) or 'propositions' (1996a, 181).

13 Hacker is right that one can lie unawares, but we don't do so *by default*. Rather, lying unawares is a form of pathology akin to confabulation; confabulation being 'the production of false or erroneous memories without the intent to deceive' (Chlebowski et al, 2009).

14 See Chapter 8, 'Wittgenstein on Knowledge and Certainty', in this volume.

15 I cannot here engage in a discussion of the link between spontaneous utterances and what Wittgenstein calls 'secondary meaning', where expressions are governed by criteria, not of truth, but of *truthfulness* or sincerity (cf. PI 222).

16 I agree with John Koethe's view on the 'pervasiveness of showing and seeing' in Wittgenstein's work, but not with his interpretation of the distinction (1996 *passim*). I believe that what is *shown* is what, though verbally articulated, in fact cannot *logically* be *said* inasmuch as it is not propositional (in Wittgenstein's consistently bipolar view of the proposition), not susceptible of truth or falsity. I believe Wittgenstein to have focused on two large classes of cases where words do not *meaningfully* say, but only show. These are rules (grammatical and others – Tractarian remarks belong here, as well as the 'hinge certainties' of *On Certainty*) and spontaneous utterances. This will be fleshed out throughout the volume.

17 Norman Malcolm (*Nothing Is Hidden: Wittgenstein's Criticism of His Early Thought*. (Oxford: Blackwell, 1986) and *Wittgensteinian Themes: Essays 1978–1989*, ed. G. H. von Wright (New York: Cornell University Press, 1995) and Paul Johnston (*Wittgenstein: Rethinking the Inner* (London: Routledge, 1993)) in particular have contributed to elucidating this crucial aspect of Wittgenstein's thought.
18 My thanks to Laurence Goldstein, Anat Matar, Constantine Sandis and Daniel Statman for their constructive comments at various stages of this chapter.

4 Literature as the Measure of our Lives

1 For a fully fledged argument against the view that Wittgenstein was a linguistic idealist, see Moyal-Sharrock (2016a).
2 '... the aim of the book is to draw a limit to thought, or rather – not to thought, but to the expression of thoughts: for in order to be able to draw a limit to thought, we should have to find both sides of the limit thinkable (i.e., we should have to be able to think what cannot be thought). It will therefore only be in language that the limit can be drawn' (TLP 3).
3 For a more in-depth discussion, see Moyal-Sharrock (2007b).
4 See Chapter 8, 'Wittgenstein on Knowledge and Certainty', in this volume.
5 'The philosophical problem is an awareness of disorder in our concepts, and can be solved by ordering them' (BT 309).
6 This struggle is also manifest in the multiple times Wittgenstein begins his sentences with: 'I want to say ...'.
7 'The work of art is the object seen *sub specie aeternitatis*; and the good life is the world seen *sub specie aeternitatis*. This is the connexion between art and ethics.' (NB 83)
8 See Moyal-Sharrock (2016b).
9 'What is [...] difficult here is to put this indefiniteness, correctly and unfalsified, into words' (PI 227).
10 See Chapter 7, 'Wittgenstein on Psychological Certainty', in this volume.
11 'But you do speak of *understanding* music. You understand it, surely, while you hear it! Ought we to say this is an experience which accompanies the hearing?' (Z 159).
12 Alluding to Aristotle's notion of tragedy in the *Poetics*, Amelie Rorty writes: 'While there is sorrow, grief, loss, pain in life, there is *tragedy* only when the actions and events that compose a life are organized into a story, a structured representation of that life' (1992, 3–4; my emphasis).
13 Including Chateaubriand's *René* (1802) which was hailed as the first to diagnose this French *mal du siècle*. *Madame Bovary* was published in 1856, one year before Baudelaire's *Les Fleurs du Mal*, which starts off its section on *Spleen et Idéal* with a poem referring to 'l'Ennui, ce monster délicat'.
14 This is the first verse of Lawrence's poem 'Song of a man who has come through'.
15 I am grateful to Constantine Sandis and Keith Farman for their valuable and sensitive comments on the final draft of this chapter. I feel prompted by their comments to dispel the impression that I do not value the role of *saying*, or indeed of philosophy, in moral understanding. In fact, having argued against Cora Diamond for the importance of philosophical ethics for moral understanding (Moyal-Sharrock (2012)), my aim in this chapter was to highlight and flesh out the important difference of *showing* and of literature for moral understanding. The 'perspicuous presentations' of philosophy are of a different kind from those of literature; because philosophy's mode

is *saying* rather than *showing*, it lacks the tools to transmit the fine-grained texture of being. However, philosophy has other tools. Take, for instance, Russell's sentence 'I cannot see how to refute the arguments for the subjectivity of ethical values, but I find myself incapable of believing that all that is wrong with wanton cruelty is that I don't like it' (1999, 165). It summarizes in a nutshell one of the deepest and most persistent problems of ethics; and if one were to replace the ethical values in that passage with aesthetic ones, it would be a brilliant summary of Kant's third critique. Literature is not able to do this: it takes philosophy to make perspicuous presentations of that kind. Russell's sentence describes, without literary texture, the problem we have with ethical objectivity or intersubjectivity, and elucidates beautifully in articulating the problem simply.

5 From Deed to Word

1. Professor Emeritus at the University of Toronto, Jack (as he liked to be called) was an eminent philosopher of language, philosopher of mind, Wittgenstein scholar – and a dear friend. Among his many publications are: 'The Community View (*Philosophical Review*, 1996); 'The rudiments of language' (*Language & Communication*, 1995); 'The Passage into Language: Wittgenstein and Quine' (in *The Cambridge Companion to Wittgenstein*, 1996); 'Pretence and the Inner' (in *The Third Wittgenstein*, 2004); 'Back to the Rough Ground: Wittgenstein and ordinary language' (in *Wittgenstein and Analytic Philosophy: Essays for P. M. S. Hacker*, 2009); and *Becoming Human: The Development of Language, Self and Self-Consciousness* (2007). This chapter pays tribute to his deep and sensitive understanding of what it means to be(come) human.
2. 'According to REC [Radical Enactive account of Cognition], the basic sorts of cognition that our brains help to make possible are fundamentally interactive, dynamic, and relational. REC's signature view is that such basic forms of cognition do not involve the picking up and processing of information that is used, reused, stored and represented in the brain. The usual form of what REC calls basic, contentless cognition is nothing short of organisms actively engaging with selective aspects of their environment in informationally sensitive, spatiotemporally extended ways' (2017, xiv)
3. In fact, this – 'the claim that we must recognize a sharp discontinuity . . . in the natural history of our species' – is what Bar-On calls the *diachronic* deep-chasm claim which she distinguishes from the *synchronic* deep-chasm claim 'that there are deep and important differences between present-day humans and all the nonhuman animals around us' (2013, 294).
4. The continuity thesis – the idea that things change gradually, not by leaps or bangs – is explicitly maintained by many language acquisition theorists, who stand in stark opposition to Chomsky's Big Bang theory. According to Chomsky (see 1988), language suddenly appears as a kind of evolutionary accident where humans, to the exclusion of all other animals, were somehow accidentally blessed with a fully functioning prefabricated language organ. Deacon (1997) abundantly demonstrates that Chomsky's scenario is unsupported by evolutionary anthropology which evidences a *gradual* adaptation of the human brain and vocal chords to the use of language rather than the sudden appearance of a language organ containing a complete set of parameters enabling all grammars – Chomsky's 'Big Bang' theory. (For a more general discussion of Chomsky's view, see Chapter 2, 'Universal Grammar', in this volume).

5 Though some sophisticated higher-level practices (e.g., mathematics) are exclusive to humans, it will become clear in the chapter that I don't see 'content-involving cognition' as exclusive to humans.
6 Though in principle remaining open to animals.
7 See Chapter 3, 'Words as Deeds', in this volume.
8 It is a 'well-known fact that animals are able to learn small sets of arbitrary signal-meaning relationships. The most celebrated trained apes, Kanzi (Savage-Rumbaugh and Lewin, 1994) and Nim (Terrace, 1987), have been able to acquire arbitrary symbolic vocabularies of several hundred items' (Hurford 2004, 554–5).
9 Bruce Richman (1976) found that gelada monkeys can produce sounds hitherto thought to be exclusive to human speech, such as vowel and consonant sounds and sounds articulated in different parts of the vocal tract such as labials and dentals. Richman (1987) also notes that the gelada's highly synchronized exchanges of contact calls share many of the rhythmic and melodic properties of human speech patterns (see also Richman 1978), and relates this to the need to resolve emotional conflicts inherent in many social situations.
10 'The difference in mind between man and the higher animals, great as it is, certainly is one of degree and not of kind' (1871) *The Descent of Man*.
11 For a related, perhaps complementary, set of sufficient, general holding conditions at the basis of language, see Gallagher: 'With exceptions for pathological cases, we arrive on the scene already attuned to other people's faces and their emotional expressions; we come already perceptually attentive to biological motion; we come already prepared for embodied interaction with others – and we are immediately pulled into such processes by caregivers and other persons' (2012, 208). I see these – which Gallagher proposes as 'social interaction processes of primary intersubjectivity' that get 'social cognition off the ground' – as more of the pre-symbolic interaction conditions or necessary starting points of language:
12 '*This* is how calculation is done, in such circumstances a calculation is *treated* as absolutely reliable, as certainly correct' (OC 39); '*This* is how one calculates. Calculating is *this*. What we learn at school, for example. Forget this transcendent certainty, which is connected with your concept of spirit' (OC 47).
13 Their being conditioned by facts that unassailably pertain to *the human form of life* makes some of our rules of grammar *universal* – that is, they are the bounds of sense from which *any* normal human being must begin to make sense. Alongside these, more local grammars emerge from *the different forms of human life*. See Chapter 1, 'Wittgenstein's Grammar: Through Thick and Thin', in this volume.
14 This passage provides an apt illustration of Doris Bar-On's suggestion that 'our commonsense descriptions of the expressive behavior we share with existing nonhuman animals – as well as those provided by ethologists – can guide us towards a natural intermediate stage in a diachronic path connecting the completely unminded parts of the animal world with the fully minded, linguistically infused parts that we humans now occupy' (2013, 39).
15 On this, see Chapter 3, 'Words as Deeds', in this volume.
16 There is no space here to rehearse the argument, amply made by Wittgenstein and Merleau-Ponty, that other minds are not, by default, hidden to us. See inter alia McGinn (1998), Gallagher (2012), Zahavi and Satne (2016).
17 As psychologist Richard Gipps summarizes: 'In place of ... an intellectualist, disengaged, cognition-focused psychology, we are offered perspectives that stress the

primitive foundational character of our prereflective (noncognitive) engagement with one another, our emotion, our expression, and our embodiment' (2004, 195).
18 See especially Tomasello (2016), but also Tomasello et al (2016): That great apes operate, at least on an implicit level, with an understanding of false beliefs suggests that this essential TOM skill is likely at least as old as humans' last common ancestor with the other apes' (p. 113). But Tomasello is not alone; see Jill Byrnit's 'Primate Theory of Mind: a state-of-the-art review' *Journal of Anthropological Psychology* 17: 2006, 1–21.
19 In philosophy, a similar position is adopted by Michael (2011) who claims that interaction complements, and may even contribute to mindreading, but does not replace, and Kim Sterelny who similarly defends a gestural origins hypothesis while hanging on to a complementary representationalist Theory of Mind (e.g., Sterelny 2012).
20 We do not normally theorize about whether other human beings have mental states (and only in some cases do we even ask ourselves what our interlocutor is *really* thinking or feeling). Our 'certainty' about someone having a mind is not an implicit conclusion we come to, but an instinctive, nonepistemic attitude; not resulting from inference, it is not open to falsity or mistake. It may be open to pathological failure, but then this is only the exception that confirms the rule (see Chapter 8, 'Wittgenstein on Knowledge and Certainty', in this volume). Wittgenstein rightly rejects the notion that we can never really be certain of what another thinks or feels, so it is spurious to attribute to us a Theory of Mind: 'But of course it isn't true that we are never certain about the mental processes in someone else. In countless cases we are' (LW II, 94); 'It is only in particular cases that the inner is hidden from me; and in those cases it is not hidden because it is the inner' (LW II, 33) (see Chapter 7, 'Wittgenstein on Psychological Certainty', in this volume). Indeed, in many cases where a feeling or thought is explicitly manifested, it may not be a *genuine* feeling or thought.
21 Dunbar imports the mentalistic picture elsewhere (e.g., Dunbar (2009), 568), but it is sufficiently absent in this paper to offer a clearly enactive hypothesis.
22 Dunbar suggests that the switch from manual to vocal grooming began with the appearance of Homo erectus, around two million years ago (1996, 115).
23 It is – to use the terminology used by Dunbar on his website – one of many 'cognitive tricks' used to overcome the constraints that time places on an individual's ability to manage their relationships. Dunbar notes that 'this explanation clearly stands in direct contrast to the conventional wisdom that language developed, and brain size increased, in the context of hunting communication and tool-making development. In fact, 'the markedly improved tool designs of the Upper Palaeolithic can . . . be better interpreted as a consequence rather than a cause of enlarged brain size.' (1993, 15).
24 He sees this development as a 'small step' (1996, 141). Dunbar notes that Cheney and Seyfarth (1982) have shown that slight differences in the acoustical form of the calls allow the audience to infer a great deal about the event or situation on which the caller is commenting, *even in the complete absence of any visual information*' (Dunbar 1993, 17; my emphasis). Of course, I disagree that what is being understood here is so as a result of inference.
25 In the broader, Wittgensteinian, sense of grammar: as the often unarticulated, customary rules that govern our use of words and, by extension, our intentional actions (gestures) or nonverbal vocalizations.
26 See Chapter 3, 'Words as Deeds', in this volume.
27 'A dog believes his master is at the door. But can he also believe his master will come the day after to-morrow? – And *what* can he not do here? – How do I do it?' (PI, p. 174)

6 Wittgenstein and the Memory Debate

1. Though there has been that too: for example, M. Chapman and R. Dixon (eds) *Meaning and the Growth of Understanding: Wittgenstein's Significance for Developmental Psychology* (Berlin: Springer-Verlag, 1985).
2. As exemplified by the protest by psychologists against the BBC's general perception of the mental as all in the brain, which implicitly signals the influence of Wittgenstein's thought on psychology; after all, it was he who said 'by "psychological" I don't mean "inner"' (RPP II, 612).
3. On this, see Hutto (2009).
4. For an insightful and original gloss on this often misunderstood passage see McDonough (2004, esp. pp. 322–3).
5. In a chapter of this length, I can only point to the ambiguity of the word 'memory' and not attempt to clarify it. In perusing the literature, it has seemed to me that this ambiguity and the frequent interchangeability of 'memory' with the equally ambiguous 'remembering', have obstructed research. A conceptual elucidation of these terms would hugely benefit the neuroscience of memory. The only elucidatory effort I have found is Endel Tulving's inelegant 'remembery' to denote the neural record of encoded information (1993, 294).
6. M. R. Bennett and Peter Hacker are clear on this: 'It may well be the case that but for certain neural configurations or strengths of synaptic connections, one would not be able to remember the date of the Battle of Hastings and would not recollect being told it. But it does not follow from that idea that what one remembers must be, as it were, written down in the brain, or that there must be some neural configuration in the brain from which one could in principle read off what is remembered. *Nor can it be said that this neural configuration is a memory*.... The expression of a memory must be distinguished from the neural configurations, whatever they may be, which are conditions for a person's recollecting whatever he recollects. But these configurations are not the memory; nor are they representations, depictions or expressions of what is remembered' (2003, 170–1; my emphasis). As Stéphane Chauvier notes: 'That a lesion in a part of her brain prevents an individual from recognizing certain familiar faces informs us about the neural conditions required for someone to recognize a face, but the recognition of a face is not itself a neuronal process' (2007, 46). Recognizing is not a neuronal process, though a neuronal process enables recognizing. The same can be said of remembering.
7. On this, see Susswein and Racine (2009).
8. And thereby to make a category mistake; for the brain is a material object, the mind a capacity.
9. An engram is 'the transient or enduring change in our brain that results from encoding an experience' (Shacter 1996, 58).
10. As David Stern puts it: '... postulating a place where mind meets matter is a *deus ex machina* which does not solve the problem, for it does nothing to explain how this interaction is possible' (1991, 205).
11. Bennett and Hacker (2003, Part I, Chapter 3). A fallacy first noted by Aristotle: 'Yet to say that it is *the soul* which is angry is as inexact as it would be to say that it is the soul that weaves webs or builds houses. It is doubtless better to avoid saying that the soul pities or learns or thinks, and rather to say that it is the man who does this with his soul' (*De An* 408b12–15); and then Wittgenstein: 'Only of a human being and what resembles (behaves like) a living human being can one say: it has sensations; it sees, is blind; hears, is deaf; is conscious or unconscious' (PI 281).

12 Indeed, Wittgenstein even suggests that the capacity for memory necessitates the capacity for linguistic expression: 'Anyone with a soul must be capable of pain, joy, grief, etc. etc. And if he is also to be capable of memory, of making decisions, of making a plan for something, with this he needs linguistic expression' (LW II, 67).
13 'Note also how sure people are that to the ability to add or to multiply or to say a poem by heart, etc., there *must* correspond a peculiar state of the person's brain, although on the other hand they know next to nothing about such psycho-physiological correspondences' (BB 118).
14 E.g., Tulving, who speaks of 'stored information' in some memory systems as 'representational – isomorphic with what is, or could be, in the world' (2005, 11).
15 Though this interchangeability has since been questioned; cf. Tulving (2002), 271.
16 In fact, 'nondeclarative memory' is a larger category, which subsumes procedural memory, but these terms are often used interchangeably, and I will use them thus here.
17 Cf. also Hunter: although everyday speech suggests that memory is an object we possess in the same way as we possess a head or a big toe, 'it is true, although alarming, to say that there is no such thing as memory' (1957, 13).
18 Cf. e.g., Tulving (1993); Schacter (1996, p. 5); but also Toth and Hunt (1999, 257).
19 What about the Freudian unconscious? However much our present behaviour and personality are (adversely) affected by our past experiences, those experiences cannot be said to be stored in memory (memory is not a storage space, and experiences cannot be stored). When impressions or pictures from the past present themselves to us (prodded or unprodded), we rightly speak of remembering or of memory, but it does not follow that these memories had been previously stored as unconscious memories.
20 I have classified these into *linguistic, local, universal and personal hinges* (see Chapter 8, 'Wittgenstein on Knowledge and Certainty', in this volume. It turns out that these classifications roughly correspond to what is deemed to be the content of semantic memory (linguistic, local, universal hinges), and episodic (or autobiographical) memory (personal hinges).
21 Later, when she comes to use language, hinges will regulate the child's *speaking* within the bounds of sense in the same way they now regulate her *acting* within the bounds of sense. It must be stressed that Wittgenstein sees logic or grammar as rooted in instinct and action: 'I want to regard man here as an animal; as a primitive being to which one grants instinct and ratiocination. As a creature in a primitive state. Any logic good enough for a primitive means of communication needs no apology from us. Language did not emerge from some kind of ratiocination' (OC 475). See also PG, pp. 62–3. (On this, see Chapter 1, 'Wittgenstein's Grammar: Through Thick and Thin', in this volume)
22 See Chapter 8, 'Wittgenstein on Knowledge and Certainty', in this volume.
23 Similarly hinges are immune to *mistake* (but not to mechanical slips, such as slips of the tongue (OC 625) or to pathological confusion, both of which Wittgenstein prefers not to call 'mistakes'), 'In certain circumstances a man cannot make a *mistake*' (OC 155): 'How might I be mistaken in my assumption that I was never on the moon?' (OC 661); 'Can I be making a mistake, for example, in thinking that the words of which this sentence is composed are English words whose meaning I know?' (OC 158). By ruling out the possibility of mistake in such cases, Wittgenstein does not mean to rule out the possibility that an English speaker might believe that the words of which this sentence are composed are *not* English, or that someone could believe they'd been to the moon when they hadn't; only we 'should not call this a *mistake*, but rather a mental disturbance' (OC 71).

24 Or so I have called them (see note 20 above). Examples from *On Certainty* are: '2 x 2 = 4', 'What the colour of human blood is called', 'What is called "a slab" / "a pillar"', 'Which colour is meant by the word blue', 'The words composing this sentence are English' (OC 455, 340, 565, 545, 158)
25 Covered in *On Certainty* by what I have classified as *local hinges*; e.g.: 'There is an island, Australia', 'The earth is round', 'Trains normally arrive in a railway station' (OC 159, 291, 339) – and *universal hinges*; e.g.: 'The earth exists', 'Things don't systematically disappear when we're not looking', 'If someone's head is cut off, the person will be dead and not live again', 'Trees do not gradually change into men and men into trees', 'I have a brain', 'I am a human being', 'I have forbears' (OC 209, 234, 274, 513,159, 4, 234).
26 Nor is the expression not susceptible of slips of the tongue, the way even the most expert typists mistype some words.
27 E.g.: 'I come from such and such a city', 'For months I have lived at address A', 'I have never been on the moon', 'I have just had lunch', 'The person opposite me is my old friend so and so' (OC 67, 70, 419, 111, 659, 613) – these, I have called *personal hinges*.
28 Amnesia affects some parts of the brain and those have been termed 'autobiographical memory', 'long-term storage', 'declarative memory' etc. This makes it sound as if amnesia is an erasing of the memory tape or an emptying of the memory box, whereas memory is an ability. It isn't that the film has gone blank or blurry, but that we are unable to recall. Again, as Bennett and Hacker explain, it isn't that declarative and non-declarative memories are stored in different brain areas, for there is no such thing as storing memories in the brain, but '[r]ather the capacity to remember various kinds of things is *causally dependent* on different brain areas and on synaptic modifications in these areas' (2003, 159). Here again, confusion results from the failure to distinguish the retention of an ability from the neural conditions for the possession of that ability, and from the storage of information in inscribed or otherwise recorded form (2003, 160). Moreover, what is *pathologically* possible is not an indicator of norm. In normal circumstances, I am not cognitively certain of having a body. Losing proprioception is a pathological condition that makes the only awareness I can have of my body a cognitive one, but this does not have any resonance on the normal case. For further discussion, see Moyal-Sharrock (2007a, 127–9). For the same argument applied to autism and dyssemia, see Chapter 7, 'Wittgenstein on Psychological Certainty', in this volume).
29 Exact reproduction and verbatim recall are rare instances of recall; they often demand by rote or focussed memorization, and are seldom conditions for successful remembering. As Tulving notes, memory can be absolutely veridical, as in memorized poems, speeches, dates, addresses, phone numbers and passwords that we can recall, but 'a good part of the activity of memory consists not in reproduction, or even in reconstruction, but in sheer reconstruction. And constructed memories do not always correspond to reality' (2002, 273).
30 According to which remembering involves interaction with an external element (e.g., amnesiac's notebook). This is an offshoot of the Extended Mind thesis: the thesis that cognitive processes and the individual itself can extend into the environment.
31 For discussions of extensive *mind*, see Hutto (2012) and Hutto and Myin (2013).
32 This is a radically situated model of memory according to which organisms simply embody their cognitive capacities, rather than derive these from internal description. (*ibid.* 126). 'The conception of memory as embodied capacity which we have come to, departs from internalism from the very beginning. According to this conception, memory cannot be extended, because it never has been internal, but always *extensive*' (*ibid.*, 127).

33 University of York, 2011.
34 It should be noted that Craik's stance was uncharacteristic.
35 Which is not to say that Wittgenstein is championing behaviourism; Wittgenstein does not do away with the inner; he merely revises its importance and its nature.
36 As, for instance, the importance of myelin, the insulating material surrounding the wiring that connects neurons, for learning and memory (Douglas Fields 2020).
37 I am greatly indebted to Jason Leboe, Steve Lindsay, Ulrich Mueller and Tim Racine for their invaluable comments on an earlier draft of this chapter. I am also grateful to audiences at the universities of Barcelona and Hertfordshire.

7 Wittgenstein on Psychological Certainty

1 See Chapter 8, 'Wittgenstein on Knowledge and Certainty', in this volume.
2 The only mentions, in *On Certainty*, of what can be called 'psychological certainties', are to our *basic* reliance on / certainty about our memory (cf. OC 66, 201, 337, 345, 346, 416, 419, 497, 506, 632); to one's certainty of being in pain as the benchmark for basic, nonepistemic certainty (cf. OC 41, 178, 504); and to one's claim that someone else is in pain as epistemic (OC 555) or perhaps not (OC 563).
3 The writings focused on here are PI, Part II; RPP I and II; LPP; LW I and LW II. For a discussion of a 'third' Wittgenstein, see Moyal-Sharrock, ed. (2004) as well as the 'Introduction: Discovering Wittgenstein' in this volume.
4 '[The] characteristic [of psychological verbs] is this, that their third person but not their first person is stated on grounds of observation.' (RPP I, 836); cf. also RPP II, 63.
5 Knowledge requires justification, and so cannot be the kind of assurance Wittgenstein is looking for here: 'Whether I *know* something depends on whether the evidence backs me up or contradicts me. For to say one knows one has a pain means nothing' (OC 504; my emphasis); 'If "I know..." means: I can convince someone else if he believes my evidence, then one can say: I may well be as certain about his mood as about the truth of a mathematical proposition, but it is still false to say that I *know* his mood. [...] That is: 'knowing' is a psychological concept of a different kind from 'being certain', 'being convinced', 'believing', surmising', etc. The evidence for knowing is of a different kind' (LW II, 88; original emphasis). On this, see Chapter 8, 'Wittgenstein on Knowledge and Certainty', in this volume.
6 In later work, I stopped using the term 'objective certainty' because of the possible confusion with other understandings of the term 'objective' (e.g., scientific), and refer to the kind of logical certainty described by Wittgenstein as 'hinge certainty'. I decided, however, to maintain the use of 'objective certainty' in this chapter to preserve coherence with Wittgenstein's use of the expressions 'objectively certain' (LW II, 23), as well as 'objective uncertainty' (LW I, 888); and so the expressions 'hinge certainty' and 'objective certainty' are used, in this chapter, interchangeably.
7 'As if giving grounds did not come to an end sometime. But the end is not an ungrounded presupposition: it is an ungrounded *way of acting*' (OC 110; my emphasis); 'I want to say: it's not that on some points men know the truth with perfect certainty. No: perfect certainty is only a matter of their *attitude*' (OC 404; my emphasis). But if certainty is a way of acting, should we call it certainty? At some point, Wittgenstein's answer would have been negative: 'There isn't any question of certainty or uncertainty yet in their language-game. Remember: they are learning to

do something' (Z 416); but at that point he hadn't yet firmly come to the notion of a nonepistemic certainty, of a certainty *in deed*, that he will come to later, particularly in *On Certainty* (cf. OC 342).

8 Doubt-behaviour is not the same as pretending to doubt; in the former case, the person may well believe they are doubting (indeed, this is the case of most philosophers who purport to have doubts about the existence of other minds etc.), but the doubt here does not translate itself in practice; it is, as Wittgenstein puts it, only that 'they talk rather more about certain things than the rest of us' (OC 338). And, again: 'So how does the doubt get expressed? That is: in a language-game, and not merely in certain *phrases*' (RPP II, 342; original emphasis).

9 For example, 'The frame of reference to which we fasten these words is ordinary human behaviour. The further away a human being is from this the less we could know how to teach him' (LPP 158–9); and: 'Again, having been taught, the child must use the word in a normal way. There will be exceptions, but the centre of reference is ordinary human life, and the further we go from ordinary human life the less meaning we can give such expressions' (LPP 37).

10 'Is there such a thing as 'expert judgement' about the genuineness of expressions of feeling? – Even here, there are those whose judgement is 'better' and those whose judgement is 'worse'. / Correcter prognoses will generally issue from the judgements of those with better knowledge of mankind. / Can one learn this knowledge? Yes; some can. Not, however, by taking a course in it, but through 'experience'. – Can someone else be a man's teacher in this? Certainly. From time to time he gives him the right tip. – This is what 'learning' and 'teaching' are like here. – What one acquires here is not a technique; one learns correct judgements. There are also rules, but they do not form a system, and only experienced people can apply them right. Unlike calculating-rules' (PI, p. 227); 'To be sure, there is this: acquiring a knowledge of human nature; it is also possible to help someone with this, to give lessons, as it were, but one only points to cases, refers to certain traits, gives no hard and fast rules' (RPP II, 607).

11 'What is [...] difficult here is to put this indefiniteness, correctly and unfalsified, into words' (PI, p. 227).

12 This is characteristic of logical positivists who attempted to eradicate this indeterminacy of sense by translating ordinary psychological language into a more precise language, with the help of (different versions of) 'protocol sentences'. See ter Hark (2004, 126) on Carnap's treatment of indeterminacy of sense as a defect that has to be repaired by replacing psychological language with a language suitable for use in rigorous (physical) science.

13 Though elsewhere, he does call the *uncertainty* constitutional (see RPP II, 657).

14 See also: '"But you can't recognize pain with *certainty* just from externals." – The *only* way of recognizing it is by externals, and the uncertainty is constitutional. It is not a shortcoming. // It resides in our concept that this uncertainty exists, in our instrument. Whether this concept is practical or impractical is really not the question' (RPP II, 657).

15 Ter Hark sees here 'a categorial difference between psychological concepts and concepts for the description of all sorts of physical facts' (2004, 142).

16 Here, we might speak, with Gordon Bearn of a 'Superficial Essentialism' (Bearn 1997, 110), as does Jeff Coulter: '"Essence", a term that Wittgenstein uses at several junctures in his later writings, has taken on a new significance.... In his mature work, for Wittgenstein, it no longer means (as it had for generations before him) a hidden, unitary core or commonality across instances, revealed as such only by philosophical

analysis and abstraction, but rather, 'essence' now encompasses those myriad cases of the use of a word which perspicuously exhibits its grammar of use, the ways in which it can (and contrastively, cannot) be used intelligibly, thus constituting what concept it expresses. In Bearn's helpful phrase, "grammatical investigations would uncover superficial essences" – i.e., what constitutes the intelligibility of a concept is to be discovered by laying out many richly-detailed examples of the roles it plays in the weave of our lives as we observably live them (including, of course, in the weave of our discursive actions and interactions)" (Coulter 1999, 150–1).

17 See ter Hark 1990, 151.
18 On this, see Moyal-Sharrock (2020).
19 '"One can't pretend like that". – This may be a matter of experience – namely that no one who behaves like that will later behave in such-and-such a way; but it also may be a conceptual stipulation ("That wouldn't still be pretence"); and the two may be connected. / That can no longer be called "pretence"' (Z 570).
20 '"Human beings think, grasshoppers don't." [...] one could impart this to a person who doesn't understand the English word "thinking" and perhaps believes erroneously that it refers to something grasshoppers do.' (RPP II, 23). See also: 'Could a legislator abolish the concept of pain? / The basic concepts are interwoven so closely with what is most fundamental in our way of living that they are therefore unassailable.' (LW II, 43–4).
21 For not all first-person psychological statements are nondescriptive: 'Surely one doesn't normally say "I wish ..." on grounds of self-observation [*Selbstbeobachtung*], for this is merely an expression [*Äusserung*] of a wish. Nevertheless, you can sometimes perceive or discover a wish by observing your own reactions' (RPP II, 3). On this see Chapter 3, 'Words as Deeds', in this volume; and for a discussion of Wittgenstein's 'thesis of asymmetry', see Chauvier (2007).
22 In *most* cases, not *all*, as Peter Winch reminds us: 'That is not to deny that often our reactions *are* based on reflections about others' states of mind, or probable future behaviour. The point is, first that it is not always so; and second, that our *un*reflective reactions are part of the primitive material out of which our concept of a human person is formed and which makes such more sophisticated reflections possible' (1980–1, 147).
23 Which, however, is not to be confused with a tacit presupposition (cf. PI, pp. 179–80), or with what Wittgenstein calls an 'intuitive conviction', which manifests itself as follows: 'I am sure, *sure*, that he isn't pretending; but someone else isn't. Can I convince him? And if not – do I say that he [the person who can't see it] can't think? (The conviction could be called "intuitive".)' (RPP II, 688).
24 Although this of course does not prevent uncertainty from being 'hopeless' in particular cases: 'And then there is what I should like to call the case of hopeless doubt. When I say, "I have no idea what he is really thinking –". He's a closed book to me. When the only way to understand someone else would be to go through the same upbringing as his – which is impossible' (RPP II, 568). Indeed, such a possibility constitutes a foil against which we measure our ordinary unproblematic grasp: 'It is important for our view of things that someone may feel concerning certain people that their inner life will always be a mystery to him. That he will never understand them. (Englishwomen in the eyes of Europeans.)' (CV, p. 74)
25 In *On Certainty* and works contemporaneous with it, one must be wary of Wittgenstein's use of 'know', particularly when it appears in italics or scare quotes. In such cases, Wittgenstein is not referring to knowing as he understands it (i.e. as

justified true belief; cf. *inter alia* OC 91, 504), but to the objective, nonepistemic certainty that is mistaken for knowledge (by philosophers like Moore, or in ordinary language): 'I should like to say: Moore does not *know* what he asserts he knows, but it stands fast for him, as also for me; regarding it as absolutely solid is part of our *method* of doubt and inquiry' (OC 151). I discuss this in more detail in Moyal-Sharrock (2007a), 25–7.
26 Cf. also LW II, p. 85.
27 For example, my objective certainty that someone lying there with a gaping wound is in pain manifests itself in my spontaneous, unhesitating *treating* him as such, my *tending* to him, and my informing someone on the telephone that a person is lying next to me in great pain, and asking how I can alleviate it.
28 Cf. particularly Lagerspetz (1998), 32–3. Elsewhere (Moyal-Sharrock, 2007a, 191–8), I have addressed Lagerspetz's objections to calling primary trust a 'trust'; here, I shall be applying these objections to the legitimacy of calling primitive or objective certainty a 'certainty'.
29 See Frith and Happé (1999), but also Toichi et al (2002), 'A Lack of Self-Consciousness in Autism', *Am. J. Psychiatry*, 159: 1422–4, and R. P. Hobson and J. A. Meyer (2006) 'Foundations for self and other: a study in autism', *Developmental Science*, 8 (6): 481–91.
30 I would argue that there is no Theory of Mind at all in minds that are not thus challenged – that is, there is no default Theory of Mind. For a brief discussion, see section 7 in Chapter 5, 'From Deed to Word', in this volume.
31 For an explanation of these, see Davies and Coltheart (2000).
32 (1992, 86). Also, "the average fifth-grader can recognize twenty-nine out of a possible thirty-two facial expressions correctly" (1992, 136).
33 'They are residual because they would be the "rules" left over after we hypothetically write down all of the official and formal rules of society that are codified by our systems of etiquette and justice. Examples of residual rules are plentiful because their number is nearly infinite. One rule, for instance, says that when we are sitting in a room involved in almost any activity, we do not touch anyone else. We know that this is a rule, because if we break it, we ask forgiveness from those we've offended by saying, "Oh I am so sorry, pardon me". The term 'residual rules' is Thomas Scheff's (1984, 55).
34 And, less seriously, as Wittgenstein suggests, where we would need to explain our form of life to aliens: 'I meet someone from Mars and he asks me "How many toes have human beings got?" – I say "Ten. I'll show you" 'shew' in the original – early 20th c spelling, but I don't mind your changing it, and take my shoes off. Suppose he was surprised that I knew with such certainty, although I hadn't looked at my toes – ought I to say "We humans know how many toes we have whether we can see them or not"?' (OC 430).
35 Taking up the challenge from G. E. Moore. For a discussion, see Moyal-Sharrock (2007a), and Chapter 8, 'Wittgenstein on Knowledge and Certainty', in this volume.
36 Of course, there is a sense in which we rightly say that we 'know' ourselves, and can therefore predict our behaviour – for example, 'I know myself, I won't be able to hide my feelings from her' – but this is not the knowledge arising from indefeasible, justified true belief due to indubitable and exclusive acquaintance with, or introspection of, our own mind that is put forward as the only acceptable target by the sceptic.

8 Wittgenstein on Knowledge and Certainty

1. The notes that make up *On Certainty* were inspired by discussions with Norman Malcolm in 1949 of G. E. Moore's 'Proof of an External World' (1939) and 'A Defence of Common Sense' (1925).
2. Williams contends that we are individually epistemically *entitled to* basic propositions – that is, to holding them as true *by default*, without evidence of any kind (1999, 188) – provided evidential justification can, on demand, be given by *someone else* (2001, 37).
3. The reference to 'hinge certainty / certainties' is important if we are to distinguish Wittgenstein's notion of basic certainties from traditional notions which take basic certainty to be epistemic (a brand of knowledge). Indeed, a new branch of epistemology called 'Hinge Epistemology' has emerged (see Coliva and Moyal-Sharrock (eds) 2016) and the Introduction in this volume). Note: to say that hinges have a role to play in epistemology does not imply that hinges are epistemic.
4. It is worth noting that some Wittgensteinian scholars do not mark the difference Wittgenstein makes between knowledge and logical certainty (e.g., Stephen Mulhall in 'Could there be a private language?', *Arts & Ideas,* Wed 8 Jan 2020, BBC Radio 3); others would rather we not speak here of certainty at all (e.g., Olli Lagerspetz (1998); Genia Schönbaumsfeld (2016a; 2016b)). For my response to Lagerspetz, see Chapter 7, 'Wittgenstein on Psychological Certainty', in this volume, and Moyal-Sharrock (2007a), 191–8; for my response to Schönbaumsfeld, see Moyal-Sharrock (2019).
5. Even Descartes thought as much: '. . . how could it be denied that these hands or this whole body are mine? Unless perhaps I were to liken myself to madmen' (1641, 12), whilst at the same time, however, maintaining that these beliefs are derived from the senses (1641, 13). Wittgenstein argues that they are not (see section 5 in this chapter).
6. For a corrective, proto-Wittgensteinian, reading of Hume, see Sandis (2019).
7. That is, an identical sentence can function in one context as a hinge; and in other contexts as an empirical or an epistemic proposition. For example, the sentence 'There are human beings other than myself' can function as a descriptive proposition (and therefore be open to doubt) when addressed to a Martian in a sci-fi film, but in philosophical discussion, it can only functions as an indubitable basic belief. To see it as a defeasible empirical or epistemic proposition in that context is to make a category mistake.
8. Unless Moore indicates that he would like to deviate from the standard philosophical definition of knowledge, which he is precisely intent on not doing.
9. Of course, our hinge certainties are susceptible of philosophical *examination* (indeed, this is what *On Certainty* and this chapter are engaged in), but *to examine is not to doubt*.
10. But on this, see note 5 above.
11. See Williams (2005); other commentators who have denied it are Wright (1985, 469), Phillips (1988, xv, 40, 54, 89; 2003, 182). For pro-foundationalist positions, see Stroll (1994), Conway (1989) and Mounce (2005).
12. Avrum Stroll (2004) has counted more than seventy entries in which Wittgenstein uses explicitly foundational language, with many more passages containing less explicit locutions having the same foundational thrust.

13　Conditioning includes training as well as repeated exposure; for a fuller account of how facts condition grammar, see Chapter 1, 'Wittgenstein's Grammar: Through Thick and Thin', in this volume; and Moyal-Sharrock (2013a); (2016a).
14　See e.g., AWL 101; PLP 288; BT 61 [76]. I argue elsewhere that, for Wittgenstein, a proposition is essentially *bipolar* – which means that it must be susceptible of truth *and* falsity (see Moyal-Sharrock (2007a, 35–9)), but *bivalence* suffices for my argument here.
15　'We can draw the distinction between hypothesis and grammatical rule by means of the words "true" or "false" on the one hand, and "practical" and "impractical" on the other. The words "practical" and "impractical" characterize rules. A rule is not true or false.' (AWL 70)
16　For a more complete and detailed explanation, see Moyal-Sharrock (2007a), Chapter 2.
17　For a more developed argument of Coliva's position, see Moyal-Sharrock (2013b).
18　Remember that for Wittgenstein, nonsense is not uniquely a violation of sense; '*the negation of nonsense is nonsense*' (CL 2.7.1927). 'This rod has a length' is, on his view, as nonsensical as: 'This rod has no length'. The latter is nonsense in that it contravenes a rule of grammar, the other in that it *expresses* a rule of grammar: '. . . when we hear the two propositions, "This rod has a length" and its negation "This rod has no length", we take sides and favour the first sentence, *instead of declaring them both nonsense* [*Unsinn*]' (PG 129; my emphasis)
19　However, although rules are *always* devoid of sense, when they are formulated in heuristic circumstances where the formulation of the rule *is* needed, this does not cause perplexity or arrest proceedings. Heuristic utterances are outside the language-game; they are *preparatory* to the game (MWL 72; BT 38; PI 26, 49). The formulation of a hinge certainty is never an *occurrence* of certainty but, at best, the formulation of a rule.
20　Moreover, implicatures do not function as rules of grammar.
21　It seems counterintuitive to think of sentences such as 'I am here' or 'I know that's a tree' as ineffable. The key is not to confuse 'ineffable' or 'unsayable' (in Wittgenstein's technical sense) with unutterable or non-vocalizable, and to remember that these sentences are not ineffable in all their uses. As we noted, identical sentences can have different *uses* and therefore different *statuses*. It is not because a certain combination of words is *sayable* and *falsifiable* in one context or use, that it is *sayable* and *falsifiable* in another.
22　Note, also, that hinges do not lose their nonsensicality in the philosopher's study: they are nonsensical by dint of being grammatical. The philosophical examination of hinges is an examination of rules of grammar, not of claims that can be subjected to doubt.
23　In the pathological case of the loss of proprioception, this certainty is no longer occurrent; see Oliver Sacks (1985), where Sacks himself makes the link with *On Certainty*.
24　I have counted approximately 300 occurrences of 'hinges' in approximately 200 of the 676 passages that constitute *On Certainty*.
25　See, e.g., OC 448 and 657.
26　For a discussion of the processes by which some of our hinges become 'fixed' (and, conversely, 'unhinged'), see Moyal-Sharrock (2007a), 104–16; 137–47. Wittgenstein speaks of conditioning, hardening, fossilization and fusing ('This fact is fused into the foundations of our language-game' (OC 558)), making it clear that entry into and exclusion from bedrock is not due to reasoning, falsification or verification.

9 Too Cavellian a Wittgenstein

1. This reductively Therapeutic vision of Wittgenstein was promoted by the New Wittgensteinians, thus called because of the publication of what might be called their manifesto volume, *The New Wittgenstein* (2000). Notable 'New Wittgensteinians' are Cora Diamond, James Conant, Alice Crary, Rupert Read.
2. For Hutchinson and Read, 'Wittgenstein's elucidations (and perspicuous presentations) throughout his career have to be recognized as of *transitional*, purpose-relative and "personal" use only' (2006, 3).
3. As also Wittgenstein's acknowledgment, in a letter to Ludwig Ficker, that the important part of the *Tractatus* was the silent part: 'My work consists of two parts: the one presented here plus all that I have *not* written. And it is precisely this second part that is the important one.'
4. For a reading of Tractarian nonsense as neither merely gibberish (as it is for Diamond) nor merely a *violation* of sense (as it is for Hacker), see Moyal-Sharrock (2007b).
5. This is a precursor to Wittgenstein's notion that the non-scientific aspect of human life is not susceptible of exact statement or of evidence, but only of 'imponderable evidence'.
6. Where literature is concerned, this is mostly the ethical. For a discussion, see Moyal-Sharrock (2016b).
7. See Chapter 4, 'Literature as the Measure of Our Lives', in this volume.
8. On the ineffability of basic certainty, see Chapter 8, 'Wittgenstein on Knowledge and Certainty', in this volume, and Moyal-Sharrock (2007a), 94–7.
9. Cavell speaks of 'the uncanniness of the ordinary' or 'the extreme oddness of the everyday world' (1988, 105). In French translations of Cavell (which he approved), 'uncanniness' is translated as 'inquiétante étrangeté' (literally, 'worrisome strangeness') thereby stressing the 'worrisome' connotation in the notion of the uncanny.
10. For a more balanced view, see Constantine Sandis (2015) on what he calls the 'unproblematic' tension between the *public* Wittgenstein's optimism about knowledge of other minds and the *private* Wittgenstein's pessimism about understanding others.
11. 'There seem to be propositions that have the character of experiential propositions, but whose truth is for me unassailable. That is to say, if I assume that they are false, I must mistrust all my judgements' (RC III, 348). 'And don't I have to admit that sentences are often used on the borderline between logic and the empirical, so that their meaning shifts back and forth and they are now expressions of norms, now treated as expressions of experience? For it is not the "thought" (an accompanying mental phenomenon) but its use (something that surrounds it), that distinguishes the logical proposition from the empirical one' (RC III, 19).
12. '... I am inclined to believe that not everything that has the form of an empirical proposition *is* one' (OC 308); 'But wouldn't one have to say then, that there is no sharp boundary between propositions of logic and empirical propositions? The lack of sharpness *is* that of the boundary between *rule* and empirical proposition.' (OC 319); 'I want to say: propositions of the form of empirical propositions, and not only propositions of logic, form the foundation of all operating with thoughts (with language)' (OC 401).
13. 'In fact, all the propositions of our everyday language, just as they stand, are in perfect logical order' (TLP 5.5563).

14 'Philosophical troubles are caused by not using language practically but by extending it on looking at it. We form sentences and then wonder what they can mean. Once conscious of 'time' as a substantive, we ask then about the creation of time' (AWL 15).
15 The 'truth of scepticism', according to Cavell, being 'the standing threat to thought and communication, that they are only human' (1979, 47).
16 Cavell: '… in our desperation for closure or order or sublimity in our concepts – in our disappointment with our criteria for their application – we ask criteria to do something or to go somewhere that they are not fit to do or to go, and so we repudiate, as it were, their intelligence' (2001, 357).
17 It would seem then, that at the close of his last writings on philosophical psychology – and we should note here that the passage is dated 'April 15 1951', and that the last dated passage of *On Certainty* is '27 April 1951' – Wittgenstein is no longer saying that uncertainty is a *constitutional* or *essential* trait of our psychological ascriptions. He has come to see that, in some cases, we *are* as *objectively* certain about 'He is in pain' as about 'I am in pain'. On this, see Chapter 3, 'Words as Deeds', in this volume.
18 See McDowell's gloss here: 'The terror of which Cavell writes at the end of this marvellous passage is a sort of vertigo, induced by the thought that there is nothing that keeps our practices in line except the reactions and responses we learn in learning them. The ground seems to have been removed from under our feet. In this mood, we are inclined to feel that the sort of thing Cavell describes is insufficient foundation for a conviction that some practice really is a case of going on in the same way. What Cavell offers looks, rather, like a congruence of subjectivities, not grounded as it would need to be to amount to the sort of objectivity we want if we are to be convinced that we are really going on in the same way' (2000, 43).
19 'Just as in writing we learn a particular basic form of letters and then vary it later, so we learn first *the stability of things as the norm*, which is then subject to alterations' (OC 473; my emphasis). On language-acquisition, see Chapter 2, 'Universal Grammar: Wittgenstein versus Chomsky', in this volume'
20 Wittgenstein's rule-following argument shows precisely that generating new sentences is nothing but an instance of knowing how to go on, 'how to extend the speech that [we] have into new contexts' (Bruner 1983, 39). As H.-J. Glock rightly notes, the early Wittgenstein's was also concerned with what is now known as the problem of 'the creativity of language': the number of propositions being indefinite although the number of words is finite (NL 98; TLP 4.02, 4.027 etc.) (1996, 298).
21 Of course, that is unlikely, even if the index in *The Claim of Reason*, whose subtitle includes 'Wittgenstein' and 'Skepticism', does not list *On Certainty*.
22 *Pace* Genia Schönbaumsfeld (2016b), the concept of groundlessness is needed in that it helpfully underlines the absence of reasoning or justification or grounds; its use by Wittgenstein needn't imply that groundlessness is an absence where there ought to be a presence (i.e. grounds); it is simply a helpful contrast to cases of assurance which are reliant on grounds (such as knowledge).
23 Moreover, though groundlessness means absence of justification or reasoning, it does not mean detachment from reality: our hinges are *conditioned* by how the world is, by 'very general facts of nature'; they are rooted, albeit not ratiocinatively, in our human form of life and in the various forms of human life (see Chapter 1, 'Wittgenstein's Grammar: Through Thick and Thin', in this volume).
24 Indeed, the images used by Wittgenstein are images of stability and fixity: the hard rock of the river is 'subject to no alteration or only to an imperceptible one' (OC 99); the foundations (OC 167, 248, 411, 414, 558); les hinges that stay fixed so that the door

can turn (OC 343). Far from succumbing to the threat of sceptical vertigo, Wittgenstein repeats that certain things are solidly or unshakeably fixed for me and others (e.g., OC 112, 116, 144).
25 See Chapter 8, 'Wittgenstein on Knowledge and Certainty', in this volume.
26 See for example: '... the fact that both skepticism and tragedy conclude with the condition of human separation, with a discovering that I am I; and the fact that the alternative to my acknowledgment of the other is not my ignorance of him but my avoidance of him call it my denial of him' (1979, 389).
27 I argue against a more recent expression of scepticism as an existential human condition which occurs in Duncan Pritchard's notion of 'epistemic angst' (influenced by Cavell) in Moyal-Sharrock (2016c).
28 I am indebted to Paul Standish and Anat Matar for invaluable comments on a previous draft of this chapter.

10 Fighting Relativism

1 See the Introduction, 'Discovering Wittgenstein', and Chapter 11, 'Beyond Hacker's Wittgenstein', in this volume, as well as Moyal-Sharrock, ed. (2004).
2 See, e.g., Alexander Bird (2002). Bird notes that Kuhn mentions Wittgenstein just twice in his writings (1996, 44–5; 1977, 121), but that he may well have absorbed much Wittgenstein indirectly from discussions with Stanley Cavell at Berkeley (2000, 295n11).
3 No attempt was made in this chapter to define or distinguish the terms 'world', 'reality' and 'nature' used by philosophers quoted in the chapter to refer, more or less metaphorically, to unconceptualized or raw reality – or what Wittgenstein refers to as the 'reality lying behind the notation' (PI 562). My use of these terms usually follows theirs but I have also tried to navigate as best I could to avoid confusion (1) with the sense of 'reality' as comprising and often constituted by our conceptual constructions; and (2) with the sense of 'nature' about which our accounts or conceptualization would sound too close to those of a botanist or zoologist.
4 See Thomas Nagel, *The View from Nowhere* (Oxford University Press, 1986).
5 A point dramatically highlighted by quantum physics – the mere presence of a viewer necessarily distorts reality. This is at least one interpretation; another is that there is no (objective) reality.
6 As Norman Malcolm writes: 'To suppose that there is an "objective basis" in terms of which one language-game could be judged to be more adequate or more "true" than the other, is to suppose that the true concept of pain is stowed away somewhere like the standard meter, available for comparison when differences arise between merely human concepts. But we may be certain that there are no principles of justification which lie outside of all human conceptual frameworks and world-pictures' (1982, 99).
7 Wittgenstein would not speak of theory-ladenness, but he views language as necessarily conditioned by, and embedded in, our forms of life; they are therefore, one could say 'reality-soaked' (see Chapter 1, 'Wittgenstein's Grammar: Through Thick and Thin', in this volume). I am not concerned in this chapter with the conceptuality of *perception*. Suffice it to say that for Kuhn, there is no access to a nonconceptualized world; even observation is theory-laden. Wittgenstein would not go that far: animals and pre-linguistic children are concept-free (e.g., 'As children we learn concepts and what one does with them simultaneously' (LW II, 43)). Kuhn can go this far in that he believes a

prelinguistic 'mental module' or 'taxonomic module' is possessed also by animals (2000, 93). This brings Kuhn much closer to Kant than Wittgenstein could ever be.
8   Kuhn repeatedly corrects his readers' assumption that when he spoke of theories as incommensurable he meant that they could not be compared (e.g., 2000, 189).
9   Of course, many languages (most European and many Asian ones) may have derived from a common Indo-European one, but the latter isn't a *neutral* language.
10 Though these are not synonymous, Wittgenstein often uses them interchangeably to refer to our modes of classification, and I shall also do so here. On Wittgenstein's connected use of grammar and concepts, see Chapter 1, 'Wittgenstein's Grammar: Through Thick and Thin', section 4, in this volume.
11 There is a possible debt here to *family resemblance*, but the reference to 'patterns' is not likely to have been inspired by Wittgenstein, though he, too, spoke of *patterns of experience* – a term he used with specific regard to psychological concepts (cf. LW I, 211; LW II, 42). On the latter, see Chapter 7, 'Wittgenstein on Psychological Certainty', in this volume.
12 Ilham Dilman: 'Think of the similarity we may find between a deep well and a deep sorrow. Is it not clearer here that were it not for our language we would not find a similarity here?' (2002, 71)
13 As previously noted (Chapter 1, note 20), Wittgenstein's does not always mark the distinction between language and grammar.
14 Suggesting Wittgenstein knows full well that the problem is that empiricists confuse facts and concepts, and so take sentences like 'The earth is a planet' to express a fact or an empirical proposition. This confusion between the empirical and the formal (or grammatical) is at the heart of what both Wittgenstein and Kuhn are combating.
15 Wittgenstein even speaks here of correspondence – 'Indeed the correspondence [*Entsprechung*] between our grammar and general (seldom mentioned) facts of nature does concern us' (RPP I, 46) – however, as all his other formulations and descriptions make clear, not in the sense of a strict or veridical correspondence.
16 Thus summarized by Boghossian: '"The world which we seek to understand and know about is not what it is independently of us and our social context; rather, all facts are socially constructed in a way that reflects our contingent needs and interests" ("*Constructivism about Facts*")' (2006, 22) Or indeed from nominalism; see Hacking: 'The realist, in the sense that matters here, may well echo the first half of Wittgenstein's first sentence in the *Tractatus*: "The world is made up of facts". The nominalist retorts that we have a good deal to do with organizing what we call a fact. The world of nature does not just come with a totality of facts; rather it is we who organize the world into facts' (1999, 174).
17 This does not mean that *all* our concepts are susceptible of change: our *basic* concepts are unalterable: 'Sometimes it happens that we later introduce a new concept that is more practical for us. – But that will only happen in very definite and small areas, and it presupposes that most concepts remain unaltered. / Could a legislator abolish the concept of pain? / The basic concepts are interwoven so closely with what is most fundamental in our way of living that they are therefore unassailable.' (LW II, 43–4).
18 '... we lay down the rule, we hold the measuring-rod: "The certainty with which I call the colour "red" is the rigidity of my measuring-rod, it is the rigidity from which I start' (RFM 329).
19 Indeed, Kuhn does not believe that scientific progress is truth-related (unless truth be taken intra-theoretically); that we can compare theories as statements about 'what is really there' (2000, 159), but this absence of *truth* as a goal, does not mean that science

has no goal at all, and therefore that any theory is as good as another: Kuhn sees the progress of science in evolutionary and pragmatic terms. For Kuhn, science is a cognitive empirical investigation of nature that exhibits a unique sort of progress – that is, it does not progress towards some goal (truth), but instead progresses away from its primitive, earlier stages (cf. Bird 2000, 27). Kuhn defined this progress as increasing fitness over time, including the fitness of the exemplars themselves, where fitness means consonance with the state of the art as defined by the scientific community, not directly to reality itself (cf. Nickles 2003, 169). Not truth, but 'accuracy, precision, scope, simplicity, fruitfulness, consistency, and so on, simply *are* the criteria which puzzle solvers must weigh in deciding whether or not a given puzzle about the match between phenomena and belief has been solved' (2000, 251).

20 Kuhn and Wittgenstein, in their rejection of a human-independent objective description of the world, explicitly and implicitly hold that correspondence and causal theories of truth are not valid. Kuhn: '. . . what is fundamentally at stake is rather the correspondence theory of truth, the notion that the goal, when evaluating scientific laws or theories, is to determine whether or not they correspond to an external, mind-independent world. It is that notion, whether in an absolute or probabilistic form, that I'm persuaded must vanish together with foundationalism. What replaces it will still require a strong conception of truth, but not, except in the most trivial sense, correspondence truth.' (2000, 95)

21 Sharrock and Read clarify this aspect of Kuhn and Peter Winch's position, which makes them, they write, 'the true "anti-Relativists"' (as we shall see, Wittgenstein can be added to the picture): 'Far from arguing that we have to accept that the convictions of the pre-Copernicans or those of believers in magic are true, Kuhn is in fact arguing that we *cannot possibly* make their way of thinking our own. . . . Kuhn and Winch aspire to present the point of view of "the Other" to us in such a way that we can understand how that point of view could be compelling to them, how, *in those same circumstances and under those conditions,* we ourselves would have thought . . . in exactly those same ways – and how, in the circumstances in which we actually are, those other / older ideas *are complete non-starters.*' (2002, 161).

22 Wittgenstein wrote this fifteen years before Armstrong set foot on the moon.

23 Putnam uses this phrase, which he attributes to David Wiggins (1981, 55).

24 On this, see Chapter 8, 'Wittgenstein on Knowledge and Certainty', in this volume. By 'universal' I mean 'across the human world', not across 'all possible worlds'.

25 See Carpendale and Lewis: 'It might seem that if we endorse the Wittgensteinian idea that children learn about the mental world through learning how to express their feelings, plans, and goals, etc. in language, and learning the criteria for the third person use of various psychological terms, then we must endorse an enculturation position in which mentalistic concepts are imported from the social world to the individual. As mentioned above, this is one interpretation of Wittgenstein and it implies a cultural relativism, by which children would just learn the mental concepts used in their particular culture. However, we do not endorse this interpretation for two reasons. First, *at the basic level of* social understanding (e.g., seeing, looking, intentions, desires and beliefs) children's understanding is built onto shared practices that we expect would be common across cultures because these are common aspects of human experience . . . . This does not rule out that there may be cross-cultural variability, such as in complex emotions.' (2004, 20; my emphasis).

26 For a more in-depth discussion of the difference between the one human form of life and the many forms of human life, see Moyal-Sharrock (2015).

27 '... it belongs to the logic of our scientific investigations that certain things are *in deed* not doubted' (OC 342).
28 Malinowski in Young (1979), 207.
29 Wittgenstein also sees the purpose of some ritualistic action as expressivist: 'Burning in effigy. Kissing the picture of one's beloved. That is *obviously not* based on the belief that it will have some specific effect on the object which the picture represents. It aims at satisfaction and achieves it. Or rather: it *aims* at nothing at all; we just behave this way and then we feel satisfied' (GB 123).
30 '... the characteristic feature of ritualistic action is not at all a view, an opinion' (GB 129); 'magic is always based on the idea of symbolism' (GB 125).
31 'I should like to say: nothing shows our kinship to those savages better than the fact that Frazer has on hand a word as familiar to himself and to us as "ghost" or "shade" in order to describe the views of these people.... much too little is made of the fact that we count the words "soul" and "spirit" as part of our educated vocabulary. Compared with this, the fact that we do not believe that our soul eats and drinks is a trifling matter' (GB 133).
32 'As simple as it sounds: the distinction between magic and science can be expressed by saying that in science there is progress, but in magic there isn't. Magic has no tendency within itself to develop.' (GB 141).
33 I also discuss the nonsensicality of equating possibility with conceivability (all possible worlds) in Chapter 1, 'Wittgenstein's Grammar: Through Thick and Thin', section 7, in this volume.

11 Beyond Hacker's Wittgenstein

1 See *The Third Wittgenstein: the post-Investigations works* (Aldershot: Ashgate 2004).
2 This position is notably represented and articulated by Peter Hacker who, in *Connections and Controversies*, notes the division of Wittgenstein's philosophy into 'two powerful complete philosophical world-pictures crystallized respectively in the *Tractatus* and the *Investigations*' producing 'two diametrically opposed philosophical masterpieces, the *Tractatus Logico-Philosophicus* (1921) and the *Philosophical Investigations* (1953)' (2001, viii and 1).
3 This resulted in three collections of essays: *The Third Wittgenstein* (op. cit.), *Readings in Wittgenstein's On Certainty* (Basingstoke: Palgrave Macmillan, 2007), and *Perspicuous Presentations: Essays on Wittgenstein's Philosophy of Psychology* (Basingstoke, UK: Palgrave Macmillan, 2007).
4 It may be objected that the intention had nevertheless been there to publish some version of PI. The fact remains that Wittgenstein did not intend to publish the version Hacker calls one of Wittgenstein's two books; nor, as Malcolm notes, did Wittgenstein think 'he could give the final polish to it in his lifetime' (1984, 75).
5 As Alois Pichler and Michael Biggs remark: 'The expression "Wittgenstein's works" may be interpreted in a number of ways' (1993, 7), but what is clear is that any stringent definition of 'a work' would leave us with a much diminished Wittgenstein corpus. Indeed, it would consist of a single work. The *Tractatus*, as Guido Frongia and Brian McGuinness write, is 'the sole work that Wittgenstein considered finished enough to be printed', and we would be hard put to find, after the *Tractatus*, any of his own writings that Wittgenstein would have regarded as a 'finished work' (1990, 3).
6 We would simply consider those pages as drafts or discards.

7. Anscombe and von Wright in the Preface: 'The material falls into four parts; we have shown the divisions at §65, p. 10, §192, p. 27 and §299, p. 38. What we believe to be the first part was written on twenty loose sheets of lined foolscap, undated.... The rest is in small notebooks, containing dates.'
8. PI, on the other hand, as Wittgenstein himself writes in the Preface, is the *precipitate* of *sixteen years*' work (from 1929 to 1945); 'concern[s] many subjects'; and is 'really only an album'.
9. I make a book-length case for this – and for my claim that *On Certainty* is a 'masterpiece', Wittgenstein's *third* – in Moyal-Sharrock (2007a).
10. Wittgenstein is reported as saying that 'No fact can be a paradigm for grammar. It you try to find facts to justify grammar, when you try to *say* that they are, they are no longer paradigms, you are using the same grammar to describe both the facts and the grammar you are justifying. [...] Grammar is not determined by facts.' (LWL 95). Note, however, that Wittgenstein is here countering the idea that grammar can be *justified* by facts; something which of course he will never retract and which he also expresses by saying that grammar is 'autonomous'; not 'answerable' or 'accountable' to any reality (BT 184–6). However, as he clarifies in Part II of PI and in OC, grammar can be *conditioned* by facts. More on this in the main body of the chapter below.
11. Or what, according to Peter Hacker and Joachim Schulte's new translation (and I concur), is not really part of the *Investigations* at all, but a 'fragment' of his philosophy of psychology. I will, however, for ease of reference, go on speaking of Part II of the *Investigations*.
12. Hacker of course acknowledges this: 'Such systems of rules as we adopt, unlike the logical syntax of all possible languages as envisaged in the *Tractatus*, are conditioned by empirical facts – facts about us and our nature, and facts about the world around us' (1996b, 78).
13. Grammar is not justified but *conditioned* by the facts: 'Indeed doesn't it seem obvious that the *possibility* of a language-game is conditioned by certain facts?' (OC 617; my emphasis; see also RFM 80, 116).
14. The function Wittgenstein accords to a rule of grammar is not only the narrow one of instructing us in the use of individual words (e.g., 'A rod has (what we call) a length' or 'This(is a hand'); but more generally that of expressing the *conditions* for making sense (PG, p. 88). Such 'conditions' include not only straight-forward *definitions*, or expressions of rules 'used to explain the use of certain symbols' (LFM 282); precise *prescriptions* and *proscriptions* (e.g., 'The truth is: it makes sense to say about other people that they doubt whether I am in pain; but not to say it about myself' (PI 246); 'Certainly it makes no sense to say that the colour red is torn up or pounded to bits' (PI 57)); *conceptual elucidations* – that is, reminders of the kinds of statement we are making (e.g., 'We remind ourselves, that is to say, of the *kind of statement* that we make about phenomena.... Our investigation is therefore a grammatical one' (PI 90)); and anything that is 'a preparation for a description' (MWL 72): this includes samples, tables, and any other 'object' or 'instrument of the language' (cf. PI 16). The scope of what Wittgenstein means by rules of grammar is perceptible in this remark: 'By *grammatical* rule I understand every rule that relates to the use of language' (VOW 303). In *On Certainty*, Wittgenstein considers our basic beliefs – because they underpin our making sense – as rules of grammar (e.g., OC 53, 57–9, 136, 151). On this, see Chapter 1, 'Wittgenstein's Grammar: Through Thick and Thin', in this volume.
15. And this extension of grammar to include less general facts than had been envisaged in PI, part 2 is a realization Wittgenstein comes to in *On Certainty*.

16 The mention of 'method' is another confirmation of Wittgenstein's referring to grammar here (cf. PG, p. 88).
17 As in the following, where having explained that for Wittgenstein '… the negation of a proposition with sense, which describes how things are, is itself a proposition with sense', he qualifies this in a footnote: 'There are, as Wittgenstein realized, exceptions to this principle, e.g. certain conditionals and some propositions of the *Weltbild*.' (Hacker 1996b, 77). And a variant of this in the revised 1996c edition: 'If the negation of a proposition makes sense …, then the proposition negated must make sense', with Hacker's footnote: 'There are exceptions to this: grammatical propositions themselves … and, *in a different way*, some of the propositions of one's "world-picture" (*Weltbild*) which are discussed in *On Certainty*, etc.' (1996c, 113; my emphasis). We are not told in what different way.
18 And indeed several Wittgenstein scholars insist that bipolarity is a constant in Wittgenstein's work, from beginning to end: G.H. von Wright (1982, 174); Jacques Bouveresse (1981, 93); Newton Garver (1996, 148-9); Anthony Kenny (1973, 229).
19 Hacker takes rules of grammar to be bounds of sense, but without that occasioning a broadening of his conception of grammar: 'The expression "bounds of sense" is not Wittgenstein's but Strawson's Kantian phrase. Nevertheless, it is apt for Wittgenstein's conception of the limits of language, since the limits of language are precisely the bounds of sense, and transgressing the limits of language, like transgressing the bounds of sense, does not yield a description of impossible possibilities, but nonsensical forms of words' (2012, 5n4).
20 For a discussion of how such 'propositions' become rigid by dint of conditioning and/or repeated exposure, see Chapter 1, 'Wittgenstein's Grammar: Through Thick and Thin', in this volume.
21 Of course, these same sentences may be formulated in contexts in which they express empirical propositions – e.g., in a sci-fi novel, aliens are discussing the human world and coming to conclusions about it, such that it has existed for many years; a headline in a 21 July 1969 newspaper referring to Armstrong and Aldrin's first steps on the moon) – but these sentences can also express certainties that act as norms of representation, or rules of testing (OC 96-8). So that although a sentence that expresses a hinge certainty may have a doppelgänger that functions as an empirical proposition; it is itself, qua *hinge*, not an empirical proposition but a rule of testing or rule of grammar.
22 In *On Certainty*, Wittgenstein shows such personal certainties not to be empirical or epistemic conclusions we come to. This, contra Descartes' claim, that such 'beliefs' as 'I am here, sitting by the fire, wearing a winter dressing-gown, holding this piece of paper in my hands, and so on' are derived from the senses (1641, 12-13).
23 Although Wittgenstein's post-Tractarian conception of grammar differed from his Tractarian one, it was not miles apart: his aim there was to avoid, with the help of a 'logical grammar' (TLP 3.325), the fundamental confusions produced by the misleading uniformity of language (see especially TLP 3.323-3.325). Although it is crucial to point out differences in Wittgenstein's philosophical journey, it is also important to trace any continuous or unifying preoccupation which may have informed it: as mentioned in my introduction to *The Third Wittgenstein*, I believe the single track of Wittgenstein's philosophy is the discernment and elucidation of grammar – its nature and scope.
24 In *Last Writings on the Philosophy of Psychology*, Wittgenstein writes: 'Don't think of being certain as a mental state, a kind of feeling, or some such thing. The important

thing about certainty is the way one behaves...' (LW II, p 21) / Ask not "What goes on in us when we are certain – ?", but "How does it show?"' (LW II, p. 21) [see PI , p. 225: 'Ask, not: "What goes on in us when we are certain that...?" – but: How is "the certainty that this is the case" manifested in human action?']. These are all 'third Wittgenstein' (i.e. post-PI Part I) writings.

25 And there appear to be *negative* theses as well; for example: 'The employment of a word is not: to designate something' (RPP I, 614). Or, this one: 'You don't need any *knowledge* to find a smell repulsive' (LW I, 758) – which can be read as a precursor to a noncognitive theory of emotion, whereby basic emotions, such as disgust or repulsion, are nonpropositional or noncognitive.

26 Short for 'the philosopher, as understood by Wittgenstein'.

27 Remember also: '... it is, rather, of the essence of our investigation that we do not seek to learn anything *new* by it. We want to *understand* something that is already in plain view. For *this* is what we seem in some sense not to understand' (PI 89).

28 Hutto suggests 'wrong' be changed to 'poor' or 'incomplete', as more properly describing the lack in an elucidation, not a theory. On the other hand, in response to my view that a map should be seen as analogous to a tool, instrument, model or template, but not a theory: a tool can be flawed and not work properly, and is therefore *rejected* as a proper working tool, *not refuted*, Oliver Petersen argues (in personal communication) that a map can be like a theory in that it can be refuted. He suggests the following dialogue: 'No, you can't go to station X by underground; look at the map.' Reply: 'You are wrong, the map is not correct: there is an underground-connection between station Y and station X now; the map is out of date.' The map can be said to be refuted by the respondent or it is refuted (in another sense of 'refuted') by the facts about the underground system.

29 Hutto's response is well worth quoting: 'Surely not. I can underdescribe or misdescribe the contents of this room. Someone else can do a better, more illuminating, more revealing job. But neither I nor the other are offering "theories". Theories seek to explain things – they make posits and stand in need of justification. That's not true of the two descriptions just mentioned. Sure we can say why one is better than another but we don't evaluate them in the way we evaluate theories. Someone once said: "I teach differences." That applies here too.'

30 'Not empiricism and yet realism in philosophy, that is the hardest thing' (RFM VI, 23).

31 See Chapter 5, 'From Deed to Word', in this volume.

32 See Chapter 6, 'Wittgenstein on Memory', in this volume.

33 'Is scientific progress useful to philosophy? Certainly. The realities that are discovered lighten the philosopher's task, imagining possibilities' (LW I, 807); 'The rule we lay down is the one most strongly suggested by the facts of experience.' (AWL 84).

34 Special thanks to Dan Hutto for his valuable comments on this chapter.

References

Anderson, S. R. and D. W. Lightfoot (2000), 'The Human Language Faculty as an Organ', *Annu. Rev. Physiol.*, 62: 1–23.
Baddeley, A. (1992), 'What is autobiographical memory?', in M. A. Conway, D. C. Rubin, H. Spinnler and W. A. Wagenaar (eds), *Theoretical Perspectives on Autobiographical Memory*, 13–29, Dordrecht: Kluwer Academic Publishers.
Baddeley, A. (1999), 'Memory', in R. A. Wilson and F. C. Keil (eds), *The MIT Encyclopedia of the Cognitive Sciences*, 514–17, Cambridge, MA: MIT Press,.
Bar-On, D. (2013), 'Expressive communication and Continuity Skepticism', *Journal of Philosophy*, 110 (6): 293–330.
Barrett, L. (2018), 'Picturing Primates, and Looking at Monkeys: Why 21st Century Primatology Needs Wittgenstein', *Philosophical Investigations* 41: 161–87.
Bates, E. and B. MacWhinney (1989), 'Functionalism and the competition model', in B. MacWhinney and E. Bates (eds), *The Crosslinguistic Study of Sentence Processing*, 3–76, Cambridge: Cambridge University Press,.
Bates, E. (1993), 'Comprehension and Production in Early Language Development: Comments on Savage-Rumbaugh et al.', in *Monographs of the Society for Research in Child Development*, 58: 3–4, 222–42.
Beardsmore, R. W. (1971), 'Art and Understanding', in J. Haldane & L. Lloyd (eds), *Art, Morality and Human Nature: Writings by Richard W. Beardsmore*, 55–79, Exeter: Imprint Academic, 2017,.
Bearn, G. C. F. (1997), *Waking to Wonder: Wittgenstein's Existential Investigations*, New York: SUNY Press.
Bennett, M. R., D. Dennett, P. M. S. Hacker and J. Searle (2007), *Neuroscience & Philosophy: Brain, Mind, & Language*. With an introduction & conclusion by D. Robinson, New York: Columbia University Press.
Bennett, M. R. and P. M. S. Hacker (2003), *Philosophical Foundations of Neuroscience*, Oxford: Blackwell.
Bickerton, D. (1984), 'The language bio-program hypothesis', *Behavioral and Brain Sciences*, 7: 173–212.
Biggs, M. and A. Pichler (1993), *Wittgenstein: Two Source Catalogues and a Bibliography*. Working Papers from the Wittgenstein Archives at the University of Bergen. No.7.
Bird, A. (2000), *Thomas Kuhn*, Slough, UK: Acumen.
Bird, A. (2002), 'Kuhn's wrong turning', *Studies in History and Philosophy of Science* 33: 443–63.
Bishop, D. (2014), 'What Chomksy doesn't get about child language', Figshare.
Boghossian, P. (2006), *Fear of Knowledge: Against Relativism and Constructivism*, Oxford: Clarendon Press.
Bouveresse, J. (1981), 'Wittgenstein et la philosophie du langage' in *Hermeneutique et linguistique*, 73–99, Combas, Editions de l'Eclat, 1981.
Bruner, J. (1983), *Child's Talk: Learning to Use Language*, New York: Norton.

Bühler, K. (1934), *Theory of Language: The Representational Function of Language*, trans. D. F. Goodwin, Amsterdam: Benjamins.

Byrne, R. (1999), *The Thinking Ape: Evolutionary Origins of Intelligence*, Oxford: Oxford University Press.

Calonne, D. S. (2006), 'Creative Writers and Revision' in A. Horning & A. Becker (eds), *Revision: History, Theory, and Practice*, 142–76, Indiana: Parlor Press.

Canfield, J. V. (1975; 1986), 'Anthropological Science Fiction and Logical Necessity' in J. V. Canfield (ed.), *The Philosophy of Wittgenstein; Vol. 10: Logical Necessity and Rules*, 105–17, New York: Garland.

Canfield, J. V. (1995), 'The Rudiments of Language', *Language and Communication*, 15 (3): 195–211.

Canfield, J. V. (1996), 'The Community View', *The Philosophical Review*, 105 (4): 469–88.

Canfield, J. V. (1997), 'Wittgenstein's Later Philosophy', in J. V. Canfield (ed.), *Philosophy of Meaning, Knowledge and Value in the Twentieth Century. Routledge History of Philosophy*, Vol. X., 247–85, London: Routledge.

Canfield, J. V. (2007), *Becoming Human: The Development of Language, Self, and Self-Consciousness*, Basingstoke: Palgrave Macmillan.

Carpendale, J. and C. Lewis (2004), 'Constructing an Understanding of Mind: The Development of Children's Social Understanding within Social Interaction', *Behavioral & Brain Sciences*, 27: 79–96.

Cavell, S. (1969), *Must We Mean What We Say: A Book of Essays*, New York: Cambridge University Press.

Cavell, S. (1979), *The Claim of Reason: Wittgenstein, Skepticism, Morality, and Tragedy*, Oxford: Oxford University Press.

Cavell, S. (1981), *The Senses of Walden*, San Francisco: North Point Press.

Cavell, S. (1986), *The Uncanniness of the Ordinary. The Tanner Lectures on Human Value*, delivered at Stanford University.

Cavell, S. (1988), *In Quest of the Ordinary: Lines of Skepticism and Romanticism*, Chicago: University of Chicago Press.

Cavell, S. (1996), 'Declining Decline' in S. Mulhall (ed.), *The Cavell Reader*, 321–52, Oxford: Blackwell, 1996.

Cavell, S. (2001), 'Silences Noises Voices' in J. Floyd, J. & S. Shieh (eds), *Future Pasts: The Analytic Tradition in Twentieth-Century Philosophy*, 351–8, Oxford: Oxford University Press, 2001.

Cavell, S. (2002a), 'L'ordinaire et l'inquiétant' *Rue Descartes* 1/2003 (no. 39), 88–98. URL: www.cairn.info/revue-rue-descartes-2003-1-page-88.htm. Excerpt of an interview for France-Culture, Paris, 22 November 2002.

Cavell, S. (2002b), *Must We Mean What We Say?*, 2nd ed. Cambridge, UK: Cambridge University Press.

Cavell, S. (2005), 'Responses' in R. B. Goodman (ed.), *Contending with Stanley Cavell*, 157–76, Oxford: Oxford University Press,.

Cavell, S. and P. Standish (2012). 'Stanley Cavell in Conversation with Paul Standish', *Journal of Philosophy of Education*, 46 (2): 155–76.

Chauvier, S. (2007), 'Wittgensteinian Grammar and Philosophy of Mind' in D. Moyal-Sharrock (ed.), *Perspicuous Presentations: Essays on Wittgenstein's Philosophy of Psychology*, 29–51, Basingstoke: Palgrave Macmillan.

Chauviré, C. (2012), 'L'Art Incorporé: A propos des réactions esthétiques' in C. Romano (ed.), *Wittgenstein*, 225–51, Paris: Cerf,.

Cheney, D. L. and R. M. Seyfarth (1982), 'How vervet monkeys perceive their grunts', *Animal Behaviour*, 30: 739–51.
Cheney, D. L. and R. M. Seyfarth (1996), 'Function and intention in the calls of nonhuman primates', *Proceedings of the British Academy*, 88: 59–76.
Chlebowski, S. M. et al (2009), 'Confabulation: A Bridge Between Neurology and Psychiatry?', *Psychiatric Times* 26 (6). https://www.psychiatrictimes.com/cognitive-disorders/confabulation-bridge-between-neurology-and-psychiatry
Chomsky, N. (1980a), *Rules and Representations*, Oxford: Blackwell.
Chomsky, N. (1980b), 'On cognitive structures and their development: A reply to Piaget', in M. Piatelli-Palmarin (ed.), *Language and Learning: The Debate between Jean Piaget and Noam Chomsky*, 35–54, Cambridge, MA: Cambridge: Harvard University Press.
Chomsky, N. (1983), '"Things No Amount of Learning Can Teach." Noam Chomsky interviewed by John Gliedman', *Omni*, 6 (11). http://www.chomsky.info/interviews/198311--.htm
Chomsky, N. (1988), 'Language and the problems of knowledge', The Managna Lectures, Cambridge, MA: MIT Press.
Chomsky, N. (1993), *Language and Thought*, London: Moyer Bell.
Chomsky, N. (1995), *The Minimalist Program*, Cambridge, MA: MIT Press.
Chomsky, N. (2000), 'The "Chomskyan Era"', Extracted from *The Architecture of Language*, N. Mukhergi, B. N. Patniak, and R. K. Agnihotri (eds), New Dehli: Oxford University Press [Oxford India Paperbacks]. Online.
Chomsky, N. (2012), 'The Minimalist Program and Language Acquisition', Lectio Magistralis, International School for Advanced Studies (SISSA), Trieste 17 September 2012.
Christiansen, M. H. and N. Chater (2008), 'Language as shaped by the brain', *Behavioral & Brain Sciences*, 31: 489–58.
Cioffi, F. (1998), *Wittgenstein on Freud and Frazer*, Cambridge: Cambridge University Press.
Cioffi, F. (2007), 'The Sort of Explanation One Longs For', in D. Moyal-Sharrock (ed.) *Perspicuous Presentations: Essays on Wittgenstein's Philosophy of Psychology*, 173–93, Basingstoke: Palgrave Macmillan,.
Clark, A. (1997), *Being There: Putting Brain, Body, and World Together Again*, Cambridge, MA: MIT Press.
Coliva, A. and D. Moyal-Sharrock, eds (2016), *Hinge Epistemology*, Leiden: Brill.
Coliva, A. (2010), *Moore and Wittgenstein: Scepticism, Certainty, and Common Sense*, Basingstoke: Palgrave Macmillan.
Conway, G. (1989), *Wittgenstein on Foundations*, Atlantic Highlands, NJ: Humanities Press International.
Cook, V. J. and M. Newson (2007), *Chomsky's Universal Grammar: An Introduction*, 3rd ed. Oxford: Blackwell Publishing.
Coulter, J. (1999), 'Discourse and Mind', rpt in S. Shanker and D. Kilfoyle (eds), *Ludwig Wittgenstein: Critical Assessments*, 2nd series, III, 143–61, London: Routledge, 2002,
Cowie, F. (2008), 'Innateness and Language', *Stanford Encyclopaedia of Philosophy*. http://plato.stanford.edu/entries/innateness-language/#toc
Cowley, S. (2007), 'The Cradle of Language: Making Sense of Bodily Connexions', in ed. D. Moyal-Sharrock (ed.), *Perspicuous Presentations: Essays on Wittgenstein's Philosophy of Psychology*, 278–98, Basingstoke: Palgrave Macmillan.
Craig, D. (2013), 'Thank God for the Leavisites', *London Review of Books* 35 (20), 24 October 2013. https://www.lrb.co.uk/v35/n20/letters#letter9

Crane, T. (2015), 'The Mental States of Persons and their Brains', in A. O'Hear (ed.) *Mind, Self, and Person*, Royal Institute of Philosophy Supplement 76, 253–70, Cambridge: Cambridge University Press.

Crane, T. (2016), 'Wittgenstein, bewitched', review of I. Ground and F. A. Flowers III (eds), *Portraits of Wittgenstein, Times Literary Supplement*, 24 February. Available online: https://www.the-tls.co.uk/articles/bewitched/

Crick, F. (1994), *The Astonishing Hypothesis: The Scientific Search for the Soul*, New York: Charles Scribner's Sons.

Curtiss, S, et al. (1997), 'The development of language in Genie: a case of language acquisition beyond the "critical period"', *Brain and Language*, 1 (1): 81–107.

Dabrowska, E. (2010), 'Native vs. expert intuitions: an empirical study of acceptability judgements', *The Linguistic Review*, 27: 1–23.

Dalla Barba, G. (2000), 'Memory, Consciousness, and Temporality: What Is Retrieved and Who Exactly Is Controlling the Retrieval?', in E. Tulving and F. I. M. Craik (eds), *The Oxford Handbook of Memory*, 138–55, Oxford: Oxford University Press.

Davies, M. and M. Coltheart (2000), 'Pathologies of Belief', *Mind & Language: Pathologies of Belief*, 15 (1): 1–46.

Dawkins, R. (1993), *The Independent*, September 1993; cited by D. Macarthur (2008) 'Quinean Naturalism in Question', *Philo*, 11 (1): 1–14.

Deacon, T. (1997), *The Symbolic Species: The Co-evolution of Language and the Human Brain*, New York: Penguin.

Descartes, R. (1641), *Meditations on First Philosophy*, rev. ed., John Cottingham (trans. and ed.), Cambridge: Cambridge University Press, 1996.

Diamond, C. (1989), 'Rules: looking in the right place', in D. Z. Phillips (ed.), *Wittgenstein: Attention to Particulars: Essays in Honour of Rush Rhees*, 12–34, London: Macmillan.

Diamond, C. (1991), *The Realistic Spirit: Wittgenstein, Philosophy, and the Mind*, Cambridge, MA: MIT Press.

Dilman, I. (2002), *Wittgenstein's Copernican Revolution: The Question of Linguistic Idealism*, Basingstoke: Palgrave Macmillan.

Douglas Fields, R. (2020), 'The Brain Learns in Unexpected Ways', *Scientific American*, March: 67–71.

Dunbar, R. I. M. (1993), 'Coevolution of neocortical size, group size and language in humans', *Behavioral and Brain Sciences*, 16 (4): 681–735.

Dunbar, R. I. M. (1996), *Grooming, Gossip, and the Evolution of Language*, Cambridge MA: Harvard University Press.

Dunbar, R. I. M. (2003), 'The Social Brain: Mind, Language, and Society in Evolutionary Perspective, *Annual Review of Anthropology*, 32: 163–81.

Dunbar, R. I. M. (2009), 'The social brain hypothesis and its implications for social evolution', *Annals of Human Biology*, 36: 562–72.

Dunn, M., S. J. Greenhill, S. C. Levinson and R. D. Gray (2011), 'Evolved structure of language shows lineage-specific trends in word-order universals', *Nature*, 473: 79–82.

Dye, M. (2010), 'The Advantages of Being Helpless: Human brains are slow to develop – a secret, perhaps, of our success', *Scientific American*, February. http://www.scientificamerican.com/article/advantages-of-helpless/

Engel, S. (1999), *Context is Everything & the Nature of Memory*, New York: W.H. Freeman.

Evans, N. and S. C. levinson (2009), ' The myth of language universals: Language diversity and its importance for cognitive science', *Behavioral and Brain Sciences*, 32: 429–92.

Evans, V. (2014), *The Language Myth: Why Language Is Not an Instinct*, Cambridge: Cambridge University Press.

Everett, D. (2012), 'There is no such thing as universal grammar', Interview by R. McCrum. *The Guardian*, 25 March http://www.theguardian.com/technology/2012/mar/25/daniel-everett-human-language-piraha

Fogelin, R. (1987), *Wittgenstein*, 2nd ed, London: Routledge & Kegan Paul.

Fortis, J.-M. (2008), 'Le langage est-il un instinct? Une critique du nativisme linguistique de Chomsky à Pinker', *Texto!* 13 (4), http://www.revue-texto.net/index.php?id=1870.

Foster, J.K. and M. Jelicic, eds, (1999), *Memory: Systems, Process, or Function?*, Oxford: Oxford University Press.

Frith, U. and F. Happé (1999), 'Theory of Mind and Self-Consciousness: What Is It Like to Be Autistic?', *Mind & Language*, 14 (1): 1–22.

Frongia, G. and B. McGuinness (1990), *Wittgenstein: A Bibliographical Guide*, Oxford: Basil Blackwell.

Gaita, R. (1990), 'Introduction' in *Value and Understanding: Essays for Peter Winch*, ix–xiii, New York: Routledge, 1990.

Gallagher, S. (2012), 'In Defense of Phenomenological Approaches to Social Cognition: Interacting with the Critics', *Rev. Phil. Psych*, 3 (2): 187–212.

Garver, N. (1996), 'Philosophy as Grammar' in H. Sluga and D. G. Stern (eds), *The Cambridge Companion to Wittgenstein*, 139–70, Cambridge: Cambridge University Press.

Gennaro, R. (n.d.), 'Consciousness' *Internet Encyclopaedia of Philosophy*, http://www.iep.utm.edu/consciou/

Gipps, R. (2004), 'Autism and Intersubjectivity: Beyond Cognitivism and the Theory of Mind', *Philosophy, Psychiatry, & Psychology*, 11 (3): 195–8.

Glock, H.-J. (1996), *A Wittgenstein Dictionary*, Oxford: Blackwell.

Green, C. D. and J. Vervaecke (1997), 'But What Have You Done for Us Lately? Some Recent Perspectives on Linguistic Nativism', in D. M. Johnson and C. E. Erneling (eds), *The Future of the Cognitive Revolution*, 149–63, Oxford: Oxford University Press.

Gutting, G. (2012), 'Philosophy – What's the Use?', *The Stone*, 25 January 2012. https://opinionator.blogs.nytimes.com/2012/01/25/philosophy-whats-the-use/?mtrref=www.google.com&gwh=BA0FB28652ADDDFE91EE347CB9372A12&gwt=pay&assetType=REGIWALL

Hacker, P. M. S. (1989), *Insight and Illusion: Themes in the Philosophy of Wittgenstein*, Corrected edition, Bristol: Thoemmes Press, 1997.

Hacker, P. M. S. (1993), *Meaning and Mind. Volume 3 of An Analytical Commentary on Wittgenstein's Philosophical Investigations, Part 1: Essays*, Oxford: Blackwell.

Hacker, P. M. S. (1996a), *Wittgenstein's Place in Twentieth-Century Analytic Philosophy*, Oxford: Blackwell.

Hacker, P. M. S. (1996b), *Wittgenstein: Mind and Will. Volume 4 of An Analytical Commentary on Wittgenstein's Philosophical Investigations. Part I: Essays*, Oxford: Basil Blackwell.

Hacker, P. M. S. (1996c), *Wittgenstein: Mind and Will. Volume 4 of An Analytical Commentary on the Philosophical Investigations*, rev. ed., Oxford: Basil Blackwell.

Hacker, P. M. S. (2000), 'Was he trying to whistle it?' in A. Crary and R. Read, *The New Wittgenstein* 353–88, London: Routledge.

Hacker, P. M. S. (2001), *Connections and Controversies*, Oxford: Oxford University Press.

Hacker, P. M. S. (2007a), 'The Relevance of Wittgenstein's Philosophy of Psychology to the Psychological Sciences', *Deutsches Jahrbuch Philosophie*, special edition, 'Wittgenstein: Zu Philosophie und Wissenschaft' 2012, Vol. 3, 205–23.

Hacker, P. M. S. (2007b), 'Passing by the naturalistic turn: On Quine's cul-de-sac' in G. Gasser (ed.), *How Successful Is Naturalism?*, 147–58, Heusenstamm: Ontos Verlag.

Hacker, P. M. S. (2010), 'Wittgenstein's Anthropological and Ethnological Approach', in J. Padilla Galvez (ed.), *Philosophical Anthropology: Wittgenstein's Perspective*, 15–32, Ontos Verlag: Open Library.

Hacker, P. M. S. (2012), 'Wittgenstein on Grammar, Theses and Dogmatism', *Philosophical Investigations*, 35 (1): 1–17.

Hacker, P. M. S. (2013), 'Wittgenstein's Philosophy of Psychology as a Critical Instrument for the Psychological Sciences', in T. P. Racine and K. L. Slaney (eds), *A Wittgensteinian Perspective on the Use of Conceptual Analysis in Psychology*, 10–27, Basingstoke: Palgrave Macmillan.

Hacker, P. M. S. (2015a), 'Philosophy and Scientism: What cognitive neuroscience can, and what it cannot, explain' in R. N. Williams and D. N. Robinson (eds), *Scientism: The New Orthodoxy*, 97–116, London: Bloomsbury Academic.

Hacker, P. M. S. (2015b), 'Forms of Life', *Nordic Wittgenstein Review*, October, 1–20.

Hacking, I. (1999), *The Social Construction of What?*, Cambridge, MA: Harvard University Press.

Hagberg, G. (1995), *Art as Language: Wittgenstein, Meaning and Aesthetic Theory*, Ithaca, NY: Cornell University Press.

Hanfling, O. (2004), 'The Use of "Theory" in Philosophy', in E. Ammereller and E. Fischer (eds), *Wittgenstein at Work: Method in the Philosophical Investigations*, 183–200, London: Routledge.

Harrison S. J, et al (2013), 'Calling, Courtship, and Condition in the Fall Field Cricket' *Gryllus pennsylvanicus*' *PLoS ONE*, 8 (3) http://journals.plos.org/plosone/article?id=10.1371/journal.pone.0060356

Harrison, B. (1991), *Inconvenient Fictions: Literature and the Limits of Theory*, New Haven, CT: Yale University Press.

Harrison, B. (ms), 'Making room for the human: on the unity of a philosophical project'.

Haugeland, J. (2002), 'Andy Clark on Cognitive and Representation', in H. Clapin (ed.), *Philosophy of Mental Representation*, 21–36, Oxford: Clarendon Press.

Hawking, S. and L. Mlodinow (2010), *The Grand Design*, London: Transworld.

Hinzen, W. (2012a), 'The philosophical significance of Universal Grammar', *Language Sciences*, 34 (5): 635–49.

Hinzen, W. (2012b), 'Human Nature and Grammar', *Royal Institute of Philosophy Supplement*, 70: 53–82.

Hobson, P. (2008), 'Wittgenstein and the developmental psychopathology of autism', in *New Ideas in Psychology*, 30: 1–15.

Hudson-Kam, C. L. and E. L. Newport (2009), 'Getting it right by getting it wrong: When learners change languages', *Cognitive Psychology*, 59: 30–66.

Hume, D. (1748), *An Enquiry concerning Human Understanding*, ed. with an Introduction by P. Millican, Oxford: Oxford University Press, 2007.

Hume, D. (1932), *The Letters of David Hume*, ed. J. Y. T. Greig, Oxford: Clarendon Press.

Hunter, Ian M. L. (1957), *Memory: Facts & Fallacies*, Baltimore: Penguin [1976].

Hurford, J. R. (2004), 'Human uniqueness, learned symbols and recursive thought', *European Review*, 12 (4): 551–65.

Hutchinson, P. and R. Read (2006), 'An Elucidatory Interpretation of Wittgenstein's *Tractatus*: A Critique of Daniel D. Hutto's and Marie McGinn's Reading of *Tractatus* 6.54', *International Journal of Philosophical Studies* 14 (1): 1–29.

Hutto, D. D. (2007), 'Getting Clear About Perspicuous Representations: Wittgenstein, Baker and Fodor' in D. Moyal-Sharrock (ed.), *Perspicuous Presentations: Essays on Wittgenstein's Philosophy of Psychology*, 299–322, Basingstoke: Palgrave Macmillan.
Hutto, D. D. (2009), 'Lessons from Wittgenstein: Elucidating folk psychology', *New Ideas in Psychology*, 27: 197–212.
Hutto, D. D. (2012), 'Truly Enactive Emotion' *Emotion Review*, 4 (2): 176–81.
Hutto, D. D. (2014), 'Contentless Perceiving: The very idea' in M. Campbell (ed.), *Wittgenstein and Perception*, 64–84, London: Routledge.
Hutto, D. D., M. D. Kirchhoff and E. Myin (2014), 'Extensive enactivism: why keep it all in?' *Front. Hum. Neurosci.* 25 September 2014 | https://doi.org/10.3389/fnhum.2014.00706
Hutto, D. D. and E. Myin (2013), *Radicalizing Enactivism: Basic Minds without Content*, Cambridge, MA: MIT Press.
Hutto, D. D. and E. Myin (2017), *Evolving Enactivism: Basic Minds Meet Content*, London: MIT Press.
Hutto, D. D. and G. Satne, G. (2015), 'Searching for the Natural Origins of Content: Challenging Research Project or Benighted Quest?', *Philosophia* 4 (3): 505–19.
Izquierdo-Torres, E. and I. Harvey (2006), 'A Situated, Embodied and Dynamical Systems Approach to Understanding Learning and Memory'. Paper delivered at the 50th Anniversary Summit of Artificial Intelligence. Monte Verita, Switzerland, 9–14 July 2006.
Kenny, A. (1973), *Wittgenstein*, London: Penguin Press.
Knobe, J. (2011), 'Experimental Philosophy: Thoughts Become the New Lab Rats', *Scientific American*, November 2011. https://www.scientificamerican.com/article/thought-experiments-philosophers/
Koethe, J. (1996), *The Continuity of Wittgenstein's Thought*, Ithaca, NY: Cornell University Press.
Kuhn, T. (1977), *The Essential Tension: Selected Studies in Scientific Tradition and Change*, Chicago: University of Chicago Press.
Kuhn, T. (1996), *The Structure of Scientific Revolutions*, 3rd ed. Chicago: University of Chicago Press.
Kuhn, T. (2000), *The Road since Structure: Philosophical Essays, 1970–1993*, ed. J. Conant and J. Haugeland, Chicago: University of Chicago Press.
Lagerspetz, O. (1998), *Trust: The Tacit Demand*, Dordrecht: Kluwer Academic Publishers.
Lancaster, J. B. (1975), *Primate Behavior and the Emergence of Human Culture*, New York: Holt, Rinehart and Winston.
Lawrence, D. H. (1961), *Phoenix I: The Posthumous Papers of D.H. Lawrence*, ed. E. D. McDonald, London: Heinemann.
Lawrence, D. H. (1964), *Studies in Classic American Literature*, London: Heinemann.
Leavis, F. R. (1948) *The Great Tradition* (London: Chatto and Windus).
Leavis, F. R. (1975), *The Living Principle: 'English' as a Discipline of Thought*, London: Chatto & Windus.
Leavis, F. R. (1976), *Thought, Words and Creativity: Art and Thought in Lawrence*, London: Chatto & Windus.
Leavis, F. R. (1982), *The Critic as Anti-Philosopher*, ed. G. Singh, London: Chatto & Windus.
Leavis, F. R. (1986), *Valuation in Criticism and other Essays* (posth.), ed. G. Singh, Cambridge: Cambridge University Press.
Lewis, D. (1971), 'Counterparts of Persons and Their Bodies', in *Philosophical Papers: Vol. 1*, 47–54, Oxford, Oxford University Press [1983].

Locke, J. (1689), *An Essay Concerning Human Understanding*, abridged and edited by A. S. Pringle-Pattison, Oxford: Clarendon Press [1929].
MacWhinney, B. (1993), 'The (il)logical problem of language acquisition', in *Proceedings of the Fifteenth Annual Conference of the Cognitive Science Society*, Hillsdale, NJ: Lawrence Erlbaum Associates.
Malcolm, N. (1958), *Ludwig Wittgenstein. A Memoir*, Oxford: Oxford University Press.
Malcolm, N. (1977), *Memory and Mind*, Ithaca, NY: Cornell University Press.
Malcolm, N. (1980), 'Wittgenstein: The Grammar of Reality', *The Washington Post*, 13 July 1980. https://www.washingtonpost.com/archive/entertainment/books/1980/07/13/wittgenstein-the-grammar-of-reality/9cb285d8-ec17-453f-9123-861e06ccb8f1/
Malcolm, N. (1982), 'Wittgenstein and Idealism' in Norman Malcolm, *Wittgensteinian Themes: Essays 1978-1989*, ed. G. H. von Wright, 87-108, Ithaca, NY: Cornell University Press [1995].
Malcolm, N. (1984), *Ludwig Wittgenstein: A Memoir*, 2nd ed., Oxford: Oxford University Press.
Malcolm, N. (1986), 'Language as expressive behaviour', in *Nothing is Hidden: Wittgenstein's Criticism of his Early Thought*, Oxford: Basil Blackwell.
Matar, A. (2006), *Modernism and the Language of Philosophy*, London: Routledge.
Maupassant, de, G. (1884), *Etude sur Gustave Flaubert* in *La Revue bleue*, quoted in and translated by Walter Pater in *Appreciations*, London: Macmillan [1910].
McDonough, R. (2004), 'Wittgenstein, German organicism, chaos, and the center of life', *Journal of the History of Philosophy*, 42: 297-326.
McDowell, J. (2000), 'Non-cognitivism and Rule-Following' in A. Crary and R. Read (eds), *The New Wittgenstein*, 38-52, London: Routledge.
McGinn, M. (1998), 'The Real Problem of Others: Cavell, Merleau-Ponty and Wittgenstein on Scepticism about Other Minds', *European Journal of Philosophy*, 6 (1): 45-58.
McGuinness, B. (2012), 'Two Cheers for the "New" Wittgenstein?' in J. Zalabardo (ed.), *Wittgenstein's Early Philosophy*, 26-72, Oxford: Oxford University Press, 2012.
Medina, J. (2002), *The Unity of Wittgenstein's Philosophy: Necessity, Intelligibility, and Normativity*, Albany, NY: SUNY Press.
Meijers, A. W. M. (2000), 'Mental Causation and Searle's Impossible Conception of Unconscious Intentionality', *International Journal of Philosophical Studies*, 8 (2): 155-70.
Michael, J. (2011), 'Interactionism and mindreading', *Review of Philosophy and Psychology*, 2 (3): 559-78.
Moerk, E. L. (1994), 'Corrections in first language acquisition: Theoretical controversies and factual evidence', *International Journal of Psycholinguistics*, 10: 33-58.
Monk, R. (1991), *Ludwig Wittgenstein: The Duty of Genius*, London: Vintage.
Montgomery, D. E. (2002), 'Mental Verbs and Semantic Development;, *Journal of Cognition and Development*, 3 (4): 357-84.
Moore, G. E. (1925), 'A Defence of Common Sense', in *Philosophical Papers*, 32-59, London: George Allen & Unwin [1959].
Moore, G. E. (1939), 'Proof of an External World' in *Philosophical Papers*, 127-50, London: George Allen & Unwin [1959].
Mounce, H. O. (2005), 'Wittgenstein and Classical Realism' in D. Moyal-Sharrock and William H. Brenner (eds), *Readings of Wittgenstein's On Certainty*, 103-21, Basingstoke: Palgrave Macmillan.
Moyal-Sharrock, D., ed. (2004), *The Third Wittgenstein: The Post-Investigations Works*, London: Routledge.

Moyal-Sharrock, D. (2007a), *Understanding Wittgenstein's On Certainty*, Basingstoke: Palgrave Macmillan.
Moyal-Sharrock, D. (2007b), 'The Good Sense of Nonsense: A Reading of Wittgenstein's *Tractatus* as Nonself-repudiating', *Philosophy*, 82 (1): 147–77.
Moyal-Sharrock, D., ed. (2007c), *Perspicuous Presentations: Essays on Wittgenstein's Philosophy of Psychology*, Basingstoke: Palgrave Macmillan.
Moyal-Sharrock, D. (2009), 'Introduction. *The Third Wittgenstein Conference*', special issue, *Philosophia*, 37 (4): 557–62.
Moyal-Sharrock, D. (2012), 'Cora Diamond and the Ethical Imagination', *British Journal of Aesthetics*, 52 (3): 223–40.
Moyal-Sharrock, D. (2013a), 'Realism, but not empiricism: Wittgenstein versus Searle', in T. P. Racine and K. L. Slaney (eds), *A Wittgensteinian Perspective on the Use of Conceptual Analysis in Psychology*, 153–71, Basingstoke: Palgrave Macmillan.
Moyal-Sharrock, D. (2013b), 'On Coliva's Judgmental Hinges', *Philosophia*, 41 (1): 13–25.
Moyal-Sharrock, D. (2015), 'Wittgenstein's Forms of Life, Patterns of Life and Ways of Living', *Nordic Wittgenstein Review,* special issue on *Wittgenstein and Forms of life*, 21–42.
Moyal-Sharrock, D. (2016a), 'Wittgenstein, No Linguistic Idealist' in S. Greve and J. Mácha (eds), *Wittgenstein and the Creativity of Language*, 117–40, Basingstoke: Palgrave Macmillan.
Moyal-Sharrock, D. (2016b), 'Wittgenstein and Leavis: Literature and the Enactment of the Ethical', *Philosophy and Literature*, 40 (1): 24–64.
Moyal-Sharrock, D. (2016c), 'The Animal in Epistemology: Wittgenstein's Enactivist Solution to the Problem of Regress' in A. Coliva & D. Moyal-Sharrock (eds), *Hinge Epistemology*, 24–47, Leiden: Brill.
Moyal-Sharrock, D. (2017), 'The Myth of the Quietist Wittgenstein' in J. Beale & I. J. Kidd (eds), *Wittgenstein and Scientism*, 152–74, London: Routledge.
Moyal-Sharrock, D. (2019), 'Restoring Certainty', *International Journal for the Study of Skepticism*, 20 Oct 2019 https://brill.com/view/journals/skep/aop/article-10.1163-22105700-20191419/article-10.1163-22105700-20191419.xml?language=en
Moyal-Sharrock, D. (2020), 'Literature as the measure of our lives' in H. Appelqvist (ed.), *Wittgenstein and the Limits of Language*, 270–87, Abingdon: Routledge.
Moyal-Sharrock, D. and W. H. Brenner, eds (2007), *Readings of Wittgenstein's On Certainty*, Basingstoke: Palgrave Macmillan.
Mulligan, K. (1997), 'The Essence of Language: Wittgenstein's Builders and Bühler's Bricks', *Revue de Métaphysique et de Morale*, 2: 193–215.
Myin, E. and K. Zahidi (2012), 'Het bereik van het mentale: van uitgebreid naar omvattend geheugen', *Tijdschrift voor filosofie*, 74 (1): 103–27.
Narboux, P. (2004), 'Jeux de langage et jeux de dressage: Sur la critique éthologique d'Augustin dans les *Recherches philosophiques*', in C. Lecerf (ed.), *Ludwig Wittgenstein. Europe*, 130–42.
Nelson, K. (2009), 'Wittgenstein and contemporary theories of word learning', *New Ideas in Psychology*, 27: 275–87.
Newport, E. L., H. Gleitman and L. A. Gleitman (1977), 'Mother, I'd rather do it myself: Some effects and non-effects of maternal speech style', in C. E. Snow and C. A. Ferguson (eds), *Talking to Children: Language Input and Acquisition*, 109–49, Cambridge: Cambridge University Press.
Nickles, T., ed (2003), *Thomas Kuhn*, Cambridge: Cambridge University Press.

Nowicki, S. and M. P. Duke (1992), *Helping the Child Who Doesn't Fit In*, Atlanta, GA: Peachtree Publishers.
Nowicki, S. and M. P. Duke (2002), *Will I Ever Fit In?: The Breakthrough Program for Conquering Adult Dyssemia*, New York: The Free Press.
Parkin, A. J. (1997), *Memory & Amnesia: An Introduction*, 2nd ed., Oxford: Blackwell.
Parkin, A. J. (1999), *Memory: A Guide for Professionals*, Chichester: John Wiley & Sons.
Penn, D. C., K. J. Holyoak and D. J. Povinelli (2008), 'Darwin's mistake: Explaining the discontinuity between human and nonhuman minds', *Behavioral and Brain Sciences*, 31:109–78.
Phillips, D. Z. (1988), *Faith After Foundationalism*, London: Routledge.
Phillips, D. Z. (2003), 'Afterword: Rhees on Reading *On Certainty*' in *There Like Our Life: Wittgenstein's On Certainty* by Rush Rhees, ed. D. Z. Phillips, 133–82, Oxford: Wiley-Blackwell, 2003.
Plooij, F. (1978), 'Some Basic traits in Wild Chimpanzees', in Andew Lock (ed.), *Action Gesture and Symbol*, 111–32, London: Academic Press.
Prinz, J. (2009), 'Is Consciousness Embodied?', in P. Robbins and M. Aydede (eds), *Cambridge Handbook of Situated Cognition*, 419–36, Cambridge: Cambridge University Press,.
Pritchard, D. (2011), 'Epistemic Relativism, Epistemic Incommensurability and Wittgensteinian Epistemology' in S. Hales (ed.), *The Blackwell Companion to Relativism*, 266–85, Oxford: Wiley-Blackwell.
Pritchard, D. (2012), 'Wittgenstein and the Groundlessness of our Believing', *Synthese*, 189: 255–72.
Putnam, H. (1981), 'Two Philosophical Perspectives', in *Reason, Truth and History*, 49–74, Cambridge: Cambridge University Press.
Putnam, H. (1995), *Pragmatism: An Open Question*, Oxford: Blackwell.
Ramscar, M. and D. Yarlett (2007), 'Linguistic self-correction in the absence of feedback: A new approach to the logical problem of language acquisition', *Cognitive Science*, 31: 927–60.
Ramscar, M., M. Dye and S. M. McCauley (2013), 'Expectation and error distribution in language learning: The curious absence of "mouses" in adult speech', *Language*, 89 (4): 760–93.
Ramsey, W. (2007), *Representation Reconsidered*, Cambridge: Cambridge University Press.
Rhees, R., ed. (1981), *Ludwig Wittgenstein: Personal Recollections*, Oxford: Basil Blackwell.
Richman, B. (1976), 'Some vocal distinctive features used by gelada monkeys', *Journal of the Acoustical Society of America*, 60: 718–24.
Richman, B. (1978), 'The synchronisation of voices by gelada monkeys', *Primates* 19: 569–81.
Richman, B. (1987), 'Rhythm and melody in gelada vocal exchanges', *Primates* 28: 199–223.
Roediger, H. L. et al (1999), 'Components of Processing', in J. K. Foster and M. Jelicic (eds), *Memory: Systems, Process, or Function?*, 31–65, Oxford: Oxford University Press.
Rorty, A. (1992), 'The Psychology of Aristotelian Tragedy' in A. Rorty (ed.), *Essays on Aristotle's Poetics*, 1–22, Princeton, NJ: Princeton University Press.
Rorty, R. (2004), 'The Brain as Hardware, Culture as Software', *Inquiry*, 47: 219–35.
Rosat, J-J. (2007), 'Patterns in the Weave of Life: Wittgenstein's "Lebensmuster"', in D. Moyal-Sharrock (ed.), *Perspicuous Presentations: Essays on Wittgenstein's Philosophy of Psychology*, 199–213, Basingstoke: Palgrave Macmillan.

Russell, B. (1999), *Russell on Ethics: Selections from the Writings of Bertrand Russell*, ed. C. Pigden, London: Routledge.
Russell, B. (1912), *The Problems of Philosophy*, Oxford, Oxford University Press.
Ryle, G. (1949), *The Concept of Mind*, London: Penguin Books.
Sacks, O. (1985), 'The Disembodied Lady', in *The Man Who Mistook his Wife for a Hat*, 42–52, London: Picador.
Sandis, S. (2015), '"If Some People Looked Like Elephants and Others Like Cats": Wittgenstein on Understanding Others and Forms of Life', *Nordic Wittgenstein Review*, special issue on *Wittgenstein and Forms of Life*, 131–53.
Sandis, S. (2019), *Character and Causation: Aspects of Hume's Philosophy of Action*, London: Routledge.
Savage-Rumbaugh, S. and R. Lewin (1994), *Kanzi: The Ape at the Brink of the Human Mind*, New York: Doubleday.
Saxe, R. (2008), 'The Ape That Teaches' interview by PBS Nova. 1.1. 2008. Online.
Schacter, D. L. (1996), *Searching for Memory: The Brain, the Mind, and the Past*, New York: Basic Books.
Schacter, D. L. and E. Tulving (1994), 'What are the memory systems of 1994?' in D. Schacter and E. Tulving (eds), *Memory Systems 1994*, 1–29, Cambridge, MA: MIT Press.
Scheff, Thomas J. (1984) *Being Mentally Ill: A Sociological Theory*, 3rd ed., London: Aldine Transaction.
Schönbaumsfeld, G. (2016a), *The Illusion of Doubt*, Oxford: Oxford University Press.
Schönbaumsfeld, G. (2016b), '"Hinge Propositions" and the "Logical" Exclusion of Doubt' in A. Coliva and D. Moyal-Sharrock (eds), *Hinge Epistemology*, 94–109, Leiden: Brill.
Schoneberger, T. (2010), 'Three Myths from the Language Acquisition Literature', *The Analysis of Verbal Behavior*, 26: 107–31
Schroeder, S. (1993), '"Too Low!" Frank Cioffi on Wittgenstein's *Lectures on Aesthetics*', *Philosophical Investigations*, 16 (4): 261–79.
Seager, W. (2016), *Theories of Consciousness: An Introduction and Assessment*, 2nd ed., London: Routledge.
Searle, J. R. (1990), 'Is the Brain's Mind a Computer Program?', *Scientific American*, 262: 26–31.
Searle, J. R. (1991), 'Response to Freeman/Skarda', in E. Lepore & R. Van Gulick (eds), *John Searle & His Critics*, 141–6, Cambridge: Basil Blackwell.
Searle, J. R. (2005), 'Reply to Stevan Harnard – 'What is Consciousness?', *The New York Review of Books*, 52: 11 (online).
Searle, J. R. (2010), *Making the Social World: The Structure of Human Civilization*, Oxford: Oxford University Press.
Searle, J. R. (2011), 'Wittgenstein and the Background', *American Philosophical Quarterly*, 48 (2): 119–28.
Seyfarth, R. M. and D. L. Cheney (1984), 'Grooming, alliances and reciprocal altruism in vervet monkeys', *Nature* 308: 541–43.
Seyfarth, R. M. and D. L. Cheney (1990), 'The assessment by vervet monkeys of their own and another species' alarm calls', *Animal Behaviour*, 40: 754–64.
Seyfarth, R. M. and D. L. Cheney (2014), 'The evolution of language from social cognition', *Current Opinion in Neurobiology*, 28: 5–9.
Shapiro, L. (2014), Review of *Radicalizing Enactivism: Basic Minds without Content*, by D. D. Hutto and E. Myin, *Mind*, 123 (489): 213–20.

Sharrock, W. and R. Read (2002), *Kuhn: Philosopher of Scientific Revolution*, Cambridge: Polity Press.

Singleton, D. and L. Ryan (2004), *Language Acquisition: The Age Factor*, 2nd ed., Clevedon: Multilingual Matters.

Squire, L. R. (1999), 'Memory, Human Neuropsychology', *MIT Encyclopedia of the Cognitive Sciences*, 520–2.

Standish, P. (2007), 'Education for grown-ups, a religion for adults: scepticism and alterity in Cavell and Levinas', *Ethics and Education* 2 (1): 73–91.

Sterelny, K. (2012), 'Language, gesture, skill: the co-evolutionary foundations of language', *Phil. Trans. R. Soc. B*, 367: 2141–51.

Stern, D. G. (1991), 'Models of Memory: Wittgenstein and Cognitive Science', *Philosophical Psychology*, 4 (2): 203–18.

Stern, D. G. (1996), 'The Availability of Wittgenstein's Philosophy' in H. Sluga and D. Stern (eds), *The Cambridge Companion to Wittgenstein*, 442–76, Cambridge: Cambridge University Press.

Stroll, A. (1994), *Moore and Wittgenstein on Certainty*, Oxford: Oxford University Press.

Stroll, A. (2004), 'Wittgenstein's Foundational Metaphors' in D. Moyal-Sharrock (ed.), *The Third Wittgenstein: The Post-Investigations Works*, 13–24, Aldershot: Ashgate.

Susswein, N. and T. P. Racine (2009), 'Wittgenstein and not-just-in-the-head cognition', *New Ideas in Psychology*, 27: 184–96.

Tallis, R. (2012), 'Aping Mankind: Neuromania, Darwinitis and the Misrepresentation of Mankind', The 2012 Francis Bacon Lecture, delivered at the University of Hertfordshire, 29 February 2012.

Tejedor, C. (2017), ' Scientism as a threat to science' in J. Beale and I. A. Kidd (eds), *Wittgenstein and Scientism*, 7–27, London: Routledge.

ter Hark, M. R. M. (1990), *Beyond the Inner and the Outer: Wittgenstein's Philosophy of Psychology*, Dordrecht: Kluwer.

ter Hark, M. R. M. (1995), 'Electric Brain Fields and Memory Traces: Wittgenstein and Gestalt Psychology', *Philosophical Investigations*, 18 (1): 113–37.

ter Hark, M. R. M. (2004), 'Patterns of Life: A Third Wittgenstein Concept', in D. Moyal-Sharrock (ed.), *The Third Wittgenstein: The Post-Investigations Works*, 125–43, Routledge.

Terrace, H. S. and J. Metcalf (2005), *The Missing Link in Cognition: Origins of Self-Reflective Consciousness*, Oxford: Oxford University Press.

Terrace, H. (1987) *Nim*, New York: Columbia University Press.

Tomalin, M. (2012), 'Generative Grammar', in *The Cambridge Encyclopaedia of the Language Sciences* (CELS), 334–7, New York: Cambridge University Press.

Tomasello, M. (1999), *The Cultural Origins of Human Cognition*, Cambridge, MA: Harvard University Press.

Tomasello, M. (2008), *Origins of Human Communication*, Cambridge, MA: MIT Press.

Tomasello, M. (2014), *A Natural History of Human Thinking*, Cambridge, MA: Harvard University Press.

Tomasello, M. (2016), 'Precis of *A Natural History of Human Thinking*', *Journal of Social Ontology*, 2 (1): 59–64.

Tomasello, M. et al (2016), 'Great apes anticipate that other individuals will act according to false beliefs', *Science*, 354: 110–14.

Toth, J. P. (2000), 'Nonconscious Forms of Human Memory', in E. Tulving and F. I. M. Craik (eds) *The Oxford Handbook of Memory*, 245–61, Oxford: Oxford University Press.

Toth, J. P. and R. Reed Hunt (1999), 'Not one versus many, but zero versus any: structure and function in the context of the multiple memory systems debate', in J. K. Foster and M. Jelicic (eds), *Memory: Systems, Process, or Function?*, 232–72, Oxford: Oxford University Press.
Travis, C. (1997), 'Pragmatics', in B. Hale and C. Wright (eds), *A Companion to the Philosophy of Language*, 87–108, Oxford: Blackwell.
Tulving, E. (1993), 'Varieties of consciousness and levels of awareness in memory', in A. Baddeley & L. Weiskrantz (eds), *Attention: Selection, Awareness, and Control. A Tribute to Donald Broadbent*, 283–99, Oxford, Clarendon Press.
Tulving, E. (2002), 'Episodic Memory & Common Sense: How Far Apart?', in A. Baddeley et al (eds), *Episodic Memory: New Directions in Research*, 269–88, Oxford: Oxford University Press.
Tulving, E. (2005), 'Episodic Memory & Autonoesis: Uniquely Human?', in H. S. Terrace and J. Metcalf, *The Missing Link in Cognition: Origins of Self-Reflective Consciousness*, 3–56, Oxford: Oxford University Press.
Tulving, E. and F. I. M. Craik, eds (2000), *The Oxford Handbook of Memory*, Oxford: Oxford University Press.
Vaaja, T. (2013), 'Wittgenstein's "Inner and Outer": Overcoming Epistemic Asymmetry' *Nordic Wittgenstein Review*, 2 (1): 107–29. http://wab.uib.no/nwr/index.php/nwr/article/view/1012/pdf
Varela, F. J., E. Thompson and E. Rosch (1991), *The Embodied Mind: Cognitive Science and Human Experience*, Cambridge, MA: MIT Press.
Ware, B. (2015), *Dialectic of the Ladder: Wittgenstein, the* Tractatus *and Modernism*, London: Bloomsbury.
Whiten, A. and R. W. Byrne (1988), 'Tactical deception in primates', *Behavioral and Brain Sciences*, 11 (2): 233–44.
Williams, B. (1981), 'Wittgenstein and Idealism', in *Moral Luck*, 144–63, Cambridge: Cambridge University Press.
Williams, M. (1991), *Unnatural Doubts: Epistemological Realism and the Basis of Scepticism*, Oxford: Blackwell.
Williams, M. (1999), Afterword in M. Williams, *Groundless Belief: An Essay on the Possibility of Epistemology*, 2nd ed., 183–201, Princeton: Princeton University Press.
Williams, M. (2001), *Problems of Knowledge: A Critical Introduction to Epistemology*, Oxford: Oxford University Press.
Williams, M. (2005), 'Why Wittgenstein Isn't a Foundationalist' in D. Moyal-Sharrock and W. H. Brenner (eds), *Readings of Wittgenstein's On Certainty*, 47–58, Basingstoke: Palgrave Macmillan.
Winch P. (1980–1), 'Eine Einstellung zur Seele' in *Trying to Make Sense*, 140–53, Oxford, Basil Blackwell.
Wright, C. (1985), 'Facts & Certainty', *Proceedings of the British Academy*, 429–72.
Wright, C. (2004a), 'Warrant for Nothing (and Foundations for Free)?', *Proceedings of the Aristotelian Society* (Supplementary Volume), 78: 167–212.
Wright, C. (2004b), 'Wittgensteinian Certainties', in D. McManus (ed.), *Wittgenstein and Scepticism*, 22–55, London: Routledge.
Wright, C. (2007), 'Rule-Following without Reasons: Wittgenstein's Quietism and the Constitutive Question', in J. Preston (ed.), *Wittgenstein and Reason: Ratio*, 20: 481–502.
Wright, von G. H. (1982), *Wittgenstein*, Oxford: Basil Blackwell.
Yarlett, D. and M. Ramscar (2008), 'Language Learning Through Similarity-Based Generalization'. Unpublished manuscript.

Young, M. W., ed. (1979), *The Ethnography of Malinowski: The Trobriand Islands 1915–18*, London: Routledge & Kegan Paul.

Zahavi, D. and G. Satne (2016), 'Varieties of shared intentionality: Tomasello and classical phenomenology' in J. A. Bell et al (eds), *Beyond the Continental-Analytic Divide*, 305–25, London: Routledge.

Index

4-E cognition 202
   see also 'e-turn' in philosophy

aesthetics/aesthetic(ally) 22, 66, 68–71, 157, 158, 201, 204, 216
agreement 127, 163–4, 193, 262
   'quiet', unconcerted 5, 20
   'in practice' 20
amnesia 113, 221
Anderson, S.R. 35–6, 39, 207, 208
animal(s) 5, 6, 7, 14, 42, 44–5, 56, 58, 63–4, 79, 83–91 *passim*, 94–7, 108, 125, 135, 145, 147
   certainty/assurance/trust 1, 13, 14, 60, 110, 137, 147, 150, 152
   see also instinct(ive)/instinctual)
anthropological/anthropology 28, 29, 40–1, 93–4, 124, 203, 216, 218
   see also possibility: anthropo-*logical*
anthropomorphic/anthropomorphism 29
Aristotle 1, 3, 17, 74, 201, 202, 215, 219
Austin, J. L. 56, 214
autism/austist(ic) 130–1, 221, 225, 229
autonomy of grammar/language 21, 28, 46, 66, 76–8, 146, 174, 205, 234

Baddeley, A. 106, 109–10
Bar-On, D. 82, 96, 216, 217
Barrett, L. 95
Bates, E. 45, 208
Baudelaire, C. 72, 215
Beardsmore, R. 74
Bearn, G. 223–4
Beckett, S. 50
bedrock 89, 120, 143, 152–3, 166, 227
   'bedrock certainties' 139
   of our thought 177, 179
   psychological bedrock/grammar 28, 132
behaviourism/behaviourist 43, 50, 100, 203, 222

belief in 133, 138
   see also nonpropositional attitudes *and* trust
Bennett, M. R. 6, 102, 103, 219, 221
Bickerton, D. 33, 39
Biggs, M. 233
Boghossian, P. 24, 173, 231
bound(s) of sense 23, 26, 30–1, 46, 47, 140, 159, 189, 190, 199, 217, 220, 235
   limits of sense 29
Bruner, J. 38, 212, 229
Bühler, K. 213, 214
Byrne, R. W. 86

Calonne, D. 77
Canfield, J. V. 41–2, 46, 81, 85, 87, 88–90, 93–5, 96
Carnap, R. 223
Carpendale, J. 232
category mistake 62, 157, 166, 213, 219, 226
Cavell, S. 29, 30, 155–68, 228, 229, 230
certainties/hinges
   linguistic 111, 152, 220
   local 46, 152, 213, 217, 220, 221
   personal 52, 191, 220, 221, 235
   universal 152–3, 177–8
   see also grammar: universal
Chateaubriand, F.-R. 215
Chater, N. 40, 210
Chauvier, S. 219, 224
Chauviré, C. 71
Cheney, D. L. 86, 218
Chomsky, N. 33–48, 91, 164–5, 207–13, 216
Christiansen, M. H. 40, 210
Cioffi, F. 201
Clark, A. 108
Coliva, A. 15, 137, 147–8, 227
'common behaviour of mankind' 26–7, 42, 65, 74, 87, 135, 177, 179, 203, 213

conceivability/imaginability vs possibility 30, 233
consciousness 6–7, 9, 11, 60, 77, 103, 106, 130, 168
   hard problem of 4, 7, 11
Conway, G. 179, 226
Cook, V. J. 207, 208, 210, 211
Coulter, J. 223–4
Cowie, F. 35, 38
Cowley, S. 90, 93
Craig, D. 70
Craik, F. 116, 222
Crane, T. 10–13
Crick, F. 15

Dabrowska, E. 39
Dalla Barba, G. 103, 104, 108, 114
Darwin, C. 79, 83, 86, 210
   Darwinian 91, 177
Dawkins, R. 15
Deacon, T. 41, 210, 216
Diamond, C. 29, 30, 202, 215, 228
disease of philosophy 3, 5
Descartes, R. 49, 62, 137, 142, 185, 213, 226, 235
   Cartesian 99, 140, 213

Dilman, I. 169, 231
Doppelgänger: 141, 235
Dostoevsky, L. 74
Duke, M. 131–2
Dunbar, R. 95–6, 218
Dye, M. 37, 209
dyssemia 131–2, 221

Eliot, G. 54, 214
embodied/embodiment
   abilities/capacities 8, 94, 221
   activities/interactions 8, 81, 217
   beliefs etc 62
   brains 12
   certainty 151
   cognition/mind 10, 81, 108, 116, 201, 202
   experience ourselves as 26, 218
   grammar 22
   memory 108, 221
   principles 34
empiricism/empiricist 4–5, 29, 169, 175, 231

enactive
   certainty 13–14, 140, 151, 153
   cognition/mind 10, 14, 62, 85, 96, 116, 202, 216, 218
   enactive nature of grammar/language 17, 19, 21, 30–1, 64, 71, 82, 85, 91–3, 95
enactivism/enactivist 8, 81–2, 85, 96, 97, 202
   'extensive enactivism' 202
   see also Wittgenstein's enactivism
enactment
   in literature 17, 65, 70–1
      see also nonpropositional: expression and nonpropositional: significance
   in mathematics 92
Engelmann, P. 23, 69, 70, 158
epistemology/epistemologist(s) 15, 30, 132, 135, 137, 138, 147, 154, 168, 181, 184, 185, 192, 226
   hinge epistemology 15, 226
ethical/ethics 21–2, 66, 68–71, 76, 78, 156, 157–8, 201, 204, 215–16, 228
'e-turn' in philosophy 9
   see also 4E cognition
extended
   capabilities 94
   cognition/mind 108, 202, 216, 221
   memory 115
extensive
   enactivism 202
   memory 115, 221
   mind 221
Evans, N. 40
Evans, V. 213
Everett, D. 46
experiential vs empirical 26
explanatory gap 49–50, 62–3

family resemblance (concepts) 62, 99, 115, 119, 197, 231
Flaubert, G. 72, 74–5
Fodor, J. 50, 107
form(s) of life 40, 90, 122, 164
   our/human form of life 2, 7, 8, 19, 28, 29–30, 47, 79, 121, 165, 176, 177, 179, 190, 195, 198, 201, 206, 212, 217, 225, 229, 232

different forms of (human) life 2, 31, 85, 93, 175, 177, 201, 206, 217, 229, 230, 232
Fortis, J.-M. 39
foundational
   beliefs/certainties/hinges 140, 143–4, 150, 152–3
   engagement with others 218
   images/language 143, 226
foundationalism/foundationalist 143, 226, 232
   Wittgenstein's foundationalism 143–4
Frege, G. 29, 62
Frith, U. 130, 225
Frongia, G. 233

Gaita, R. 8. 30
Gallagher, S. 217
Gennaro, R. 203
gesture(s)/gestural/gesturing 41–3, 57, 62, 69, 71, 85–91, 92, 93–4, 96, 97, 104–5, 115, 118, 122–3, 131–2, 195–7, 211, 218
Gipps, R. 217–18
Goldstein, L. 33, 206
grammar
   reality-soaked (also: concepts, language) 19, 25–6, 29, 46, 66, 76, 93, 202, 204, 206, 230
   thick 19, 20, 26, 28, 30, 31, 46, 206
   thin 19, 20, 26, 30, 31, 46
   universal (rules of) 45–7, 212–13, 217
      see also certainties/hinges: universal
   universal (UG)/innate 33, 34–5, 37–41, 45–6, 209, 201, 213
      see also autonomy of grammar/language *and* embodied: grammar
'grammaticalization of experience' 20, 28–9
Green, C. D. 38, 208, 210
Ground, I. 12
groundless(ness) 143–4, 166, 229
Gutting, G. 203

Hacker, P. M. S. 5, 6, 11, 24, 34, 46, 49, 53, 55–61, 64, 91, 102, 103, 114, 158, 181–93, 198–9, 203, 204, 208, 214, 216, 219, 221, 228, 233, 234, 235

Hagberg, G. 70
Hanfling, O. 197
Happé, F. 130, 225
Harrison, B. 77, 204
Harrison, S. J. 85
Harvey, I. 108
Haugeland, J. 45
Hawking, S. 13, 201
Hegel, G.W.F 3
Heidegger, M. 21, 157
Hemingway, E. 77–8
heuristic 22, 23, 92, 110, 119, 137, 149, 227
hinge
   epistemology, *see* epistemology
   taxonomy 152–3, 220–1
hinges, see certainties/hinges
Hinzen, W. 46, 212
Hudson-Kam, C. L. 37, 210
Hunt, R. R. 107–8, 112, 220
Hunter, I. 109, 220
Hurford, J. R. 86, 217
Hutchinson, P. 228
Hutto, D. D. 8, 14, 81–7, 93, 96, 97, 195, 202, 208, 219, 221, 236

idealism/idealist 5, 169–70, 174–5
linguistic idealism/idealist 23–4, 65, 169–70. 172, 175, 198, 215
illusion
   of doubt 142
   of explanation 102
   of possibility 180
imaginability, *see* conceivability/imaginability vs possibility
'imponderable evidence' 71, 74, 119–20, 122–3, 128, 228
impossibility
   of knowing what goes on in someone else 128
   of hyperbolic scepticism 185
   see also conceivability
ineffability/ineffable 21–3, 66, 68, 110, 130, 140, 149–51, 152, 156–8, 204, 227, 228
Ineffabilists 158, 204
   see also unsayable/unsayability *and* unutterable
infinite regress of justification 17, 137, 144, 154, 185, 192

instinct(ive)/instinctual 14, 17, 26–7, 41–2, 48, 79, 87–9, 93, 110, 115, 129, 133, 145, 150–2, 211, 218, 220
   see also animal
Izquierdo-Torres, E. 108

Johnston, P. 215

Kant, I. 1, 176, 216, 231
Kantian 119, 172, 177, 235
know-how 6, 30, 41, 85, 106, 108, 110, 112
   see also technique
Koethe, J. 214
Kuhn, T. 169–80, 186, 230–2

Lagerspetz, O. 129–30, 132, 225, 226
language acquisition 33–5, 37–8, 40–4, 47, 55, 84, 88, 95, 198, 203, 207–13 *passim*, 216
   device (LAD) 35, 40, 44–5, 207
Lawrence, D. H. 71, 73, 76, 77, 78, 214, 215
Leavis, F. R. 1, 69, 70, 71, 73, 75, 76, 78, 201
Leboe, J. 114
Levinson, S. C. 40
Lewis, C. 232
Lightfoot, D.W. 35–6, 39, 207, 208
limits of (my) language 21, 24, 65, 156–9, 235
linguistic idealism/idealist, *see* idealism/idealist
Locke, J. 13
logical necessity 19, 29–30, 179–80

McDonough, R. 219
McDowell, J. 144, 229
McGuinn, M. 242
McGuinness, B. F. 157, 233
MacWhinney, B. 208, 209
Malcolm, N. 58, 75, 102, 105, 107, 185, 205, 215, 226, 230, 233
Malinowski, B. 233
Matar, A. 156
mathematics 81–2, 86, 91–2, 93, 182, 184, 197, 217
   see also enactment: in mathematics
Maupassant, de, G. 74
Medina, J. 43, 92, 211
Meijers, A. 6

memory 2, 9, 11, 12, 99–116 *passim*, 150, 198, 203, 206, 219–22
remember/remembering 2, 3, 8, 10, 89, 99–116 *passim*, 150, 198, 219–21
   see also embodied: memory *and* extended: memory *and* extensive: memory
Merleau-Ponty, M. 94, 217
metaphysical/metaphysics 2–4, 10, 17, 24, 67, 68, 77, 149, 155–6, 160
metaphysical urge 2
metaphysical assumption 95
Michael, J. 94, 218
mind (minded/ness) 2, 4–13, 15, 34, 40, 49–50, 52, 58, 61–3, 71, 79, 81–4, 86, 95, 105, 118, 121, 125, 128, 129, 130, 132, 135, 161, 171, 179, 196, 198, 201, 202, 205, 208, 210, 211, 213, 217, 218, 219, 224, 225, 232
mindreading 94, 101, 218
   other minds 117, 118, 129, 132–3, 167, 217, 223, 228
   see also embodied cognition/mind *and* enactive cognition/mind *and* extended: cognition/mind *and* extensive: mind *and* Theory of mind
Mlodinow, S. 13
Monk, R. 19–20, 182–3
Montgomery, D. 44, 88, 211, 212
Moore, G.E. 19, 20, 68, 137–58 *passim*, 166–7, 176, 185, 190, 191, 194, 212, 225, 226
Morrison, T. 65
Mulhall, S. 226
Mulligan, K. 213
Myin, E. 8, 14, 81–7, 93, 96, 115, 202, 208, 221

naturalism/naturalistic(ally) 69–71, 81, 82
   biological 5
   soft 169
   see also realism
Nelson, K. 211
Newport, E. L. 37, 210
Newson, M. 207, 208, 210, 211

'New Wittgenstein'/'New
    Wittgensteinians'/'Therapeutic
    reading'/'Therapeutes' 22, 156,
    158, 204, 228
Nickles, T. 232
nonpropositional
    attitude(s): 61, 138, 236
        see also belief in *and* trust
    certainty/certainties: 73, 110, 137,
        139–40, 144, 147–8, 149, 150,
        154, 185, 192
        see also certainties/hinges *and*
            embodied: certainty
    commitment 148–9
    expression/manifestation (showing) 63,
        64, 66
        see also enactment: in literature
    impact 73
    literary devices 73
    reading of hinge certainty: 137, 147–8,
        149
    significance/understanding 23, 71
        see also enactment: in literature
nonsense/nonsensical 15, 21–2, 26, 47, 51,
        61, 66–7, 145, 149–50, 154,
        157–8, 178, 190, 195, 204, 205,
        227, 228, 233, 235
    elucidatory nonsense 22
    important nonsense 22–3
    regulative nonsense 22–3
Nowicki, S. 131

objectivity 118, 170, 175–6, 179–80
ontogenetic development/origin 41–2, 79,
    82, 85, 202, 211

Parkin, A. 100, 106
pathology/pathological 114, 130, 132–3,
    163, 179, 213, 214, 218, 220
    act(s) 178, 213
    cases/condition 118, 130, 177, 217, 221,
        227
    causes 142
    circumstances/contexts 13, 20, 133
    exceptions 130
    flipside 132
    nonpathological 110, 113
patterns of action/behaviour: 42–3, 87,
    89–90, 92, 114

'patterns of life'/'patterns of experience' 19,
    20, 27–8, 31, 120–1, 125, 126,
    204, 206, 231
Penn, D. C. 83
'perspicuous presentation(s)' 4, 7, 13, 47,
    69, 71–2, 77, 159, 194–5, 198,
    215–16, 228
philosophical theories (theorizing)/theses
    28, 33, 103, 132, 156, 171, 181,
    192–8, 213, 223, 224, 236
proprioception/proprioceptive 221, 227
phylogenetic development/origin 41–2, 79,
    82, 85, 95, 96, 202, 203, 211
physicalism/physicalist 3, 5, 8, 10, 100, 202
physicalist presumption 2
Pichler, A. 233
Plato/Platonic 3, 4, 11, 17. 99, 119, 202, 213
Plooij, F. 89
possibility 206
    anthropo-*logical* 17, 19, 21, 29–30, 125
    illusion of 180
    limits of 29–30, 177
        see also limits of sense
    logical 19, 26, 29, 118, 129, 190
    of a language-game 65, 145, 173, 234
    of certainty 122, 131
    of communication 172
    of doubt 129–30, 135, 163–4
    of error/mistake 60, 128, 163, 220
    of pretence/deception/dissimulation
        54, 58–61, 126–7, 163
    of recollection 103
    of scepticism 160, 162, 165, 185
    of understanding 94, 224
        see also conceivability/imaginability vs
            possibility
poverty of stimulus argument 33–5, 37–9,
    207
pragmatic, pragmatism 140, 142, 143–4,
    156, 214, 232
Prinz, J. 116
Pritchard, D. 15, 137, 147–9, 154, 230
'proto-language games' 42, 44, 88–90
proto-language(s) 96, 209
'prototypes of thought' 27, 42, 87, 89, 211
Putnam, H. 171, 232

Ramscar, M. 47, 209
Ramsey, W. 6

Read, R. 228
realism/realist 5, 10, 174–5, 231
  see also naturalism
realism without empiricism 4–5, 29, 175, 196, 236
  scientific 169
  soft 5, 177, 202
    see also naturalism: soft
reality-soaked concepts/grammar, see grammar
reflex (action)/reflexes 49, 53, 56, 64, 112, 115, 119
  reflex-like 14, 119
  reflexive 214
reification/reify: 2–3, 11, 67, 107, 115, 149, 198
relativism 169–70, 172, 175–9, 232
Rhees, R. 19
Richman, B. 217
Roediger, H. L. 109–10
Rosch, E. 202
Rorty, A. 74, 215
Rorty, R. 44
Russell, B. 67, 160, 216
Ryan, L. 210
Ryle, G. 7, 62, 107, 213

Sacks, O. 227
Sandis, C. 226, 228
Satne, G. 83, 217
Saxe, R. 45
sayable/sayability 22–3, 66, 150, 157, 227
  see also unsayable/unsayability
saying/showing distinction 62, 68–73, 78, 151, 158, 204, 215–16
scaffolding
  cognitive 108
  of sense/thought 22, 23, 26, 47, 119
  of the world 119
socio-cultural 82–3
sceptic(al)/scepticism 117, 132, 137, 140–1, 153, 154, 155, 159–63, 166–8, 185, 225, 230
  continuity 81, 82–3, 86, 96
  external world 132, 167, 185
  hyperbolic/radical/universal 126, 135, 140, 142, 163, 185
  linguistic 158, 160–5, 229
  other minds 118, 132

Schacter, D. L. 105–6, 108–9, 220
Schönbaumsfeld, G. 226, 229
Schoneberger, T. 38, 209
Seager, W. 11
Searle, J. 5–8, 12, 50
Seyfarth, R. M. 86, 218
Shapiro, L. 92
Sharrock, W. 232
showing
  what cannot be said, but only shown/shows itself 17, 23, 65, 66, 68–9, 70–1, 78, 150–1, 157–8, 214
  what shows itself/is shown
    in action 63, 110, 119, 140, 150–2, 236
  meaning 70
    the ethical 69–70, 75, 157–8
    through language 17, 23, 65, 66, 110, 119, 140, 151, 152
    through literature 17, 23, 65, 68–75, 78, 158, 215–16; see also enactment: literature
    through silence 158
  see also saying/showing distinction
Singleton, D. 210
spontaneous utterance(s) 10, 23, 49–64, 96, 214
Standish, P. 165–8
Sterelny, K. 218
Stern, D. 156, 219
Squire, L. R. 106

Tallis, R. 11
technique 30–1, 41, 43–4, 47, 85, 91, 112, 164–5, 211, 223
  see also know-how
Tejedor, C. 203
ter Hark, Michel 101, 121, 122, 126, 132, 213, 223, 224
theories, see philosophical theories/theses
theory-ladenness/judgment-ladenness
  of language 171, 230
  of observation/perception 24, 230
Theory of Mind 24, 94–5, 101–2, 117, 129, 130, 132, 205, 218, 225
Therapeutic reading/Therapeutes, see 'New Wittgenstein'
Theses, see philosophical theories/theses
thick/thin grammar, see grammar

Third Wittgenstein 15, 19, 20–1, 28, 117, 120, 163, 181–6, 192, 204, 222, 233, 235, 236
Thompson, E. 202
Tomasello, M. 48, 94–5, 218
Toth, J. P. 107–8, 109, 112, 220
training 31, 42–4, 91–2, 106, 110, 130, 152, 194, 203, 211, 227
Travis, C. 150
trust 78, 130, 138, 144, 149, 150, 225
  see also belief in
Tulving, E. 105, 106, 108, 109, 219, 220, 221

universal grammar, see grammar: universal and certainties/hinges: universal
unsayable/unsayability 150, 157, 227
  see also ineffable/ineffability and unutterable
unutterable 23, 69–70, 158, 227
  see also ineffable/ineffability and unsayable/unsayability

Varela, F. J. 202
Vervaecke, J. 38, 208, 210

Vigotsky, L. 38
von Wright, G. H. 184, 186, 215, 234, 235

Ware, B. 67, 156
Weltbild (world picture) 169, 175, 191, 230, 233, 235
  'propositions' 190, 235
Whiten, A. 86
Williams, B. 65
Williams, M. 137, 138–9, 140–2, 143, 144, 150, 226
Winch, P. 30, 129, 132, 224, 232
Wittgenstein's
  enactivism 8–10, 82, 85, 87–8, 154, 202
  foundationalism, see foundationalism: Wittgenstein's foundationalism
  Razor 9–10, 116, 202
  soft naturalism/realism: 5, 169, 177, 202
Wright, C. 137, 143–4, 145, 146–7, 151, 226

Yarlett, D. 47, 209

Zahavi, D. 250
Zahidi, K. 115

www.ingramcontent.com/pod-product-compliance
Lightning Source LLC
Chambersburg PA
CBHW072133290426
44111CB00012B/1865